SOA Patterns with BizTalk Server 2013 and Microsoft Azure

Second Edition

Learn how to create and implement SOA strategies on the Microsoft technology stack using BizTalk Server 2013 and Azure Integration platforms

Richard Seroter

Mark Brimble

Johann Cooper

Colin Dijkgraaf

Mahindra Morar

[PACKT] enterprise
PUBLISHING
professional expertise distilled

BIRMINGHAM - MUMBAI

SOA Patterns with BizTalk Server 2013 and Microsoft Azure

Second Edition

First published: April 2009

Second edition: June 2015

Production reference: 1250615

Published by Packt Publishing Ltd.
Livery Place
35 Livery Street
Birmingham B3 2PB, UK.

ISBN 978-1-78439-646-6

www.packtpub.com

Credits

Authors
Richard Seroter
Mark Brimble
Johann Cooper
Colin Dijkgraaf
Mahindra Morar

Reviewers
René Brauwers
Sandro Pereira
Abdul Rafay

Commissioning Editor
Nadeem N. Bagban

Acquisition Editors
Harsha Bharwani
Richard Brookes-Bland

Content Development Editor
Rohit Kumar Singh

Technical Editor
Mrunmayee Patil

Copy Editors
Pranjali Chury
Brandt D'mello
Neha Vyas

Project Coordinator
Mary Alex

Proofreader
Safis Editing

Indexer
Mariammal Chettiyar

Graphics
Disha Haria

Production Coordinator
Conidon Miranda

Cover Work
Conidon Miranda

About the Authors

Richard Seroter is the VP of Product for the CenturyLink platform, and a Microsoft MVP for application integration. He is also an instructor for the developer-centric training company Pluralsight, the lead InfoQ editor for cloud computing, and the author of multiple books on application integration strategies. As the VP of Product for CenturyLink, he is responsible for product strategy, sprint planning, and community contribution. He also leads an expert team of product owners and analysts there. He maintains a blog (https://seroter.wordpress.com/) that he updates regularly on the topics of architecture and solution design and can be found on Twitter at @rseroter.

Mark Brimble is a solution integration architect with over 17 years of experience in the field of designing, building, implementing, and supporting integration solutions. He has experience in integrating Windows, Unix, and AS/400 platforms, SQL Server, SAP, Oracle, Microsoft CRM, and other web service technologies. He also has experience of eGate (Java CAPS), SSIS, BizTalk Server, MuleSoft, Boomi, and Flow integration products. His main interest at the moment is to help people choose the best architecture patterns. He has been active in the integration community for many years and posts regularly on his blog at https://connectedpawns.wordpress.com/. He also contributes to BizTalk Map Documenter (http://biztalkmapdoc.codeplex.com/) and is the coordinator for BizTalk 2013 Documenter (https://biztalk2013documenter.codeplex.com/). He can be found on Twitter at @BrimbleMark.

I would like to thank my coauthors, Mahindra, Johann, and Colin, who have travelled with me on this very interesting journey over the last 6 months. I would also like to acknowledge the members of the BizTalk community who, over the years, have helped me understand the integration patterns better. If this vibrant community did not exist, I would have missed being part of something very special.

Finally, I would like to thank my lovely wife, Margaret, and my big girl, Rebecca, for being so patient with me and understanding me while I wrote my chapters for this book.

Johann Cooper is an integration specialist who currently holds the role of a principal integration consultant at Datacom, New Zealand, and focuses on Microsoft Stack. He is well-versed with the usage of BizTalk Server, WCF, and RESTful services. He recently delved into the cloud space and successfully delivered projects that leverage the Microsoft Azure platform. He is a keen advocate of following and defining best practices, and is a big believer in automated testing.

He is the creator and curator of the *BizTalk BRE Pipeline Framework* CodePlex project, the author of the blog *Adventures inside the Message Box*, and is the author of the whitepaper *The A-Y of running BizTalk Server in Microsoft Azure*. He is also part of the Microsoft P-TSP program that is tasked with the goal of promoting the usage of BizTalk Server and the Microsoft Azure platform in New Zealand.

I would like to acknowledge Richard Seroter for writing the original edition of this book, which gave us a fantastic base to start working from. I'd also like to acknowledge my fellow coauthors who all worked hard to put this book together; it has truly been a labor of love.

A big thank you goes out to my parents who introduced me to the world of personal computing at the early age of 5 and sparked a lifelong passion in me.

Most of all, I would like to thank my lovely wife, Jeska, and my little girl, Isla, for being so patient with me and understanding me while I burrowed away with my laptop working on this book. I don't think my grammar would have been anywhere near the quality that it is without Jeska's help, so we can all thank her for that.

Finally, thank you dear readers for reading this book. It makes all the effort worthwhile.

Colin Dijkgraaf started dabbling in programming as a teenager in the days when the Internet was still called FidoNet and the modem speed was around 2400 baud. After getting a bachelor's of commerce degree in information systems, he did various different IT-related jobs, including image banking and digital imaging. He finally started full-time development for Datacom in 2000. In 2004, he first came across BizTalk while developing the frontend for an interchange to process invoices and purchase orders for a large New Zealand company and also worked on some maps. He has become a full-time developer of BizTalk since then and also a codeveloper of BizTalk Server 2013 Documenter.

I would like to thank my coauthors, Mahindra, Johann, and Mark, for all the hard work they did on their chapters, as well as for helping me out with the reviewing process of my chapters.

Finally, I would like to thank my lovely wife, May, for being so patient with me and understanding me while I edited my chapters for this book.

Mahindra Morar has been working in the IT sector since 1997, developing Windows and website enterprise applications. In the last 8 years, he has focused primarily on integrating systems as a principal integration consultant.

Having come from an electronics engineering background, he is able to use this knowledge to design solutions that integrate wetware, software, and hardware. He has worked in many industries, including manufacturing, financial institutions, insurance, retail/wholesale, and power utilities.

His areas of interest include exploring new technologies and deciding how to use them in the world of integration.

You can view his blog at https://connectedcircuits.wordpress.com.

The last 6 months have been a great learning experience in writing this book. I now truly appreciate the hard work and dedication authors endure to complete a book. I take my hat off to you all.

I would like to thank the three precious people in my life, Vanita, my lovely wife and my two joyful boys, Ameesh and Jayan, who gave me the time to coauthor this book.

About the Reviewers

René Brauwers started his IT career as a web developer/designer and was primarily engaged in the work of building websites using classic ASP. Soon, his focus got drawn toward developing client/server applications using the 3GL language Centura/Gupta Team Developer.

Around the end of 2002, he got involved in the integration space, starting off with webMethods and did this for the next 3 years, with an occasional side step that he took to develop .NET. This occasional side step got him in touch with BizTalk Server in 2005 and, since then, he has been involved with most of the integration offerings Microsoft offers both in the cloud (Microsoft Azure) as on-premise.

Until March 2015, he was employed as a Microsoft integration specialist for Motion10 (http://www.motion10.nl) in the Netherlands, and since April 2015, he has been employed as a solution architect at Breeze (http://www.breeze.net) in Sydney, Australia.

Breeze specializes in application development, cloud integration, and business intelligence solutions based on Microsoft technologies that drive real business efficiencies through cutting-edge technologies and the imaginative use of people and systems. Breeze has achieved global recognition, including the Worldwide Application Partner of the Year recognition for 2012 and 2014 from Microsoft. Some proprietary software solutions for Breeze include Cloud Lab Manager, Cloud Feeds Manager, and Cloud Data Manager.

René can be contacted via e-mail (rene@brauwers.nl), Twitter (@ReneBrauwers), LinkedIn (http://www.linkedin.com/in/renebrauwers), through his blog *Me, .NET, and BizTalk* (http://blog.brauwers.nl), or via http://www.integrationofthings.com.

> Thank you Tom, JoAnn, Steef-Jan, Mick, Nicki, Rimonda, Nino, Sandro, Daan, Wilfred, Gijs, Wesley, Rob, Maik, and Migael for being part of my professional and personal life. I cherish our friendship and would like to thank all of you, as every single one of you has played a part in making my Australian dream come true. Last but not least, I would like to thank Miranda, the future is ours to grasp!

Sandro Pereira lives in Portugal and currently works at DevScope (www.devscope.net) as a BizTalk consultant. In the last few years, he has been implementing integration scenarios and cloud provisioning at a major telecommunications service provider in Portugal.

His main focus is on integration technologies where he has been using .NET, BizTalk, SOAP/XML/XSLT, and Microsoft Azure since 2002. He is very active in the BizTalk community as a blogger (http://sandroaspbiztalkblog.wordpress.com/), member, and moderator on the MSDN BizTalk Server forums. He is the author of TechNet Wiki and a member of the council. He is a Code Gallery and CodePlex contributor, a member of the BizTalk Brazil (http://www.biztalkbrasil.com.br/) community, the NetPonto community (http://netponto.org/), and the BiztalkAdminsBlogging community (http://www.biztalkadminsblogging.com/). He is also the editor of the magazine *Programar* (http://www.revista-programar.info/) and is a public speaker. He has also technically reviewed *BizTalk Server 2010 Cookbook*, *Packt Publishing*, and authored *BizTalk Mapping Patterns and Best Practices*.

He has been awarded the Microsoft Most Valuable Professional (MVP) award in January 2011 for his contributions to the worldwide BizTalk Server community and is a certified MCTS: BizTalk Server BizTalk Server 2006 and BizTalk Server 2010

Abdul Rafay (http://abdulrafaysbiztalk.wordpress.com) has been working on integration with BizTalk and other Microsoft technologies for more than 9 years. He works as an integrator in a bank at Qatar, where he is involved in architecture, design, development, and the testing of integration solutions built on Microsoft platforms, which mainly include BizTalk, WCF, and Windows Server AppFabric.

He has vast experience of integration projects in the banking domain and has been involved in projects to integrate banking applications with core banking systems and B2B partners. He previously worked with the largest implementations of BizTalk in the region, such as United Bank Ltd. in Pakistan and SADAD in KSA.

He has won the award of Microsoft Most Valuable Professional (MVP) three times at BizTalk and likes to share his knowledge and technical expertise on his blog, MSDN, and other forums.

Other than integration projects and BizTalk, he has previously worked as a web developer with technologies such as ASP, ASP.NET, Sharepoint, and other open source web applications.

I would like to thank my fantastic wife, Hira, for making this project and my life successful. Thank you for your understanding, patience, and support that lead me to success. I would like to thank God Almighty for giving me all that I have today. I would like to thank all my friends who were there when I needed them, especially my in-laws. I would like to thank all those who contributed to my success and were part of my life.

www.PacktPub.com

Support files, eBooks, discount offers, and more

For support files and downloads related to your book, please visit www.PacktPub.com.

Did you know that Packt offers eBook versions of every book published, with PDF and ePub files available? You can upgrade to the eBook version at www.PacktPub.com and as a print book customer, you are entitled to a discount on the eBook copy. Get in touch with us at service@packtpub.com for more details.

At www.PacktPub.com, you can also read a collection of free technical articles, sign up for a range of free newsletters and receive exclusive discounts and offers on Packt books and eBooks.

https://www2.packtpub.com/books/subscription/packtlib

Do you need instant solutions to your IT questions? PacktLib is Packt's online digital book library. Here, you can search, access, and read Packt's entire library of books.

Why subscribe?

- Fully searchable across every book published by Packt
- Copy and paste, print, and bookmark content
- On demand and accessible via a web browser

Free access for Packt account holders

If you have an account with Packt at www.PacktPub.com, you can use this to access PacktLib today and view 9 entirely free books. Simply use your login credentials for immediate access.

Instant updates on new Packt books

Get notified! Find out when new books are published by following @PacktEnterprise on Twitter or the *Packt Enterprise* Facebook page.

Table of Contents

Preface

Repeat after me: SOA is something you do, not something you buy.

– David Linthicum

This may seem an odd quote to use when beginning a book about employing a particular product to facilitate the implementation of a service-oriented architecture (SOA). However, I think it sets the tone.

I prefer to define SOA as an architectural discipline based on loosely-coupled, autonomous chunks of business functionality, which can be used to construct composite applications.

This is how the first edition of this book started, and like so many words in that book, they are timeless. As I updated chapters, I was continuously struck by how little had changed. We also added new chapters, *Chapter 4, REST and JSON Support in BizTalk Server 2013, Chapter 5, Azure BizTalk Services*, and *Chapter 6, Azure Service Bus* to cover some of the newer technologies that give us more ways to implement SOA. For sure, there are newer technologies and we are embracing the brave new world of the cloud, but the underlying patterns that we use in integration do not change. For example, the words in *Chapter 7, Planning Service-oriented BizTalk Solutions* just as true today as they were seven years ago. SOA might not be a trendy word anymore, but call it what you will, the pattern does not go away.

– Mark Brimble, June 2015

From writing desktop and web-based Line of Business (LOB) applications in the early 2000, I find integration is the adhesive that connects all these disparate systems together. Without integration, I wonder how many businesses would survive in today's world where information exchange is essential. This book describes how BizTalk Server and Microsoft Azure create the adhesive that bonds these systems together.

When writing the chapters on REST and hybrid systems, I pondered how the Internet has grown to become the conduit of connecting systems and devices together. The trend now seems to be all about providing RESTful services and hosting them in the cloud. With this in mind, new integration patterns have emerged, which are discussed in this book.

– Mahindra Morar, June 2015

In the information technology industry, if you aren't constantly learning, then you are falling behind due to the technology and methodology constantly changing. Some examples of this changing landscape include the move toward cloud-based services and REST web services, both of these are covered in this updated book.

I'm lucky enough to be part of a team of BizTalk developers with whom I can share and receive ideas and concepts, and we can learn from each other. Another source of these ideas and concepts come from books like this where others have shared their expertise. So, I hope this book helps you to keep learning and growing.

– Colin Dijkgraaf, June 2015

BizTalk Server is equivalent to a Swiss army knife in that there are so many options available to solve integration problems. Like a weapon, it is possible to attack your problems with brute force or finesse. Typically, the end result seems similar, but the amount of effort expended is vastly different, not to mention the amount of cleanup required after the exercise.

When I was still in the early stages of my journey toward becoming a seasoned BizTalk developer, I came across the first edition of this book, and it opened my eyes to the fact that there is a right way to do integration, and an expensive way to do integration, even if the costs are not instantly evident. The differentiating factors between these two end results typically come down to applying the right integration patterns and making early architectural decisions that will guide you down a path toward building efficient solutions.

Now, I'm not just talking about the 40,000 feet in the air high level types of architectural decisions, which are obviously very important, but the low level detail as well. Having an understanding of the inner workings of the toolsets you are working with as well as an appreciation for how and when to apply various integration principles and patterns can make or break a solution. These patterns and principles are timeless, and will serve you well regardless what technology you are using to solve your integration problems, but having a keen understanding of their relevance to a given product empowers you even more.

The first edition of this book would have already given you great insight into the inner workings of BizTalk Server and how to apply SOA principles to the platform. This updated edition will take things further, firstly by extending the existing material from a BizTalk Server perspective with all the new insights that have been gleaned in the last few years. Moreover, we have also explored some previously untrodden territory by exploring how SOA and BizTalk Server can be used to build effective solutions leveraging RESTful architectures as well as by extending the reach of the integration platform through the use of Azure Service Bus. Finally, we end the book by giving you a taste of the newest technologies to be released by Microsoft, which will hopefully inspire you to get your hands dirty playing with these new platforms.

Thank you for reading our book, and I hope you enjoy reading it as much we enjoyed writing it.

– Johann Cooper, June 2015

What this book covers

Chapter 1, Building BizTalk Server 2013 Applications, looks at what exactly BizTalk Server is, reviews the core architecture of the application, and shows you how to build an end-to-end solution.

Chapter 2, Windows Communication Foundation Primer, looks at the problems that WCF attempts to solve, and how to actually build and host WCF services.

Chapter 3, Using WCF Services in BizTalk Server 2013, builds a number of common scenarios using BizTalk and WCF services.

Chapter 4, REST and JSON Support in BizTalk Server 2013, covers the fundamentals of REST-based services and the BizTalk WCF-WebHttp adapter.

Chapter 5, Azure BizTalk Services, looks at one of the newer integration offerings from Microsoft, reviews how it works, and shows how to build an end-to-end solution. Although this platform has been superseded by Azure Logic Apps while we were writing this book, we decided to keep this chapter for historical completeness.

Chapter 6, Azure Service Bus, discusses the different types of services available and the characteristics of each type. You will also learn about creating Azure Topics and Subscriptions.

Chapter 7, Planning Service-oriented BizTalk Solutions, investigates exactly what a service-oriented BizTalk solution looks like. What types of services you should expose. How you can exchange messages through the BizTalk bus. We'll answer these questions and many more at this stage of the book.

Chapter 8, Schema and Endpoint Patterns, explores various patterns for building schemas and endpoints, and discusses what scenarios each pattern is applicable to.

Chapter 9, Asynchronous Communication Patterns, looks at how to take advantage of asynchronous messaging to build robust service-oriented solutions. We'll also cover the tricky concept of providing acknowledgements or results to clients that call services in a fire-and-forget fashion.

Chapter 10, Orchestration Patterns, explores advanced patterns used to build loosely-coupled orchestrations that cater for advanced functionality without compromising flexibility.

Chapter 11, Versioning Patterns, covers proven methods to version your BizTalk components, ensuring that you don't introduce changes that will cause unintended disruption.

Chapter 12, Frameworks and Tools, introduces you to a variety of tools and frameworks that can be leveraged to support your SOA aspirations.

Chapter 13, New SOA Capabilities in BizTalk Server 2013 – Azure Hybrid Patterns, covers the pros and cons of hybrid solutions. This chapter also describes the different integration patterns available when connecting on-premise resources to the resources hosted in the cloud.

Chapter 14, What's New and What's Next?, will touch upon some of the latest offerings from Microsoft, cover how they are relevant to you, and give you a taste of how to implement solutions with these platforms.

What you need for this book

The requirements for this book are as follows:

- An Internet connection.

- An Azure subscription.

- A MSDN account or access to BizTalk Server 2013 and 2013 R2 media as well as to corresponding SQL Server media (refer to `https://msdn.microsoft.com/en-us/library/jj248697.aspx` for corresponding SQL Server versions).

- A development VM with Visual Studio 2012 on which you can install BizTalk Server 2013 and a corresponding SQL Server instance. You can alternatively create a VM based on the Azure template for BizTalk Server 2013 Developer Edition. Refer to `https://msdn.microsoft.com/en-us/library/jj248697.aspx` for minimum hardware requirements and software prerequisites.

- A development VM with Visual Studio 2013 on which you can install BizTalk Server 2013 R2 and a corresponding SQL Server instance. You can alternatively create a VM based on the Azure template for BizTalk Server 2013 R2 Developer Edition. Refer to `https://msdn.microsoft.com/en-us/library/jj248697.aspx` for minimum hardware requirements and software prerequisites.

Who this book is for

If you are a developer who has been tasked with building service-oriented BizTalk Server solutions or cloud-based integration solutions using Microsoft Azure, this book is for you. Architects, designers, and technical leads who want to envision an enterprise solution and implement the software blueprint to deliver solutions will also find this book useful.

Conventions

In this book, you will find a number of text styles that distinguish between different kinds of information. Here are some examples of these styles and an explanation of their meaning.

Code words in text, database table names, folder names, filenames, file extensions, pathnames, dummy URLs, user input, and Twitter handles are shown as follows: "The "schema generators" need to be installed from VB scripts in the C:\Program Files (x86)\Microsoft BizTalk Server 2013\SDK\Utilities\Schema Generator folder before the first use."

A block of code is set as follows:

```
<xs:schema
  xmlns:xs="http://www.w3.org/2001/XMLSchema">
    <xs:element name="Person>
    <xs:complexType>
        <xs:sequence>
            <xs:element name="FirstName" type="xs:string"/>
            <xs:element name="LastName" type="xs:string"/>
            <xs:element name="Age" type="xs:int"/>
        </xs:sequence>
    </xs:complexType>
    </xs:element>
</xs:schema>
```

When we wish to draw your attention to a particular part of a code block, the relevant lines or items are set in bold:

```
Svcutil.exe http://localhost:8081/VServiceBase?WSDL /
out:WCFProxy.cs /language:c#  /config:app.config /mergeConfig
```

New terms and **important words** are shown in bold. Words that you see on the screen, for example, in menus or dialog boxes, appear in the text like this: "When a new BizTalk project is added to a Visual Studio solution, you should immediately right-click on the project and select the **Properties** option."

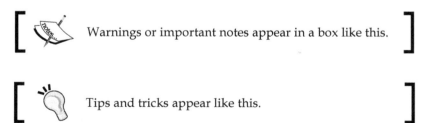

> [Warnings or important notes appear in a box like this.]

> [Tips and tricks appear like this.]

Reader feedback

Feedback from our readers is always welcome. Let us know what you think about this book—what you liked or disliked. Reader feedback is important for us as it helps us develop titles that you will really get the most out of.

To send us general feedback, simply e-mail feedback@packtpub.com, and mention the book's title in the subject of your message.

If there is a topic that you have expertise in and you are interested in either writing or contributing to a book, see our author guide at www.packtpub.com/authors.

Customer support

Now that you are the proud owner of a Packt book, we have a number of things to help you to get the most from your purchase.

Downloading the example code

You can download the example code files from your account at http://www.packtpub.com for all the Packt Publishing books you have purchased. If you purchased this book elsewhere, you can visit http://www.packtpub.com/support and register to have the files e-mailed directly to you.

Errata

Although we have taken every care to ensure the accuracy of our content, mistakes do happen. If you find a mistake in one of our books—maybe a mistake in the text or the code—we would be grateful if you could report this to us. By doing so, you can save other readers from frustration and help us improve subsequent versions of this book. If you find any errata, please report them by visiting http://www.packtpub.com/submit-errata, selecting your book, clicking on the **Errata Submission Form** link, and entering the details of your errata. Once your errata are verified, your submission will be accepted and the errata will be uploaded to our website or added to any list of existing errata under the Errata section of that title.

To view the previously submitted errata, go to https://www.packtpub.com/books/content/support and enter the name of the book in the search field. The required information will appear under the **Errata** section.

Piracy

Piracy of copyrighted material on the Internet is an ongoing problem across all media. At Packt, we take the protection of our copyright and licenses very seriously. If you come across any illegal copies of our works in any form on the Internet, please provide us with the location address or website name immediately so that we can pursue a remedy.

Please contact us at copyright@packtpub.com with a link to the suspected pirated material.

We appreciate your help in protecting our authors and our ability to bring you valuable content.

Questions

If you have a problem with any aspect of this book, you can contact us at questions@packtpub.com, and we will do our best to address the problem.

1
Building BizTalk Server 2013 Applications

Creativity is the power to connect the seemingly unconnected.

– William Plomer

Let's begin our journey by investigating what BizTalk Server actually is, why one would use it, and how to craft a running application. This chapter will be a refresher on BizTalk Server for those of you who have some familiarity with the product.

In this chapter, you will learn:

- How to articulate BizTalk Server, when to use it, and how it works
- How to outline the role of BizTalk schemas, maps, and orchestrations
- BizTalk messaging configurations

What is BizTalk Server?

So what exactly is BizTalk Server, and why should you care about it? In a nutshell, Microsoft BizTalk Server 2013 uses adapter technology to connect disparate entities and enable the integration of data, events, processes, and services. An entity may be an application, department, or a different organization altogether that you need to be able to share information with. A software adapter is typically used when we need to establish communication between two components that do not natively collaborate. BizTalk Server adapters are built with a common framework; which results in system integration implemented via configuration, not coding.

Traditionally, BizTalk Server has solved problems in the following three areas:

- Enterprise Application Integration
- Business-to-Business
- Business Process Automation

First, BizTalk Server acts as an **Enterprise Application Integration (EAI)** server that connects applications that are natively incapable of talking to each other. The applications may have incompatible platforms, data structure formats, or security models. For example, when a new employee is hired, the employee data from the human resources application needs to be sent to the payroll application so that the new employee receives his/her paycheck on time. Nothing prevents you from writing the code necessary to connect these disparate applications with a point-to-point solution. However, using such a strategy often leads to an application landscape that looks like this:

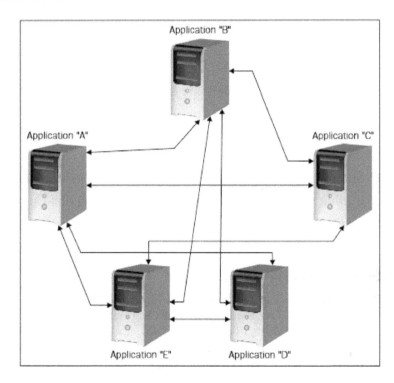

Many organizations choose to insert a communication broker between these applications, as shown in the following figure:

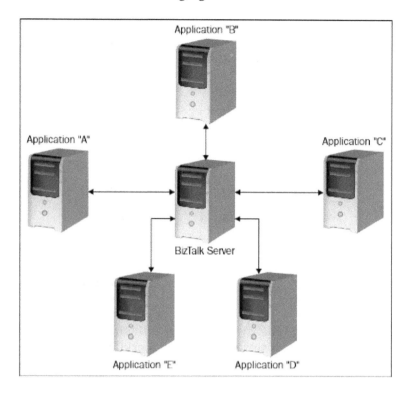

Some of the benefits that you would realize from such an architectural choice include:

- Loose coupling of applications where one does not have a physical dependency on the other
- Durable infrastructure that can guarantee delivery and queue messages during destination system downtime
- Centralized management of system integration endpoints
- Message flow control such as in-order delivery
- Encouragement for the reuse of core components
- Insight into cross-functional business processes through business activity monitoring

BizTalk Server solves a second problem by filling the role of a **Business-to-Business (B2B)** broker that facilitates communication across different organizations. BizTalk supports B2B scenarios by offering Internet-friendly adapters, industry standard EDI message schemas, and robust support for both channel- and message-based security.

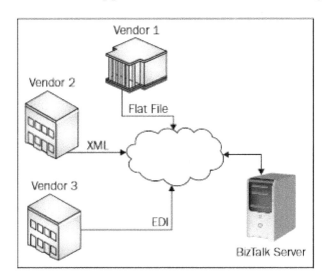

The third broad area that BizTalk Server excels in is **Business Process Automation (BPA)**. BPA is all about taking historically manual workflow procedures and turning them into executable processes. For example, consider an organization that typically receives a new order via e-mail, and the sales agent manually checks inventory levels prior to inserting the order into the fulfillment system. If the inventory is too low, then the sales agent has to initiate an order with their supplier and watch out for the response so that the inventory system can be updated. The inevitable problems of this scenario are as follows:

- Poor scalability when the number of orders increases
- Lack of visibility into the status of orders and supplier requests
- Multiple instances of redundant data entry, ripe for mistakes in one system and not the other
- Unreliable resources when a sales agent is sick

By deciding to automate this scenario, the company can reduce human error while streamlining communications between applications and organizations.

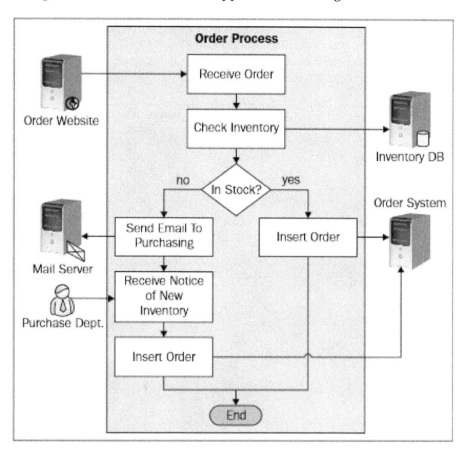

The beginning of the second decade of the 21st century saw the disruption of the traditional ways in which EAI and B2B problems were solved because of the rise of **Software as Service (SaaS)**. SaaS is a software that is hosted external to your business, and is paid for on a subscription basis; its best known example is Salesforce.com. Many organizations have chosen to modify their EAI and B2B solutions with BizTalk Server to access SaaS applications using hybrid solutions, as shown in the following figure:

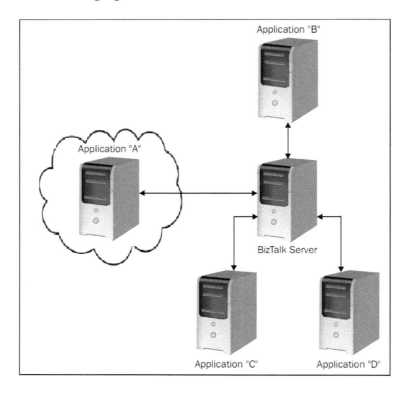

Four new adapters, the WCF-BasicHTTPRelay, WCF-WebHTTP, WCF-NetTCPRelay, and SB-Messaging adapter, have been added to BizTalk 2013 to support hybrid solutions, and are nicknamed the "cloud adapters". New chapters on RESTful services and the Azure Service Bus have been added to this edition of the book to describe how these cloud adapters enhance the BizTalk Server story.

Microsoft Azure BizTalk Service (MABS) has been created as a SaaS offering that can abstract B2B problems to Azure. We have added a chapter that shows how to use BizTalk Server 2013 with this new SaaS model. Examples of how to use all these new components to add new SOA capabilities to BizTalk Server have been added to this book.

Azure App Services is Microsoft's next generation SaaS offering that will supersede MABS. While the platform is still very fresh, we have outlined the underlying concepts for you in the final chapter of this book to help you get a head start on usage of this platform.

What's the one thing that all of these BizTalk Server cases have in common? They all depend on the real-time interchange and processing of discrete messages in an event-driven fashion. This partially explains why BizTalk Server is such a strong tool within a service-oriented architecture. We'll investigate many of BizTalk's service-oriented capabilities in later chapters, but it's important to note that the functionality that exists to support the three top-level scenarios mentioned earlier (EAI, B2B, and BPM) fits well into a service-oriented mindset. Concepts such as contract-first design, loose coupling, and reusability are soaked into the fabric of BizTalk Server.

 BizTalk Server should be targeted for solutions that exchange real-time messages as opposed to **Extract Transform Load** (**ETL**) products that excel at bulky, batch-oriented exchanges between data stores.

BizTalk Server 2013 is the eighth release of the product, the first release being BizTalk Server 2000. Back in those days, developers had access to four native adapters (filesystem, MSMQ, HTTP, and SMTP). Development was done using a series of different tools, and the underlying engine had some fairly tight coupling between components. Since then, the entire product has been rebuilt and reengineered for .NET and a myriad of new services and features have become part of the BizTalk Server suite. The application continues to evolve and take greater advantage of the features of the Microsoft product stack, while still being the most interoperable and platform-neutral offering that Microsoft has ever produced.

BizTalk architecture

So how does BizTalk Server actually work? At its core, BizTalk Server is an event-processing engine based on a conventional publish-subscribe pattern. Wikipedia defines the publish-subscribe pattern as:

"An asynchronous messaging paradigm where senders (publishers) of messages are not programmed to send their messages to specific receivers (subscribers). Rather, published messages are characterized into classes, without knowledge of what (if any) subscribers there may be. Subscribers express interest in one or more classes, and only receive messages that are of interest, without knowledge of what (if any) publishers there are."

This pattern enforces a natural loose coupling and provides more scalability than an engine that requires a tight connection between receivers and senders. In the first release of BizTalk Server, the product *did* have tightly coupled messaging components, but thankfully, the engine was completely redesigned for BizTalk Server 2004.

Once a message is received by a BizTalk adapter, it runs through any necessary preprocessing (such as decoding and validations) in BizTalk pipelines before being subjected to data transformation via BizTalk maps, and finally being published to a central database called the MessageBox. Then, the parties that have a corresponding subscription for that message can consume it as they see fit. While introducing a bit of unavoidable latency, the MessageBox database makes up for that by providing us with durability, reliability, and scalability. For instance, if one of our subscriber systems is offline for maintenance, outbound messages are not lost, but rather the MessageBox ensures that the messages are queued until the subscriber is ready to receive them. Worried about a large flood of inbound messages that steal processing threads away from other BizTalk activities? No problem! The MessageBox ensures that each and every message finds its way to its targeted subscriber, even if it must wait until the flood of inbound messages subsides.

There are really two ways to look at the way BizTalk is structured. The first is the traditional EAI view, which sees BizTalk receiving messages and routes them to the next system for consumption. The flow is very linear and BizTalk is seen as a broker between two applications, shown as follows:

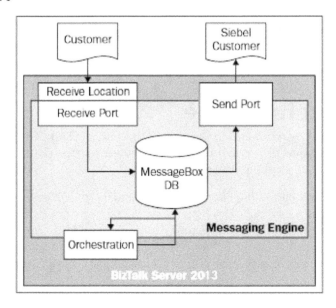

However, the other way to consider BizTalk, and the focus of this book, is as a Service Bus, with numerous input/output channels that process messages in a very dynamic way. That is, instead of visualizing the data flow as a straight path through BizTalk to a destination system, consider BizTalk exposing services as on-ramps to a variety of destinations. Messages published to BizTalk Server may fan out to dozens of subscribers, who have no interest in what the publishing application actually was. Instead of thinking about BizTalk as a simple connector of systems, think of it as a message bus that coordinates a symphony of events between endpoints.

This concept is an exciting way to exploit BizTalk's engine in this modern world of service orientation. In the following figure, I've shown how the central BizTalk bus has receiver services hanging from it, and has a multitude of distinct subscriber services that are activated by relevant messages reaching the bus:

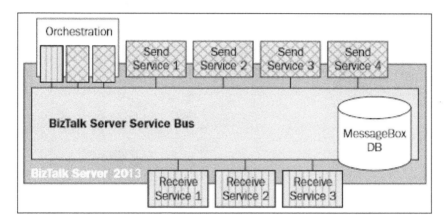

 If the on-ramp concept is a bit abstract to understand, consider a simple analogy. In designing the transportation for a city, it would be foolish to create distinct roads between each and every destination. The design and maintenance of such a project would be lunacy. It would be smart to design a shared highway with on and off ramps, which enable people to use a common route to get to the numerous locations around town. As new destinations in the city emerge, the entire highway (or road system) doesn't need to undergo changes, but rather, only a new entrance/exit point needs to be appended to the existing shared infrastructure.

What exactly is a message anyway? A message is data processed through BizTalk Server's messaging engine, whether that data is transported as an XML document, a delimited flat file, or a Microsoft Word document. The message content may contain a command (for example, `InsertCustomer`), a document (for example, `Invoice`), or an event (for example, `VendorAdded`). A message has a set of properties associated with it. First and foremost, a message may have a type associated with it, which uniquely defines it within the messaging bus. The type is typically comprised of the XML namespace and the root node name (for example, `http://CompanyA.Purchasing#PurchaseOrder`). The message type is much like the class object in an object-oriented programming language; it uniquely identifies entities by their properties. The other critical attribute of a message in BizTalk Server is the property bag called the message context, as shown in the following screenshot:

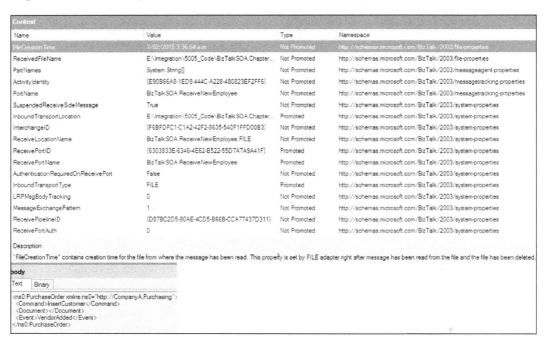

The message context is a set of name/value properties that stay attached to the message as long as it remains within BizTalk Server. These context values include metadata about the transport used to publish the message and attributes of the message itself. Properties in the message context that are visible to the BizTalk engine, and therefore available for routing decisions, are called promoted properties.

How does a message actually get into BizTalk Server? A receive location is configured for the actual endpoint that receives messages. The receive location uses a particular adapter that knows how to absorb the inbound message. For instance, a receive location may be configured to use the FILE adapter, which polls a particular directory for XML messages. The receive location stores the file path to monitor, while the adapter provides transport connectivity. Upon receipt of a message, the adapter stamps a set of values into the message context. For the FILE adapter, values such as `ReceivedFileName` are added to that message's context property bag.

Note that BizTalk has both application adapters, such as SQL Server, Oracle, and SAP, as well as transport-level adapters, such as HTTP, MSMQ, and FILE. The key point is that the adapter configuration user experience is virtually identical regardless of the type of adapter chosen. Some of the adapters available are shown in the following figure:

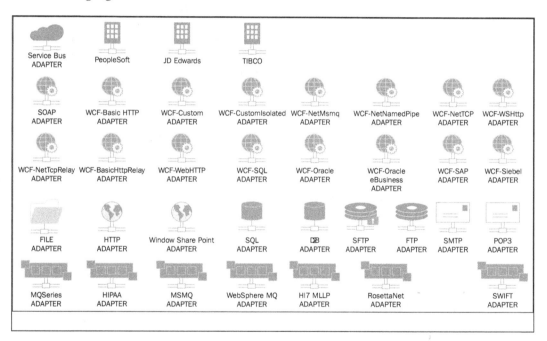

Receive locations have a particular receive pipeline associated with them. A pipeline is a sequential set of optional operations that is performed on the message in preparation of being parsed and sent to the message box database by the BizTalk adapter. For instance, I would need a pipeline in order to decrypt, unzip, or validate the XML structure of my inbound message. One of the most critical roles of the pipeline is to identify the type of the inbound message and put the type into the message context as a promoted property. Custom pipelines can serve as preprocessing stages to make the message useful for processing. As discussed earlier, a message type is the unique characterization of a message. Think of a receive pipeline as performing all the preprocessing steps necessary for putting the message in to its most usable format.

A receive port contains one or more receive locations. Receive ports have XSLT maps associated with them that are applied to messages prior to publishing them to the `MessageBox` database. What value does a receive port offer? It acts as a grouping of receive locations where capabilities such as mapping and data tracking can be applied to all of the associated receive locations. It may also act as a container that allows us to publish a single entity to BizTalk Server regardless of how it came in, or what it looked like upon receipt. Let's say that my receive port contains three receive locations, which all receive slightly different "invoice" messages from three different external vendors. At the receive port level, I have three maps that take each unrelated message and maps it to a single, common format, before publishing it to BizTalk.

Now that we have a message cleaned up (by the pipeline) and in the final structure (via an XSLT map), it's published to the BizTalk Server `MessageBox` where message routing can begin. For our purposes, there are two types of subscribers that we care about. The first type of subscriber is a send port. A send port is conceptually the inverse of the receive location and is responsible for transporting messages out of the BizTalk "bus".

It has not only the adapter reference, adapter configuration settings, and pipeline (much like the receive location), but also the ability to apply XSLT maps to outbound messages. If a send port subscribes to a message, it first applies any XSLT map to the message, then processes it through a send pipeline, and finally uses the adapter to transmit the message out of BizTalk.

The other type of subscriber for a published message is a BizTalk orchestration. An orchestration is an executable business process that uses messages to complete operations in a workflow. We'll spend plenty of time working with orchestration subscribers throughout this book.

Setting up new BizTalk projects

What do you need to set up a brand new BizTalk project? First, you will need a development environment with Windows Server 2008 R2 SP1 or 2012 or 7 SP1 or 8; IIS 7.0, 7.5 or 8; SQL Server 2008R2 SP1 or 2012, Visual Studio 2012, and BizTalk Server 2013 with developer tools and SDK, installed in that order.

Consider using a standard structure for all of your BizTalk Server solutions. This makes it easier to package and share source code, while also defining a consistent place to store solution artifacts in each project. To build the following structure, we used a Visual Studio extension (VSIX), which is available at `http://connectedpawns.wordpress.com/2014/10/10/biztalk-2013-solution-template/`.

Note that BizTalk Server 2013 solutions can (and should) be centrally persisted in standard source control applications, such as Subversion or Microsoft Team Foundation Server.

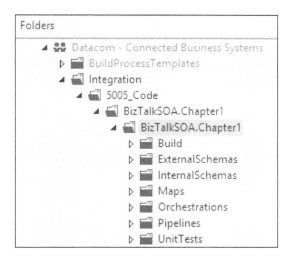

You can tell whether you have successfully installed BizTalk Server in your development environment if you are able to see BizTalk Projects in the **New Projects** menu option of Visual Studio:

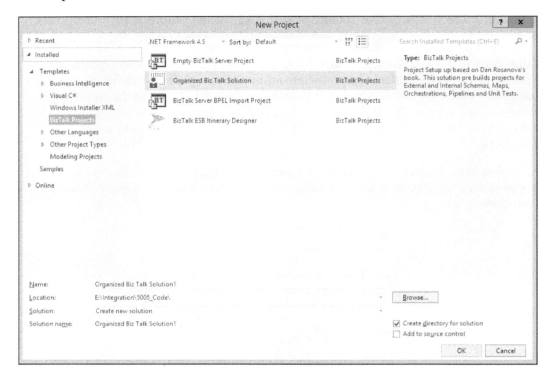

When a new BizTalk project is added to a Visual Studio solution, you should immediately right-click on the project and select the **Properties** option.

The first value that you need to set is under the **Signing** section. You can either point to an existing strong name key, or generate a new key on the fly. BizTalk Server projects are deployed to **Global Assembly Cache (GAC)**, and must be strong named prior to deployment. After setting the necessary key value, navigate to the BizTalk-specific **Deployment** section, and set **Application Name** to something meaningful such as BizTalkSOA as shown in the following screenshot:

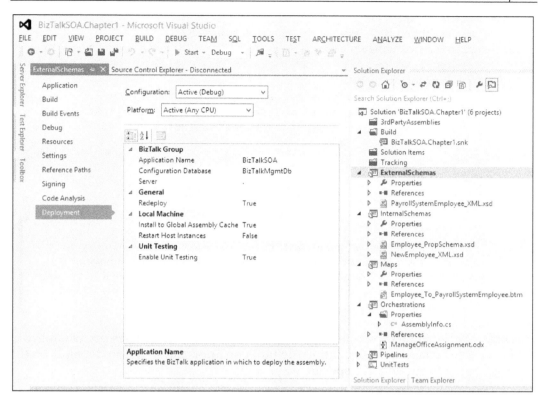

Once you have a project created, the strong name key set, and application name defined, you're ready to start adding development artifacts to your project.

What are BizTalk schemas?

Arguably, the building block of any BizTalk Server solution (and general SOA solution) is the data contract, which describes the type of messages that flow through BizTalk Server. A contract for a message in BizTalk Server is represented using an industry standard **XML Schema Definition** (**XSD**). For a given contract, the XSD spells out the elements, their organizational structure, and their data types. An XSD also defines the expected ordering of nodes, whether or not the node is required, and how many times the node can appear at the particular location in the node tree; it can even be used to enforce further constraints based on lengths or regular expressions to name a few. The following is an example XSD file:

```
<xs:schema
  xmlns:xs="http://www.w3.org/2001/XMLSchema">
    <xs:element name="Person>
    <xs:complexType>
        <xs:sequence>
            <xs:element name="FirstName" type="xs:string"/>
            <xs:element name="LastName" type="xs:string"/>
            <xs:element name="Age" type="xs:int"/>
        </xs:sequence>
    </xs:complexType>
    </xs:element>
</xs:schema>
```

Downloading the example code

You can download the example code files from your account at http://
www.packtpub.com for all the Packt Publishing books you have
purchased. If you purchased this book elsewhere, you can visit http://
www.packtpub.com/support and register to have the files e-mailed
directly to you.

Having a strict contract can reduce flexibility, but it greatly increases predictability as the message consumer can confidently build an application, which depends on the message being formatted in a specific way.

Schema creation and characteristics

While producing completely valid XSD syntax, the BizTalk Schema Editor takes a higher level approach to defining the schema itself. Specifically, instead of working purely with familiar XML concepts of elements and attributes, the BizTalk Schema Editor advances a simpler model based on records and fields, which is meant to represent the hierarchical nature of a schema in a better way. Do not let this fact mislead you to believe that the BizTalk Schema Editor is just some elementary tool designed to accommodate the drooling masses. In fact, the Editor enables us to graphically construct relatively complex message shapes through a fairly robust set of visual properties and XSD annotations.

There are multiple ways to create schemas in the BizTalk Schema Editor, namely:

- You can generate a schema from an existing XML file. The BizTalk Editor infers the node names and structure from the provided XML instance. In many integration projects, you start off knowing exactly what the transmission payload looks like. If you are fortunate enough to start your project with a sample XML file already in place, this schema generation mechanism is a big time-saver. However, there are caveats to this strategy. The BizTalk Editor can only build a schema structure based on the nodes that are present in the XML file. If optional nodes were omitted from the instance file, then they will be missing from the schema. Also, the schema will not mark "repeating" structures unless the XML file represents a particular node multiple times. Finally, the generated schema will not try to guess the data type of the node, and will default all nodes to a type of string. Despite these considerations, this method is a fantastic way to establish a head start in schema construction.

The "schema generators" need to be installed from VB scripts in the `C:\Program Files (x86)\Microsoft BizTalk Server 2013\SDK\Utilities\Schema Generator` folder before the first use.

- XSD schemas may also be manufactured through the BizTalk adapters. For example, the BizTalk adapters for SQL Server and Oracle will generate XSD schemas based on the database table or stored procedure that you are targeting. As we will see shortly, BizTalk Server also generates schemas for services that you wish to consume. Using adapters to harvest metadata and automatically generate schemas is a powerful way to make certain that your messages match the expected system format.

- New schemas can actually be created by importing and including previously created schemas. If XSD complex types are defined in a schema (for example, `Address`), then new schemas can be built by mixing and matching existing types. Because these inherited types are merely referenced, not copied, changes to the original content types cascade down to the schemas that reuse them. If you are inclined to design a base set of standard types, then building schemas as compositions of existing types is a very useful way to go.

- Finally, you have the option to roll up your sleeves and build a new XSD schema from scratch. Now, while you can switch to a text editor and literally type out a schema, the BizTalk Editor allows you to graphically build a schema tree from the beginning. Note that because of BizTalk Server's rigorous support for the XSD standard, you can even fashion your XML schemas with alternate tools such as **Altova's XML Spy**. We will handcraft many of our schemas in the BizTalk Editor for the schemas that we build together in this chapter and throughout the book.

If you're like me, you often sketch the schema layout first, and only later worry about concepts such as data types, repeating nodes, and entry restrictions. By default, each new node is assigned a string data type and is assumed to only exist once in a single XML document. Using the BizTalk Server Schema Editor, you can associate a given node with a wide variety of alternate data types such as dateTime, integer, and base64Binary. One thing to remember is that while you may use a more forgiving schema for inbound data (unless you intend to validate inbound data before it is accepted), you should be strict in what you send out to other systems. We want to ensure to only produce messages that have clean data and stand little chance of being outright rejected by the target system.

Changing the number of times a particular node can appear in an XML document is as simple as highlighting the target node and setting the Max Occurs property. It's also fairly straightforward to set limits on the data allowed within certain nodes. What if we want a **ZipCode** field to only accept a maximum of 10 characters? Alternately, what if the data stored in an **AddressType** node has to be constrained to only three allowable choices? By default, these options are not visible for a given node. To change that, you can select a node and set the **Derived By** equal to **Restriction**. A flurry of new properties such as **Maximum Length** or **Enumeration** become available. This is illustrated as follows:

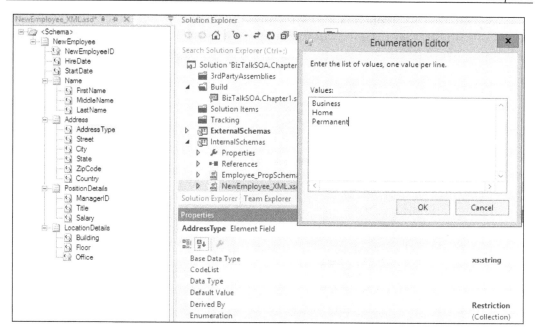

Property schemas

A critical BizTalk schema concept to examine is the property schema. These schemas are internal to BizTalk and do not represent any message which will be exchanged with an external system. Earlier in this chapter, I mentioned the notion of promoted properties, which expose a message's data content to the BizTalk messaging layer. This, in turn, allows for a message to be routed to subscribers who are specifically interested in data condition (for example, `Order Number == 12345`). Promoted properties are defined in a property schema, which is a special schema type within BizTalk Server. The property schema contains a flat list of elements (no records allowed) that represent the type of data we want the BizTalk messaging engine to know about. Once the property schema is created, we can associate specific fields in our message schema with the elements defined in the property schema. As we will see in practice later in this book, one key benefit of property schemas is that they can be used by more than one XSD schema.

For instance, we can create `NewEmployee` and `ModifiedEmployee` message, both containing an `EmployeeID` element that maps to a single `EmployeeID` property field. In this manner, we can associate messages of different types: that have common data attributes:

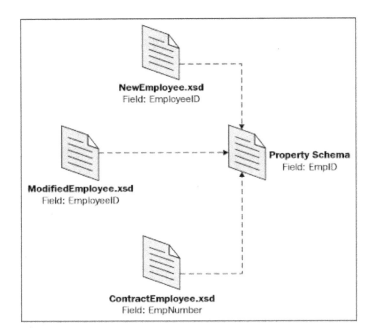

The BizTalk Schema Editor is a robust tool for building industry standard XSD schemas. In a service-oriented architecture, the data contract is key, and understanding how to construct an XSD contract within BizTalk Server is an important skill.

What are BizTalk maps?

Rarely does data emitted from one system match the structure and content expected by another system. Hence, some sort of capability is needed to translate data so that it can be digested by a variety of consumers. **Extensible Stylesheet Language Transformations (XSLT)** is the industry standard for reshaping XML documents, and the BizTalk Mapper is the tool used by BizTalk developers to graphically build XSLTs.

When creating a map, the BizTalk Mapper uses a straightforward design paradigm where the source schema is identified on the left-hand side and the destination schema resides on the right-hand side of the tool:

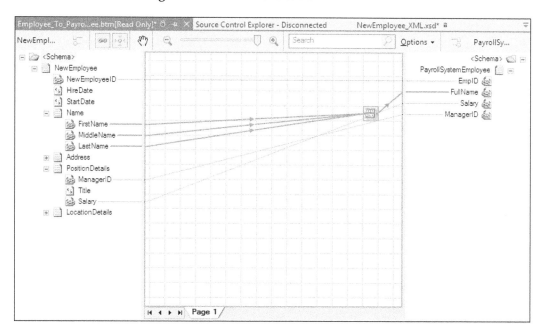

We are often lucky enough to be able to make direct connections between nodes. For instance, even though the node names are different, it is very easy to drag a link between a source node named **FName** and a destination node named **FirstName**. However, you are frequently required to generate new data in a destination schema that requires reformatting or reshaping the source data. This is where the BizTalk Mapper functoids come to the rescue. What in the world is a functoid? Well, it is a small component that executes data manipulation functions and calculations on source nodes in order to meet the needs of the destination schema. There are over 75 out-of-the-box functoids available in the BizTalk Mapper, which span a variety of categories such as string manipulation, mathematical calculations, logical conditions, and cumulative computation. This can be extended with the custom functoids that you can add to your project.

If you don't see exactly what you're looking for, you can use the `Scripting` functoid that enables you to write your own XSL script or .NET code to be executed within the map.

An example of the concatenate string functoid configuration screen is shown as follows:

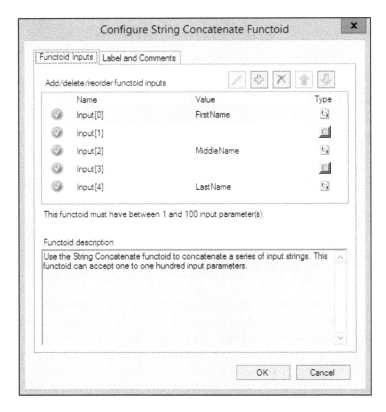

It's important to understand that the BizTalk Mapper is for data normalization logic only, *not* business logic. If you need to make business decisions, a map is not the right place to store that logic. For example, you would not want to embed complex discount generation logic within a BizTalk map. That sort of business logic belongs in a more easily maintained repository than in a map file. As a simple rule, the map should only be responsible for shaping the output message, not for altering the meaning of the data in its fields. Maps are great for transformation instructions, but a lousy place to store mission-critical business algorithms.

Configuring BizTalk messaging

Understanding how to design and arrange BizTalk messaging settings is an absolutely critical part of designing any BizTalk solution, let alone a service-oriented one.

Earlier in this chapter on BizTalk Server, we discussed the BizTalk messaging architecture and its foundation in a publish and subscribe routing model. One of the most important parts of a messaging configuration is enabling the receipt of new messages. Without the ability to absorb messages, there's not much to talk about. In BizTalk Server, messages are brought onboard through the combination of receive ports and receive locations.

Receive ports can be configured from within the BizTalk Server Administration Console. Receive ports support both "one-way" and "two-way" message exchange patterns. On the left-hand side of a receive port configuration, there is a series of vertically arranged tabs that display different sets of properties. Choosing the **Receive Locations** tab enables us to create the actual receive location, which defines the URI that BizTalk will monitor for inbound messages. In the **Transport** section of a receive location's primary configuration pane, we can choose from the list of available BizTalk adapters. Once an adapter is chosen from the list, the **Configure** button next to the selected transport type becomes active. For a receive location exploiting the FILE adapter, "configuration" requires entering a valid file path into the Receive folder property as illustrated in the following screenshot:

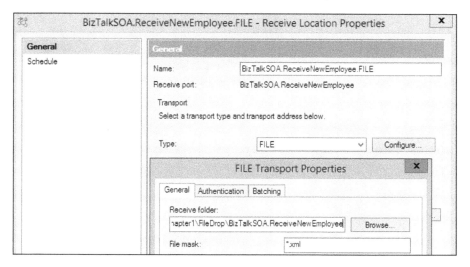

The next step in configuring BizTalk messaging is to create a subscriber for the data that is published by this receiving interface. BizTalk send ports are an example of a subscriber in a messaging solution. Much like receive locations, send ports allow you to choose a BizTalk adapter and configure the transmission URI for the message. However, simply configuring a URI does not complete a send port configuration as we must pinpoint what type of message this subscriber is interested in. On the left-hand side of a send port configuration window, there is a vertical set of tabs. The **Filters** tab, as shown in the following screenshot, is where we can set up specific interest criteria for this send port. For example, we can define a subscription that listens for all messages of a particular type that reach the MessageBox database:

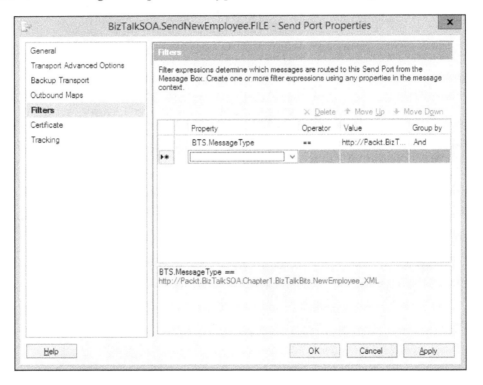

A send port can be in three distinct states. By default, a send port is unenlisted. This means that the port has not registered its particular subscription with BizTalk, and would not pull any messages from the MessageBox. A send port may also be enlisted, which is associated with ports that have registered subscriptions but are not processing messages. In this case, the messages targeted for this port stay in a queue until the port is placed in the final state, Started. A started port has its subscriptions active in MessageBox is heartily processing all the messages it cares about.

The BizTalk Server messaging engine is the heart and soul of a BizTalk solution. Here, we saw how to create new input interfaces and define subscribers for the published data.

Working with BizTalk orchestration

BizTalk Server includes a workflow platform, which allows us to graphically create executable, long-running, stateful processes. These workflows, called orchestrations, are designed in Visual Studio and executed on by BizTalk Server. The Orchestration Designer in Visual Studio includes a rich palette of shapes that we can use to build robust workflows consisting of control flow, message manipulation, service consumption, and much more. The orchestration runtime is responsible for executing the orchestrations and managing their state data.

Orchestration is a purely optional part of a BizTalk solution. You can design a complete application that consists solely of message routing ports. In fact, many of the service-oriented patterns that we visit throughout this book will not require an orchestration. Having said that, there are a number of scenarios where injecting orchestrations into the solution makes sense. For instance, instead of subscribing directly to the "new employee" message, perhaps a payroll system will need additional data (such as bank information for a direct deposit) not currently available in the original employee message. We can decide to create a workflow, which first inserts the available information into the payroll system, and then sends a message to the new employee asking for additional data points. The workflow will then wait for and process the employee's response, and conclude by updating the record in the payroll system with the new information. BizTalk orchestrations are a good fit for automating manual processes or choreographing a series of disconnected services or processes to form a single workflow.

Orchestration "shapes" such as **Decide**, **Transform**, **Send**, **Receive**, and **Loop** are used to build our orchestration diagrams like the one shown here. The following diagram shows a message leaving the orchestration, and then another message returning later on in the flow. How does that message know which running orchestration instance to come back to? What if we have a thousand of these individual processes in flight at a single point in time? BizTalk Server has the concept of **correlation**, which means that you can identify a unique set of attributes for a given message; this will help it find its way to the appropriate running orchestration instance. A correlation attribute might be as simple as a unique invoice identifier, or a composite key made up of a person's name, order date, and zip code.

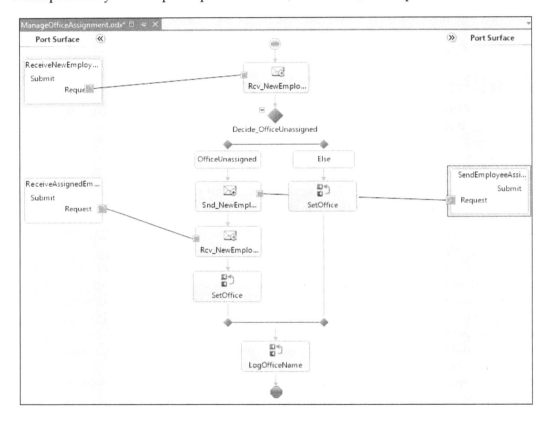

 Orchestration is a powerful tool in your development arsenal and we will make frequent use of it throughout this book.

Summary

In this chapter, we looked at what BizTalk is, its core use cases, and how it works. In my experience, one of the biggest competitors to BizTalk Server is not another product, but custom-built solutions. Many organizations engage a "build versus buy" debate prior to committing to a commercial product. In this chapter, I highlighted just a few aspects of BizTalk that make it a compelling choice for usage. With BizTalk Server, you get a well-designed scalable messaging engine with a durable persistence tier, which guarantees that your mission-critical messages are not lost in transit. The engine also provides native support for message tracking, recoverability, and straightforward scalability. BizTalk provides you with more than 20 native application adapters that save weeks of custom development time and testing. We also got a glimpse of BizTalk's integrated workflow toolset, which enables us to quickly build executable business processes that run in a load-balanced environment. These features alone often tip the scales in BizTalk Server's favor, not to mention the multitude of features that we are yet to discuss, such as Enterprise Single Sign On, the Business Rules Engine, Business Activity Monitoring, and so on.

I hope that this chapter also planted some seeds in your mind with regards to thinking about BizTalk solutions in a service-oriented fashion. There are best practices for designing reusable, maintainable solutions that we will investigate throughout the rest of this book. In the next chapter, we'll explore one of the most important technologies for building robust service interfaces in BizTalk Server, which is Windows Communication Foundation.

Windows Communication Foundation Primer

2

Good communication is as stimulating as black coffee, and just as hard to sleep after.

– Anne Morrow Lindbergh

Windows Communication Foundation (WCF) is a critical part of the Microsoft services strategy and a key part of BizTalk Server 2013 platform. WCF is a rich and expansive topic, so this chapter will only focus on the key aspects of WCF, which prepares us for its usage in later chapters.

In this chapter, you will learn:

- What WCF is and why it matters
- How to construct and configure new WCF services
- Service hosting options
- How to call a WCF service from a client application

What is WCF?

In a nutshell, WCF is a framework for building and hosting services. WCF services make use of standard technologies to offer a wide range of cross-platform security, transaction, and communication capabilities.

Before WCF came along, .NET developers who built distributed applications had to choose between communication schemes such as ASP.NET web services, .NET remoting, and **Message Queuing (MSMQ)**. This choice carried with it implications for how the component was designed, developed, deployed, and consumed. If you went with ASP.NET web services, you were committing to XML message formats and were handcuffed by limitations of the HTTP transport protocol. If you chose .NET remoting, you were able to process messages in an efficient fashion, but have immediately limited yourself to .NET-only service clients. MSMQ is wonderful for disconnected applications, but in choosing it you've eliminated any chance at having a synchronous, request-response conversation with a software client.

The goal of WCF is to unify these many technologies and provide a single transport-neutral development paradigm with common aspects for security, transactions, and exception handling. The service is implemented independent of the communication protocol strategy. This is a fairly revolutionary concept that introduces immense flexibility to service designers. Instead of building services with tightly coupled and rigid endpoints that do not welcome change, we can design flexible services that are capable of supporting a wide range of current and future consumers.

The service endpoint is king, and endpoints in WCF are defined using the easy-to-remember **ABC** acronym.

- The letter **A** stands for **addressing**, which refers to the actual URL of the service
- The letter **B** stands for **binding**, which describes how we communicate with the service
- Finally, the letter **C** stands for **contract**, which defines the operations and data elements that this service exposes

Let's look at each of these in detail.

Defining the contract

Unlike ASP.NET web services, WCF truly promotes a "contract first" design style where developers need to thoughtfully consider how the outside world will interact with their service. There is a clean separation between the interface definition and the actual implementation of the service. When building ASP.NET services, the developer typically takes a code-first approach, where .NET classes are decorated with attributes and exposed as services. In the WCF model, we focus first on the data being shared and what our interface to the outside world should look like (the contract). Only after this critical step is complete does the WCF developer begin to design the actual service implementation logic.

There are actually three different contracts that you may define for a WCF service:

- Service contract
- Data contract
- Fault contract

There's actually a fourth contract type corresponding to the message, but I won't be covering that here. We'll investigate the service and data contract types right now, but save the fault contract for the *Throwing custom service faults* section in this chapter.

Service contracts

The **service contract** explains what your service can do. It's built using a .NET interface class and decorated with WCF attributes that identify it as a service contract. A basic service contract looks like this:

```
[ServiceContract()]
public interface IVendorContract
{
    [OperationContract()]
    void InsertVendor(string vendorId, string vendorName);

    [OperationContract()]
    bool DeleteVendor(string vendorId);
}
```

Note that the interface has a ServiceContract attribute and that each operation that we wish to expose publicly on our contract has an OperationContract attribute. Each of these metadata attributes has a series of optional parameters that let us explicitly define public characteristics of the service. For instance, we can add the Name and Namespace properties to ServiceContract to better characterize this service in our environment. We can also add a series of properties to OperationContract to control what the operation is named and what the SOAPAction value is set to. Why give an alternate name to a service operation? Consider scenarios where you have an overloaded operation in your WCF service contract and need each WSDL operation to have a unique public name. C# (and .NET) support overloading, but the WSDL standard no longer does. Examples of service contracts are shown as follows:

```
[ServiceContract(Name="VendorService",
  Namespace="http://BizTalkSOA/Contracts")]
public interface IVendorContract
{
    [OperationContract(Name="InsertVendor")]
    void InsertVendor(string vendorId, string vendorName);
    [OperationContract(Name="InsertVendorWithContact")]
    void InsertVendor(string vendorId, string vendorName,
      string vendorContactName);

    [OperationContract(Name="DeleteVendor")]
    bool DeleteVendor(string vendorId);
}
```

Data contracts

As you can probably imagine, services often need to accept and return comprehensive data entities in addition to simple type parameters. I might want to model a data entity such as customer instead of having a service operation accept 15 individual string parameters. Complex data parameters are categorized as **data contracts** in WCF. Data contracts can be replica of schemas, or we can think of contracts as .NET class representation of schemas. Contracts can have the same level of hierarchy and structure as schemas. A data contract is a .NET class decorated with the DataContract attribute and whose public properties are flagged with DataMember attributes. Public service operation definitions can only include complex types identified as data contracts as illustrated in the following code:

```
[DataContract()]
public class VendorType
{
    private string vendorId;
    private string vendorName;
    private string vendorContactName;

    [DataMember()]
    public string VendorId
    {
        get { return vendorId; }
        set { vendorId = value; }
    }

    [DataMember()]
    public string VendorName
    {
```

```
        get { return vendorName; }
        set { vendorName = value; }
    }

    [DataMember()]
    public string VendorContactName
    {
        get { return vendorContactName; }
        set { vendorContactName = value; }
    }
}
```

Much like the service contract, the attributes of the data contract allow for more fine-grained control of the entity definition. For instance, we may provide Name and Namespace to DataContract while also adding some useful node ordering and existence attributes to the member elements:

```
[DataContract(Name="Vendor" Namespace = "http://BizTalkSOA/Types")]
public class VendorType
{
    private string vendorId;
    private string vendorName;
    private string vendorContactName;

    [DataMember(IsRequired=true, Order=0)]
    public string VendorId
    {
        get { return vendorId; }
        set { vendorId = value; }
    }

    [DataMember(IsRequired=true, Order=1)]
    public string VendorName
    {
        get { return vendorName; }
        set { vendorName = value; }
    }

    [DataMember(IsRequired=false, Order=2)]
    public string VendorContactName
    {
        get { return vendorContactName; }
        set { vendorContactName = value; }
    }
}
```

If you omit the Order property from the DataMember attribute, the nodes are ordered alphabetically, which may not be how you wish to organize your public schema.

Implementing contracts in services

Once we have decided upon an interface definition for a service, we are able to move forward with the service which implements this interface. For those of you who have previously built .NET interface classes and then realized those interfaces in subsequent concrete classes, the WCF model is quite natural. In fact, it's the same. We build a concrete service class and choose to implement the WCF service contract defined earlier. For this example, we will take the previously built interface (which has since had its Insert operations replaced by a single operation that takes a data contract parameter) and implement the service logic.

Consider creating distinct Visual Studio projects to house the service contract and the service implementation. This allows you to share the contract project with service consumers without sharing details of the service that realizes the contract. This idea is shown in the following screenshot:

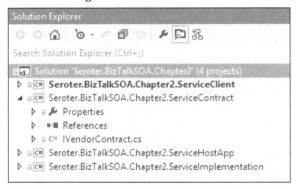

An example code for the service contract is as follows:

```csharp
public class VendorService : IVendorContract
{
    public void InsertVendor(VendorType newVendor)
    {
        System.Console.WriteLine("Vendor {0} inserted by service ...",
newVendor.VendorId);

    }
```

```
    public bool DeleteVendor(string vendorId)
    {
        System.Console.WriteLine("Vendor {0} deleted ...", vendorId);

        return true;
    }
}
```

A WCF service may have metadata attributes applied to it in order to influence or dictate behavior. For instance, WCF has very robust support for creating and consuming transactional services. While specific attributes are applied directly to the service contract to affect how the service respects transactions, the attributes on the concrete service itself establish the way the service processes those transactions. In order to identify whether a service will accept transactions or not, an attribute is added to the service contract.

```
[ServiceContract(Name="VendorService", Namespace="http://BizTalkSOA/
Contracts")]
    public interface IVendorContract
    {
        [OperationContract(Name="DeleteVendor")]
        [TransactionFlow(TransactionFlowOption.Allowed)]
        bool DeleteVendor(string vendorId);
    }
```

However, this doesn't dictate the implementation details. That is left to the attributes on the service itself. The ServiceBehavior attribute has numerous available properties used to shape the activities of the service. Likewise, OperationBehavior applied to the implemented contract operations enables us to further refine the actions of the operation. In the following code snippet, I've instructed the service to put a tight rein on the transaction locks via the Serializable isolation level. Next, I commanded the DeleteVendor operation to either enlist in the flowed transaction or create a new one (TransactionScopeRequired) and to automatically commit the transaction upon operation conclusion (TransactionAutoComplete), as shown:

```
[ServiceBehavior(TransactionIsolationLevel=
  System.Transactions.IsolationLevel.Serializable)]
public class VendorService : IVendorContract
{
    [OperationBehavior(TransactionAutoComplete=true,
      TransactionScopeRequired=true)]
    public bool DeleteVendor(string vendorId)
    {
        System.Console.WriteLine("Vendor {0} deleted
          ...", vendorId);
```

```
          return true;
    }
}
```

Be aware of the nuances of where WCF attributes may be applied (for example, service contract, concrete service, and service operation) and the rich capabilities that these metadata tags can offer you.

While this example showed how to attach transactions to services, you need to be extremely cautious and judicious with the usage of transactions across service boundaries. While WCF makes this seem transparent, try to make your services as encapsulated as possible so that they have few explicit or implied dependencies on other services

Throwing custom service faults

Whenever possible, you should avoid returning the full exception stack back to the service caller. You may inadvertently reveal security or implementation details that allow a malicious user to engage in mischief. The preference is to throw friendly/ business and typed faults for the clients to handle.

Alternatively, in the config file in the service behavior section, we can set includeExceptionDetailInFaults="false" to avoid sending exception details to clients.

Within WCF, a fault contract is a custom data contract that allows you to shape the exception being returned to the service consumer. Let's say we defined a controlled fault contract that looks like this:

```
[DataContract(Name = "InsertFault")]
public class InsertFaultType
{
    private string friendlyMessage;

    [DataMember()]
    public string FriendlyMessage
    {
        get { return friendlyMessage; }
        set { friendlyMessage = value; }
    }
}
```

So far, this looks like any old data contract. And in reality, that's all it is. However, we can associate this fault contract with a particular operation by adding the FaultContract attribute to the operation in the service contract:

```
[OperationContract(Name="InsertVendor")]
[FaultContract(typeof(InsertFaultType))]
void InsertVendor(VendorType newVendor);
```

While implementing the service, we explicitly produce and throw these custom exception types back to the service consumer. This is done by catching the .NET exception and creating a new fault object from the custom fault we created earlier. Then, we throw a new FaultException typed to our custom fault definition:

```
public void InsertVendor(VendorType newVendor)
{
    try
    {
        //do complex database update ...
    }
    catch (System.Data.SqlClient.SqlException sqlEx)
    {
      //log actual fault to admin log

      //throwing SQL exception back to caller is bad.
      //Create new exception out of custom fault contract
      InsertFaultType insertFault = new InsertFaultType();
      insertFault.FriendlyMessage = "Insert operation failed";

      //throw custom fault
      throw new FaultException<InsertFaultType>(
          insertFault,
          "illegal insert");

    }
}
```

By defining and throwing custom service faults, you achieve better control over how your service communicates to the outside world and can better insulate yourself from critical implementation leakage.

Choosing an endpoint address

It's great that we've talked about the important **C** (the contract) in the **ABCs** of WCF endpoints, but the story is far from complete. So far, we have a service definition completely devoid of transport information. Where does someone go to consume this service? The goal of the endpoint address is to:

- Tell us the communication scheme
- Tell us the location of the service

WCF provides a number of out-of-the-box communication schemes for accessing WCF services. These include options such as:

- HTTP
- TCP
- MSMQ

When looking at a service URI such as `https://packt:8081/VendorService/` `SecureVendorService.svc`, what am I able to infer from this WCF address? First, I can see that I'm using an HTTP/S scheme in order to secure my HTTP transmission channel via SSL certificates. Next, I can tell that the domain hosting this service is called `packt` and uses port `8081` for the HTTP/S traffic. Finally, I can gather the path of the service that I wish to call.

We'll see shortly how to actually set up a WCF service to listen on the address of your choice. For now, simply note that the address of a service is a key part of the whole service endpoint.

The role of service bindings

The WCF service binding (or the **B** in the WCF endpoint **ABCs**) is the channel stack that ties up how a service actually transmits data across the wire. The stack is made up of individual elements that make up the message communication. This includes elements that control security options, session capacity, and transaction capabilities. They are also used to determine how a message is actually encoded during transmission, whether that is in text/XML, binary format, or the new **Message Transmission Optimization Mechanism (MTOM)** format.

WCF provides a series of bindings for the available WCF transports, which offer the most compatible and logical component order for a given transport. Let's review the key bindings that are also available with BizTalk Server 2013 as adapters:

- `BasicHttpBinding`: This binding works great for ASMX SOAP clients that only support **the SOAP 1.1 Basic Profile**. By default, there is no security aspect enabled, no session or transaction capabilities, and its default data encoding is plain text. This is your "safe bet" binding that is the most interoperable for clients that don't support the latest `ws*` web services standards.

- `BasicHttpRelayBinding`: Use this binding when you expose services via Microsoft Azure Service Bus relays, if you want them to have the same capabilities as `BasicHttpBinding`. Configuration of authentication is all that is required because an outbound connection initiates a session to receive messages from the Service Bus relay endpoint.

- `WSHttpBinding`: Like `BasicHttpBinding`, this binding is for HTTP and HTTP/S traffic. This is a rich HTTP-based binding with full support for transactions, sessions, and a default message-based security scheme. With `WSHttpBinding`, you have the choice of not only encoding the payload in plain text but also the more compressed MTOM format.

- `NetTCPBinding`: If you need fast, secure connectivity between WCF endpoints, `NetTCPBinding` is an excellent choice. Data is transferred over TCP in binary format while still getting full support for sessions, transactions, and the full range of security options. Note, however, that this binding will only work for .NET-based service clients.

- `NetTCPRelayBinding`: This replaces `NetTCPBinding` for the exposing of services via Microsoft Azure Service Bus relays using a publicly reachable TCP endpoint. A secure outbound TCP connection creates a TCP listener that receives messages from the Service Bus relay.

- `NetNamedPipeBinding`: If your client communicates with a WCF service and both reside on the same physical server, this is the binding for you. `NetNamedPipeBinding` uses IPC (named pipes) to transport data in a binary encoding with a secure transmission channel.

- `NetMsmqBinding`: This binding uses queuing technology that is ideal for disconnected applications. Data is transferred in a binary encoding with rich security options available, but there is no support for sessions or request/response scenarios. That makes sense because, in a queue scenario, the publisher and subscriber are not aware of each other.

- `WebHTTPBinding`: This supports integration scenarios with RESTful APIs. Security can be configured in the same way as with `BasicHTTPBinding`. Transactions and data encoding do not come out of the box. RESTful services are simple and easy to use and this is what this binding delivers.

The `BasicHttpRelayBinding` and `NetTCPRelayBinding` Service Bus bindings only became available as adapters in BizTalk 2013. *Chapter 6, Azure Service Bus* and *Chapter 13, New SOA Capabilities in BizTalk Server 2013 – Azure Hybrid Patterns* have been added to this version of the book to describe how to use them. For now, you should realize that these open up exciting new possibilities where an on-premise WCF service can be exposed securely in Azure without having to change your corporate infrastructure. For example, there is no requirement to open up a firewall port to facilitate the connection if ports `9350`, `9351`, `9352`, `9353`, and `80/443` are already open.

If a situation arises where none of these bindings meet your needs, you can always craft a custom binding to mix and match available binding elements to your liking. What if your service consumer can only send binary messages over HTTP? The out-of-the-box HTTP bindings don't support such an encoding, but we could configure a custom binding that matches this business requirement. Or what if you need a transmission protocol not offered in the standard WCF toolset? We'll see in *Chapter 9, Asynchronous Communication Patterns*, that the WCF SQL Server Adapter delivers a custom binding, which includes SQL Server communication as a valid service transport. Such control over the WCF channel stack is a key aspect of the framework's flexibility.

Note that there are additional bindings provided by WCF in .NET Framework 4.5, which are not explicitly set up as BizTalk adapters. These include `WSDualHttpBinding` (for duplex communication between endpoints), `WS2007FederationHttpBinding` (which supports federated security scenarios), and `NetPeerTcpBinding` (for peer-to-peer networking).

Hosting services

Now that we've identified the core components of a WCF endpoint, the giant remaining question is: how do I make this service available to consumers? You are able to host your service in a variety of places, including:

- **Self-hosting**: You can create a managed .NET application such as a Windows Form or Console application that acts as the host for your service. A self-hosted service can use any of the available WCF bindings but offers the least infrastructure for service hosting. This avenue is typical of demonstration or proof-of-concept scenarios and is not really considered enterprise grade.

- **Windows Service**: You could choose to build a Windows Service that hosts your service in a more managed fashion. Also considered a form of self-hosting; it too can support the full range of WCF bindings. This is a bit better than manually building a service host because, through the Windows Services platform, you get more manageability and support for failure recovery, automatic startup, and association with a specific Windows identity.

- **IIS**: You can serve up WCF services that have HTTP and HTTP/S endpoints. Here you get the full power of an enterprise web server and the availability, process separation, and host lifecycle management that comes along with it.

- In-process WCF: The premier WCF hosting environment is IIS 7.0 or above, alongside **Windows Process Activation Service (WAS)**. This is available in Windows Server 2008, Windows Vista, and more recent Windows versions. With IIS 7.0 and above, you can host services that rely not only on HTTP communication, but also on three other WCF protocols (TCP, MSMQ, and Pipes). So you get an integrated IIS experience regardless of the transport protocol. This is a fantastic way to get web server benefits (process recycling, health monitoring, and so on) for non-HTTP based services.

For our examples here, I'll use a self-hosted service. While it is very simple to use IIS 7.0 to host our services, the self-hosted paradigm forces us to create (and learn) the host activation plumbing that IIS nicely hides from you. In our case, the host is a Console Application project in Visual Studio. Let's look at the complete host and then dissect it a bit:

```
using System.ServiceModel;
using System.ServiceModel.Channels;

class Program
{
    static void Main(string[] args)
    {
      string address = "http://localhost:8081/VServiceBase";
      Binding httpBinding = new BasicHttpBinding();
```

```
ServiceHost vendorHost = new ServiceHost(
    typeof(VendorService),
    new Uri(address));

vendorHost.AddServiceEndpoint(
    typeof(IVendorContract),
    httpBinding, "");

vendorHost.Open();
Console.WriteLine("Vendor host opened ...");

Console.ReadLine();

vendorHost.Close();
    }
}
```

So what do we have here? First, I created a string to hold my base address. A base address acts as a root for the service from which a series of endpoints with relative addresses may be based upon.

Next, I created an object for `BasicHttpBinding`. We could have used any WCF binding here, but given that I chose an HTTP base address, I chose one of the available WCF bindings that supports HTTP.

Now comes the important part. The `ServiceHost` object essentially instantiates the service, configures the endpoint, applies security, and starts to listen on the requested URI. The constructor I used for `ServiceHost` first accepts the service implementation class object. The second parameter is an array of base addresses for the service. Note that we could have multiple base addresses, but only one per URI scheme. for instance, I could have both an HTTP base address and a TCP base address for my service and then have endpoints defined that use either of the available base addresses.

On the next line of the Console Application, I call the `AddServiceEndpoint` operation on my `ServiceHost` instance. This operation accepts the contract used by the service, the binding of the endpoint, and optionally, the relative address. Note that our endpoint has the full **ABCs** of WCF applied. Finally, I opened the host which led to the service endpoint being available for consumption.

Now, you may look at this and wonder why you'd want to hardcode this type of connection information into your host. How do you deal with service promotion through multiple environments where the address constantly changes or achieve all this flexible goodness that WCF evangelists always talk about? This is where we gently shift into the concept of storing service configurations in an external XML file. If there is one thing you will learn from your forays into WCF, it's that configuration is key and configuration files get pretty darn big.

If we add an application configuration to the Console Application in Visual Studio, all the address, binding, and endpoint decisions are moved from code to configuration. The self-hosted service we just saw has much simpler code when a configuration file is used, as shown:

```
class Program
  {
    static void Main(string[] args)
    {
        ServiceHost vendorHost =
            new ServiceHost(typeof(VendorService));

        vendorHost.Open();
        Console.WriteLine("Vendor host opened ...");

        Console.ReadLine();
        vendorHost.Close();
    }
  }
```

Much shorter, eh? The application configuration (app.config) file associated with this self-hosted service looks like this:

```
<configuration>
  <system.serviceModel>
    <services>
      <service name="BizTalkSOA.Chapter2.
        ServiceImplementation.VendorService">
      <endpoint
        address=""
        binding="basicHttpBinding"
         contract="BizTalkSOA.Chapter2.
            ServiceContract.IVendorContract" />
        <host>
```

```
        <baseAddresses>
          <add baseAddress=
            "http://localhost:8081/VServiceBase" />
        </baseAddresses>
      </host>
    </service>
  </services>
  </system.serviceModel>
</configuration>
```

Note how the values (for example, base address, binding, contract, and service implementation) previously spelled out in code are now all present in a configuration file. As you can imagine, it's quite simple to add new endpoints, change base addresses, and switch binding parameters in an XML configuration file.

 As far as I can determine, the only reason you would choose to embed WCF endpoint details in the service host code would be when either (a) the address and channel stack are *never* expected to change or (b) the address and channel stack are set dynamically based on runtime conditions. Other than this, storing these transport values in an external configuration file provides the greatest level of flexibility and extensibility for WCF host solutions.

Is this all there is to a hosted WCF service? Hardly so. Once the endpoint has been defined, we decide which binding settings to modify. For instance, I could explicitly set up a basicHttpBinding configuration and define service timeout values, message size limits, and a specific security scheme. There are a wide array of service variations that may be designed by manipulating these binding configurations.

While binding configurations play a key role in refining the way the service operates over the wire, WCF behaviors are used to provide custom extensions to the WCF runtime. There are four places where behaviors may be applied in a WCF solution:

- Contract
- Operation
- Endpoint
- Service

For example, we can apply a `serviceMetadata` behavior to the service in order to allow clients to investigate the service WSDL. Also, at the service level, we are capable of controlling the number of concurrent calls via the `serviceThrottling` behavior. Most importantly, it's fairly straightforward to build new behaviors that can be customized and reused by multiple services. For instance, we could build a custom interceptor, which logs all inbound messages to a database. We'll see examples of custom behaviors in future chapters.

Consuming WCF services

Now comes the most important part: using the service! How you go about consuming a WCF service depends greatly on the type of client application used.

Non-WCF clients

If you plan on calling a WCF service from a non-WCF client, have no fear, you're still in great shape. One of the design goals of WCF (and any quality SOA solution) is interoperability, which means that WCF services should be consumable on a wide variety of platforms and technology stacks.

Now, it is still the responsibility of the service designer to construct a service that's usable by non-WCF applications. For instance, a broadly used service would offer `basicHttpBinding` to ensure that applications based on .NET Framework 2.0, or JRE 1.4 would have no problem consuming it. An interoperable service would also use security schemes that rely upon commonly available certificates for transport security.

Let's assume that a WCF service with a basic HTTP endpoint has been exposed. Let's also assume that this service has a metadata "behavior" attached to it so that we can interrogate its WSDL contract. If you have a .NET Framework 2.0 application that typically consumes classic ASMX services (ASP.NET web services), they can consume a WCF service in the exact same fashion. That is, add a new web reference to the WCF service metadata definition.

If you have Visual Studio 2012 installed, the **Add Web Reference** option isn't immediately available on the project.

1. You first right-click the project and choose the **Add Service Reference** menu item. Click on the button labeled **Advanced**, which you'll find at the bottom of the window:

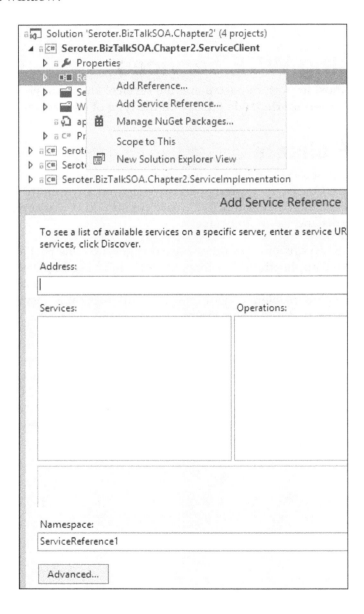

2. The next window that opens is a settings window, which has a button at the bottom for those who wish to add a traditional "web reference" that leverages older .NET technology:

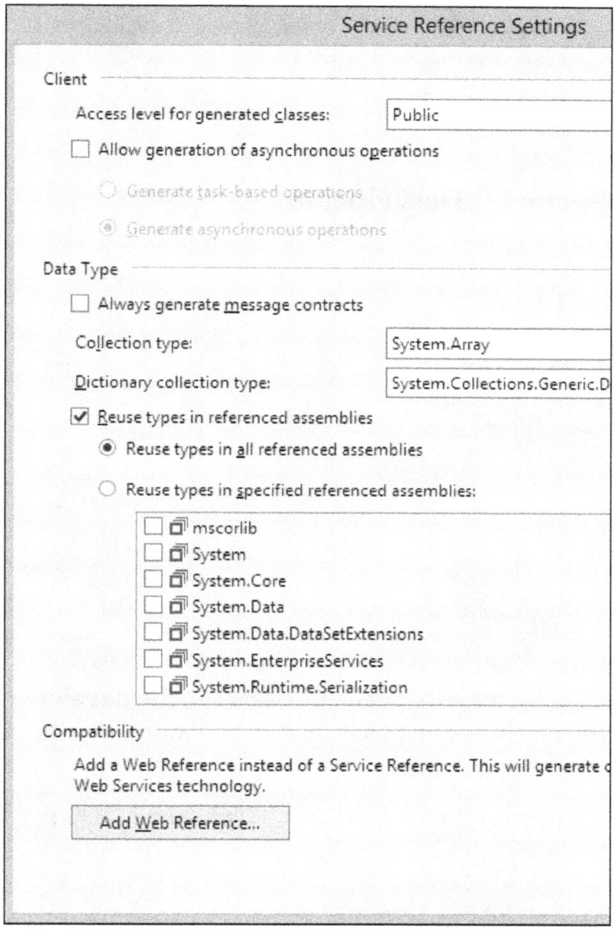

Service Reference Settings

Client

Access level for generated classes: Public

☐ Allow generation of asynchronous operations

○ Generate task-based operations

◉ Generate asynchronous operations

Data Type

☐ Always generate message contracts

Collection type: System.Array

Dictionary collection type: System.Collections.Generic.D

☑ Reuse types in referenced assemblies

◉ Reuse types in all referenced assemblies

○ Reuse types in specified referenced assemblies:

☐ mscorlib
☐ System
☐ System.Core
☐ System.Data
☐ System.Data.DataSetExtensions
☐ System.EnterpriseServices
☐ System.Runtime.Serialization

Compatibility

Add a Web Reference instead of a Service Reference. This will generate ⌀
Web Services technology.

Add Web Reference...

3. Choosing the **Add Web Reference** button finally opens up the traditional service browser, where we plug in the URL of our service and see the corresponding metadata:

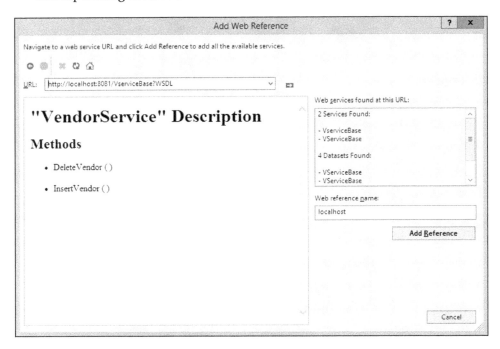

4. In the subsequent code that calls this service, the developer would use the assigned web reference just as if they were calling any standard SOAP web service:

```
Console.WriteLine("Vendor client launched ...");
try
{
  AsmxProxy.VendorService svc = new
    AsmxProxy.VendorService();
  AsmxProxy.Vendor newVendor = new AsmxProxy.Vendor();
  newVendor.VendorId = "1234";
  newVendor.VendorName = "Watson Consulting";
  newVendor.VendorContactName = "Watson Seroter";
```

```
      svc.InsertVendor(newVendor);
      Console.WriteLine("Vendor " + newVendor.VendorId +
        " inserted ...");
      Console.ReadLine();
    }
    catch (System.Web.Services.Protocols.SoapException ex)
    {
    //grab "insert fault" part of message
      Console.WriteLine(ex.Detail.InnerText);
      Console.ReadLine();
    }
```

The result? The HTTP host was opened successfully by WCF, and after the client executed the insert operation, the service wrote its confirmation message to the host console:

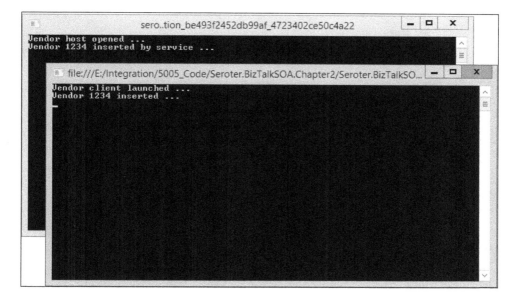

However, if our service fails and throws our custom fault message, our client code catches it as a SOAP exception and still has access to the custom fault details. Note that the exception's detail object contains the XML message of the `InsertFault` type, in the following screenshot:

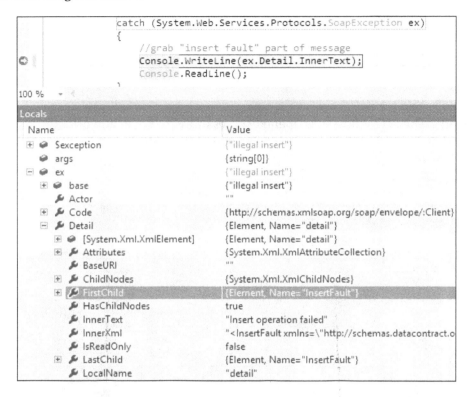

WCF clients

If you have the benefit of using a WCF-enabled application to call a WCF service, the full might of Microsoft's communication stack is laid before you. You are no longer constrained by HTTP-only communication and you can exploit a wide range of encoding, security, and transaction capabilities in your service consuming application.

> While WCF-to-WCF communication scenarios offer a rich set of communication options, technically any `WS*`-compliant application should be able to take advantage of a majority of WCF's service characteristics. For example, an Oracle application that understands WS-Security can effectively participate in secure conversations with a WCF service.

The easiest way to consume WCF services from a WCF application is to generate a proxy class that shields us from the plumbing necessary to call the service. A WCF proxy can be generated in one of two ways. First, we use the **ServiceModel Metadata Utility** tool (`svcutil.exe`) command-line tool if we want full control of the way the proxy class is generated. This tool takes the service metadata and generates a .NET source code file that may be used to call the WCF service.

The power in this little utility lies in the ability to apply a cornucopia of command-line parameters that define attributes of the .NET source code file, such as its programming language, namespace, output location, and a whole lot more. For instance, executing the following command on our service results in a full WCF proxy class and merges the new WCF configurations with the existing configuration file of the client application:

```
Svcutil.exe http://localhost:8081/VServiceBase?WSDL /
out:WCFProxy.cs /language:c#  /config:app.config /mergeConfig
```

Because I built the WCF service proxy manually, my client application must have both the `System.ServiceModel` and `System.Runtime.Serialization` assemblies added as project references.

Consuming the WCF proxy class looks quite similar to consuming the ASMX proxy class. In fact, the only real difference that you'll notice here is more explicit interaction with the client proxy class. Note that we work with the proxy class within a `try` block and catch any exceptions (including our custom one) in well-defined `catch` blocks. While it is tempting to apply the C# `using` statement to WCF proxies, that practice can actually lead to swallowed exceptions and should be avoided. See `http://msdn.microsoft.com/en-us/library/aa355056.aspx` for more details. The other slight difference is that the WCF proxy class has an overloaded constructor. In this case, I'm passing in the name of the service endpoint name that resides in the application configuration file:

```
WcfProxy.VendorServiceClient svc = new
  WcfProxy.VendorServiceClient
  ("BasicHttpBinding_VendorService");

try
  {
WcfProxy.Vendor newVendor = new WcfProxy.Vendor();
  newVendor.VendorId = "9876";
  newVendor.VendorName = "Noah Partners";
  newVendor.VendorContactName = "Noah Seroter";

  svc.InsertVendor(newVendor);
```

```
Console.WriteLine("Vendor " + newVendor.VendorId +
  " inserted ...");

svc.Close();
}
catch (System.ServiceModel.FaultException
  <WcfProxy.InsertFault> ex)
  {
    Console.WriteLine(ex.Detail.FriendlyMessage);

    Console.ReadLine();
  }
catch (System.ServiceModel.CommunicationException)
  { svc.Abort(); }
catch (System.TimeoutException) { svc.Abort(); }
catch (System.Exception) { svc.Abort(); throw; }
```

If you're looking for an easier way to generate a WCF proxy class, look no further! Visual Studio also offers an **Add Service Reference** option, which enables us to generate our proxy class from within our development environment. This is depicted as follows:

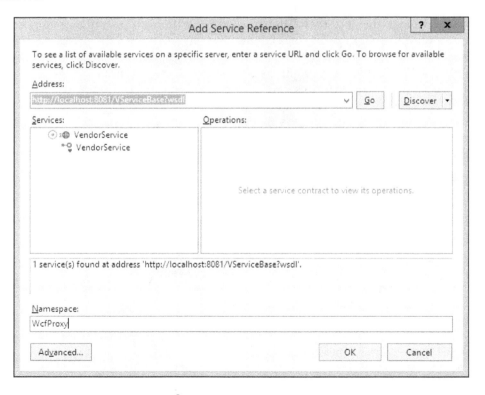

By either using the ServiceModel Metadata Utility tool explicitly to generate proxy classes or, instead, using Visual Studio (which uses `svcutil.exe` underneath the covers), you have some efficient options for generating WCF-compliant code for use by service clients.

Summary

In this chapter, we learned that Windows Communication Foundation is a broad and powerful framework for designing, building, hosting, and consuming services. WCF unifies the many distributed application technologies in the Microsoft platform under a single programming model. The service developer is now freed from programming to the constraints of a given transport and can instead focus on building robust services that take advantage of the latest industry standards for security, transactions, stateful sessions, and more.

The importance of WCF to BizTalk Server 2013 cannot be understated. In the next chapter, we will look at how to both expose and consume powerful WCF services from the BizTalk Server engine.

3
Using WCF Services in BizTalk Server 2013

The path to greatness is along with others.

– Baltasar Gracián

Now that I've whetted your appetite with a quick look at BizTalk and WCF development, we're ready to start the main course. Let's dig into how BizTalk Server takes advantage of the power of WCF to consume and expose services. We will start this chapter with a look at how BizTalk and WCF complement each other and then explicitly show how to both consume and expose WCF services from BizTalk Server. Then we'll see how to interact with both one-way and two-way messaging patterns and conclude by seeing how to consume services with and without orchestration in the middle. Throughout this chapter, I will demonstrate integration with numerous WCF bindings including WSHttp, NetTcp, and NetPipe.

In this chapter, you will learn:

- The different roles of BizTalk Server and WCF in a solution
- Where WCF fits into the BizTalk architecture
- How to generate WCF services out of BizTalk artifacts
- How to consume WCF services from BizTalk artifacts

The relationship between BizTalk and WCF

So, are WCF and BizTalk Server competing technologies or complementary ones? Let's review the role of each:

BizTalk Server 2013	• Enterprise offering for messaging solutions that require consistent life cycle for design, build, and deployment
	• Process orchestration made available through a stateful, durable workflow engine
	• Adapters to numerous protocols, technologies, and line-of-business systems
	• Route data through high-performing, scalable, and persistent publish-subscribe message broker
	• Runtime services with built-in scalability and load balancing
	• Supplementary modules such as Business Activity Monitoring, Single Sign On, and Business Rules Engine
Windows Communication Foundation	• Unify existing .NET communication technologies under a single umbrella
	• Offer rich cross-platform support for WS* extensions targeting security, transactions, and stateful sessions
	• Variety of flexible service host containers available
	• Significant amount of service configuration exists outside compiled code

Given this information, we see that the intersection of these two technologies occurs at the point where the BizTalk messaging and orchestration engine needs to communicate effectively with the outside world. WCF extends BizTalk Server's base capability to provide and consume rich service interfaces through powerful security and customization options. BizTalk Server provides WCF solutions with an enterprise-class messaging engine, which brings along service orchestration and access to numerous adapters that WCF does not have out-of-the-box bindings for.

BizTalk WCF adapters

BizTalk Server 2006 R2 introduced us to the BizTalk WCF adapters. In reality, BizTalk Server 2006 R2 has seven WCF adapters that directly correlate to a subset of bindings available in WCF. These adapters are:

- **WCF-BasicHttp**: Just like the built-in WCF binding, this adapter is your safest best for simple service clients that conform to SOAP Basic Profile 1.1

- **WCF-WSHttp**: When you need an HTTP endpoint juiced up with the robustness of WS* standards for greater security, transactions, and encoding, this is the ideal adapter

- **WCF-NetTcp**: If WCF technologies are on both ends of the channel, this adapter provides the most efficient means for transporting information while still providing all the hearty WS* capabilities

- **WCF-NetMsmq**: In scenarios where disconnected operations are vital, this adapter provides integration with queuing through MSMQ

- **WCF-NetNamedPipe**: When you have the source or target WCF application on the same physical server as BizTalk itself, the most adept adapter is this one

- **WCF-Custom**: When you need rich customization of the WCF endpoint, you use this adapter to manipulate the binding details and add behaviors

- **WCF-CustomIsolated**: For WCF endpoints hosted by the local web server and requiring binding or behavior customizations choose this adapter

BizTalk Server 2010 added some additional WCF adapters (deprecating some existing non-WCF adapters) via the BizTalk Server Adapter Pack 2010 which includes the following adapters:

WCF-OracleDb: This provides connectivity to the Oracle Database

- **WCF-SQL**: This provides connectivity to Microsoft SQL Server database, deprecating the SQL adapter

- **WCF-SAP**: This provides connectivity to SAP

- **WCF-OracleEBS**: This provides connectivity to Oracle E-business Suite

- **WCF-Siebel**: This provides connectivity to the Siebel eBusiness Suite

BizTalk Server 2013 added the following adapters:

- **WCF-BasicHttpRelay**: Microsoft BizTalk Server uses the WCF-BasicHttpRelay adapter when receiving and sending WCF service requests through the BasicHttpRelayBinding, which allows you to leverage Azure Service Bus Relays to expose your on-premise services to the outside world without any reverse proxy or other infrastructure changes.

- **WCF-NetTcpRelay**: Microsoft BizTalk Server uses the WCF-NetTcpRelay adapter when receiving and sending WCF service requests through the NetTcpRelayBinding which allows you to leverage Azure Service Bus Relays to expose your on-premise services to the outside world without any reverse proxy or other infrastructure changes.

- **WCF-WebHttp**: This adapter allows you to expose or target RESTful services.

> Note that there are additional WCF bindings available in .NET Framework 4.5 but they do not have specific BizTalk adapters. These include WS2007HttpBinding, WsFederationHttpBinding, NetPeerTcpBinding, and NetMessagingBinding. But these can be used with the WCF-Custom adapter.

You can see all the bindings available by creating a new send or receive location, selecting **WCF-Custom**, clicking on **Configure**, selecting the **Binding** tab, and dropping down **Binding Type**, as shown in the following screenshot:

So how do these adapters actually fit into the BizTalk architecture? As they are adapters, they reside at the edges of BizTalk Server. A message sent to a **WCF-BasicHttp** receive location might follow this path:

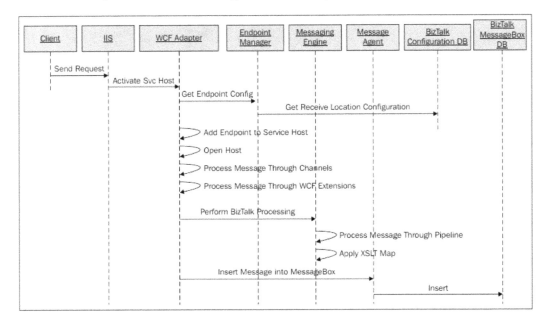

The inbound message arrives from the client to **Internet Information Services (IIS)**, which determines the service endpoint to instantiate. The WCF service host is activated, and BizTalk Endpoint Manager is called in order to retrieve the settings of the receive location that matches the service endpoint. The message is processed through any relevant WCF channels and extensions before the message is passed off to the BizTalk Messaging Engine (residing in an isolated host). The Messaging Engine cycles through any receive pipeline components and maps before sending the message to the MessageBox via the BizTalk Message Agent.

In *Chapter 2, Windows Communication Foundation Primer*, we saw how WCF services require a service host in order to operate. In the BizTalk Server world, a **host** is a processing container that encompasses a wide range of runtime activities. BizTalk has the concept of an in-process host and an isolated host. An in-process host simply refers to a Windows Service that is owned and operated by BizTalk Server. In-process hosts manage most BizTalk adapters, run the Orchestration Engine, and contain the Messaging Engine. A BizTalk isolated host is used when BizTalk Server does not own the life cycle of the container process. For all practical purposes, this refers to processes hosted within Microsoft IIS. The BizTalk web-based receive adapters (such as SOAP and HTTP) have to run in the same domain as IIS; therefore, they run in the special BizTalk isolated host.

All this all matters because the BizTalk WCF adapters have some flexibility when it comes to BizTalk hosting. All of the WCF bindings (including the HTTP-based ones) can be technically hosted by an in-process BizTalk host by using a WCF-Custom adapter. The following adapters will only run in isolated hosts for a Receive Port:

- WCF-BasicHttp
- WCF-CustomIsolated
- WCF-WebHttp
- WCF-WSHttp

If you wish to maintain an HTTP-based receive endpoint within an in-process host, you may use the WCF-Custom adapter and choose one of the HTTP-based bindings. For all these in-process adapters, the BizTalk Server receive location actually acts as the WCF service host. When you start the receive location, you are opening the WCF host. Likewise, when you disable the receive location, the WCF host is closed.

For adapters hosted in isolated hosts, while the BizTalk receive location still plays a role in the availability of the service, the adapter lifetime is actually managed by IIS. Starting and stopping the receive location linked to an isolated host impacts the ability to call the related service but does not physically impact the service host.

Is there any reason that you would host HTTP endpoints within a BizTalk in-process host instead of inside IIS? On the plus side, you get greater control over the service life cycle and can define any URL you like. On the downside, you make it more difficult to participate in web server load balancing and give up the rich set of service management features that IIS offers.

Let's now take a look at how we actually use these WCF adapters to generate both services and metadata as well as hosts for WCF endpoints.

Exposing WCF services from orchestrations

Our first task is to take a BizTalk orchestration workflow and expose one of its ports as a WCF-enabled web service. Fortunately for us, this is a fairly straightforward undertaking that requires no actual coding.

Setting up the project

The use case we will use throughout this chapter involves the ordering of pharmaceutical products. Our initial assignment is to define the shape of the data representing a "new order". I've built a schema named NewOrder_XML.xsd with a root node name of NewOrder and a structure that holds the characteristics of the order, the particular items that made up the order, and the corresponding sales territory information. The namespace of my schema, http://BizTalkSOA. Chapter3.OrderManagement.BizTalk/Contract, will surface again once the service WSDL is generated. As shown in the following screenshot:

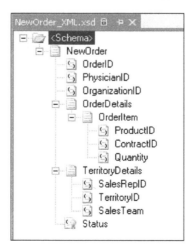

Now that we have a contract definition representing a new order where we have distinguished the Status field, we will assemble an orchestration workflow that consumes this data entity. Recall from *Chapter 1, Building BizTalk Server 2013 Applications* that a BizTalk orchestration depends on messages which equate to the data being sent and received by the orchestration. These messages are immutable so their data cannot be manipulated by the orchestration except during message creation. For our first simple orchestration, we have a message representing the inbound request and a separate message for the acknowledgement returned to the caller. In this case, both messages are of the same schema type, as shown in the following screenshot:

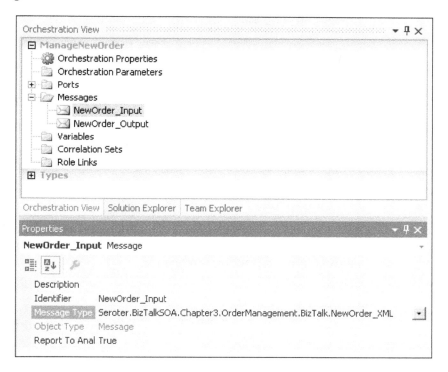

Once our messages have been defined, we sketch out the orchestration's sequential flow. In this case, let's do a very simple orchestration that receives the new order and then constructs and returns a response message with an altered Status value:

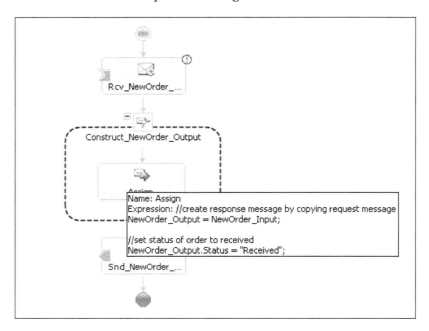

Finally, I set up a public, request-response logical port, which acts as the interface and entry point to the orchestration. This port has a single operation named SubmitNewOrder, as shown in the following screenshot:

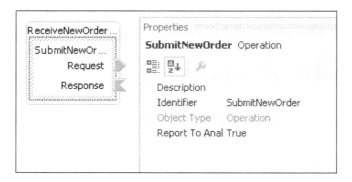

The final orchestration looks like this:

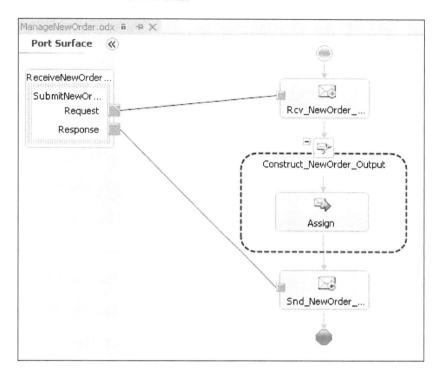

Note that absolutely nothing we've done within this orchestration hints at its role as the realization of a WCF service. Ideally, an orchestration's ports are not tightly coupled to a runtime transport scheme, which in return means greater flexibility and reuse. The orchestration port only dictates a message type and message exchange pattern while remaining transport neutral.

 Before continuing, I built and deployed this project to the BizTalkSOA.Chapter3 application to ensure that my BizTalk application was created and refreshed.

Generating the WCF endpoint

Unlike most BizTalk receive adapters, which poll or listen to existing URIs (such as file locations, databases, queues), the WCF adapters require us to create new endpoints that BizTalk uses to get data absorbed into the system. Fortunately, Microsoft makes generating such endpoints fairly easy by introducing the **BizTalk WCF Service Publishing Wizard** tool.

Pitfall

Unlike the classic ASMX-based BizTalk Web Services Publishing wizard, the BizTalk project in Visual Studio does not have to be deployed in the Global Assembly Cache in order for the BizTalk WCF Service Publishing Wizard to locate it. However, if the BizTalk project assembly had been deployed at any time previously, the freshly updated assembly must be deployed to the GAC so that the Visual Studio wizard pulls the latest version of the assembly.

While one can launch the BizTalk WCF Service Publishing Wizard from the Microsoft BizTalk Server 2013 folder on the **Start** menu, it's much simpler to trigger this wizard from within Visual Studio itself. We initiate this wizard by going to the **Tools** menu of Visual Studio and choosing **BizTalk WCF Service Publishing Wizard**. What we see next is a new window that will walk us through all the steps necessary to generate the service and endpoint we desire.

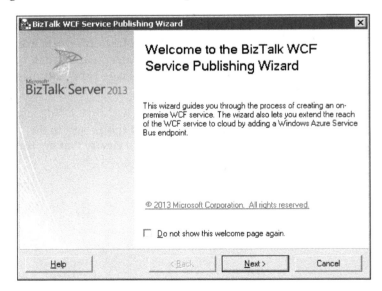

You need to perform the following steps:

1. The first thing that this wizard needs to know is what type of WCF service we'd like to produce. Our choices are as follows:

Endpoint type	Usage scenario
Service endpoint	If you choose this type of endpoint, then this wizard will be responsible for generating a consumable WCF service that is hosted outside of BizTalk Server itself. Only WCF adapters that reside in the BizTalk isolated host (WCF-BasicHttp, WCF-CustomIsolated, WCF-WebHttp, and WCF-WSHttp) can be chosen here. Note that you are able to allow metadata browsing of this service (through a WCF behavior) by selecting the **Enable metadata endpoint** checkbox. If you'd like the wizard to automatically create the BizTalk receive port/location which is linked to this freshly generated WCF service, then you may also select the corresponding checkbox that performs this action.
Metadata only endpoint (MEX)	Use this option if you have an existing in-process BizTalk WCF endpoint whose metadata description you wish to expose in an IIS application. Because BizTalk receive locations are never "typed" to a particular message schema, the in-process endpoints can't share any metadata that explains their expected data contract. Using a MEX, we can generate an IIS service that does nothing but expose the contract of the in-process endpoint. We'll see more of this option in the next section.

2. Choose the **Service endpoint** with a **WCF-WSHttp** transport while also enabling the metadata endpoint and auto-generation of a receive location in the BizTalk application named `BizTalkSOA.Chapter3`:

3. After selecting the desired service type, our next task is to identify which artifacts the wizard should use to generate the WCF service. Our current scenario will use the **Publish BizTalk orchestrations as WCF service** option, which means that key service attributes such as data contract, communication pattern, and operation name are all retrieved from an existing orchestration's logical port.

4. On the next page is a new feature of BizTalk Server 2013, which will ask if you want to **Add a Service Bus endpoint**. This will be covered in *Chapter 6, Azure Service Bus* so we will leave this unchecked for now and click **Next**. As shown in the following screenshot:

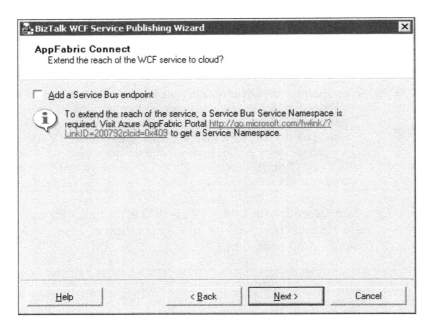

5. On the following screen, leave it at the default selection of **Publish BizTalk orchestrations as WCF service** and click **Next**:

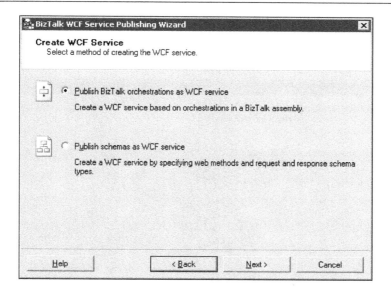

6. On the next screen of the wizard, we are asked to designate which .NET assembly contains the orchestration that we'd like to use to generate the service. If you launched this wizard from within Visual Studio with the BizTalk project open, then the assembly's file path will already be populated by the wizard.

7. If the orchestration was successfully loaded by the wizard, we should see the (public) orchestration ports available for selection:

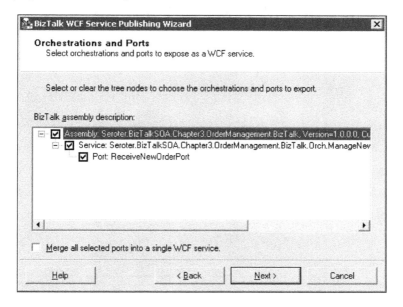

8. After accepting the currently selected items, we enter a namespace for the service. In this case, I supplied the namespace `http://BizTalkSOA. Chapter3/Service`, as shown in the following screenshot:

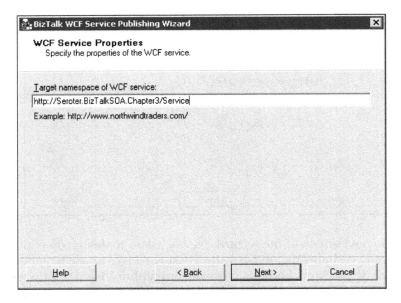

9. Finally, we need to specify the web server and address where our shiny new service will be deployed:

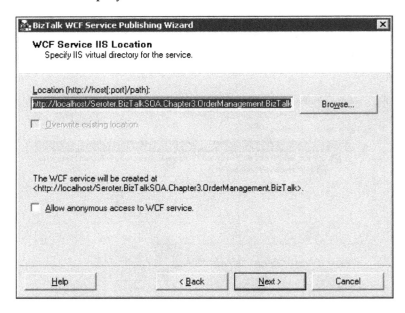

10. Once we've picked a valid URL, we see a read-only view of the pending WCF service configuration. If everything looks good, click on **Create**, wait for confirmation that all the necessary actions succeeded, and click on **Finish**.

Configuring the generated components

We told the **BizTalk WCF Service Publishing Wizard** to build a receive location for us, so we should investigate exactly what we got as a result of that choice. In opening **BizTalk Administration Console** and probing the `BizTalkSOA.Chapter3` application, we should see a new receive location with a staggeringly long name that is hard to miss. Like all auto-generated messaging ports, this receive location is in a **Disabled** state. The next step is to enable this receive location, and in the **Orchestrations** section of the application, both bind and start the deployed orchestration.

Double-clicking this new receive location reveals that it has been set up using the WCF-WSHttp adapter and the BizTalk isolated host. However, the real meat of this endpoint lies in the adapter configuration. We inspect this by clicking the **Configure** button next to the chosen adapter. The standard (non-custom) WCF adapters all have a similar look and feel to their configuration pages, with the same set of tabs along the top. Here, we see the first critical piece of the endpoint: the address:

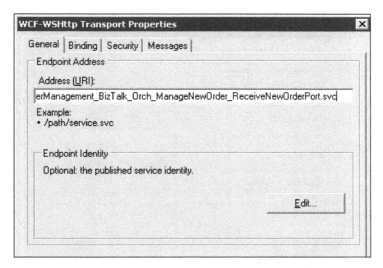

The second tab in this receive location configuration, named `Binding`, shows a subset of available WCF-WSHttp binding switches that we may alter for the adapter. Take note of the fact that, while the default number of concurrent calls for a WCF service is `16`, the BizTalk WCF endpoint sets this value to `200` for performance reasons. If we desire deeper control over this binding configuration or wish to affix service behavior extensions, then the WCF-CustomIsolated adapter should be used instead.

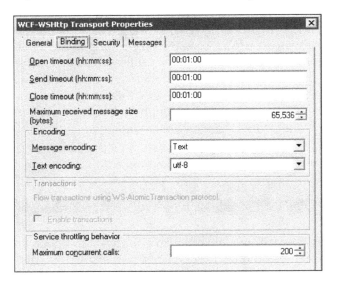

The third tab is named **Security** and provides us with a fairly straightforward way to apply standard WCF security schemes to our endpoint. We'll stick with the default **Message security** mode shown here:

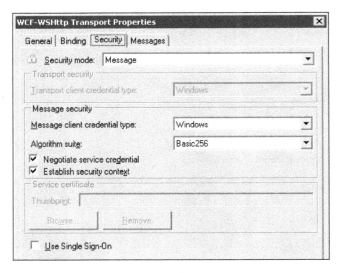

Finally, the last tab, named **Messages**, is where we tell BizTalk where to extract the message body from the WCF payload. We could send the entire SOAP payload to the BizTalk `MessageBox` (SOAP envelope included) or even rip out a specific node in the SOAP body. In our case, we just need the message body:

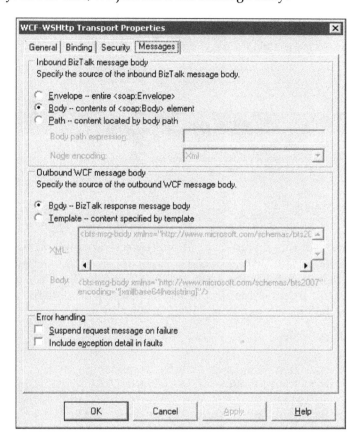

You may have noticed that nowhere in this receive location do we designate the C in the *ABCs* of WCF. Where is the *contract*? All BizTalk receive locations are typeless, and the WCF receive locations are no different. A BizTalk WCF endpoint exposes a generic contract that will accept any valid SOAP message. This is why the generation of a metadata endpoint is critical; otherwise, we'd have no clear way to tell consumers how to structure the payload their service requests.

If you recall, our preceding run through the BizTalk WCF Service Publishing Wizard produced this receive location and an actual WCF service hosted in IIS 8.0. If we had tried to visit the service in our web browser immediately after the wizard had completed, we would have seen an error telling us that the receive location was offline. Note that the receive location for the associated WCF service must be enabled in order to browse the service. Once the receive location gets enabled, we should see a standard WCF service metadata page instead of an exception.

Let's take advantage of this metadata endpoint by referencing and consuming our new WCF service. In a new Visual Studio console application, we choose **Add Service Reference** and point to the generated WCF service WSDL. Only a small bit of code is needed to consume this simple service. However, note the unwieldy type names that the orchestration-generated WCF service imparts upon us:

```
static void Main(string[] args)
{
  OrchSvc.BizTalkSOA_Chapter3_OrderManagement_
    BizTalk_Orch_ManageNewOrder_ReceiveNewOrderPortClient client =
  new OrchSvc.BizTalkSOA_Chapter3_OrderManagement_
    BizTalk_Orch_ManageNewOrder_ReceiveNewOrderPortClient
    ("WSHttpBinding_ITwoWayAsync");

  try
  {
    OrchSvc.NewOrder order = new OrchSvc.NewOrder();
    order.OrderID = "123";
    order.OrganizationID = "987";
    order.PhysicianID = "555";
    order.Status = "submitted";

    Console.WriteLine("Calling WCF service ...");

    client.SubmitNewOrder(ref order);
```

```
            Console.WriteLine("Result status is: " +
                order.Status);
            client.Close();
            Console.ReadLine();
        }
        catch (System.ServiceModel.CommunicationException) {
            client.Abort(); }
        catch (System.TimeoutException) { client.Abort(); }
        catch (System.Exception) { client.Abort(); throw; }
    }
```

At this point, we've designed an orchestration, exposed its port interface as a WCF service, and consumed that service from a WCF client.

Anatomy of a generated WCF WSDL

Attributes set while building a BizTalk project seep into the WSDL of a generated WCF service. Here is a quick look at which design-time properties map to runtime WSDL attributes.

BizTalk project attribute	WCF WSDL attribute
Value set for the **Service Namespace** in the WCF Service Publishing wizard	`<wsdl:definitions name="BizTalkServiceInstance" targetNamespace="http://BizTalkSOA. Chapter3/Service" xmlns:tns="http://BizTalkSOA. Chapter3/Service">`
Value set for the **Service Namespace** in the WCF Service Publishing wizard	`<xsd:schema targetNamespace="http://BizTalkSOA. Chapter3/Service/Imports">`
Value set for **Target Namespace** in the BizTalk Schema	`<xsd:import schemaLocation="..." namespace="http://BizTalkSOA. Chapter3.OrderManagement.BizTalk/ Contract" />`
Value of the orchestration's **Namespace** attribute combined with the **Typename** of the orchestration, the name of the logical port being exposed, and the name of the port **Operation**	`<wsdl:message name="BizTalkSOA_ Chapter3_OrderManagement_ BizTalk_Orch_ManageNewOrder_ ReceiveNewOrderPort_SubmitNewOrder_ InputMessage">`
Value of the orchestration's **Namespace** attribute combined with the **Typename** of the orchestration and the name of the logical port being exposed	`<wsdl:portType name="BizTalkSOA_ Chapter3_OrderManagement_ BizTalk_Orch_ManageNewOrder_ ReceiveNewOrderPort">`

BizTalk project attribute	WCF WSDL attribute

Value of the orchestration's **Namespace** attribute combined with the **Typename** of the orchestration and the name of the logical port being exposed	`<wsdl:binding name="WSHttpBinding_`
	`ITwoWayAsync" type="tns:BizTalkSOA_`
	`Chapter3_OrderManagement_`
	`BizTalk_Orch_ManageNewOrder_`
	`ReceiveNewOrderPort">`

Value of the exposed orchestration port's **Operation** name	`<wsdl:operation` `name="SubmitNewOrder">`

Exposing WCF services from schemas

In the previous section, we looked at accepting a new product order in an orchestration and returning a response to the submitter. What if we only want a one-way channel and want multiple consumers to subscribe to this new order? This screams for a more event-driven scenario where the publisher asynchronously sends data that is handled and acted upon by unknown downstream systems (for example, fulfillment systems and billing systems). In this case, we aren't interested in creating an orchestration that dictates our service contract but rather want to build a service on-ramp that simply gets data onto the message bus.

For this scenario, we will do the following:

- Configure a TCP endpoint in BizTalk Server
- Generate a WCF metadata service hosted in IIS that clients use to discover the service and its true service URI
- Build the metadata endpoint using only schemas and no orchestrations

We will reuse the previously built `NewOrder_XML.xsd` schema as the input message to the new service. This means that this new scenario requires no new development on our part. The scenario begins with the creation of a new receive port and location in the `BizTalkSOA.Chapter3` application found in the BizTalk Administration Console. The receive port has the following attributes:

Attribute	Value
Port type	One-way
Name	`BizTalkSOA.Chapter3.ReceiveNewOrder`

Next, we'll take this receive port and add a new receive location to it with the following attributes:

Attribute	Value
Name	`BizTalkSOA.Chapter3.ReceiveNewOrder`
Transport Type	WCF-NetTcp
Receive Pipeline	XMLReceive
Transport Endpoint Address	`net.tcp://localhost:9900/`
	`BizTalkSOA.Chapter3.ReceiveNewOrder`

Once the receive location is created, it should be started to ensure that it was configured correctly. An example of an incorrect configuration would be the designation of a URI port that was already in use by other processes. If this situation occurs, a message is added to the Application Event Log explaining the port collision.

Now, as we mentioned before, BizTalk receive locations are never associated with a particular XSD schema. So, if we are assuming that our service client(s) does not have a copy of the service contract already, then we must provide a metadata endpoint that explains the type of message that our in-process receive location expects. In the previous section, we saw that the WCF endpoints generated from BizTalk orchestrations have verbose descriptions and burden you with lengthy attribute names. In many cases, you will want more fine-grained control over the service definition than what the Publish BizTalk orchestrations as WCF service selection in the BizTalk WCF Service Publishing Wizard can give you. In fact, unless you are desperate for the quickest possible way to generate WCF services and/or descriptions, there is no discernible reason to ever choose the Publish BizTalk orchestrations as WCF service option.

The alternative to using orchestrations to define the service contract and communication pattern is to build up the service definition graphically using a schema-only model. Selecting this alternative option allows us to manually name the service, choose a communication pattern, name the service operation, and choose the data contract(s).

To create such an endpoint, fire up the BizTalk WCF Service Publishing Wizard once again and choose **Metadata only endpoint (MEX)** as **WCF Service Type**. When we are asked which receive location we wish to produce metadata for, select `BizTalkSOA.Chapter3.ReceiveNewOrder` and click **Next**; and also click **Next** on the **AppFabric Connect** screen. After choosing **Publish schemas as WCF service** on the next screen of the wizard, we are given the opportunity to manually describe the new service.

Here, we apply friendlier names for service attributes, starting with the service description at the top. Note that this attribute cannot have dot operators in the name, so I called it BizTalkSOAChapter3. This value does not show up anywhere in the service itself but rather is the name of the Visual Studio solution file that the wizard generates for the web service. After renaming the service node **OrderService**, the existing two-way operation should be deleted. Next, add a new operation by right-clicking on the service, selecting **Add web method**, and choosing a **one-way** operation. After changing the operation name to SubmitNewOrder, we need to right-click on the **Request** message and choose **Select schema type**. This is where we indicate the input message type that our service expects. Browse to the appropriate BizTalk project assembly and pick the NewOrder_XML schema. Our service definition will now look like this:

On the next page of the wizard, set the service namespace to http://BizTalkSOA. Chapter3/Service. For the service location, I chose http://localhost/ BizTalkSOA.Chapter3.OrderManagement.BizTalkMEX. Once the wizard is completed, we have an IIS-deployed metadata endpoint that can be interrogated by WCF clients to reveal the contract and URL for our BizTalk-hosted service. Note that the status of the actual BizTalk endpoint (that is, whether the receive location is enabled or disabled) does not impact the availability of the MEX endpoint.

Consuming WCF services from orchestrations

For BizTalk Server to play a full role within the service bus, it must be able to not only expose service endpoints but also easily consume them. Let's take a look at how to create an orchestration that accepts messages through the WCF-NetTcp receive location created earlier and also calls a WCF service that reveals a single endpoint based on Named Pipes.

We start by adding a new orchestration file named `LookupOrderContact.odx` to our existing BizTalk project in Visual Studio. The orchestration starts up when a new order arrives. Therefore, we should create a new orchestration message of type `BizTalkSOA.Chapter3.OrderManagement.BizTalk.NewOrder_XML`, named `NewOrder_Input`. After the order is received, we call an existing WCF service, which provides us with more details about the customer placing the order. What do we need to know to call the WCF service from our orchestration? If you guessed the following, you'd be right:

- Schema contract(s) used
- Message exchange pattern (request/reply, request only)
- Service address and binding

Instead of having to manually produce these artifacts and configurations, we should use BizTalk-provided tools to do the work for us. If you wanted to reference a WCF service from a standard Visual Studio project (for example, class library, ASP.NET application), you could use the **Add Service Reference** option available by right-clicking on the project. However, adding WCF references to BizTalk projects works a bit differently.

First let's start by off creating a running service with a WCF-NetNamedPipe endpoint and an explicit MEX endpoint by starting a command prompt (Run as Administrator) and browsing to the `BizTalkSOA.Chapter3.OrderService\bin\Release` folder in the accompanying source code and running `BizTalkSOA.Chapter3.OrderService.exe`. It should come up with Order service host opened....

To add a WCF service reference, first right-click on the BizTalk project and choose **Add** and then **Add Generated Items**. We are presented with a window that Visual Studio uses to auto-construct BizTalk artifacts, such as schemas based on adapter endpoints. Choose the **Consume WCF Service** option and click on **Add**.

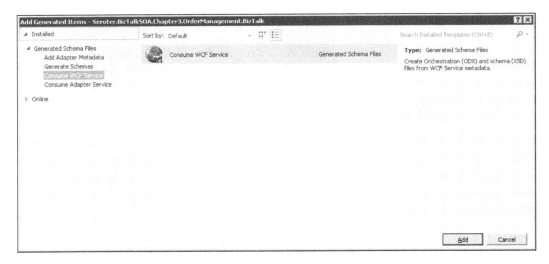

Now we get the pleasure of working with the BizTalk WCF Service Consuming wizard. This is a twin of the BizTalk WCF Service Publishing Wizard, except that instead of generating new services, it produces the artifacts necessary to consume existing ones.

The first thing the wizard has to find out is where to get the metadata needed to craft the artifacts for BizTalk. If you only have a physical XSD and WSDL file (assuming someone went the true contract-first design route), then the second option in the wizard (**Metadata Files**) is best. However, if the target service is live and allows metadata queries, we can choose the first option.

After choosing **Metadata Exchange Endpoint** as the metadata source, we plug in the address of the metadata URL. In my case, this value is `net.pipe://localhost/BizTalkSOA.Chapter3.OrderService/mex`. Note that while only http(s) endpoints actually produce browsable metadata, any WCF endpoint can still expose metadata to query.

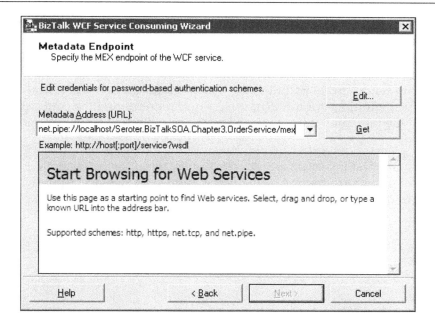

On the next screen of the wizard (assuming that our service was accessible), we see a summary of what the wizard is about to import.

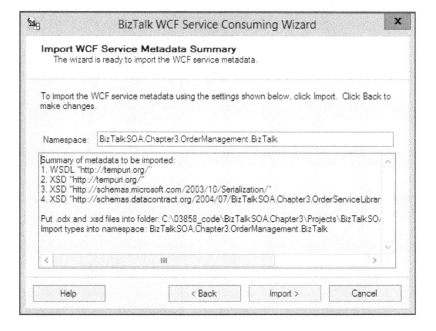

A number of files are generated, including three different XSD schemas. These schemas describe the data types contained in the service contract. We also get two BizTalk binding files: one for the adapter type used in the metadata request (in our case, WCF-NetNamedPipe) and another we can optionally use to configure a WCF-Custom send port. In addition, the wizard emitted a new orchestration, which contains type definitions for multi-part messages representing the contract schemas and a port type that reflects the message exchange pattern of the target service.

Back in our primary orchestration, we now add the messages used for calling the service and handling the response. These messages (`Contact_Request` and `Contact_Response`) are created by using the multi-part message types defined in the wizard-generated orchestration.

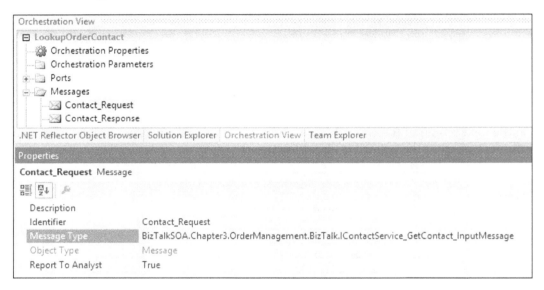

The service input message is represented as a complex (schema) type, so a BizTalk map is necessary to instantiate the new orchestration message. This means our orchestration requires a **Construct** shape in concert with a **Transform** shape that points to a new map. The map is quite simple as all we need to do is transfer the data in the target schema's `PhysicianID` XML node to the destination schema's `contactId` node.

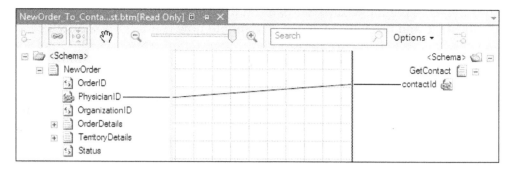

Once the map is finished, we add the **Send** and **Receive** shapes to the orchestration. The orchestration will send the `request` message and receive the `response` message. Once the shapes are dropped on the orchestration, and the corresponding **Message** properties are set on them, we create the logical port used by the orchestration to communicate with the service. After choosing to create and name a **New Configured Port**, we want to choose an *existing* port type for this port.

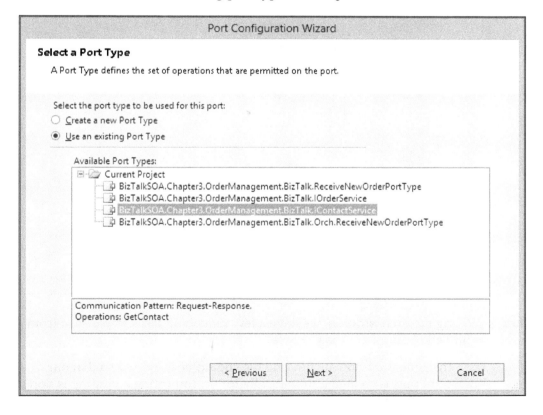

On the next screen of the wizard, we confirm that the direction of the port is set to send a message and receive a response. We should now connect the service's send and receive shapes with the connectors on the logical port operation. Our final shape in the orchestration should be an **Expression** shape, where a success confirmation is printed. If we want to extract data from the response message as proof that the response was successfully received, then we need to distinguish a field within the service response schema. In my case, I distinguished the Name element and printed that value out. To complete the orchestration, I added a new logical receive port for accepting the inbound order. The finished orchestration looks like this:

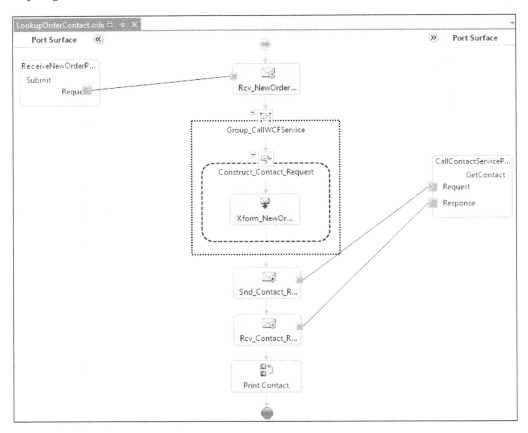

After deploying the orchestration, we have a few remaining tasks to perform from inside the BizTalk Administration Console.

1. First, the generated BizTalk binding file should be imported so that our WCF send port is created automatically for us. Importing a binding is done by right-clicking the BizTalk application (in our case, named BizTalkSOA. Chapter3) and choosing **Import** and then **Bindings**.

2. Point this dialog box to the adapter-based binding (in our case, named `ContactService.BindingInfo.xml`) instead of the custom binding.

3. After the import succeeds, we see a new (un-enlisted) send port that utilizes the WCF-NetNamedPipes adapter. That port should be turned on by right-clicking on it and choosing **Start**.

4. Our final step is to bind and enlist the orchestration. We created a one-way WCF-NetTcp receive channel in the previous exercise and can reuse that receive port as our input to the orchestration. The orchestration binding is represented as follows:

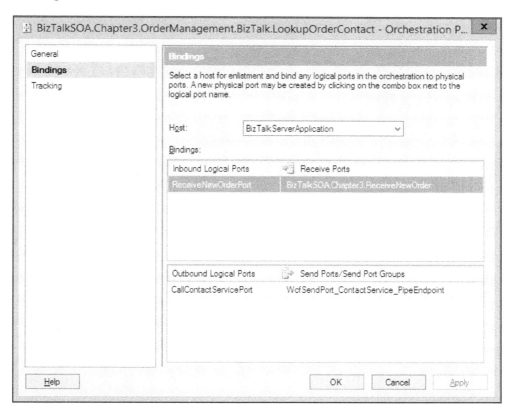

Once we start the orchestration and ensure that the downstream service is up-and-running, we should trigger our client service. From the following screenshot, you can see that the client succeeded; the downstream service registered an invocation, and the orchestration successfully sent a trace message to the application Event Log.

Consuming WCF services without orchestration

There are plenty of scenarios where orchestration is an unnecessary addition to service bus processing. Recall that an orchestration's prime benefit is the injection of a stateful, sequential series of steps to message processing. If the "processing" of a message can consist solely of the core BizTalk messaging components (receive ports, send ports, pipelines, maps, and subscriptions), then a messaging-only solution is the way to go. A general rule among BizTalk architects is that you avoid orchestration and concentrate on pure messaging when at all possible. This isn't because orchestration is intrinsically bad but rather because many situations actually don't require the overhead and complexity of a workflow.

That said, how nicely does the BizTalk bus play with WCF services when no orchestration is involved? Quite well, thank you. Let's look at how we may route inbound data to a WCF subscriber using only the message bus.

In our new scenario, we have a target service in our **enterprise resource planning (ERP)** system that accepts new order notices and uses WCF's WsHttpBinding. We'd like to call this service whenever a new product order enters the MessageBox. This subscriber does not need any direct knowledge of the upstream publisher or how the message arrived to the bus.

1. We start this example by referencing the target service from within Visual Studio. This is done by once again right-clicking the BizTalk project and choosing **Add** and then **Add Generated Items**.

2. The **Consume WCF Service** is selected, and when the BizTalk WCF Service Consuming wizard launches, the **Metadata Exchange Endpoint** is picked as the source of the service metadata.

3. Now we plug in the valid HTTP endpoint URI of our WCF service:

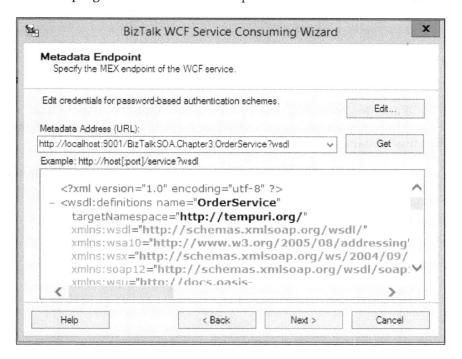

When the wizard completes, we have a set of metadata files (schemas, bindings, and orchestrations) that help describe the service and how to consume it. This example doesn't use orchestration, but we do still require one hand-built BizTalk artifact—a map. The WCF service expects the order data to be in a particular format, so we should design a map that gets applied by the outbound send port. The BizTalk map takes the repeating set of order items and puts them into their appropriate fields in the target schema.

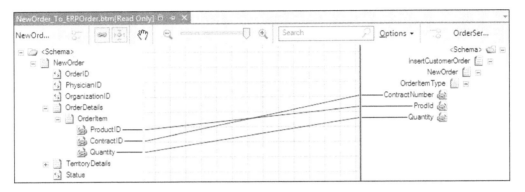

Now we build and deploy our updated project. Once that deployment has succeeded, we import the binding generated by the BizTalk WCF Service Consuming wizard. For this scenario:

1. Let's import the custom binding (`OrderService_Custom.BindingInfo.xml`) so that we can see the different properties this adapter exposes.

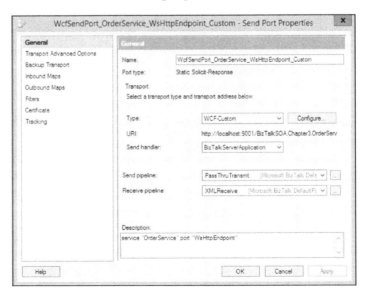

2. A send port is created for the WCF-Custom adapter, but note that the binding specified by the adapter matches that of our service endpoint, `wsHttpBinding`.

On the **General** tab of the adapter configuration, observe that there is a section called **SOAP action header**. This contains the SOAP action that will be attached to the outbound messages for this send port.

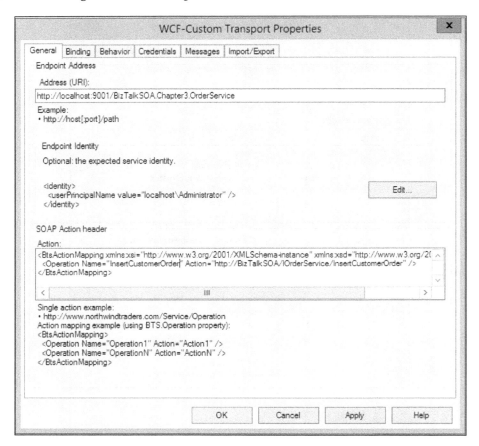

The `BtsActionMapping` wrapper in this textbox is used to support multiple `SOAPAction` values. However, this also means that something needs to set the `BTS.Operation` value, which the WCF adapter uses to choose the appropriate SOAP action from this collection. Typically, this is set by the orchestration's logical send port operation name, but in the absence of an orchestration, we would have to set the `BTS.Operation` value in a custom pipeline component. Before throwing up your hands and swearing loudly at this unnecessary complexity, breathe deeply and relax. Luckily, this textbox also supports an alternate format that is more supportive of simple content-based routing scenarios. A single SOAP action URI in this textbox is used when you want to apply the same `SOAPAction` header to all messages transmitted by the send port. For our scenario, let's switch this to the single `SOAPAction` header that corresponds to our target service operation.

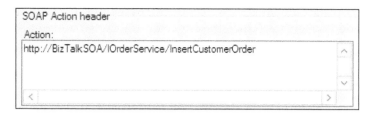

Next, we must apply our XSLT map to this send port. The map is a required component because our service is expecting a very specific data format that does not match the original structure of the data.

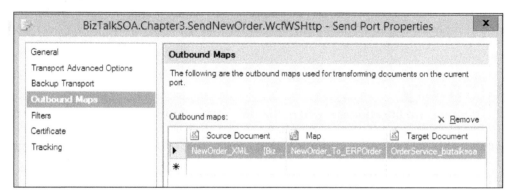

Our final step is to introduce a valid subscription for this send port. Without one, this port will never receive any messages published to the bus. Because we'd like to pull every order from the MessageBox, our subscription should be type-based, not context-based. A context-based subscription would say that we are subscribing to properties of the message (for example, which port it arrived at) instead of anything relating to the message itself. We want to subscribe to all messages of a particular type. The subscription applied can be seen in the following screenshot:

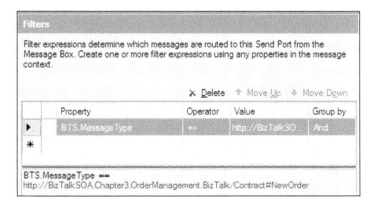

Now, technically we are finished. If we send a message into BizTalk, it should route to a listening send port and produce the expected tracing statements. However, see the following *Pitfall* to resolve an error with our current configuration.

Pitfall

The solution, as it stands now, will raise an exception. Why? The WCF service that BizTalk calls does not return a response message. However, the auto-generated BizTalk binding file was for a two-way send port. So, when the WCF service is called, the request is successful but we end up with a **subscription not found** exception on the (empty) response message. We can fix this by creating a new one-way send port with configuration settings (adapter type, URI, binding, SOAPAction, and subscription) identical to those of the auto-generated port.

Summary

In this chapter, we began to see where BizTalk Server and Windows Communication Foundation intersect. WCF greatly enhances BizTalk Server by providing a flexible and extensible set of service endpoints that are capable of supporting a wide range of transmission, security, and encoding configurations. We now know how to generate services from BizTalk artifacts, whether those artifacts are schemas or orchestrations. We also looked at consuming existing services via orchestration or messaging-only patterns.

Later, in *Chapter 7, Planning Service-oriented BizTalk Solutions*, we will investigate how to take the implementation knowledge we now have and use it to actually architect service-oriented BizTalk solutions.

4
REST and JSON Support in BizTalk Server 2013

Computers make excellent and efficient servants, but I have no wish to serve under them

Spock, Star Trek

Representable State Transfer (REST) is an architectural style for developing software services, based on the HTTP transport protocol. The first edition of this book did not go into great detail on REST, however, in this edition, we will cover the fundamentals of REST-based services and the BizTalk WCF-WebHttp adapter.

REST's popularity is mainly due to its familiarity among those who perform website development. It allows a developer to consume a web service in the client's browser using languages such as Ajax or jQuery instead of processing the request server side.

Also with the rise of smart devices, such as mobile phones and tablets, which favor lightweight messages, REST services have gained momentum.

Most cloud-based services now offer REST APIs to use their services.

In this chapter, you will learn:

- Why REST services are gaining preference over SOAP-based services
- What URL resources are and how best to structure them
- Different techniques of versioning a REST-based service
- How to publish and consume REST-based services using the WCF-WebHttp adapter, and how to handle XML- and JSON-formatted messages

Why REST services

A REST-based service is best suited for limited bandwidth and resources where you need to process simple **Create, Read, Update, Delete (CRUD)** type operations using the following verbs:

- GET
- POST
- PUT
- DELETE

Also, REST is a platform and language independent service, which makes it ideal as an integration protocol.

It uses a lightweight protocol such as HTTP to send messages in a simple XML format, or other formats such as JSON or plain text. TCP may also be used, but HTTP is more commonly used.

REST services are totally stateless in operation. This allows greater scalability since the server does not have to maintain the session state. What this essentially means is that the client must include all the information required for the server to fulfill each request.

For a comparison between messaging based on SOAP and REST, please refer to the blog post at `http://connectedcircuits.wordpress.com/2013/02/16/what-to-use-soap-or-rest/`.

A RESTful API should adhere to the following specifications:

- Honor HTTP request verbs
- Use of proper HTTP status code
- No version numbers in the URIs
- Response message format defined in the HTTP Accept header

URL deciphering

The URL is one of the most important components in describing a service. It should be short and descriptive, and should provide a natural hierarchy path structure to the resource. The resource names should be nouns; verbs should be avoided.

A well designed API should be intuitive and easy to use. If done poorly, it can make the service difficult to use and understand. URL query strings should only be utilized for filtering and specifying the ordering of the result set.

JSON versus XML

One of the primary reasons why XML was created in the nineties was that it allowed open data sharing by providing an interchangeable data serialization format. It was able to handle native data types and also other formats such as images, audio, documents and so on.

While it is possible to attach any file format to an XML message, JSON on the other hand, only supports simple data structures stored as arrays. Both formats have their advantages, but data transfers will be easier and faster if the data serialization resembles the structure of the data it represents. JSON makes it very easy to import the data into languages such as JavaScript, Ruby, Python, and many others.

XML is the ideal format for transferring documents as it can be used to define the structure or format of the data along with the actual data. When returning XML, it should be without the namespaces present.

JSON is best used for data sharing as it is only suitable for transferring the data component.

> More information about JSON can be found at `http://www.json.org/`.

Resource representation

Resource representation defines the data format of the response. The response message may be in any one of the following formats:

- Plain text
- Form-encoding
- XML
- HTML
- JSON
- Any other Internet media type, provided that it is a valid hypertext standard

You can specify the format of the delivery content by setting the Content-Type header value in the request headers to the service. REST APIs commonly use either the `application/json` or `application/xml` media type.

Here is an example of a header request for JSON:

```
Content-Type: application/json
Host: localhost:65437
Content-Length: 69
```

Now, we'll see an example for XML:

```
Content-Type: application/xml
Host: localhost:65437
Content-Length: 69
```

> Remember to use XML to transfer documents and JSON for data transfers.

Handling message versioning in REST

All services change over time, mainly because of new business requirements. More often than not, this includes changes to the entity structure.

Following are several options available to handle entity versioning:

- **URL versioning**: Here the URL determines the version that is to be returned. This option seems to be the most common method used, although this goes against the RESTful nature of the URL, which expresses the resource. Although this provides a very simple mechanism for versioning, it requires the server to maintain multiple versions of the URL even though you are fetching the same information.

    HTTP GET: https://my_rest_service.com/api/v2/account/10043

- **Query string versioning**: This option appends the required version number to the query string. The disadvantage of using this method is that some browsers and **Internet Service Providers** (**ISPs**) do not cache response messages when the request URL includes a query string.

    HTTP GET:

    ```
    https://my_rest_service.com/api/account/10043?version=2
    ```

- **Custom header versioning**: This option adds a custom property to the request header and requires the client to append the custom property with each server request.

    HTTP GET: https://my_rest_service.com/api/account/10043

    ```
    X-api-version = 2
    ```

Normally, custom header properties are prefixed with *X*, although there are no standards on the correct naming convention.

- **Media type versioning**: This method is more in line with the REST specifications. The version is specified in the accept header property of request headers.

  HTTP GET:

  `https://my_rest_service.com/api/account/10043`

- **Accept**: `application/vnd. my_rest_service -v2.0+json`, `application/vnd.account+json`

  The appended second part `/vnd.account+json` of the `my_rest_service` accept header informs the service to return any version if version 2.0 cannot be found. Also the `+json` keyword informs the server to return the response as JSON.

  To request different versions of the account object, set the accept header as follows:

  ```
  1.0: vnd. my_rest_service -v1.0+json
  1.1: vnd. my_rest_service -v1.1+json
  2.0: vnd. my_rest_service -v2.0+json
  ```

Unfortunately, there is no silver bullet to resolve which option to use as there are pros and cons for each one. The custom header and media type versioning strategy, require the server to examine these properties for every request in order to determine which entity version to return. The client also needs to configure the header properties with each request. The other method of using URL versioning or query string versioning is cache friendly to browsers and ISPs. However, this is not the purest form of creating a RESTful API.

The bottom line comes down to who will be consuming your services and what will be their preferred method. Most of the early adopters of REST-style services used the URL versioning strategy.

Documenting contracts

Unlike soap style messages where the **Web Services Description Language (WSDL)** defines a robust contract between the consumer and service provider as an XML document, there was no such metadata exchanged when consuming a REST service until WSDL 2.0 was released.

Textual documentation still seems to be popular with developers to describe the available methods and entities. There is a NuGet package available for MS Visual Studio, which automatically generates help page content for Web API projects. It can be installed using the Package Manager Console using the following command: PM> `Install-Package Microsoft.AspNet.WebApi.HelpPage`.

Swagger, which is an open source product is also very popular among developers for generating interactive documentation and client SDK generation and discoverability. More information can be found at `http://swagger.io/`. Swagger appears to be Microsoft's tool of choice for API documentation as it has been adopted in many products in the Azure suite.

Another tool is **RESTful API Modeling Language (RAML)**, which provides a contract first approach of modeling web APIs. This uses a derivative of YAML (YAML ain't markup language) and JSON to create a human- and machine-readable document. More information can be found at `http://raml.org/index.html`.

To help the consumers of the service, the messages should be self-descriptive, and you should be able to understand the requests and responses after spending minimal time using the service and reading the documentation. In the end, the URL structure has a large part to play in the overall usability of the service.

Security

REST offers no built-in security features, however, there are various options available to secure your API. The right solution will depend on your requirements, but remember that REST is meant to be stateless by nature and you should not rely on session states.

Basic authentication is quite easy to implement, but provides the lowest level of security. Usernames and passwords are normally passed around as encoded base64 strings. You should always use **Transport Layer Security (TLS)**, also known as SSL, to encrypt the channel to ensure that the credentials can not be intercepted and inspected.

API keys are another form of basic authentication as described previously, but instead of using a username/password, a token value is passed around. The key is either placed in the header section of the request or in the URL as a query string. Once again, it is best to use TLS when making use of API keys to guarantee privacy.

OAuth is another authentication process, whereby authentication is handled by another authority by redirecting your initial service API request to a login page where you enter your credentials. If authenticated successfully, you will receive an access token in the response message. You must then present this token to each REST API method call.

BizTalk 2013 and REST

With the release of BizTalk Server 2013, BizTalk now supports REST-based services using the new WCF-WebHttp adapter. This has been long anticipated by BizTalk developers as a majority of the cloud-based services are REST-based. This adapter supports both synchronous and asynchronous communications.

When Microsoft initially released BizTalk 2013, the WCF-WebHttp adapter only supported XML message types.

If you were required to support JSON, you would have to create a custom pipeline to convert JSON context into XML. Now, in BizTalk 2013 R2, Microsoft has included a JSON Encode and Decoder pipeline component together with a JSON Schema Wizard for both consuming and sending messages in the JSON format. In this chapter, we will cover only the version released with BTS2013, but we also cover how to handle JSON message formats. We will discuss the BizTalk 2013 R2 features further in *Chapter 14, What's New and What's Next?*

Exploring the WCF-WebHttp Adapter

The WCF-WebHttp adapter adds support for specific context properties to handle REST-based messages using the verbs GET, POST, PUT and DELETE. However, the underlying technology is still WCF, as most of the properties are similar to the other WCF adapters available in BizTalk.

There are several new context properties specifically to handle REST. For a complete list of all the properties, refer to the following link: `http://msdn.microsoft.com/en-us/library/wcf(v=bts.80).aspx`.

When using a standard send port, you cannot update the HttpHeader properties as the adapter uses the properties on the port by design. To get around this issue, set the BTS.IsDynamicSend context property to true on an outbound message, then a static send port will respect the HttpHeader context property.

As an example, when a consumer requires information about a resource in a RESTful manner, it uses the HTTP GET verb on the resource. The request would be similar to GET http://myservice.com/products/10045. This instructs the server to return the product with an ID of 10045. Note that there is no message body, just a verb and a resource location identified by the URL.

This is where the WCF-WebHttp adapter comes into play. It extracts the parameters from the URI and writes them to the message context using a new feature called **variable mapping** when receiving a request. Also, when sending a request, the message context properties can be written into the URL at the specified variable mapping locations.

The main configuration feature of the new adapter is the HTTP method and URL mapping shown in the following screenshot:

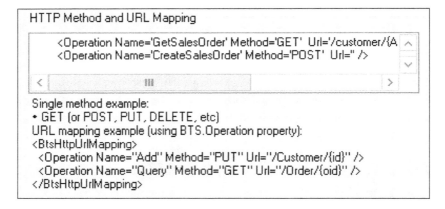

This is used for both sending and receiving HTTP requests, and this is where you further define the resource locations. You can use either single or multiple operation methods for both receiving and sending REST-based resources.

The single method operation just takes a single verb operation (GET, POST, PUT, DELETE, and so on) without specifying any URL mapping variables. A single verb operation is used when sending or receiving an HTTP request with no parameterized resource locations, or a POST method where the content is in the message body.

If multiple operations are required or variables are to be used in the URL for either receive locations or send ports, they must be wrapped inside the `BtsHttpUrlMapping` elements.

When using multiple operations on a receive location, the HTTP method and URL subpath are used to match against a set, consisting of an HTTP verb method and a URI template. If a match is found, the adapter adds the value of the `BTS.Operation` name to the BizTalk message context of the received message. If multiple operations are to be used for a send adapter, the `BTS.Operation` name must be set before it reaches the send port. The operation name is used to determine which `BTS.Operation` to use when the message is sent to the send port.

Note, the placeholders {id} and {oid} in the examples provided in the following `Url` attribute:

```
Single method example:
• GET (or POST, PUT, DELETE, etc)
URL mapping example (using BTS.Operation property):
<BtsHttpUrlMapping>
  <Operation Name="Add" Method="PUT" Url="/Customer/{id}" />
  <Operation Name="Query" Method="GET" Url="/Order/{oid}" />
</BtsHttpUrlMapping>
```

These form a part of the resource location and are used as variable placeholders where the actual values are swapped at runtime.

The last section on this tab is variable mapping. If you specify any placeholders for the variables in the URL subpath of the "HTTP method and URL mapping" section, you are required to set up mappings between the variable names and the promoted properties in the property schema that you will need to add to your solution. Pressing the **Edit** button in this section will open the **Variable Mapping** form.

In some cases the `Url` attribute may require an & symbol in the URL query string. This is normally written as `/Customer?from={start}&to={end}`, where the {start} and {end} values are the variables. For this to work correctly, the & symbol needs to be escaped using the normal XML escaping characters &.

So, the final URL with the escape characters added is rewritten as follows: `/Customer?from={start}&amp;to={end}`.

When using the adapter to consume a RESTful service (Send Port adapter), and if using either the GET or DELETE operations, you cannot send a payload to the RESTful service. There is provision on the **Messages** tab to suppress the message body being sent from the adapter for the specified verbs as shown here:

For POST and PUT requests, the adapter will use the BizTalk message body part as the HTTP content/payload and it will be sent formatted as XML by default.

Exposing a RESTful web service using BizTalk

Here, we will publish a request/response RESTful service that will simulate a simple sales query by a service consumer using **Content based routing (CBR)** based on the BTS.Operation name. A direct bound orchestration will subscribe to this message and return a response message containing the received account and order numbers. We will use two variable mappings on the receive location for the account and order number.

The URL will have two variables representing the account and order numbers, which represent the request resource location. The response message will simply return the account and order numbers found in the resource location and a unique identifier as an XML formatted message.

For this example, the receive pipeline will be set to `PassThruReceive` and an orchestration will be direct bound to subscribe to the `BTS.Operation` type. Later on in this chapter, we will use a custom pipeline to publish a typed message to the message box.

The request URL will be in the form `http://localhost/sales/customer/` `{AccountNumber}/salesorder/{OrderNumber}`, where `{AccountNumber}` is the customer account number and `{Ordernumber}` is the sales order number that we are interested in retrieving.

Before we get started:

1. Let's create a new BizTalk application called Sales. We are creating the application now, so that we can select it when running the WCF Service Publishing Wizard later.

2. Now, let's define the schema for the request and response. The key point here is to promote the `AccountNumber` and `OrderNumber` elements, these will be used later to map the URL variables. Also, take note of the property namespace `https://Packt.RestServices.Schemas.PropertySchema` as this will be required when we map the URL variables:

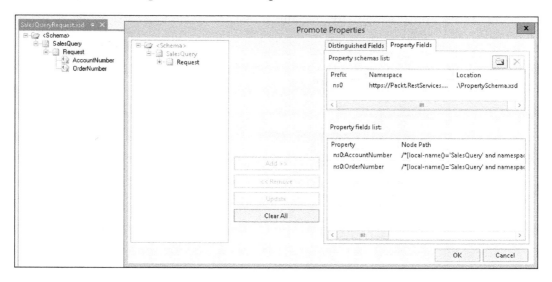

The AccountNumber and OrderNumber elements in the property schema are set to MessageContextPropertyBase as these values will only exist in the message context, as there is no message body present with a GET method.

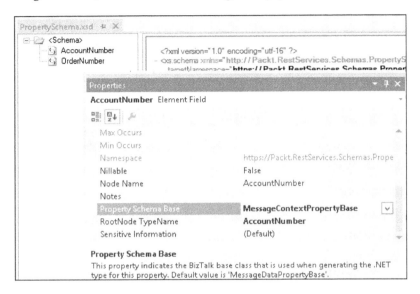

3. Now, we are ready to publish a WCF Service endpoint using the BizTalk WCF Service Publishing Wizard.

4. Set the **Adapter name (Transport type)** to **WCF-WebHttp**, and set the **BizTalk application name** to **Sales**:

Note that the WCF-WebHttp adapter can only be run under the context of Isolated Host. This effectively means it is normally hosted in IIS.

5. Keep clicking the **Next** button until you reach the option to either choose a One-Way or Request-Response port. For this example, select **Create a Request-Response Receive Port**.

    BizTalk developers who are accustomed to publishing a WCF service based on either the WCF-BasicHttp or WCF-WSHttp adapter will notice that the wizard does not ask for the schema type for the operation contracts at this point. This is because with REST-based services, there is no metadata to define the service contracts.

6. On the next page, set the **Location** to `http://localhost/sales` and check the **Allow anonymous access to WCF service** checkbox. We are not planning to add any security requirements:

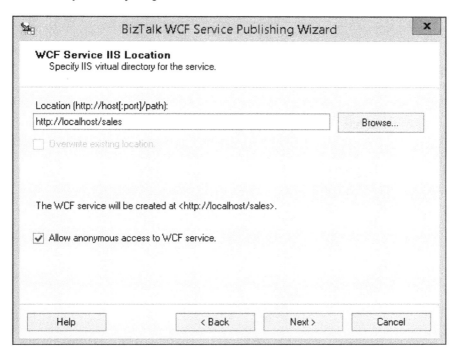

7. Click on **Next** to display the WCF Service Summary page. Now, click on **Create** and the wizard will create a `sales` virtual directory under the default website, as shown here:

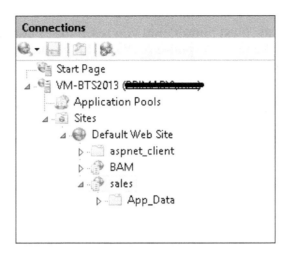

The wizard will use the same application pool used by the default website. Ideally, a new application pool should be created with appropriate access to the BizTalk Message Box.

Note that you must create a separate application pool for different protocols, for example, a receive location using SOAP cannot use the same application pool used for another receive location using the HTTP protocol.

If this happens, you may receive the following error: "Registering multiple adapter types within the same process is not a supported configuration. For e.g. HTTP and SOAP receive adapters cannot co-exist in the same process"

Now, let's see if we can view the site in Internet Explorer. The first task is to navigate to the Sales BizTalk application using the BizTalk Server Administration console and enable the created **WcfService_sales/Service1** receive location. Next, open a browser and type the following URL in the address bar: `http://localhost/sales/service1.svc`.

 Note that the wizard will create the name `service1.svc` as the default page. We will leave this as it is for now and later on, in this chapter, I will show how you can change this to a more RESTful address.

If all is working correctly, you should see the following **Service** webpage displayed. As this is meant to be a RESTful-style web service, the metadata publishing for this service should remain disabled:

Now that we have proved that IIS is serving up the page correctly, we can continue with the configuration of the adapter properties. Using the BizTalk Server Administration console, navigate to the **Sales** application and double-click on the **WcfService_sales/Service1** receive location to open the properties window shown here:

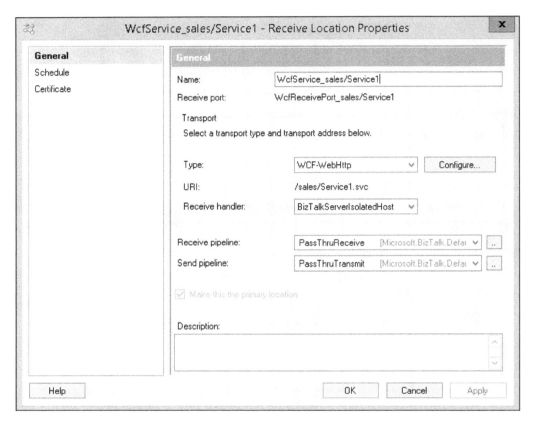

The **Receive pipeline** property can be left as **PassThruReceive** as our request is a simple GET operation, which has no message body.

Setting **Receive pipeline** to **XMLRecieve** will generate an error as there is normally no message body for the verbs GET or DELETE. We will discuss creating a custom receive pipeline later in this chapter to create a strongly typed message in the disassembly stage.

Now, we need to configure the transport properties to accept a GET verb. When the wizard creates the receive location, it sets the HTTP method and URL mapping value to the following default configuration:

```
<BtsHttpUrlMapping>
<Operation Name='Op1' Url='' />
<Operation Name='Op2' Url='/*' />
</BtsHttpUrlMapping>
```

For our example solution, we need to change this to the following configuration:

```
<BtsHttpUrlMapping>
<Operation Name="GetSalesOrder" Method="GET"
Url="/customer/{AccountNumber}/salesorder/{OrderNumber}" />
</BtsHttpUrlMapping>
```

Before you can save the configuration, you are required to map the variables `AccountNumber` and `OrderNumber` in the URL to the message context properties we defined earlier in our `SalesQuery` request schema.

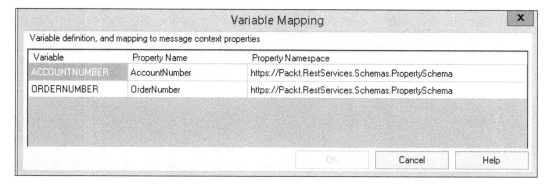

Without making any other configuration changes except enabling the receive location, you should be able to use the local browser on the BizTalk server and navigate to the URL entering random numbers for the account and order number variables. For example: `http://localhost/sales/service1.svc/customer/122/salesorder/3243`.

The browser should display an internal error message similar to following:

This error is expected because we have not completed the solution as yet. Using the BizTalk Server Administration console, you should be able to see one routing failure report error for the receive location.

If you look at the message properties of the failed message, you will see the values for the `AccountNumber` and `OrderNumber` that are written to the message context but not promoted. These are the variables defined in the URL and mapped to the `PropertySchema.xsd` file.

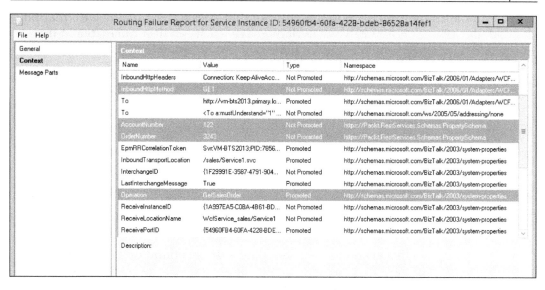

The two other important context properties are `InboundHttpMethod` and `Operation`. The `InboundHttpMethod` property describes the HTTP verb, and again is only written to the message context. In this example, the request was a GET. The other property is `Operation`, which is the only property that is promoted for a WCF-WebHttp adapter. This is the value we entered for the operation name when configuring the port properties.

 Non promoted properties cannot be used for message routing using filter expressions on send ports or orchestrations.

If you enter a resource location in the browser that does not match the URL mapping defined, the adapter will throw the fault message **AddressFilter mismatch at the EndpointDispatcher**, which is shown here:

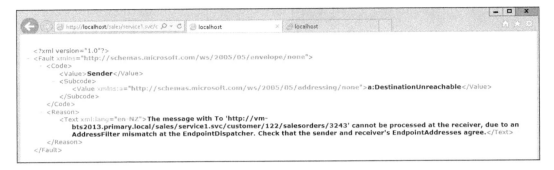

Now, let's complete this example by developing a direct bound orchestration, which subscribes to the BTS.Operation value of GetSalesOrder. The Receive message shape has a message type of System.Xml.XmlDocument (thus untyped) as the message sent by the receive pipeline has an empty message body. The Filter Expression on the Receive shape is set to (BTS.Operation == "GetSalesOrder").

In the message assignment shape, we initialize a response message and assign the Account and Order values using the message context properties. The ID element is just set to a GUID value.

The final orchestration should look like this:

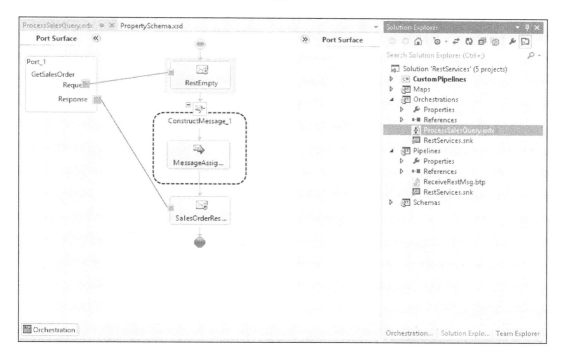

After deploying the solution to the BizTalk server environment, use SoapUI to navigate to the published REST service. For the endpoint value, use `http://localhost` and in the **Resource** value, use `/sales/service1.svc/customer/122/salesorder/3245`. Set the method to GET, and click on the submit button.

All being well, you should get a response message back in XML format and an HTTP status of 200.

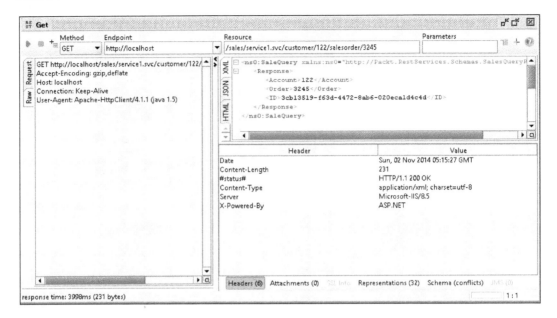

The same method may also be used to handle the HTTP DELETE verb. You will need to modify the HTTP method and URL mapping on the WCF-WebHttp Transport properties, and add the DELETE method.

Pipeline to publish a typed message

In some circumstances, it may be necessary to publish a typed message to the message box when receiving a message using the HTTP GET or DELETE verbs. As you know, there is no message body to publish, therefore we need to create one in the receive pipeline. More information about how to develop custom pipelines can be found at https://msdn.microsoft.com/en-us/library/aa548050.aspx.

In the disassemble stage of the receive pipeline, we inspect the value of the InboundHttpMethod property; if it is a GET method, we call the helper method ResourceLocationBasedMsg to instantiate a message and populate the promoted elements:

```
public void Disassemble(IPipelineContext pContext, IBaseMessage
pInMsg)
{
```

```
IBaseMessageContext context = pInMsg.Context;
//Get the http verb from the context properties
var httpVerb = context.Read("InboundHttpMethod", "http://schemas.
microsoft.com/BizTalk/2006/01/Adapters/WCF-properties");
//Check if the method is a GET
if(httpVerb.Equals("GET"))
{
var pOutMsg = ResourceLocationBasedMsg(pContext, pInMsg);
_mgsOutQueue.Enqueue(pOutMsg);
}
}
```

Here is the code for the helper method that does the work to instantiate a message and populates the elements by iterating through the context properties:

```
/// <summary>
/// Method to publish a typed message and de-promote the context
/// properties defined in the variable mappings
/// </summary>
private static IBaseMessage ResourceLocationBasedMsg(IPipelineContext
pContext, IBaseMessage pInMsg)
{
//Get a reference to the SalesQueryRequest BizTalk Schema
//Ideally this should be dynamically resolved using BRE or some other
technique
var msgTypeToLoad =    "http://Packt.RestServices.Schemas.
SalesQuery#SalesQuery";
var documentSpec = (DocumentSpec)pContext.GetDocumentSpecByType(msgTy
peToLoad);
var annotations = documentSpec.GetPropertyAnnotationEnumerator();
var doc = new XmlDocument();
var sw = new StringWriter(new StringBuilder());

//create a new instance of the schema.
doc.Load(documentSpec.CreateXmlInstance(sw));
sw.Dispose();

//iterate through the context properties and demote the property //
values to the message content.
while(annotations.MoveNext())
{
var annotation = (IPropertyAnnotation)annotations.Current;
        var node = doc.SelectSingleNode(annotation.XPath);
        var propertyValue = pInMsg.Context.Read(annotation.Name,
annotation.Namespace);
```

```
              if (propertyValue != null)
              {
//write the value into the actual element in the XML //document
                  node.InnerText = propertyValue.ToString();
              }
    }
    var ms = new MemoryStream();
    doc.Save(ms);
    ms.Seek(0, SeekOrigin.Begin);
    var pOutMsg = pInMsg;
    pOutMsg.BodyPart.Data = ms;
    pOutMsg.Context.Promote("MessageType", "http://schemas.microsoft.com/
    BizTalk/2003/system-properties", documentSpec.DocType);
    pOutMsg.Context.Promote("SchemaStrongName", "http://schemas.microsoft.
    com/BizTalk/2003/system-properties", documentSpec.DocSpecStrongName);
    return pOutMsg;
    }
```

Add the custom component to the disassemble stage of a custom receive pipeline, deploy the custom pipeline, and set the receive pipeline on your receive location to use this custom version. Now, you are able to submit a GET request and publish a typed message of the SalesQueryRequest schema to the message box.

Receiving XML and JSON messages via the Post method

Now that we have successfully published a RESTful service that handles the GET verb, let's discuss the options to accept messages using the HTTP POST verb and how to receive the message body content in XML and JSON formats.

In order to receive an XML message, a schema that matches the posted message body and setting the receive pipeline to XMLReceive is required. In this scenario, the WCF-WebHttp adapter behaves very similar to a WCF-BasicHttp adapter.

However, if you are required to receive JSON formatted messages, you need to convert them to XML first before publishing them to the message box. Before you can do this, you must also have an XML schema representation of the JSON message. There are tools on the Internet that will take a JSON message online and convert it to an equivalent XML format.

There are a couple of options that can be used to covert JSON to XML.

Note that BizTalk Server 2013R2 now includes a JSON Decoder Pipeline Component in the toolbox that converts JSON to XML.

The first option is to develop a custom receive pipeline to perform the conversion. Using the Json.Net library available on CodePlex (`https://json.codeplex.com/`) makes transforming JSON to XML fairly easy as it does all the heavy work for you. You can also use this same library to convert XML to JSON in a send port pipeline component. Later on in this chapter, I will show you how this can be achieved.

First, you need to add a reference to the Json.NET libraries in your custom pipeline component project. The easiest way to do this is from the Nuget Package Manager Console, in which you must type in the following command: `Install-Package Newtonsoft.Json`

In the disassemble stage of the custom receive pipeline, we check the `InboundHTTPHeaders` context property to get the content type. The header should contain the following content type `Content-Type: application/json` and we also check the `InboundHttpMethod` context property to confirm that it is a POST:

```
public void Disassemble(IPipelineContext pContext, IBaseMessage
pInMsg)
{
//Get the list of inbound header properties
        var inboundHeaders = context.Read("InboundHttpHeaders",
"http://schemas.microsoft.com/BizTalk/2006/01/Adapters/WCF-
properties");

//Check if method is a POST and content type is JSON
if (inboundHeaders.ToString().Contains("Content-Type: application/
json") && httpVerb.Equals("POST"))
        {
            //call the helper function
var pOutMsg = JsonBasedMsg(pContext, pInMsg);
                _mgsOutQueue.Enqueue(pOutMsg);
        }

}
```

Here is the helper code that uses the Newtonsoft.Json component to transform the JSON message to XML:

```csharp
/// <summary>
/// Method to convert a json message to a typed xml document
/// </summary>
private static IBaseMessage JsonBasedMsg(IPipelineContext pContext,
IBaseMessage pInMsg)
{
//Get a reference to the BizTalk Schema to load.
        //Ideally this should be dynamically resolved using BRE or some
other technique
        var msgTypeToLoad = "http://Packt.RestServices.Schemas.
SalesAddRequest#SalesOrder";
        var documentSpec = (DocumentSpec)pContext.GetDocumentSpecByType
(msgTypeToLoad);
        var docRoot = new XmlDocument();
        var sw = new StringWriter(new StringBuilder());

        //create a new instance of the schema.
        docRoot.Load(documentSpec.CreateXmlInstance(sw));
        sw.Dispose();



        Stream sm = pInMsg.BodyPart.GetOriginalDataStream();
         var content = string.Empty;
        using (StreamReader sr = new StreamReader(sm))
        {
            content = sr.ReadToEnd();
        }

        //Convert JSON to XML
        XmlNode jsonNode = (XmlNode)JsonConvert.DeserializeXmlNode(cont
ent,"Request");

        //Replace the inner xml with the converted json message
        docRoot.DocumentElement.InnerXml = jsonNode.OuterXml;

        byte[] bytes = Encoding.ASCII.GetBytes(docRoot.OuterXml);
        MemoryStream ms = new MemoryStream();
        ms.Write(bytes, 0, bytes.Length);
        ms.Position = 0;
```

```
        var pOutMsg = pInMsg;
        pOutMsg.BodyPart.Data = ms;


        pOutMsg.Context.Promote("MessageType", "http://schemas.
microsoft.com/BizTalk/2003/system-properties", documentSpec.DocType);
        pOutMsg.Context.Promote("SchemaStrongName", "http://schemas.
microsoft.com/BizTalk/2003/system-properties", documentSpec.
DocSpecStrongName);

        return pOutMsg;
}
```

The first part of the code creates an instance of the BizTalk XML message that we want to publish to the message box.

Then, we can use the component from Newtonsoft to convert JSON to XML, wrapping the resultant XML inside the specified Request node name.

 Note that we are loading the whole JSON message into an XmlNode object, which will cause high memory utilization if the message is very large.

We then replace the inner XML of the BizTalk message with the converted JSON message and then promote the message type and schema strong name.

After deploying the solution to BizTalk, use SoapUI to POST a JSON message. Remember to set the **Media Type** to **application/json**.

In our sample solution, we posted the following JSON message and mapped the CustomerNumber and OrderNumber to a response message:

```
{
"CustomerNumber":"89438",
        "OrderNumber": "3432",
        "ProductNumber": "PQ-739",
"Qty": "10"
}
```

Here is the request and response message as XML:

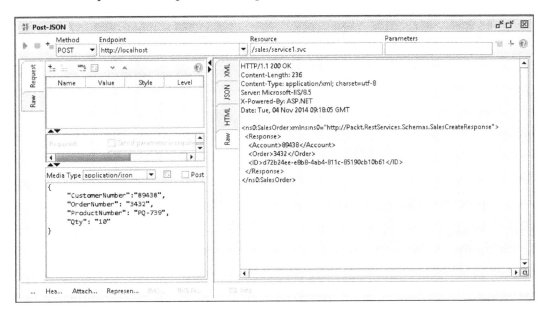

The other option is to develop a custom WCF endpoint behavior. More information about developing custom WCF behaviors can be found at `https://msdn.microsoft.com/en-us/magazine/cc163302.aspx`.

The BizTalk WCF-* adapters provide an extensibility mechanism using the `ServiceBehavior` and `EndPointBehavior` extensions. One of the main differences between the two is that `ServiceBehavior` applies only on a service, while `EndpointBehavior` applies on both client and service. For the receive adapter, we override the `AfterReceiveReply` method and implement the decoding of the JSON message to XML inside this method:

```
public void AfterReceiveReply(ref Message reply, object
correlationState)
{
// add your json to xml conversion here...
}
```

Consuming a web service

Now that you learned how to publish and receive XML and JSON formatted messages, it's time to explore how to consume a RESTful service.

For our REST service, we will use Visual Studio to create a Web API project using the ASP.Net MVC 4 web application template. This creates the following stub code for each HTTP verb:

```
// GET api/values
public IEnumerable<string> Get()
{
return new string[] { "value1", "value2" };
}

// GET api/values/5
public string Get(int id)
{
return "value";
}

// POST api/values
public void Post([FromBody]string value)
{
}

// PUT api/values/5
public void Put(int id, [FromBody]string value)
{
}

// DELETE api/values/5
public void Delete(int id)
{
}
```

The **General** tab on the WCF-WebHttp Transport properties is configured as shown here:

As we are only requesting a GET method, the WCF send adapter will want to send a message body regardless of what the HTTP verb is. To suppress this, we will need to go to the Messages tab on the WCF-WebHttp adapter and add the verbs where the message body should be suppressed.

To get BizTalk to send a request to the web service, we will use a messaging only solution. The process will be triggered by dropping a file into a pickup folder that is monitored by a BizTalk file receive location. A WCF-WebHttp Solicit/Response send port will have a filter expression BTS.ReceivePortName set to the receive port name. A file send port will also be created and its filter expression BTS.SPName will be set to the WCF-WebHttp port name to receive the response message. The response message will simply be written to the filesystem.

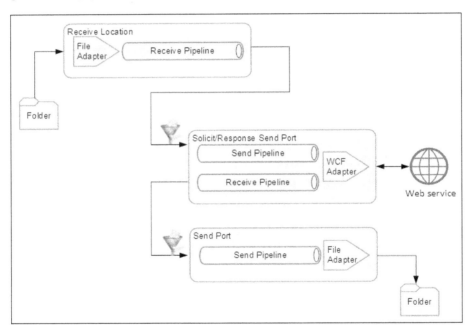

By modifying the outbound headers on the **Messages** tab, you can define the format of the response message, provided that the web service understands the Content-Type property. To request the response message to be XML, you would specify Content-Type: application/xml, and if you require a JSON formatted message, you would set the content type property to Content-Type: application/json.

This is the response message when content type is set to XML:

```
<ArrayOfstring xmlns:i="http://www.w3.org/2001/XMLSchema-instance"
xmlns="http://schemas.microsoft.com/2003/10/Serialization/Arrays">
```

```
    <string>value1</string>
    <string>value2</string>
</ArrayOfstring>
```

This is the response message when content type is set to JSON:

```
["value1","value2"]
```

 If no content type is specified in the Outbound HTTP header, the default content type property will be set to receive XML as the response message format.

Now, let's use the URL mapping feature on the send port to call the other WebAPI method GET api/Values/{id}. This method requires an ID value as part of the resource location.

The XML message that is subscribed to by the send port requires the elements to be promoted, which can then be used for the variable mappings.

The settings for the send port are as follows:

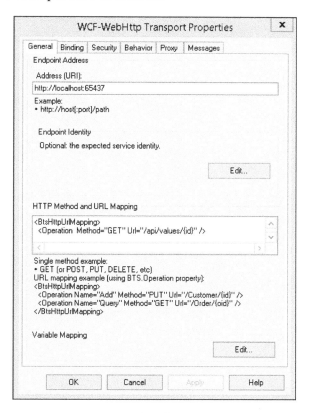

Note the absence of the `Name` property in the Operation element as this is a messaging only solution with only one operation. The following sample message is dropped into the receive location's pickup folder:

```
<ns0:SalesQuery xmlns:ns0="http://Packt.RestServices.Schemas.
SalesQuery">
  <Request>
    <AccountNumber>1234</AccountNumber>
    <OrderNumber>8979</OrderNumber>
  </Request>
</ns0:SalesQuery>
```

Once the receive location picks up the file, a request will be sent to the web service with the variables mapped.

A breakpoint is placed in the method of the web service so we can view the variable being mapped correctly by the send port adapter. For this example, we only mapped the `AccountNumber`.

```
// GET api/values
public IEnumerable<string> Get()
{
    return new string[] { "value1", "value2" };
}

// GET api/values/5
public string Get(int id)          id 1234
{
    return "value";
}

// POST api/values
public void Post([FromBody]string value)
{
}
```

We can also POST an XML message by modifying the HTTP method and URL mapping as shown here to match the specified resource location `http://localhost/api/values`:

```
<BtsHttpUrlMapping>
  <Operation  Method="POST" Url="/api/values" />
</BtsHttpUrlMapping>
```

As there were no variables defined in the `Url` property, no variable mappings were required.

Sending a JSON message to a RESTful service

In BizTalk 2013, the only data format available for posting a message to a web service was XML. This has been rectified in BizTalk Server 2013 R2 with the addition of the JSON encoder pipeline component. For BizTalk 2013, our options are to either create a WCF custom behavior or a custom send port pipeline to convert the outbound XML message to JSON.

In this section, we will discuss and build a custom pipeline to convert an XML message to a JSON message format and submit it to our Web API service. For this example, we will use a messaging only solution. The send port will subscribe to messages received by a file receive location, as we saw in our previous example.

The sample message to be picked up by the receive location will look like the following XML:

```
<ns0:SalesQuery xmlns:ns0="http://Packt.RestServices.Schemas.
SalesQuery">
  <Request>
    <AccountNumber>1234</AccountNumber>
    <OrderNumber>8979</OrderNumber>
  </Request>
</ns0:SalesQuery>
```

Before we start on the pipeline component, we will need to make a change to our Web API service. The template created a stub method for the POST verb, which expects a single string value. We will modify this to accept a JSON-style object. To do this, we will create a **Data Transfer Object (DTO)** in the `Models` folder, which represents the JSON object for the preceding XML message.

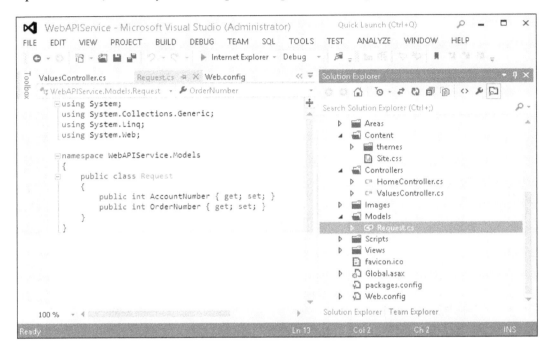

We then modify the existing `Post` method in the `ValuesController.cs` file to use the `Request` model:

```
// POST api/values
public void Post([FromBody]Request data)
{
Debug.Write(data);
}
```

Once we make the changes to the Web API service and get it running in debug mode, we can use Fiddler to compose a message to test that everything is working accordingly.

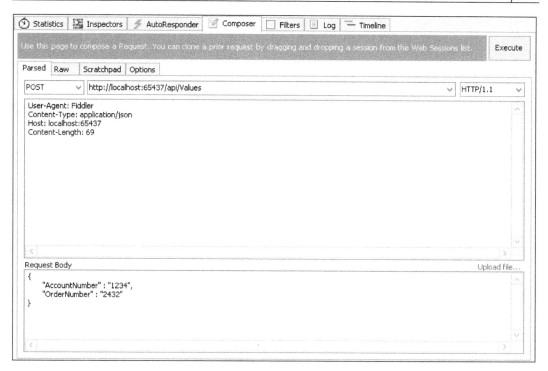

Now, we can start writing the code for the pipeline component. Just as we did for the custom receive pipeline, we will utilize the `Newtonsoft.Json` component from CodePlex.

Note that with BizTalk 2013 R2, there is no need to develop a custom send pipeline component to convert XML into JSON as this version already includes a JSON encoder pipeline component in the toolbox.

For our example, we are only interested in the inner XML of the `Request` node. The line of code—`xmlContent.LoadXml(xmlMessage.FirstChild.InnerXml);`—loads the inner XML of the message envelope:

```
#region IComponent
public IBaseMessage Execute(IPipelineContext pContext, IBaseMessage
pInMsg)
{
IBaseMessagePart bodyPart = pInMsg.BodyPart;
if (bodyPart != null)
        {
```

```
                  Stream orignalStream = bodyPart.GetOriginalDataStream();
                if (orignalStream != null)
                {
                        var xmlMessage = new XmlDocument();
                    xmlMessage.Load(orignalStream);

                    if( xmlMessage.FirstChild.NodeType == XmlNodeType.
XmlDeclaration)
            {
                            xmlMessage.RemoveChild(xmlMessage.FirstChild);
    }

    //Remove the root, only interested in the inner //xml
                    var xmlContent = new XmlDocument();
                    xmlContent.LoadXml(xmlMessage.FirstChild.
InnerXml);

    string jsonText = JsonConvert.SerializeXmlNode(xmlContent, Newtonsoft.
Json.Formatting.Indented,true);

                    byte[] outBytes = Encoding.ASCII.
GetBytes(jsonText);

                    var memStream = new MemoryStream();
                    memStream.Write(outBytes, 0, outBytes.Length);
                    memStream.Position = 0;

                    bodyPart.Data = memStream;
                    pContext.ResourceTracker.AddResource(memStream);
                }
        }
return pInMsg;
}
#endregion
```

The custom pipeline code is then placed into the Encode stage of the send pipeline. After the solution has been deployed and the filters have been set up on the WCF send port, you will need to set the outbound header properties for JSON content type.

Now, we are ready to drop a sample message into the pickup folder. We have put a breakpoint in the pipeline code so we can see the XML converted to JSON.

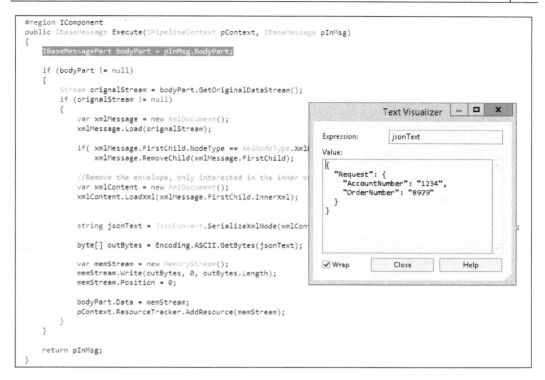

And this is the JSON received by the Web API service.

```
// POST api/values
public void Post([FromBody]Request data)
{
    Debug.Write(data);
}
                          data  {WebAPIService.Models.Request}
                             AccountNumber  1234
                             OrderNumber    8979
```

We have now completed sending an XML message from BizTalk to a RESTful JSON web service.

Hiding the SVC filename extension

With IIS7 and higher versions, you can download the URL Rewrite Module from `http://www.iis.net/learn/extensions/url-rewrite-module/using-the-url-rewrite-module`. Note that there are two versions available, one for 32 bit systems and the other for 64 bit systems.

Next, you will need to create an inbound rule to make the existing URL (`http://localhost/sales/service1.svc/customer/122/salesorder/3243`) look like `http://localhost/sales/customer/122/salesorder/3243`.

Here is the rule definition used to rewrite the URL using the URL Rewrite task under the default website:

```
<rewrite>
    <rules>
        <rule name="Remove Service1.svc">
            <match url="^sales/(.*)$" />
            <action type="Rewrite" url="sales/service1.svc/{R:1}" />
        </rule>
    </rules>
</rewrite>
```

Once the rules have been applied, you should be able type the following URL resource location `http://localhost/sales/customer/122/salesorder/3243` into the Internet browser address bar and get a response.

Summary

In this chapter, we gained an overview of RESTful services and how they are becoming more fashionable in the world of smart devices.

We covered how important it is to structure the URL resource hierarchy of a REST-based web service and how to manage versioning and security. We also discussed the format of the response message and how to specify the expected format using header properties.

Next, we discussed the WCF-WebHttp adapter that is shipped with BizTalk 2013 covering the new context properties to manage REST-based services. Then, we created some sample solutions to publish and consume a RESTful web service. In both samples, we covered creating custom receive and send pipeline components to process JSON-style messages.

5
Azure BizTalk Services

Service to others is the rent you pay for your room here on earth.

– Muhammad Ali

Microsoft Azure BizTalk Services (MABS) is a cloud-based integration service for delivering cloud and hybrid integration solutions that address some of the same B2B and EAI problems that the BizTalk Server 2013 platform does. Karthik Bharathy and Jon Fancey have recently written a primer on this subject called *Getting Started with BizTalk Services*, *Packt Publishing*. This chapter will summarize the important features of MABS and you should consult the aforementioned book for more detail.

In this chapter you will learn:

- When to use MABS and how it works
- The role of MABS schemas, maps, bridges, and hybrid connections
- MABS messaging configurations

What is MABS

Microsoft Azure BizTalk Services is a collection of integration services that run in Azure, connecting applications hosted in the cloud or a data center on the ground. Applications communicate with the service either by an HTTP Post to a bridge or via an intermediary adapter to a bridge.

The term "bridge" immediately reminds us of something that connects two end points. In the context of information systems, we are talking about a bridge connecting two or more disparate systems. A bridge is a BizTalk Services EAI and EDI component that processes, transforms, and transports data between two disparate systems. This component applies the **VETER** pattern': **Validate — Enrich — Transform — Enrich — Route**.

MABS can provide Enterprise Application and Business-to-Business integration as a service that fits nicely into service-orientated architectures. At the time of writing this book, MABS is a work in progress, and the release of more functionalities such as Business Rules Engine and Business Activity monitoring are imminent. What we can be sure of is that once MABS is finished, it will have the same rich features as its on-premises cousin, BizTalk Server. This chapter will only talk about the update released on February 20, 2014.

The MABS architecture

A simple definition of MABS is many services loosely coupled together to achieve an SOA pattern. The requirement for installation and maintenance of the services is delegated to Microsoft Azure.

Let us start by considering how we might architect the traditional EAI view from *Chapter 1, Building BizTalk Server 2013 Applications*. A message can be received by the source and passed on to a bridge. The source might be FTP, SFTP, a Service Bus Queue or a Service Bus Topic. Alternatively, the bridge can receive a message directly via an HTTP Post. The bridge is where all pre-processing and data transformations take place before publishing the message to a Service Bus Topic or Queue. Pipelines and maps perform the same task in BizTalk Server. The Service Bus performs the same function that MessageBox fulfils for BizTalk Server; namely, it queues messages until each subscriber gets the message. The publish-subscribe functionality comes in two forms: a queue with one subscription and a topic with many subscriptions.

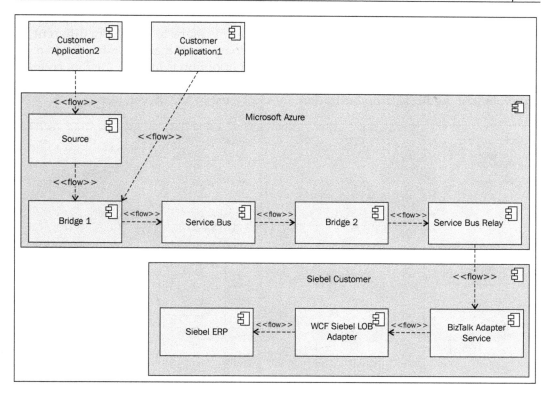

The Service Bus platform more importantly provides durability, reliability, and scalability at the cost of increasing latency. More importantly, the Service Bus platform forces you to build asynchronous services because there is no equivalent to the correlation feature found in BizTalk.

One important function of the bridge is to make sure that the message has the correct routing information and message type attached to it as metadata when it is sent to the Service Bus Queue or Topic. This metadata is then used to route the message to its final endpoint. Bridges don't have persistence (durability); instead, they are "fire-and-forget".

A bridge can also transform data using maps. Just as BizTalk Server receive ports can have many maps, a bridge can also have multiple maps to transform different message formats. The bridge is the only MABS component that can subscribe to a message on a Service Bus Queue or Topic. Another option is to write custom code that pops the message off the Service Bus and sends it to a Windows Workflow. An equivalent of the BizTalk orchestration does not exist in MABS yet.

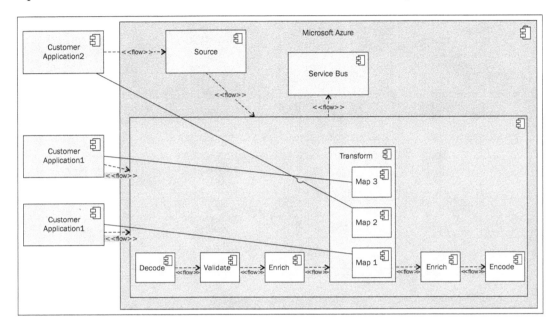

Microsoft Azure can connect synchronously with applications in a firewall-friendly way called **hybrid connectivity**. An on-premise service creates an outbound connection to an Azure Service Bus and listens for messages. Exposing a port through public-facing firewalls for the inbound connection is not required. **BizTalk Adapter Service (BAS)** and Hybrid Connections use this technology.

Internet Information Services (IIS) hosts BAS and uses the **Line of Business Adapter (LOB Adapter)** from the BizTalk Adapter pack to establish the connection to the Azure Service Bus. A client can then find the Service Bus endpoint and send messages to the LOB.

MABS Hybrid Connections use an agent that you install on-premise to connect to the LOB of interest. The agent then establishes the service connection back to Azure:

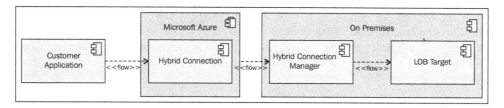

Setting up new MABS projects

Before setting up a new MABS project, you will first want to set up a MABS development environment with a Microsoft Azure subscription, a BizTalk Service provisioned from the Azure management portal, Windows 7 Service Pack 1 (or a newer Windows operating system), Microsoft Visual Studio 2012 and the Microsoft Azure BizTalk Services SDK setup.

If you have successfully installed the SDK in your development environment, you will see the **BizTalk Service** option in the **Visual Studio Projects** menu:

MABS artifacts

We saw in *Chapter 1, Building BizTalk Server 2013 Applications*, that schemas are the cornerstone of any BizTalk SOA solution, and they are also the basic building block of a MABS solution for the same reason. The MABS schema editor has a similar development experience to that of the BizTalk server version, and schemas created in BizTalk can be used without modification. Promoted properties on BizTalk schemas are ignored.

MABS uses transforms to transform messages from one structure to another in the same way that BizTalk server solutions use maps. The MABS **Transform Editor (TRFM)** is very different from the BizTalk map editor, and BizTalk maps cannot be used directly in MABS unless it uses an external XSLT file. BizTalk maps can be converted to transforms with a wizard, but this has some limitations. For example, some functoids may not get converted and are converted to an arithmetic expression functoid in the TRFM map with an empty expression value.

Selecting a BizTalk Service project template in Visual Studio creates a project that contains the `MessageFlowItinerary.bcs` and `LookupProviderConfigurations.xml` files. `MessageFlowItinerary` is where you can add bridges, sources, and destinations. Schemas and transforms can be added as artifacts to the project. The example project receives either an invoice or an order and routes it to a LOB adapter that inserts the contents into a SQL database. We illustrate two ways to receive and then publish messages, one using Service Bus Topic subscriptions and a second one that uses the message type in XML Bridge:

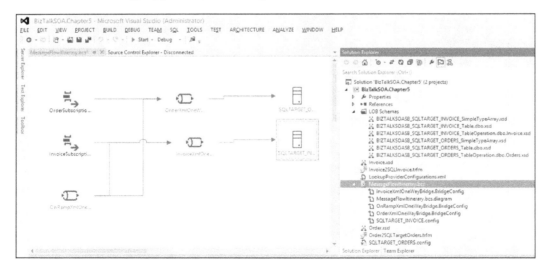

First, if a message arrives on the Service Bus with an `IsOrder` property equal to `1`, it is sent to the order subscription and if it is equal to `0`, it is sent to the invoice subscription. The order subscription source picks order messages up from the order subscription and sends them to the `OrderXMLOneWayBridge`. The invoice subscription source is configured to send invoices to the `InvoiceXMLOnewayBridge` in the same way. These are configured in the subscription rules on a Service Bus Topic. The Service Bus Topic receives any message type, and subscription rules determine which endpoint the message is sent to. In the next chapter, we will examine the Azure Service Bus in more detail.

Second, `OnRampXMLOneWayBridge` determines the message type and stamps the message with a property called `X_PIPELINE_REQUESTMESSAGE`. If this property equals `http://BizTalkSOA.Chapter5.Invoice#Invoice` then the message is routed to `OrderXMLOneWayBridge`; or if it equals `http://BizTalkSOA.Chapter5.Order#CustomerOrder`, then the message is routed to `InvoiceXMLOneWayBridge`. The XML Bridge receives any message type, and the routing rules determine which endpoint the message is sent to.

Messages can only be published to one endpoint in a MABS bridge, but we have shown that by using routing filters or subscriptions you can choose where the message goes.

Configuring messaging in MABS

The critical part of solution creation is configuring the settings of all the components that have been added to the `MessageFlowItinerary`.

MABS can receive messages from a one-way message exchange using an FTP, a Service Bus Queue, an SFTP, a Service Bus Subscription, XML One-Way Bridge, or a Pass-through Bridge source. A two-way message exchange can be configured using an XML Request-Reply XML Bridge. Configuration of MABS sources happens at design time; for example, the connection string of the Service Bus Subscription source and Subscription name are set in Visual Studio before the source is deployed to Azure.

OrderSubscriptionSource Subscription Source	
Connection String	Endpoint=sb://biztalksoasb.servicebus.windows.net/;SharedSecretIssuer=owner;SharedSecretValue
Entity Name	OrderSubscriptionSource
Initial Status	Start
Subscription Name	COorINV/subscriptions/customerorder

Destinations on the `MessageFlowItinerary` surface are also configured at design time. The following screenshot shows an XML One-Way Bridge configured to parse an XML message and transform the XML message to another XML message.

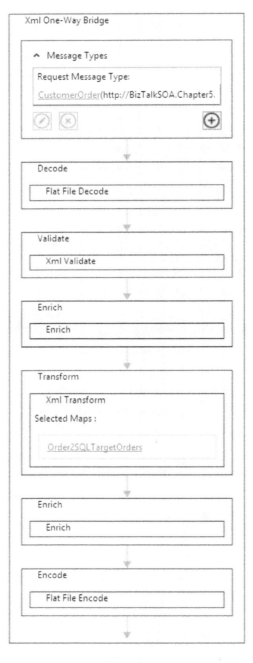

The next step is to connect the source and other components together on the message flow itinerary surface using a connector. A filter condition must be configured on the connector, and a route action can be optionally configured. The connector can select either all the messages or only messages that contain one of the message properties. The filter condition, based on the SQL 92 syntax, is similar to a send port filter in BizTalk Server.

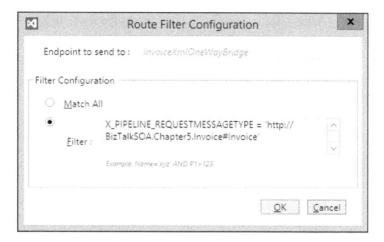

The route action can either use a property on the message or a SOAP header namespace. On a BizTalk Server send port, this corresponds to setting the SOAP Action.

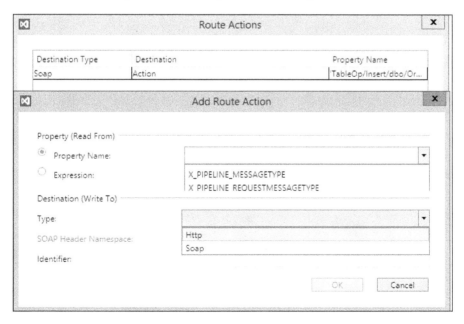

Summary

In this chapter, we learned about the MABS messaging architecture and compared it to BizTalk Server. I encourage you to consult Bharathy and Fancey's *Getting Started with BizTalk Services, Packt Publishing,* for more detailed reading. MABS is important because, as more applications move off-premises, integration solutions will be required to connect to other applications on the cloud and on the ground. We believe that, in the future, MABS will fill this space, and we hope that we have shown that it possesses the same features that BizTalk Server has, to allow you to build service-oriented solutions.

In the next chapter, we will look at Azure Service Bus, which is an asynchronous cloud-based messaging service.

6

Azure Service Bus

Live long and prosper.

– Mr Spock, Star Trek

Azure Service Bus is a multi-tenanted asynchronous messaging service based on **Platform as a Service (PaaS)** architecture. It is designed as a highly scalable and reliable messaging system used for connecting applications, services, and devices.

Service Bus supports two types of message exchange patterns, relayed messaging and brokered messaging. The main distinction between the two exchange patterns is that relayed service requires both the service consumer and provider to be online simultaneously, whereas with the brokered service, either the consumer or provider may be taken offline at any time without affecting the communication channel. Service Bus is a lightweight, messaging-only architecture, while BizTalk is a full-featured, enterprise integration engine that provides many LOB adapters out of the box.

In this chapter you will learn:

- The different types of Service Bus artifacts available in Microsoft Azure
- The two different types of queuing architectures available and some of their key characteristics
- Examples on how to create Topics and Subscriptions
- Design considerations when using Service Bus

Service Bus types

Azure Service Bus offers a collection of four different types of messaging technologies:

- **Queues**: This provides asynchronous messaging
- **Topics/Subscriptions**: This provides a publish/subscribe architecture style of integration
- **Event Hubs**: This is used to ingest event type messages on a massive scale
- **Relays**: This allows the relaying of messages through a common channel

Each type has distinctive characteristics that make it suitable for different messaging scenarios. In the following sections, we will discuss each type in more detail.

Queue types

There are two types of Queues available in the Azure stack:

- Azure Queue Storage
- Azure Service Bus Queues

Both are implementations of the message queuing architecture. While designing a solution requiring a message queuing technology, you will need to consider the features of both types of queuing mechanisms to decide the best fit.

The key differences between the two are:

- Azure Queue Storage is lightweight and offers high performance messaging, which is based on the Azure Storage infrastructure
- Azure Queue Storage provides a simple GET/PUT/Peek RESTful interface
- Service Bus queues are guaranteed First-in First-out (FIFO)
- Service Bus queues have full integration with the WCF stack, as well as RESTful and AMQP support

Scenarios in which duplicate message detection, automatic dead-lettering capabilities, and durable publish/subscribe mechanisms are required, Azure Service Bus should be considered as an option.

 More information on the differences can be found at `http://msdn.microsoft.com/en-us/library/azure/hh767287.aspx`.

Service Bus Queue characteristics

Service Bus Queues provide a one-way message exchange pattern for passing messages between distributed and loosely coupled applications using the Azure SDK, WCF, AMQP, or RESTful endpoints. These queues provide load leveling, by default, where the receiver processes messages off the queue at its own pace.

Load balancing can also be easily implemented by reading the queue length property and spinning up more processes to read the queue concurrently. As the queue length diminishes, the extra processors can be taken offline. When using multiple processors to read messages from the same queue concurrently, careful consideration must be given to the type of read lock you wish to perform. More about this is explained in the section *Retrieving messages off a Queue*.

There are many uses for this type of coupling pattern:

- Hybrid applications, which allow you to connect an on-premises application to a cloud hosted service or application

- Loosely coupled applications, where Service Bus acts as a message broker between different systems

- Mobile applications, where clients are occasionally connected to a network

- Offline/batch processing, where the queue consumer is only available for a limited time span

Queue naming convention

Before creating a queue, a namespace (a container for Service Bus artifacts) must be created first. A namespace name must be between 6 and 50 characters long and can contain only letters, numbers, and hyphens. It must start with a letter and must not end with either `-`, `-sb`, `-mgmt`, `-cache`, or `-appfabric`.

 Once a namespace has been created, its resource manifest is immutable.

The names of the queues must be in lowercase, and the length of the name must be between 3 and 63 characters long. You are once again limited to alphanumeric characters and the hyphen (-). A queue may only start with a letter or number.

Message size

While designing a queuing mechanism, consideration should be given to the size of each message. The current maximum content message size for Azure Queue Storage is restricted to 64 KB whereas for Service Bus Queues, the restriction is 256 KB. Previous versions of Queue Storage were limited to just 8 KB.

To deal with the message size restriction, there are several options available. One option would be to use blob storage to store the message content and use the queues to hold metadata about the message and URI path.

Another option is to use sessions and to break up the messages into smaller sizes (known as **chunking**). Each message chunk is placed on the queue with the same session identifier key. This instructs Service Bus to place all the received message chunks onto the same partition and in the correct sequence. The consumer would then read all the message chunks from the queue with the matching session identifier to reconstruct the entire message.

User-defined name/value pairs

If you need to send a message to an Azure Service Bus Queue with metadata, you should consider using the `BrokeredMessage` class, which is part of the `Microsoft.ServiceBus.Messaging` namespace. One of the properties of this class takes a dictionary collection of `System.Collections.Generic.IDictionary<String,Object>`.

 Note: Brokered messaging properties are not SOAP headers.

This is useful while creating a Topic with filters on user-defined values.

```
BrokeredMessage message = new BrokeredMessage()
        message.Properties["Priority"] = "High"; //used for
filtered topic subscription
        message.Properties["Location"] = "Auckland";
```

 It is not uncommon to have messages with no message bodies and simply use the messaging properties to carry the information.

Priority order

Currently, Service Bus does not natively provide a queuing mechanism that automatically sorts messages by priority. However, by using Service Bus topics with a filter, an alternative option is possible by creating two subscriptions, one for high priority messages and the other for low priority messages.

Time to live

Each message has a **time to live** (TTL) property, which specifies how long a message will be available in the queue. If the message does not get consumed within the specified TTL value, it will be deleted from the queue. The maximum TTL for Azure Queues is 7 days, whereas it is unlimited for Service Bus Queues.

Dead-lettering

Dead-lettering normally occurs when a message cannot be processed, either because the message is formatted incorrectly or because the TTL period has been exceeded.

In Azure Service Bus, the message will be placed on the $DeadLetterQueue subqueue for the following reasons:

- If the read message fails to get processed and reappears on the queue more than 10 times. This is the default maximum delivery count.

- When the message reaches the TTL threshold and the dead lettering flag has been set in the queue or subscription.

- When a subscription filter evaluation exception occurs and dead-lettering is enabled on the filter.

Automatic dead lettering does not occur for the ReceiveAndDelete read mode. This is because the message is automatically deleted from the queue once it has been read.

 Messages in a dead letter queue do not expire and must be removed manually.

If using Topics with multiple Subscriptions, each Subscription will have its own $DeadLetterQueue subqueue.

Sessions

Sessions allow grouping of related messages to be processed in a single batch by the consumer. This guarantees FIFO delivery of related messages.

Typically, the `SessionId` property on the `BrokeredMessage` class is used as the partition key. This allows all messages that have the same `SessionId` key to be handled by the same message broker.

Sessions are ideal when sending a large message (that must be broken up into smaller sizes) to a Queue. The deconstructed message parts are then reconstructed into one message at the consumer end.

Retrieving messages off a Queue

Reading a message off the queue may be requested using one of two modes. `PeekLock`, which is the default mode, reads the message of the queue and places a lock on the read message. This makes the message invisible to other consumers of the Queue. The message will reappear on the Queue if the consumer does not issue a `Complete` command within the specified `VisibilityTimeout` period. The message can also reappear if the consumer calls the `Abandon` method. This type of processing is ideal for when guaranteed processing of a message is mandatory.

The second option is `ReceiveAndDelete` mode. This is when, once the message is read, it will immediately be deleted from the Queue. This ensures that the message will get processed once only and is processed in FIFO order. However, there is a risk of the message getting lost if the process that consumed the message hangs.

To ensure your message is idempotent, there are several strategies that may be adopted:

- Setting the `VisibilityTimeout` parameter to a suitable period that will allow enough time for the message to be processed and to issue a complete command.

- Using the `DequeueCount` to check how many times the message has been read from the queue.

- Using a unique transaction identifier for each message. The identifier is persisted in Azure storage and matched when each message is de-queued in order to ensure it has not been processed again.

Service Bus also offers the ability to detect duplicate messages by tracking the value of the system `MessageId` property, which can be set to any string value. This is enabled by setting the **Duplicate Message Detection** and the **Duplication Detection History Time Window** properties. If a message arrives with the same `MessageId` value within the duplicate detection history window, it will simply be ignored.

Deferring message processing

Deferring messages allows the processing of higher priority messages first and then servicing the lower priority messages at a later time.

To use this feature, the receive mode must set to `PeekLock`. The client receiving the message then has the option to mark the message as being deferred. When the client marks the message to be deferred, they must keep track of the message sequence number in a durable store, to be retrieved later.

When a message has been deferred, it will stay in the queue until it is retrieved and the `Complete()` method has been called. The message will also be removed from the Queue if a message TTL expiry timeout occurs.

The message is read from the queue using the `QueueClient` class and passing the message sequence number that was persisted previously.

Security

The Service Bus Namespace owner account should not be shared or embedded in code. This is a highly privileged account that gives rights to delete and create Azure artifacts and should only be used for administrative tasks.

There are two options available for clients to be authenticated to allow access to the Service Bus:

- **Shared Access Signature (SAS)**: This provides authentication using a shared key configured on the namespace or on a Service Bus entity (Queues, Topics, and Subscriptions) with specific rights for Listening, Sending, or Managing. The key is then used to generate a SAS token, which the client uses to authenticate with the Service Bus.

- **Access Control Service (ACS)**: This provides identity federation with various providers. To access the Service Bus entities, the client requests a **Simple Web Token (SWT)** from the ACS. The token is then sent with every request to the Service Bus.

While creating a Service Bus Queue using the Azure Portal, the only available authentication option is SAS. To use ACS, you will need to use the following Azure PowerShell command to create the namespace and associated ACS artifacts:

```
New-AzureSBNamespace <namespaceName> "<Region>" -CreateACSNamespace
$true
```

More information on this can be found at `https://msdn.microsoft.com/en-us/library/azure/dn170478.aspx`.

Service Bus also provides three types of access rights:

- **Listen**: Receiving messages from the queue
- **Send**: Sending messages to the queue
- **Manage**: Creating, changing, or deleting entities

Topics

Topics are another communication model that provide a publish/subscribe architecture pattern. This allows a message to be consumed by many subscribers, and each subscriber is able to process the message independently.

A Topic has similar characteristics to a Service Bus Queue. When you create a topic by code, you would normally use the `NamespaceManager` class, as follows:

```
//create the token
TokenProvider token =
    TokenProvider.CreateSharedSecretTokenProvider(name, key);
//create the uri
Uri uri = ServiceBusEnvironment.CreateServiceUri("sb", "mynamespace",
string.Empty);
//create a namespace instance
NamespaceManager nsManager = new NamespaceManager(uri, token);
```

You then use the `NamespaceManager` instance to create a Topic, just as you would when you create a Queue.

```
nsManager.CreateTopic("SalesTopicQueue");
```

 Note that you cannot use the same name for a Queue and Topic within the same namespace. This will cause a `MessagingEntityAlreadyExists` exception to be thrown.

Once the Topic has been created, the subscriptions are created. The following code creates two subscriptions, `Inventory` and `Accounts`, for the topic `SalesTopicQueue`:

```
nsManager.CreateSubscription("SalesTopicQueue", "Inventory");
nsManager.CreateSubscription("SalesTopicQueue", "Accounts");
```

To send a message to a particular Topic, you would use the `MessagingFactory` and `BrokeredMessage` objects. The `BrokeredMessage` object provides the option to use a data dictionary to store metadata with the actual payload. More information on this class can be found here: `http://msdn.microsoft.com/en-us/library/microsoft.servicebus.messaging.brokeredmessage.aspx`.

```
MessagingFactory factory = MessagingFactory.Create(uri, token);
BrokeredMessage bm = new BrokeredMessage(orderData);
    bm.Label = "CustomerOrder";
    bm.Properties["StoreLocation"] = "Auckland";
    bm.Properties["SalesValue"] = "5350.40";
    bm.Properties["Priority"] = "";
//send the message to the topic
MessageSender sender = factory.CreateMessageSender("SalesTopicQueue");
    sender.Send(bm);
```

Note the use of the system property `Label` and the user defined properties. These will be used later as the arguments for filtered subscriptions.

Subscriptions

To receive messages from a Topic Queue, you would create a Subscription. A Subscription resembles a virtual Queue that receives a copy of the message sent to a topic queue.

 Note that a single subscription cannot be used for multiple topics. Instead, you need to create multiple subscriptions.

Typically the following code would be duplicated for each interested consumer, specifying the Topic and Subscription names in the constructor:

```
MessagingFactory factory = MessagingFactory.Create(uri, token);

//create a consumer for the subscription
SubscriptionClient subscriber1 = factory.CreateSubscriptionClient(topicName,
SubscriptionName,ReceiveMode.PeekLock);
```

Just like with normal queues, you can use either `ReceiveAndDelete` or `PeekLock` (receive modes) to read the message of the virtual Queue.

Once the client has created the Subscription, the messages can be read off the virtual queue as follows:

```
while ((receivedMessage = subscriber1.Receive(TimeSpan.
FromSeconds(5))) != null)
{
try
    {
        ProcessMsg(receivedMessage);
        receivedMessage.Complete();
    }
    catch (Exception e)
    {
        receivedMessage.Abandon();
    }
}
```

Subscription rules

In some scenarios, it would be helpful to filter message properties and only receive messages that satisfy the filter condition. Currently, if a subscriber creates a subscription to a topic, all messages arriving at that topic are made available to the subscriber. This is because the default filter MatchAll is applied when no filters are specified on creation of a Subscription.

Fortunately, Azure Service Bus has the concept of Subscription rules, which allows you to define filters and actions that are applied to a Topic.

More information on creating subscriptions from Microsoft can be found at http://msdn.microsoft.com/en-us/library/microsoft.servicebus.namespacemanager.createsubscription.aspx.

Rule filter

A filter is an expression in the form of a SQL 92 style predicate, for example, "StoreLocation = 'Auckland'" These filters are applied to either system or user defined application properties that are available in the BrokeredMessage class.

You may apply multiple rules for a Subscription, but bear in mind that each rule evaluating to true will result in a copy of the message being placed in the subscriber's virtual Queue.

The actual code to create a filter and subscription will look like the following example:

```
//create the filter
SqlFilter cityFilter = new SqlFilter("StoreLocation = 'Wellington'");
```

This will forward all messages to the subscription called SouthernRegion if the StoreLocation name equals Wellington.

Remember that the filter expression is based on the SQL 92 syntax, which will allow you to add more filtering options in the syntax. Here is an example:

```
SqlFilter highValuecityFilter = new SqlFilter("StoreLocation =
'Wellington' OR StoreLocation = 'Levin' AND SalesValue > 5000");
```

The filter is then added to the namespace instance and topic, using the CreateSubscription method as shown here:

```
//create a filtered subscription
nsManager.CreateSubscription("SalesTopicQueue", "SouthernRegion",
cityFilter);
```

Rule action

A rule can also define an action using the RuleDescription object. With actions you can modify the value of an existing property when the filter condition evaluates to true. The following code demonstrates how to set the value of a user-defined application property called Priority when the filtered condition evaluates to True, using SQL92 syntax:

```
var ruleLowPrice = new RuleDescription()
{
    Filter = new SqlFilter("SalesValue < 1000")
Action = new SqlRuleAction("set Priority='Low'"),
    };

var ruleHighPrice = new RuleDescription()
{
    Filter = new SqlFilter("SalesValue >= 1000")
Action = new SqlRuleAction("set Priority ='High'"),
};
```

Once the filter and actions have been defined, they can be added to the Namespace Manager, as before.

```
nsManager.CreateSubscription("SalesTopicQueue","AccountsLow",
ruleLowPrice);
nsManager.CreateSubscription("SalesTopicQueue","AccountsHigh",
ruleHighPrice);
```

 Note that the rules will be executed in the order in which they are registered.

Express Queues/Topics

Express Queues/Topics allows high throughput and low latency of messages. This is achieved by the queuing mechanism caching the received message directly to memory first. If the message is not consumed within a few seconds, it will be written to persistent storage.

If a publisher sends any crucial messages to the queue that must not be lost, the publisher must set the `ForcePersistence` property to `true`. This will force the queuing mechanism to immediately persist the message to store.

Partitioned Queues/Topics

Without partitions, a queue or topic is handled by a single message broker and stored in a single messaging store, which can constrain performance. By using partitions, a Queue or Topic can be spread across multiple brokers and stores, thereby providing a higher throughput rate than a single message broker and store. These partitions contain all the features of a non-partitioned Queue or Topic, such as transactions and sessions.

When messages arrive at the Queue or Topic, they are distributed in a round-robin fashion to all the fragments of a partitioned Queue or Topic if no partition key has been defined.

To control which fragment receives what message, the properties `SessionId`, `PartitionKey`, and `MessageId` may be used as partition keys. All messages received using the same partition key will be processed by that specific fragment. If that fragment is temporarily unavailable, an error will be returned.

When a client reads a message from a partitioned queue or topic, the Service Bus queries all fragments for the next message. Note that the client is unaware of the fragmentation while reading the Queue.

Adapters based on BizTalk cloud do not support partitioned queues. You will need to create the queues or topics in Azure using the custom create option to unselect partitioning, which is enabled by default.

Event Hubs

Event Hubs are primarily designed to ingest high volumes of event and telemetry data in a high throughput manner from a variety of devices and services. They are similar in principle to Azure Queues and Topics, but with different characteristics. While Azure Queues and Topics are used for enterprise messaging scenarios in which transaction support, dead-lettering, ordered delivery, and guaranteed delivery are of prime concern, Event Hubs are biased towards very high throughput and event processing scenarios.

Partitions

The key technology that provides this high throughput is streaming, using a partitioned consumer pattern. This is where each consumer only reads a specific subset or partition of the message stream. With Azure Queues and Topics that use a competing consumer model, if too many consumers target the same queue, this will result in resource contention and scalability issues.

Messages sent to Event Hubs can be forced to target specific partitions by using partition keys. If no partition key is supplied, the message is randomly placed on any of the allocated partitions. New messages are added at the end of the stream in the order in which they arrive. Each partition operates independently of other partitions and may have different growth rates and retention polices.

At the time of creating an Event Hub resource, you have the option to specify between 8 and 32 partitions. The chosen number of partitions should be based on the number of downstream parallel consumers. The 32-partition limit can be increased by contacting the Microsoft Azure Service Bus team.

Event Hubs are not intended to act as a permanent data store. They can only persist messages for up to 7 days in contrast to Azure Service Bus Queues/Topics, which have no limit.

Messages do not get deleted from the stream after they have been read by a consumer. Instead, the consumer is required to keep track of the last message read by using an index. The index is either based on a timestamp or an offset value. This allows a single stream to be read by multiple consumers instead of each consumer getting a copy of the message, as in Azure Service Bus Queues/Topics.

Consumer groups

While creating an Event Hub, a default consumer group is automatically created; this is how consumers read the messages. A consumer group provides isolation from other consumers and allows grouping of consumers by functionality or partition load.

Multiple consumer groups can be set up to create a publish/subscribe pattern. It is similar to the subscription concept of Service Bus Topics. Each consumer group manages its own offset and reads all the partitions at its own pace. You can create a maximum of 20 consumer groups for the standard tier Event Hub.

Connectivity

One can connect to Event Hubs by way of HTTPS or **Advance Message Queuing Protocol (AMQP)**. The main difference between the two protocols is that HTTPS provides short-lived and low-throughput messaging, whereas AMQP provides long-lived and high-throughput connections.

Event Hubs use AMQP 1.0, which maintains a session, state-aware, and bidirectional. Because of these features, creating the initial connection takes longer than HTTPS. However, once the negotiation process has completed it is faster than HTTPS, which must obtain a new session after each request.

The main benefits of using AMQP are interoperability, reliability, and the fact that it is based on open standards. More information about this protocol can be found at `http://www.amqp.org/`.

Replaying of messages

One of the benefits of Event Hubs is that you can replay messages for any period of time up to 7 days after they were first added to the messaging stream. This is achieved by changing the index pointer of the consumer to any point in the stream. When the connection is made, the reader will start processing the messages again from that point forward.

Checkpoints are managed by the consumer in order to commit the current index position within a consumer group. This provides a mechanism of marking events as being completed by downstream applications. When a consumer disconnects and reconnects at a later time, it will start to read from the last checkpoint. Reading before the checkpoint is still possible by providing a lower offset from the current checkpoint.

Poisoned messages

With Event Hubs, it is up to the receiver to handle invalid messages. Unlike Azure Service Bus Queues/Topics, messages can be rejected by placing them on the dead letter queue, where they can be processed by another processor.

If you move the receiver index back before an invalid message, you will need to handle the corrupted message again.

Security

When a device sends data to an Event Hub, it is normally to a virtual endpoint address defined by the publisher. A publisher requires a valid token to be passed with each message, which is a combination of the SAS and a publisher name. The publisher name is normally the device's unique identifier.

Although it is not recommended, you can directly connect to the Event Hub endpoint by creating a token that provides this level of access. By doing so, you lose the throttling capability and the blacklisting of devices using this token.

You can also share the same token across multiple devices or services that share the publisher.

Tokens can be generated using the following class available in the .NET Azure Service Bus SDK:

```
public static string SharedAccessSignatureTokenProvider.
GetSharedAccessSignature(string keyName, string sharedAccessKey,
string resource, TimeSpan tokenTimeToLive)
```

Here, `keyName` is the shared access policy name defined in the Azure portal, `sharedAccessKey` is the generated key from the Azure portal, and resource is defined as `//<NAMESPACE>.servicebus.windows.net/<EVENT_HUB_NAME>/publishers/<PUBLISHER_NAME>`. `tokenTimeToLive` is the TTL value of the token.

Relay Service

There are many challenges to overcome if you wish to externally expose a WCF service hosted on premise. You will need to potentially make changes to some or all of these infrastructure components within your environment: NAT, routers, hardware firewalls, and software firewalls.

Normally, a reverse proxy server would be used and firewall rules would be created to expose a WCF service. The following diagram shows the typical network infrastructure required to expose a service externally to the Internet:

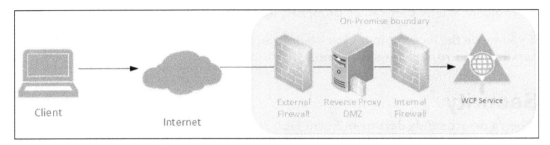

However, with the introduction of Azure Service Bus Relays, there is no requirement for proxy or firewall changes, provided outbound ports are open for HTTPS traffic. Effectively, the endpoint in Azure would be exposed to the outside world and not the endpoint locally on your server.

Here is how you would typically expose an on-premise WCF service using Relays in Azure:

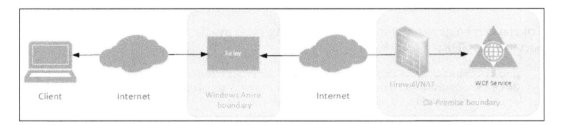

Endpoints based on WCF relay bindings open an outbound connection to Azure. Once this connection is established, bidirectional communication is enabled between the service and clients. The key point here is that an outbound request is initially being made from within the corporate network boundary and kept open, with no requirement for inbound access for external consumers. The only requirement is that specific outbound ports are to be opened. This article describes which outbound ports are required: http://msdn.microsoft.com/en-us/library/azure/ee732535.aspx.

Here are the steps for a client request:

1. The service authenticates and establishes a connection to the relay service. No consumer can access the service until this initial connection is made. At this point, the relay service registers the service endpoint and how best to call it back.

2. Next, the client authenticates and establishes a connection to the relay service.

3. The client can now send a request to the relay service.

4. The relay service forwards the request to the service that is listening at the registered endpoint.

5. The WCF service sends the response back to the relay service.

6. The relay service then forwards the response message to the client.

The sequence steps 2 and 3 may be combined depending on the connection mode used. For HTTP bindings, the authentication token would be placed in the header of the request message.

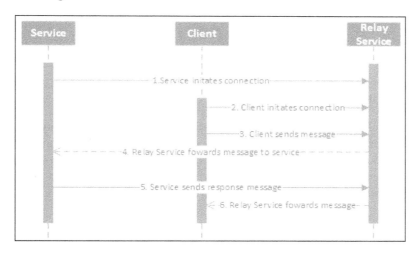

The disadvantage of this pattern is that both the service and client must be online before any messages can be passed between them, unlike Azure Service Bus Queues, where the service may be offline.

There are equivalent WCF bindings for use with Relays Services. They work in a similar way to standard WCF bindings, supporting SOAP 1.1 and SOAP 1.2 and the various WS-* security scenarios.

Both SOAP and RESTful interfaces are compatible with Relay Services.

Hosting Relay Services

One of the main differences between a normal WCF service and a WCF relay service is hosting. The relay service must be launched explicitly or must use an NT Service to host it. You cannot use versions of IIS 7 or lower and **WAS (Window Activation Service)** to host the service as these require an inbound request to initially launch the service.

With IIS 8, you can now use the built-in Application Initialization feature to warm up the WCF service.

 More information on this can be found at http://www. iis.net/learn/get-started/whats-new-in-iis-8/ iis-80-application-initialization.

Connection modes

There are two types of connection modes available for use with the TCP connection protocol:

- Relayed
- Hybrid

In relay mode, all communication is routed through the Service Bus.

If Hybrid mode is chosen, the initial connection will be relayed through the Service Bus infrastructure. This will determine the best option to call the service. It will automatically switch over to a direct socket connection for peer-to-peer connectivity between the client and service if both are behind the same firewall. If the direct connection is lost, communication will revert to the Service Bus Relay.

Authentication

The authentication mechanism is either None or via a RelayAccessToken.

With an authentication type of None, the client and service do not present an access token to the Service Bus. However, as a good security measure, the service should interrogate all requests.

If using the RelayAccessToken method, the access tokens may be SAS, Shared Secret, Web Token, or a SAML token.

Network transients

All Azure Service Bus networking connectivity is subject to network-related transients. These are microtransients commonly present on most networking infrastructures. If developing applications that use these services, it is advisable to take into consideration these micro outages.

The Client APIs that are included with Azure SDK 2.1 have built-in support for custom retry policies.

```
MessagingFactory factory = MessagingFactory.Create();
factory.RetryPolicy = RetryExponential.Default; // retry on transient
errors until the OperationTimeout is reached
factory.RetryPolicy = RetryPolicy.NoRetry; // disables retry for
transient errors
```

Also the Microsoft patterns and practices team has developed an application block that allows for a configurable retry mechanism. The application block may be downloaded from here: http://msdn.microsoft.com/en-us/library/hh680934(PandP.50).aspx.

Service Bus for Windows Server

For those who are unable to leverage Microsoft Azure (for whatever reasons, be they data sovereignty issues, unreliable internet connections, and so on) or prefer to use on-premise technologies rather than cloud technologies, **Service Bus for Windows Server (SBWS)** enables you to leverage a reasonable subset of features of the Azure Service Bus. The best part of this is that SBWS is included in the license cost of Windows Server. You can find a list of supported operating systems here: http://msdn.microsoft.com/en-us/library/dn441410.aspx.

SBWS can support multiple on-premise topologies, including a single server or a more scaled-out architecture using a farm of 3 or 5 servers if your performance or high availability requirements are more stringent. You can even build a lightweight environment based on SQL Server Express edition, if that better suits your requirements. SQL Server is required to provide persistence of messages (in contrast to MSMQ, which uses file storage) as they pass through your SBWS queues or topics and can be hosted on the same server as your SBWS farm or on a separate server.

Installation of WSSB is straightforward and can be performed via the Microsoft Web Platform Installer, which can be downloaded at http://www.microsoft.com/web/downloads/platform.aspx.

As previously alluded to, SBWS supports a subset of the features included in Azure Service Bus and also has some other differences, which might be advantageous in certain use cases. Some examples of missing features are ACS authentication (SAS authentication is still supported, as is the more traditional Windows Authentication) and relay services. One use case that is greatly simplified with SBWS is the transmission of large messages, as SBWS is able to support message sizes up to 50 MB in contrast to the Azure Service Bus limit of 256 KB. This allows you to avoid the need for complex solutions, including message splitting and aggregation. The majority of the coding techniques described within this chapter for interaction with Azure Service Bus will also work with Windows Server Service Bus, except where a feature is specifically not supported.

As SBWS is an on-premise technology, the onus falls on the enterprise to cater for server maintenance and patching, backups, and high availability. Make sure you consider this when you choose whether to leverage Service Bus queues or topics on premise or in Azure. It is also possible for a hosting provider to host their own SBWS farm in their own private cloud, which is then tenanted out to interested parties (this might even be a worthwhile consideration in larger companies in which Service Bus needs to be provisioned and managed for many different departments). To facilitate this, SBWS has a full-fledged integration with the Windows Azure pack, allowing for the provisioning and management of queues via the Management Portal, which provides a similar experience to that of the Azure Portal.

Of special note is that the BizTalk Server 2013 SB-Messaging adapter, does not support SBWS queues and topics, and will only work with Azure Service Bus. This has been rectified in BizTalk Server 2013 R2, in which the adapter is compatible with both on-premise as well as Azure Service Bus. For BizTalk Server 2013 or earlier versions of BizTalk Server that support WCF, `NetMessagingBinding` (included with the Azure SDK) can be used with SBWS (or Azure Service Bus for that matter) with the WCF-Custom adapter. `transportClientEndpointBehavior`, which is also included with the SDK, can also be leveraged to cater for authentication with your on-premise queues.

One final note is that the release cadence for Windows Server Service Bus is on a much less stringent timeline and that special consideration needs to be given to choosing the version of Azure SDK that is used to interact with your SBWS queues.

 More details on this can be found at `http://msdn.microsoft.com/en-us/library/dn282143.aspx`.

Administration tools

Being able to view and administer messages in a production environment is mandatory, especially when things go wrong. Fortunately, there is a tool available called Service Bus Explorer, which allows you to connect to a Service Bus namespace and administer the message entities. It can be downloaded at `https://code.msdn.microsoft.com/windowsazure/Service-Bus-Explorer-f2abca5a`.

Summary

Azure Service Bus provides a robust and scalable messaging infrastructure. It provides the framework to connect on-premise and cloud-based applications/ services together.

Using Topics with the Service Bus provides the framework to build scalable publish/ subscribe messaging exchange patterns.

There are basically two types of authentication mechanisms used to secure Service Bus entities, SAS and ACS. Also, both Service Queues and Relay Services provide accessibility rights for Listening, Sending, and Managing Service Bus entities and Relay Service endpoints. Exposing on-premise WCF services can be easily achieved using Relay Services. The SBWS is an option for on-premises deployments when cloud deployments are not allowed.

In the next chapter we will further build on what we have learned so far about loosely coupled messaging and dive into the world of **Service Oriented Architecture (SOA)** and how it applies to BizTalk.

Planning Service-oriented BizTalk Solutions

By failing to prepare, you are preparing to fail.

– Benjamin Franklin

Throughout the first six chapters of this book, we've looked at how to build BizTalk applications, WCF services, RESTful services, Service Bus applications, BizTalk Azure Services and BizTalk applications that use WCF services. However, simply knowing the nuts and bolts of working code doesn't mean that we're ready to architect maintainable, reusable, service-oriented applications. We need to become intimately familiar with standard patterns and always keep key principles in mind in order to truly build long-lasting SOA solutions.

In this chapter, you will learn:

- The definition of a service
- The core principles of a service-oriented architecture
- Which types of services can be exposed?
- The standard message exchange patterns for services
- How the service-orientation principles apply to a BizTalk Server solution

The core principles of an SOA

So what exactly is a service? A **service** is essentially a well-defined interface to an autonomous chunk of functionality, which usually corresponds to a specific business process. That might sound a lot like a regular old object-oriented component to you. While both services and components have commonality in that they expose discrete interfaces of functionality, a service is more focused on the capabilities offered than the packaging. Services are meant to be higher-level, business-oriented offerings that provide technology abstraction and interoperability within a multipurpose "services" tier of your architecture.

What makes up a service? Typically you'll find:

- **Contract**: Explains what operations the service exposes, types of messages, and exchange patterns supported by this service, and any policies that explain how this service is used.

- **Messages**: The data payload exchanged between the service consumer and provider.

- **Implementation**: The portion of the service which actually processes the requests, executes the expected business functionality, and optionally returns a response.

- **Service provider**: The host of the service which publishes the interface and manages the lifetime of the service.

- **Service consumer**: Ideally, a service has someone using it. The service consumer is aware of the available service operations and knows how to discover the provider and determine what type of messages to transmit.

- **Facade**: Optionally, a targeted facade may be offered to particular service consumers. This sort of interface may offer a more simplified perspective on the service, or provide a coarse-grained avenue for service invocation.

What is the point of building a service? I'd say it's to construct an asset capable of being reused which means that it's a discrete, discoverable, self-describing entity that can be accessed regardless of platform or technology.

Service-oriented architecture is defined as an architectural discipline based on loosely-coupled, autonomous chunks of business functionality which can be used to construct composite applications.

Throughout the rest of this chapter we will flesh out many of the concepts that underlie that statement. Let's go ahead and take a look at a few of the principles and characteristics that I consider most important to a successful service-oriented BizTalk solution. I'll also explain the thinking behind each principle and then call out how it can be applied to BizTalk Server solutions.

Loosely coupled

Many of the fundamental SOA principles actually stem from this particular one. In virtually all cases, some form of coupling between components is inevitable. The only way we can effectively build software is to have interrelations between the various components that make up the delivered product. However, when architecting solutions, we have distinct design decisions to make regarding the extent to which application components are coupled. Loose coupling is all about establishing relationships with minimal dependencies.

What would a tightly-coupled application look like? In such an application, we'd find components that maintained intimate knowledge of each other's' working parts and engaged in frequent, chatty synchronous calls amongst themselves. Many components in the application would retain state and allow consumers to manipulate that state data. Transactions that take place in a tightly coupled application probably adhere to a **two-phase commit** strategy where all components must succeed together in order for each data interaction to be finalized. The complete solution has its ensemble of components compiled together and singularly deployed to one technology platform. In order to run properly, these tightly-coupled components rely on the full availability of each component to fulfill the requests made of them.

On the other hand, a loosely-coupled application employs a wildly different set of characteristics. Components in this sort of application share only a contract and keep their implementation details hidden. Rarely preserving state data, these components rely on less frequent communication in which chunky input containing all the data the component needs to satisfy its requestors is shared. Any transactions in these types of applications often follow a **compensation** strategy in which we don't assume that all components can or will commit their changes at the same time. This class of solution can be incrementally deployed to a mix of host technologies. Asynchronous communication between components, often through a broker, enables a less stringent operational dependency between the components that comprise the solution.

What makes a solution loosely coupled then? Notably, the primary information shared by a component is its interface. The consuming component possesses no knowledge of the internal implementation details. The contract relationship suffices as a means of explaining how the target component is used. Another trait of loosely coupled solutions is coarse-grained interfaces that encourage the transmission of full data entities as opposed to fine-grained interfaces, which accept small subsets of data. Because loosely-coupled components do not share state information, a thicker input message containing a complete impression of the entity is best.

Loosely-coupled applications also welcome the addition of a broker which proxies the (often asynchronous) communication between components. This mediator permits a rich decoupling where runtime binding between components can be dynamic and components can forgo an operational dependency on each other.

Let's take a look at an example of loose coupling that sits utterly outside the realm of technology.

Completely non-technical loose coupling example

When I go to a restaurant and place an order with my waiter, he captures the request on his pad and sends that request to the kitchen. The order pad (the contract) contains all the data needed by the kitchen chef to create my meal. The restaurant owner can bring in a new waiter or rotate his chefs and the restaurant shouldn't skip a beat as both roles (services) serve distinct functions where the written order is the intersection point and highlight of their relationship.

Why does loose coupling matter? By designing a loosely-coupled solution, you provide a level of protection against the changes that the application will inevitably require over its life span. We have to reduce the impact of such changes while still making it possible to deploy necessary updates in an efficient manner.

Applying loose coupling to BizTalk

A good portion of the BizTalk Server architecture was built with loose coupling in mind. Think about the BizTalk `MessageBox` which acts as a broker by facilitating communication between ports and orchestrations while limiting any tight coupling. Receive ports and send ports are very loosely coupled and have absolutely no awareness of each other. The publish-and-subscribe bus thrives on the asynchronous transfer of self-describing messages between stateless endpoints. Let's look at a few recommendations of how to build loosely-coupled BizTalk applications.

Orchestrations are a prime place in which you can either go with a tightly-coupled or loosely-coupled design route. For instance, when sketching out your orchestration process, it's sure tempting to use the Transform shape to convert from one message type to another. However, a version change to that map will require a modification of the calling orchestration. When mapping to or from data structures associated with external systems, it's wiser to push those maps to the edges (receive/send ports) and not embed a direct link to the map within the orchestration. One exception is that if you need to combine two or more messages into a destination (or final) message, then you are forced to use an orchestration because these types of maps are only supported in orchestration.

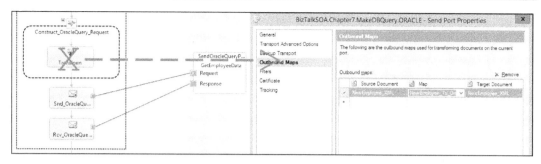

BizTalk easily generates schemas for **line-of-business** (LOB) systems and consumed services. To interact with these schemas in a very loosely coupled fashion, consider defining stable entity schemas (that is, "canonical schemas") that are used within an orchestration, and only map to the format of the LOB system in the send port. For example, if you need to send a piece of data into an Oracle database table, you can certainly include a map within an orchestration which instantiates the Oracle message. However, this will create a tight coupling between the orchestration and the database structure. To better insulate against future changes to the database schema, consider using a generic intermediate data format in the orchestration and only transforming to the Oracle-specific format in the send port.

How about those logical ports that we add to orchestrations to facilitate the transfer of messages in and out of the workflow process? When configuring those ports, the **Port Configuration Wizard** asks you if you want to associate the port to a physical endpoint via the **Specify Now** option. Once again, pretty tempting. If you know that the message will arrive at an orchestration via a FILE adapter, why not just go ahead and configure that now and let Visual Studio create the corresponding physical ports during deployment? While you can independently control the auto-generated physical ports later on, it's a bad idea to embed transport details inside the orchestration.

On each subsequent deployment from Visual Studio, the generated receive port will have any out-of-band changes overwritten by the deployment action.

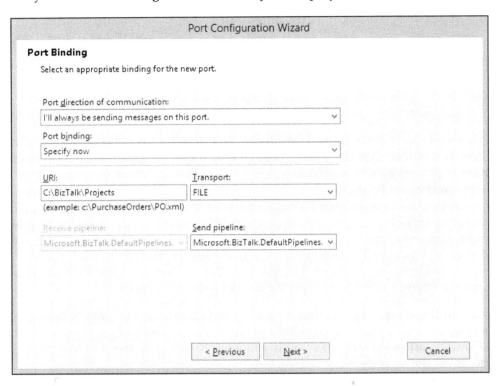

Chaining orchestration together is a tricky endeavor and one that can leave you in a messy state if you are too quick with a design decision. By "chaining orchestrations", I mean exploiting multiple orchestrations to implement a business process. There are a few options at your disposal listed here and ordered from most coupled to least coupled.

- **Call Orchestration or Start Orchestration shape**: An orchestration uses these shapes in order to kick off an additional workflow process. The **Call Orchestration** is used for synchronous connection with the new orchestration while the **Start Orchestration** is a fire-and-forget action. This is a useful tactic for sharing state data (for example variables, messages, ports) from the source orchestration to the target. However, both options require a tight coupling of the source orchestration to the target. Version changes to the target orchestration are likely to require a redeployment of the source orchestration.

- **Partner direct bound ports**: These provide you the capability to communicate between orchestrations using ports. In the **forward partner direct binding** scenario, the sender has a strong coupling to the receiver, while the receiver knows nothing about the sender. This works well in situations where there are numerous senders and only one receiver. **Inverse partner direct binding** means that there is a tight coupling between the receiver and the sender. The sender doesn't know who will receive the command, so this scenario is intended for cases where there are many receivers for a single sender. In both cases, you have tight coupling on one end, with loose coupling on the other.

- **MessageBox direct binding**: This is the most loosely-coupled way to share data between orchestrations. When you send a message out of an orchestration through a port marked for `MessageBox` direct binding, you are simply placing a message onto the bus for anyone to consume. The source orchestration has no idea where the data is going, and the recipients have no idea where it's been.

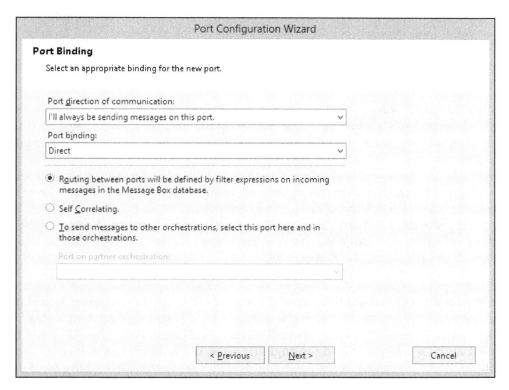

The `MessageBox` direct binding provides a very loosely-coupled way to send messages between different orchestrations and endpoints. In *Chapter 10, Orchestration Patterns*, I'll show you how to use the **BizTalk Business Rules Engine** alongside orchestrations to seamlessly link, add, and replace orchestrations in a complex business process.

> While `MessageBox` direct binding is great, you do lose the ability to send the additional state data that a **Call Orchestration** shape will provide you. So, as with all architectural decisions, you need to decide whether the sacrifice (loose coupling, higher latency) is worth the additional capabilities.

Decisions can be made during BizTalk messaging configuration that promote a loosely-coupled BizTalk landscape. For example, both receive ports and send ports allow for the application of maps to messages flying past. In each case, multiple maps can be added. This does NOT mean that all the maps will be applied to the message, but rather, it allows for sending multiple different message types in, and emitting a single type (or even multiple types) out the other side. By applying transformation at the earliest and latest moments of bus processing, you loosely couple external formats and systems from internal canonical formats. We should simply assume that all upstream and downstream systems will change over time, and configure our application accordingly.

Another means for loosely coupling BizTalk solutions involves the exploitation of the publish-subscribe architecture that makes up the BizTalk message bus. Instead of building solely point-to-point solutions and figuring that a SOAP interface makes you service oriented, you should also consider loosely coupling the relationship between the service input and where the data actually ends up. We can craft a series of routing decisions that take into account message content or context and direct the message to one or more relevant processes/endpoints. While point-to-point solutions may be appropriate for many cases, don't neglect a more distributed pattern where the data publisher does not need to explicitly know exactly how their data will be processed and routed by the message bus.

When identifying subscriptions for our send ports, we should avoid tight coupling to metadata attributes that might limit the reuse of the port. For instance, you should try to create subscriptions on either the message type or message content instead of context attributes such as the inbound receive port name. Ports should be tightly coupled to the `MessageBox` and messages it stores, not to attributes of its publisher. That said, there are clearly cases where a subscriber is specifically looking for data that corresponds to a targeted piece of metadata such as the subject line of the email received by BizTalk. As always, design your solution in a way that solves your business problem in an efficient manner.

An extensible schema design can allow the canonical data to extend easily. For example a name value structure could address additional requirements without changing the schema.

Abstraction

The SOA concept of abstraction is all about making your service a black box to consumers. All that the consumers see is an interface while possessing no visibility into the soft meaty center of the service. The underlying service could be very simple or mind-numbingly complex. It could have a very stable core, or be undergoing consistent upgrades. The service logic could integrate with a single backend system, or choreograph communication across ten applications. None of these things should matter to a service consumer who has an interface that provides an abstract perspective of the service itself.

This is where the art of service contract design plays an immense role. The contract needs to strike the right balance of information hiding, while still demanding information material for an effective service. Consider operation granularity. I have an application that requires a series of API calls in order to insert a new order for a product. First I need to check the available stock, then decrement the stock, and then add the new order to the system. If I were a brand new SOA developer, I might take those APIs, slap SOAP interfaces on them, and declare our application to be service-oriented. Wrong answer! We don't always need to expose that level of granularity to the consumer. Let's bestow upon them a nice coarse-grained interface that hides the underlying system API messiness and simply accepts the product order through a `SubmitOrder` operation.

> **Completely non-technical abstraction example**
>
> When my order is taken at a restaurant, I don't have the opportunity (or desire!) to outline the sequence of steps I wish the chef to take in preparing my meal. Instead, I am asked a simple series of questions that are recorded and forwarded on to the kitchen. Inside the kitchen, a swift, complex set of actions are taken to get the food ready all at once. From my perspective while seated at the table, I simply made a single request and will get back what I expect. If the chef decides to try to prepare a meal in a brand new way, that's of no consequence to me (unless it tastes bad). The underlying service may undergo mild or fundamental changes, but the ordering interface provided to me will remain fairly static.

Why does abstraction matter? A well-defined interface that successfully hides the service logic provides a way to change implementation details over time, while still respecting the original contract. Just because a service undergoes plumbing modifications doesn't mean that service consumers must take note of those changes or behave any differently. As long as the interface remains consistent, the service itself can accommodate either simple or radical changes. A nicely abstracted interface promotes loose coupling between the service sender and receiver while a contract that too deeply reveals implementation details can lead to tight coupling.

Applying abstraction to BizTalk server

When thinking about abstraction and information hiding in BizTalk Server, I'd like to focus on how BizTalk functionality is exposed to the outside world. Here I'll highlight two ways to respect the abstraction principle in BizTalk Server.

First, let's talk about how orchestrations are consumed by outside parties. In truth, they are never directly exposed to a service consumer. It's impossible to instantiate a BizTalk orchestration without going through the adapter layer. So when we develop external service interfaces that front orchestrations, we should be diligent and not reveal aspects of our orchestration that the service consumer shouldn't know about. We can accomplish this in part by always starting our projects in a contract-driven manner by building the schema first, and then go about building an orchestration. If we design in reverse, it is likely that the orchestration's implementation logic seeps into the schema design. For instance, let's say that my orchestration sends employee data to a SQL Server database and also interacts with a web service exposed by a TIBCO messaging server. If I built my orchestration first, and then built up my schema along the way, I might be tempted to add fields to my employee schema where I can store a `TIBCO_Response` and capture and store a `SQL_Exception`.

Then, if I used the BizTalk WCF Service Publishing Wizard to expose my orchestration as a service, I'd have an externally-facing schema polluted with information about my technical implementation. My service consumer should have no knowledge about what my orchestration does to complete its task.

Another critical way to show regard for the abstraction principle is by thoughtfully considering how to expose downstream system interfaces to upstream consumers. Let's say that you need to integrate with a Siebel application and insert new customer contacts. The WCF LOB Adapter for Siebel allows you to auto-generate the bits needed by a BizTalk orchestration to consume the target Siebel operations. When exposing that orchestration's port as a service interface, it would be a very bad decision to assign the Siebel-generated schema as our instantiating contract. There are two reasons I would avoid doing this at all costs:

- This tightly couples our service consumer to an implementation decision. Ignoring the fact that LOB system generated schemas are typically verbose and hard to digest, our service consumer should neither care nor know about how the orchestration processes the new customer. By sharing LOB system schemas as orchestration schemas, you've lost any opportunity to provide an abstract interface.

- A service typically offers a simplified interface to complex downstream activities. What if Siebel required three distinct operations to be called in order to insert a new customer? Should we expose three services from BizTalk Server and expect the service client to coordinate these calls? Absolutely not. As we discussed earlier, slapping SOAP interfaces onto existing APIs does not make an application service-oriented. Instead, we want to look for opportunities to offer services that aggregate downstream actions into a single coarse-grained exterior interface.

A good strategy for interfacing with LOB systems is to identify a single canonical schema that encapsulates all the data necessary to populate the downstream LOB systems regardless of how many individual LOB operations are needed. This strategy has two benefits. First, you obtain significant control over the structure of your service contract instead of being subjected to a data structure generated by an adapter. Secondly, we achieve a much more flexible interface that is no longer dependent on a particular implementation. What if the downstream LOB system changes its interface or the target LOB system changes completely? In theory, the service consumer can remain blissfully unaware of these circumstances as their interface is cleanly separated from the final data repository used by the service.

Interoperable

SOA-compatible services need to support cross-platform invocation and the service itself will often access a heterogeneous set of data and functions. Interoperability is all about making diverse systems work together and it is a critical component of a long-term SOA.

Similar to all of the core SOA principles, service interoperability needs to be designed early in the project lifecycle instead of being an afterthought addressed only moments before production deployment. Now Interoperability doesn't mean that the service has to accommodate a mix of runtime host environments. A service that fails to run in both Microsoft IIS and Oracle WebLogic hosting platforms doesn't mean that I've written a closed, poorly-designed service. When we talk about interoperability, we are concentrating on how a wide variety of disparate *clients* can access a single service. Is the fact that my service was written in .NET 4.5 and hosted by IIS 8.0 completely transparent to my Java, .NET, and Ruby users? If your service was written well, then the answer to that question should be *yes*.

As for service implementation, you ideally want to empower your service to yank data from any available source. To do so, the service needs a means to access diverse sets of resources that may not natively expose simple interfaces. This is where a service/integration bus can truly shine. Some applications just won't naturally play nice with each other. But a service bus with built-in adapter technology can bridge those gaps and enable unfriendly systems to share and consume data from the outside. For example, the BizTalk Adapters for Host Systems produce no-code integration solutions for IBM mainframe technology. I can write a snazzy WCF service that chews on and returns data that dwells in VSAM host file and the service client remains blissfully unaware. The adapters in BizTalk Server enable us to build rich services that penetrate existing non-service-oriented applications and seamlessly weave their data into the service result.

So how do you achieve interoperability in your service environment? First and foremost, you want to adhere to the standard entities that typically describe services and their behavior. The "big four" technologies to keep in mind are WSDL (for service contract description), XSD (for message structure definition), SOAP (the protocol for sending service messages) and UDDI (for service registration and discovery). All of these technologies are considered "cross-platform" and are readily supported by both major and minor software vendors. Do you need to use each of these technologies in order to provide an interoperable service? Definitely not. Some find WSDLs to be obtuse and unnecessary and still others find XSD to be a lousy way to organize data. However, given BizTalk's embrace of these artifact types, I'll work within these confines.

Service interoperability through services written in a RESTful manner has been described in detail in a previous chapter.

When building a service for interoperability, what do you need to consider? From my perspective, interoperability design comes in at four major points:

- **Endpoint choice**: If you truly intend for your service to be available to the widest range of consumers, then you need to pick an endpoint that is accessible to the masses. Simply put, pick a protocol like HTTP that everyone can support. Now, there's no shame in exposing WCF's `netTcpBinding` endpoint for targeted consumers, but be aware that you've instantly settled on a .NET-to-.NET only solution.

- **Data structure**: Properly selecting friendly XML data types and node behaviors is a vital part of building an interoperable service message. How are decimals handled? What's the precision of a floating point number for .NET versus. Java? For intricate calculations, those answers have a significant impact on the accuracy of data used by the service. Also don't forget about date/time handling either, as XSD has a very rigid `datetime` data type (CCYY-MM-DDThh:mm:ss), but either source or destination systems may enforce an alternate format.

- **Security scheme**: Cross-platform security can be a challenge, but without it, one cannot truly put forward an interoperable service. Even with the WS-Security standard itself, you are bound to come across existing service clients who support different versions or flavors of these standards, thus making pure interoperability impossible.

- **Transaction support**: The naturally stateless nature of most services makes the idea of a two-phase commit problematic to implement. When either exposing a service that must accept a transaction, or when the internal functions of a service require the assistance of a transaction, you want to lean heavily on standard mechanisms that can ensure the widest range of compatibility across platforms and technologies.

Completely non-technical interoperability example

For me, a true test of a quality ethnic restaurant is if the people working there are of the same ethnicity that the restaurant claims to be its specialty. However, what if the chef doesn't speak the same language as the waiter? In this case, they rely on multiple means of interoperability. First, they can use a taxonomy consisting of letter codes or numbers to represent the meals requested by patrons. Secondly, they can employ a single translator who proxies communication between the personnel who don't natively speak the same language.

Applying interoperability to BizTalk server solutions

BizTalk Server is a vendor-neutral product. Its 25+ built-in adapters allow it to readily access an impressive set of industry-standard and vendor-specific technologies. The question is, how do we make BizTalk Server's external interface as interoperable as possible in order to support the widest range of client types? Let's evaluate BizTalk's interoperability support in the four areas outlined previously.

Deciding upon an on-ramp technology for the service bus is a critical task. Do we expose a FILE-based interface that supports legacy applications? How about a very simple HTTP interface that is sure to please basic web service clients? Each choice has tradeoffs. Fortunately for BizTalk architects, this needn't be such a gut-wrenching decision. BizTalk Server walls off the interface from the implementation logic in a very loosely-coupled fashion making it possible to support a mix of inbound channel technologies. Remember that the logical ports in an orchestration are not associated with a specific technology during design time. Also recall that even when an orchestration is bound to a physical messaging artifact at runtime, it is not bound to an individual receive location, but rather to the more encompassing receive port. A single receive port can contain countless receive locations which can all accept data via different channels. As a result, we should carefully consider our service audience, and based on that assessment, configure the acceptable number of endpoints that accommodate our primary consumers. If we plan on building a very accessible service which also provides advanced capabilities for modern users, then a receive port filled with receive locations for both WCF-BasicHttp, WCF-WebHttp and WCF-WSHttp adapters makes sense. This way, our simple clients can still access the service using classic SOAP capabilities, while our forward-thinking clients can engage in a more feature-rich service conversation with us. If we later discover that we have service consumers who cannot speak HTTP at all, then BizTalk Server still affords us the opportunity to reveal more traditional endpoints such as FILE or FTP.

One place that interoperability between systems can subtly fail is when the data itself is transferred between endpoints. How one platform serializes a particular data type may be fundamentally different on an alternate platform. For instance, be sure that if you've defined a field as `nullable` that a standard mix of consumers can indeed accept a null value in that data type. Note that the `float` and `decimal` data type may have different levels of precision based on the platform so you could encounter unexpected rounding of numerical values. Also consider the handling of `dateTime` values across environments. While the XSD `dateTime` data type is quite rigid in format, you may choose to use an alternate date format embedded in a string data type instead. If you do so, you must ensure that your target service consumers know how to handle a `dateTime` in that format. In general, a reliance on simpler data types is going to go a long way towards support for the widest variety of platforms. You can stay focused on this concept by building your XSD schema first (and complying with known types) prior to building a service that adheres to the types in the schema. Fortunately for us BizTalk developers, we're used to building the contract first.

Alongside the data structure itself, a service is more interoperable when the service contract is not needlessly complicated. A complicated WSDL definition would describe an XSD contract that possessed numerous nested, imported schemas with a distinct set of namespaces. You may find that some SOAP toolkits do not properly read WSDL files with these types of characteristics. While it can initially be seen as a huge timesaver that application platforms will auto-magically generate a WSDL from a service, you are sometimes better off creating your own WSDL file that simplifies the portrayal of the service. Fortunately for us, both WCF and BizTalk Server support the usage of externally defined WSDL files as replacements for framework-generated ones.

Service security is a tricky concept due to the fact that support for cross-platform security technology has yet to extend into all major software platforms. WCF (and thus BizTalk Server) exploits the WS-Security set of standards, which offer platform-neutral security schemes, but few vendors have offerings that fully support this standard. So, when architecting service security, you can either implement modern security schemes supported through WS-I standards, or go the more traditional route of securing the transmission channel with **Secure Sockets Layer** (**SSL**) and/or securing the data throughout its journey by applying X.509 certificates and encrypting the payload.

The embrace of the service transaction standard is also slow in coming. WCF incorporates the WS-AtomicTransaction and WS-ReliableMessaging standards, but note that BizTalk Server only explicitly supports WS-AtomicTransaction. Be aware that you can make a BizTalk WCF adapter use WS-ReliableMessaging by manually constructing the binding in the WCF-Custom adapter. Also, BizTalk's support for service transactions only extends to the point of publication to the `MessageBox`, and the distribution of messages from the `MessageBox`.

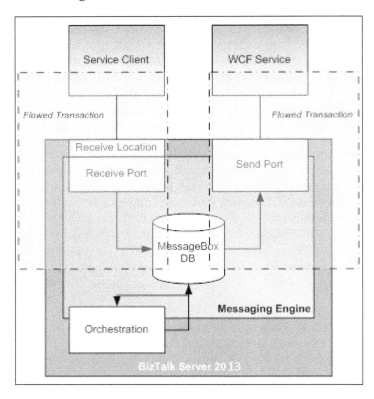

To design a BizTalk service to be interoperable, with both security and transaction concepts in mind, you may be forced to implement the security specifications available by the WS-I organization and educate service clients as to the types of frameworks and libraries they need to properly engage these advanced service capabilities.

Reusable

In my humble opinion, the principle of reusability is the most important aspect of a service-oriented architecture. I consider *reusability* to be a design time objective while *reuse* is an inadequate runtime success metric. In essence, reusability is all about effectively segmenting functionality into services which are capable of being used by others outside the scope of your immediate effort. Note the word *capable* in the previous sentence. Unless you can predict the future, it's hard to guarantee that a service module built today will satisfy all the future needs for similar capabilities. Even if no additional consumers decide that a service is of use to them, this doesn't mean that the service is a failure. By itself, the forethought and decisions made to make a service reusable makes the construction of the service a worthwhile effort.

Why does reusability matter? The answers may seem obvious, but I'll call out three explicit benefits:

- Future applications can harvest the functionality of the original service and accelerate their solution development while encouraging the adoption of composite applications. Some SOA advocates foresee a world where many applications consist of very little original functionality but rather, are simply aggregations of existing services exposed in the enterprise.

- A heavily reused service affords an organization the opportunity to make solitary changes that cascade to all consumers of that functionality. Let's say we have a service which aggregates data from multiple underlying systems and returns a single unified view of a *customer* entity. Assuming that most major applications in our enterprise use this service to get information about our customers, we can change the implementation (swap out data sources, add new sources, and change logic) of this service and each consumer instantly gets the benefits.

- The architectural choices made in designing a reusable service will inevitably encourage the implementation of the other mentioned SOA principles such as loose-coupling, abstraction, and interoperability in addition to other core principles such as composability, encapsulation, and discoverability.

A reusable service can be of many diverse shapes and sizes. First of all, such a service could exhibit a coarse-grained interface that employs a static contract while supplying a distinct business function. For instance, a service with an operation named `PublishAdverseEvent` (which takes reports of patients experiencing negative effects from a medication) can be used by every system or business process that might produce this sort of data. This service takes a very specific payload, but it can be reused by the multiple systems that encounter this category of input data. Conversely, we might define a utilitarian service that archives information to a database through a loose contract that accepts any structured data as a parameter. This service also offers a reusable interface that can be applied to a varied set of use cases. Reusable services may have very generic logic or very specific logic, flexible contracts or rigid ones, and may be business-oriented or cross-cutting functional services. A key aspect of reuse is to define the service in such a way that it can be useful to those outside of your immediate project scope.

Completely non-technical reusability example

An intelligent restaurant owner doesn't hire a chef who is only capable of preparing grilled cheese sandwiches. Instead, they seek out chefs who are adept at not only repeatedly assembling the same meal, but also skilled at delivering a wide variety of different meals. The service offered by the chef, "preparing food", is a reusable service that accepts multiple inputs and produces an output based on the request made.

Applying reusability to BizTalk server solutions

Virtually every component that comprises a BizTalk solution can be constructed in a reusable fashion. Take schemas for example. A single schema may be aggregated into other schemas, or simply applied to multiple different projects. For instance, a schema describing a standard `Address` node might be deemed an enterprise standard. Every subsequent schema that must contain an address can import that standard `Address` element. That's an example of an incomplete "part" that can only be useful as a component of another schema. You may also define an inclusive schema that depicts a standard enterprise entity such as a `Product`. Any ensuing project that requires processing on a `Product` would reference and reuse this pre-defined schema. Look for opportunities in your schemas to harvest enterprise entities and elements that may prove useful to those that follow you. When doing so, consider establishing and applying a project-neutral namespace that highlights those artifacts as multipurpose instead of project-specific.

Consider your experience when building BizTalk maps. In the development palette, you get access to 80+ functoids that provide a repeatable, consistent way to perform small fine-grained activities. When you encounter a situation where an out-of-the-box functoid won't suffice, BizTalk permits you to either build your own custom functoids, or, simply reference an external (reusable) component that holds the functionality you crave.

 While the BizTalk Scripting functoid does allow you to embed isolated code directly into the map, the window for doing so is quite small and devoid of familiar code writing comforts such as IntelliSense and debugging. This is a polite way of telling you that you should only embed simplistic code snippets in the map directly and leave complex or weighty logic to be written in externally maintained (and hopefully reusable) assemblies.

What about BizTalk pipelines and pipeline components? By nature, most pipeline components are built to serve a universal purpose well beyond the demands of a single consumer. Surely, you could choose to write an `archive` receive pipeline component that acted in a very specific way for a very specific message, but that would be bad form. Instead, a well-written archive component would accept any content and use configuration attributes to decide where to publish the archive log. When designing custom pipeline components, consider first writing all the code necessary to perform the desired function, and then scan your project for hard-coded references to aspects that are project-specific (such as XPath statements, file path directives). Take those references and turn them into configuration properties that can be substituted by other applications at a later time.

WCF behaviors are now an asset to be reckoned with in a BizTalk environment. They serve a similar function to pipeline components in that they process the raw message as it travels in and out of the BizTalk bus. Reusable WCF behaviors can be written for message logging, caching, error handling, authorization, and more. What's more, WCF behaviors can be shared between BizTalk applications and standalone WCF services. This means that a well-written enterprise service behavior does not need to be duplicated just to be used in BizTalk Server.

When should you use WCF behaviors versus BizTalk pipelines? They can both perform similar actions on the stream of data passing through BizTalk. However, BizTalk pipelines offer the advantage of knowing about the BizTalk message type and thus have clearly defined ways to deal with batching/de-batching and possess full control over creating or changing the full BizTalk message context including promoted properties. That said the ability to share WCF behaviors between BizTalk applications and standard WCF services means that where possible, you should strongly consider putting generic data processing logic into WCF behaviors instead of pipelines.

How about orchestration? On the surface, it might appear that orchestrations only serve distinct purposes and are lousy candidates for reuse. While it's true that many workflow processes are targeted to specific projects, there are clear ways to enjoy the benefits of reuse here. To begin with, consider the means by which a message enters the orchestration. It's very convenient to define a "specify later" orchestration port on the orchestration that is inevitably bound to a physical receive port. However, this type of port tightly couples itself to the receive port and thus reduces its potential for reuse. Wherever possible, look at the **Direct Binding** option and move your tight coupling to the MessageBox instead of a specific receive port. With direct binding, the orchestration simply subscribes directly on the MessageBox, so any publisher, whether a receive port or another orchestration, can flow messages into this orchestration.

We can also choose to perform orchestration decomposition and seek out reusable aspects of our orchestration that may serve other functions. For example, you may decide that every exception encountered across orchestrations should all be handled in the same fashion. Why build that same processing logic into each and every orchestration? Instead, you can define a single orchestration which accepts messages from any orchestration and logs the pertinent details to an exception log and optionally sends exception notifications to administrators. Our communal orchestration might accept *any* content and merely append the data blob to a common registry. Otherwise, the orchestration could accept a pre-defined OrchestrationException schema which all upstream orchestrations inflate prior to publishing their exception to the MessageBox. Seek out common processing logic and universal functionality that can be re-factored into a shared assembly and used across organizational projects.

Finally, let's talk about reuse in the BizTalk messaging layer. On the message receipt side, receive locations are quite multipurpose and compel no specific data format on the messages they absorb. If I define a FILE receive location, there is absolutely no reason that such a location couldn't be used to take in a broad mix of message types. However, let's be realistic and consider a case where a particular receive port is bound to a specific orchestration. This orchestration processes adverse events that have occurred with our medical products. The orchestration expects a very specific format which fortunately, the initial service consumer adheres to. Inevitably, the next consumer isn't so accommodating and can only publish a message shaped differently than what the orchestration expects. Do we need to start over with a new orchestration? Absolutely not. Instead, we can reuse the exact same receive port, and even offer to add a new receive location if the existing service endpoint is inaccessible to the new client. To support the incompatible data structure, a new map which converts the client format to the orchestration format can be added to the receive port. In this scenario, the orchestration was completely reusable, the receive port was reused, and optionally, the single receive location may have been reused.

On the message transmission side, BizTalk send ports also offer opportunities for reuse. First off, send port maps allow for a mismatched collection of messages to funnel through a single endpoint to a destination system. Let's say I have a solitary send port that updates a company's social events calendar through a service interface. Even though party notices come from varied upstream systems, we can flow all of them through this sole send port by continually affixing new maps to the send port. We don't need a new send port for each slightly different message containing the same underlying data, but rather, can aggressively reuse existing ports by simply reshaping the message into an acceptable structure. Secondly, BizTalk allows us to define dynamic ports, which rely on upstream processes to dictate the adapter and endpoint address for the port. A single dynamic port might be used by countless consumers who rely on runtime business logic to determine where to transmit the data at hand. Instead of creating dozens of static send ports, which are solely used to relay information (that is, no mapping), we can repeatedly reuse a single dynamic send port.

Identifying standard message exchange patterns

When we talk about **Message Exchange Patterns**, or **MEPs**, we're considering the direction and timing of data between the client and service. How do I get into the bus and what are the implications of those choices? Let's discuss the four primary options.

Request/response services

This is probably the pattern that's most familiar to you. We're all comfortable making a function call to a component and waiting for a response. When a service uses this pattern, it's frequently performing a **Remote Procedure Call** where the caller accesses functionality on the distant service and is blocked until either a timeout occurs or until the receiver sends a response that is expected by the caller.

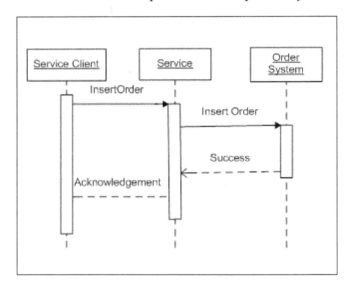

As we'll see below, while this pattern may set developers at ease, it may encourage bad behavior. Nevertheless, the cases where request/response services make the most sense are fine-grained functions and mashup services. If you need a list of active contracts that a hospital has with your company, then a request/response operation fits best. The client application should wait until that response is received before moving on to the next portion of the application. Or, let's say my web portal is calling an aggregate service, which takes contact data from five different systems and mashes them up into a single data entity that is then returned to the caller. This data is being requested for immediate presentation to an end user, and thus it's logical to solicit information from a service and wait to draw the screen until the completed result is loaded.

BizTalk Server 2013 has full support for both consuming and publishing services adhering to a request/response pattern. When exposing request/response operations through BizTalk orchestrations, the orchestration port's Communication Pattern is set to **Request-Response** and the **Port direction of communication** is equal to **I'll be receiving a request and sending a response**. Once this orchestration port is bound to a physical request/response receive port, BizTalk takes care of correlating the response message with the appropriate thread that made the request. This is significant because by default, BizTalk is a purely asynchronous messaging engine. Even when you configure BizTalk Server to behave in a request/response fashion, it's only putting a facade on the standard underlying plumbing. A synchronous BizTalk service interface actually sits on top of a sophisticated mechanism of correlating MessageBox communication to simulate a request/response pattern.

When consuming request/response services from BizTalk from an orchestration, the orchestration port's Communication Pattern is set to **Request-Response** and the **Port direction of communication** is equal to **I'll be sending a request and receiving a response**. The corresponding physical send port uses a solicit-response pattern and allows the user to set up both pipelines and maps for the inbound and outbound messages.

One concern with either publishing or consuming request/response services is the issue of blocking and timeouts. From a BizTalk perspective, this means that whenever you publish an orchestration as a request/response service, you should always verify that the logic residing between inbound and outbound transmissions will either complete or fail within a relatively brief amount of time. This dictates wrapping this logic inside an orchestration **Scope** shape with a preset timeout that is longer than the standard web service timeout interval.

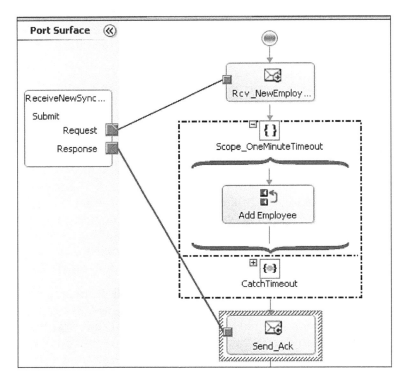

For consuming services, a request/response pattern forces the orchestration to block and wait for the response to be returned. If the service response isn't necessary for processing to continue, consider using a **Parallel** shape that isolates the service interaction pattern on a dedicated branch. This way, the execution of unrelated workflow steps can proceed even though the downstream service is yet to respond.

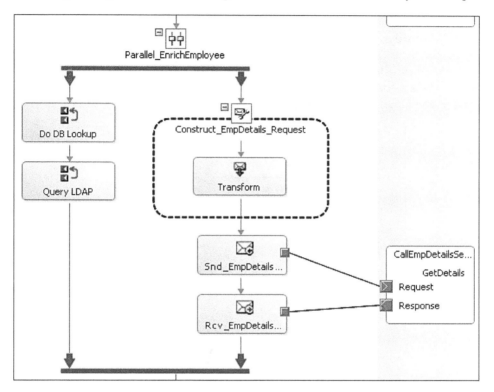

One-way services

This is your straightforward fire and forget pattern. The message is sent uni-directionally and asynchronously to a waiting receiver. If you grew up building components with fine-grained functional request/reply interfaces, this idea of throwing a message out of your application and not expecting anything back may seem a bit useless. However, this manner of service communication is a powerful way to build more event-driven applications and embrace non-blocking service invocation patterns. A one-way service interface may send a message to a single destination (a point-to-point solution), a defined list of recipients (multi-cast solution) or be a general broadcast (pub/sub solution). The key is, the caller remains unaware of the journey of the message once it is swallowed up by the service.

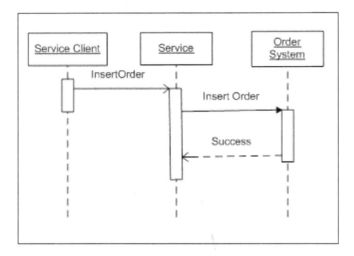

In scenarios where the sender and receiver may not both be online or active at the same time, a one-way service pattern offers a way to buffer this communication. For instance, we can build a service that offers an operation called PublishCustomerChange which takes a Customer entity possessing modified data attributes. The service itself may decide to queue up requests and only update the legacy Customer Management application during scheduled intervals throughout the day. However, the service may still receive requests all day, but because there is no expectation of a response to the submitter, the service can decide to prioritize the processing of the request until a more convenient time.

Pitfall

While the communication between endpoints may appear to be one-way, the default behavior of a WCF service returning *void* is to still provide a passive acknowledgement (or negative acknowledgement) that everything has run successfully. To prevent this completely and have a truly asynchronous service operation, set the `IsOneWay` property of an `OperationContract` attribute within the WCF service. BizTalk does not easily support true one-way WCF contracts, see `http://blogs.msdn.com/b/mdoctor/archive/2009/09/08/using-one-way-operations-with-the-wcf-adapter-in-biztalk.aspx`.

BizTalk Server 2013 is at its finest when working with one-way messaging patterns. Messages flow into the `MessageBox` and inherently cascade down to many places. When freed from the restraints of an expected service response, BizTalk Server can more powerfully chain together data and processes into far-reaching solutions. Consider a message sent to BizTalk via a one-way service interface. The loosely-coupled orchestrations and send ports can simply subscribe to this message's data, type, or attributes and act upon it. There is no concern for doing anything else but acting upon the data event. When a request/response receive port is designated as the service publisher, there can feasibly be only a single subscriber (and responder) to the request.

While all the BizTalk WCF adapters support one-way patterns, only the WCF-NetMsmq and the SB Messaging adapter requires it. MSMQ was designed for disconnected systems, and thus do not expect publishers to the queue to wait for any business data response.

Request/Callback services

There are cases where the caller of a service wants the benefits of non-blocking asynchronous service invocation, but also needs an actual data response from the service. In this case, a callback pattern can best fit your needs. In this situation, the caller acts as both, a service consumer and a service provider. That is, the caller must be able to both send a message, and host an endpoint that the service can send a subsequent response to. You can consider this an asynchronous request/response pattern.

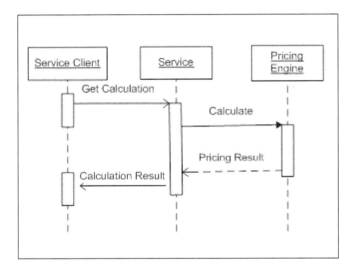

This can be a complicated pattern for service callers to accommodate. The caller has to design some intelligent strategies to correlate out-of-band responses with the original request made. During request/response invocations, the caller is blocked and doesn't proceed until the response has arrived. A sequence of processing is preserved. In a callback scenario, the client receives service responses well after the initial request. They have to make sure that:

- The response corresponds to a given request
- The response remains relevant to the application

Additionally, the client application should take into account the fact that a response may never actually arrive.

How does the service know where to send its response message back to? Typically the inbound request contains a pointer to the callback URI. The SOAP header is a good place to cram this sort of metadata instead of polluting the actual data message with context information.

WCF has some fairly rich support for callbacks through bindings such as the `NetTcpBinding` and `NetNamedPipeBinding`. While HTTP is inherently stateless and doesn't naturally support bi-directional communication, WCF provides a special HTTP binding named `WSDualHttpBinding`, which creates a matching pair of directional channels under the covers. A WCF developer can add callback *contracts* to a service contract and allow WCF clients to seamlessly call services and have an event raised when the service response is eventually received.

Sounds great, right? Unfortunately, the BizTalk WCF adapters do not openly support the **WSDualHttpBinding** or callback contracts in general. Instead, as we'll investigate in depth during *Chapter 9, Asynchronous Communication Patterns*, we need to get creative through the use of dynamic ports or polling strategies to implement a general purpose, cross platform callback pattern. That said, I will show you in *Chapter 9, Asynchronous Communication Patterns*, how you can effectively use the `WSDualHttpBinding` within a BizTalk receive location.

Publish/Subscribe services

This final MEP is actually an extension of the one-way MEP. Instead of a sender and receiver of a service, consider the parties to be a publisher and subscriber. In a publish/subscribe MEP, data objects are sent to an endpoint where a dynamic set of interested entities yank a copy of the data for their own purpose. There is a one-to-many relationship between the publisher and subscribers. The data is published to the service in an asynchronous fashion with no expectation of a direct response.

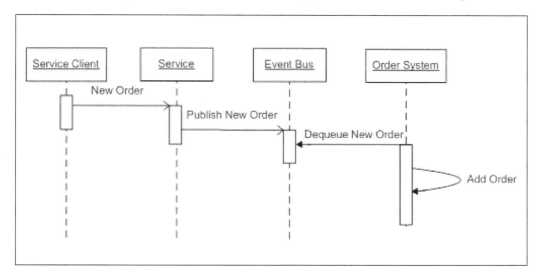

BizTalk excels at the publish/subscribe service pattern. BizTalk can optionally subscribe on three distinct pieces of information:

- **Message context**: Each message that arrives into BizTalk Server has a property bag called context attached to it. Regardless of whether the data is in a structured data format (such as XML) or a binary blob (such as a PDF file), any object reaching the BizTalk MessageBox has context attached. Message subscribers can decide to register interest in topics associated with the message metadata found in context. For instance, a subscriber might choose to listen for all messages that arrived at a specific file location. Hence, their send port subscription would equal BTS.ReceivedFileName.

- **Message type**: A message with a structured data format can be typed by the BizTalk endpoint prior to publication to the bus, typically through the use of a disassembler pipeline component. The type value is typically equal to the namespace of the XML message plus the name of the root node. BizTalk subscribers can choose to pull any message that matches the data type they are interested in.

- **Message content:** Developers can single out fields in a message schema for **promotion** which means that they are available for routing decisions within the BizTalk bus. When a message arrives into BizTalk and is processed by a disassembler. If a matching schema is found, the data elements designated for promotion have their values yanked out of the payload and put into context. Downstream subscribers can now specify data-level subscription topics. Hence, instead of pulling all new employees from the bus (based on a message type subscription), we could extract only those where EmployeeCountry == Germany using a content based subscription.

Pitfall

While BizTalk Server offers a variety of subscription topic mechanisms (context, type, or content), you are limited by the subscription operators available. For instance, you cannot create a subscription where "Organization CONTAINS Hospital". That is, you do not have options for wildcard searches or dynamic subscriptions in a send port. To achieve such a capability, you'd have to rely on orchestrations or custom pipeline components.

This manner of service invocation shifts the idea of a service from being just a functional component in a fancy SOAP wrapper to being an on-ramp to a distributed computing bus, where the publisher relinquishes knowledge and control of the data's processing path.

Types of services

There are multiple ways to look at types of services, and I've chosen to consider the types of services based on the category of message they accept.

RPC services

A **Remote Procedure Call (RPC)** is a means of executing a function on a distant object. These remote invocations are meant to appear as if they were happening locally and typically follow the request/response communication pattern. If you've written DCOM or CORBA components before, then this is a familiar concept. As SOAP gained traction, this was initially seen as just another way to execute remote functions but in a more interoperable way. However, this encourages a very point-to-point mentality.

RPC-style services follow the "Gang of Four" command pattern where objects (in our case, messages) correspond to the action you wish to perform. In essence, you are sending a message that tells the remote service what to do. For example, the payload of an RPC-style service request meant to create a new customer entity would look like this:

```
<soap:Envelopexmlns:soap="http://schemas.xmlsoap.org/soap/envelope
/">
<soap:Body>
<InsertNewCustomerxmlns="http://Seroter.BizTalkSOA.RPCExample">
<ID>010022</ID>
<Name>Amy Clark</Name>
<FacilityID>LHS2001</FacilityID>
</InsertNewCustomer>
</soap:Body>
</soap:Envelope>
```

While this type of command message may be acceptable for service requests that return a specific response (`GetCustomerDetails` or `VerifyAddress`), it is not a good practice for messaging solutions. Why? Architecturally, this is fairly tight coupling where the client confidently knows exactly what the service is supposed to do with their request and by the nature of the request, is demanding such behavior (`DeleteCustomer`). That's fairly presumptive, no? If the client truly had the ability to do this action themselves, they wouldn't need the service at all! In truth, the caller is only capable of making polite requests to the service where it remains the prerogative of the service to handle that request as it sees fit. For example, a demand to `AddNewCustomer` may not be a simple, synchronous event. The service may require human validation of the customer entry, or even decide that it doesn't want to add this new customer for reasons such as content duplication, failure of business rules, or simply irrelevance to the system.

Where does RPC play in BizTalk Server solutions? The classic ASMX service generator had a choice of producing bare or wrapped services that dictated whether the service operation followed an RPC style or not. The default style, wrapped, would enclose the message payload with the name of the service operations.

The BizTalk WCF Service Publishing Wizard offers no choice of messaging style. In fact, any WCF service generated either from schemas or orchestrations will follow the document-style outlined below. The name of the service operation is not part of the SOAP payload. If you wish to promote an RPC style service and aren't satisfied with the metadata generated by the BizTalk, you have the option to author your own RPC-oriented WSDL and provide that as the primary facade definition. Either way, the adapter is quite forgiving with each format, as it can either strip out nodes from parent elements, or conversely, add a wrapper to an inbound data object.

Document services

A document-style service is one in which the payload represents an encapsulated data structure devoid of any sort of instruction of what to do with it. As you can imagine, this type of service operation is much more coarse-grained and accepts plumper messages that are more self-describing. The service has all it needs to perform its action and doesn't rely on a stateful series of actions that provide context to the operation. If we re-factored our preceding RPC-style payload to be more document-centric, it might look like this:

```
<soap:Envelopexmlns:soap="http://schemas.xmlsoap.org/soap/envelope
/">
<soap:Body>
<NewCustomerxmlns="http://Seroter.BiztalkSOA.RPCExample">
<ID>010022</ID>
<Name>Amy Clark</Name>
<FacilityID>LHS2001</FacilityID>
</NewCustomer>
</soap:Body>
</soap:Envelope>
```

Notice that instead of having a functional directive as the focus of the message payload, we are highlighting the data entity that is travelling across the wire. Either the single recipient or the broad list of subscribers can decide how they handle a NewCustomer and what they do with the data to fit their needs.

While this type of service can be used for request/response operations, they typically make lots of sense for scenarios where one application simply needs to exchange data with another application. These services can follow a one-way MEP when data is only being shared in a point-to-point manner, or could also be a one-way MEP with a publish/subscribe flavor where any interested party could have at the data.

Does BizTalk Server support this document-centric service type? It certainly does. As mentioned above, all BizTalk-generated WCF service endpoints define a document-centric contract. We'll chat about this more in the next chapter as we analyze the best ways to construct a schema for service exposure. Specifically, we'll talk about how we should both identify and shape our schemas to avoid functional presumption and encourage reusable data entities.

Event services

Finally, let's consider the step-brother of the document-style service: the event service. For event services, when something of note occurs, the service is invoked and a message explaining the event is distributed. Unlike the document message, the event message typically contains a limited amount of information. You're basically telling the service that something important happened, but not sharing too much data or instructing it as to what to do next.

In these scenarios, it's quite possible that the service recipient will have to call back to the source system to actually get the relevant data set. Consider the NewEmployee event notification. When a new employee is added to the HR system, our service is called and the NewEmployeeEvent message is transmitted. Let's say that BizTalk fans this message out to all downstream systems that care about employee data. Our French office's security badge application has a service exposed which accepts the NewEmployeeEvent message and then peeks to see which country the new employee is associated with. If that country is France, then their service calls back to the source HR system to retrieve the full employee profile. What exactly is in this truncated event message if not the full document? Stay tuned for when we dissect the event message and consider how best to use it.

In the BizTalk sense, this sort of service is a very nice use of the event-driven message bus and is a great fit for one-way or pub/sub MEPs. Assuming that BizTalk accepts these event messages via its inbound service adapters, what are the possible outcomes? Three options are:

- Fan the message out to downstream services that have their own event-handling logic
- Spawn a new orchestration workflow that performs event processing logic
- Generate additional event messages within the bus based on content in the original message

While event messages are typically asynchronous in nature, the life cycle of event processing can actually exploit all three service types identified in this chapter. In the sequence diagram below, I show how an initial event message (Order Event) may give way to a command request (GetOrderDetails) and a document-style response (OrderDetails).

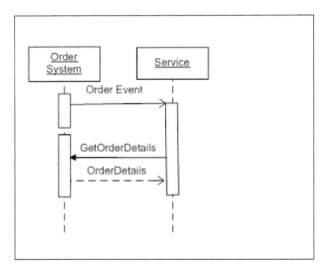

The thought of using BizTalk Server for this sort of event-style routing may be counter to classic impressions of BizTalk as a simple point-to-point broker. We've moved beyond that antiquated concept and should consider BizTalk a serious option when architecting robust service-oriented event processing systems.

Summary

We covered a lot of ground in this chapter in our quest to discover the key principles underpinning service-oriented design and evaluating how to champion these concepts within BizTalk Server 2013. Proper planning of a service oriented solution goes a long way towards ongoing agility and future return on investment that is critical to defining the success of a SOA.

BizTalk is an ideal tool for building loosely-coupled, interoperable solutions that maximize reusable components. The mix of platform-neutral technology adapters and a foundational message bus based on a publication/subscribe pattern results in BizTalk being uniquely positioned to do much more than facilitate point-to-point application interfaces. While BizTalk supports RPC messages over a request/response channel, we've also seen the benefits we can secure by rotating our thinking and embracing asynchronous messaging based on more loosely-coupled document or event messages.

In the following chapters, we will build on the concepts that we've touched upon here. In the next chapter, we'll look specifically at ways to implement many of the contract and endpoint concepts introduced so far.

8
Schema and Endpoint Patterns

A verbal contract isn't worth the paper it's written on.

– Samuel Goldwyn

How you go about designing your service interface will go a long way towards the long-term success and overall stability of your service. As we have seen in the previous chapters, a well-built service should only reveal its location, available operations, and the messages it exchanges with clients. The service's internal plumbing should remain safely tucked away from those who intend to consume the interface. We will spend the majority of this chapter looking at how to practically implement a series of key schema and endpoint patterns.

In this chapter you will learn the following topics:

- Good practices for building schemas that coincide with the service type you've chosen
- When and how to build canonical schemas
- The benefits and limits of schema reuse
- Translating data types and node characteristics into client code
- Ways to use generic schemas in your solutions
- Strategies for building contract-first endpoints

Service-oriented schema patterns

Schemas are a critical component of the service contract. They not only announce the data model that a service recognizes, but more conceptually, they allow our service to adhere to the principles laid out in previous chapters. Abstraction is a key aspect of SOA, and a well-built schema provides a sufficient level of opaqueness to the underlying service processing. Interoperability, another vital piece of a far-reaching service, should be taken into consideration at the earliest phases of schema design. Finally, the concept of reusability is readily embraced in schema design, and we will see numerous examples in this chapter.

Let's now look at a series of ways in which we can apply these service-oriented principles to schemas designed in BizTalk Server 2013. Throughout this chapter, I will use examples that revolve around receiving details about a subject's activities in an ongoing clinical drug trial. This includes actions such as enrolling into a trial, participating in a screening, and withdrawing from the trial.

Designing schemas based on service type

In the previous chapter, we defined three different service types:

- **RPC Services**: Messages correspond to actions we wish to perform
- **Document Services**: The data entity is transmitted without instructions on what to do with it
- **Event Services**: Messages represent explanations of events that have occurred

The **BizTalk WCF Service Publishing Wizard**, unlike the classic **BizTalk Web Services Publishing Wizard**, does not offer the option of **Bare** (document-style services) or **Wrapped** (RPC-style services). All BizTalk-generated WCF endpoints exhibit a document-centric pattern. Therefore, if you wanted to accept an RPC-style WCF message into BizTalk Server, you'd have to explicitly build your request schema in that RPC fashion.

So how would you build this sort of schema for a new enrollment in our drug trial? We start out with a command root node name and include the parameters we need to insert this record into our clinical trial system:

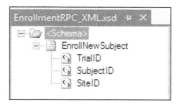

Note that by transmitting this sort of message, the caller gets the impression of invoking a function called `EnrollNewSubject` on my remote system.

What would a more document-centric design of this schema look like? In this case, we'd want to share the entire enrollment entity with the service. That is, we'd want to provide a fully encapsulated form of the data object that relies on no existing context about this interaction:

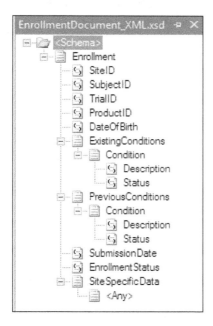

In this schema, the root is the type of document being exchanged, and no indication is given as to what the service has to do with it. Meanwhile, it contains a full spectrum of information about this particular enrollment and should not require additional enrichment prior to acting upon it.

How do event-style messages differ? In this case, the message is a reflection of something of interest that has occurred. In *Chapter 7, Planning Service-oriented BizTalk Solutions*, I mentioned that in some cases event messages trigger callbacks to the source system for more information. However, do not consider that scenario as an excuse to distribute tiny, nondescript event messages that contain nothing but foreign key pointers.

If you choose to only send data pointers in an event message, then you should ensure that one of the following points applies to your scenario:

- The user doesn't need the actual data in order to make decisions.

- The downstream consumers are guaranteed to have access to the source system for data enrichment. I consider a correctly sized event message to be one that contains enough information to be actionable by any potential recipients:

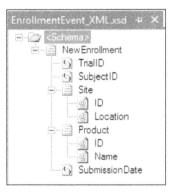

This schema is for the **NewEnrollment** event published by the business partner that manages the clinical trial process. While it's certainly possible to include the document in an event message, in my case I've chosen to include only a few pieces of data that are most critical to event subscribers. Interest in enrollments will be limited to the location of the clinical site, which product is being administered, and which trial this is part of. If the receiver of the event requires any more enrollment information than this, they will need to seek it out in their own regional systems.

Critical point

In reality, these schema structure distinctions are purely architectural ideals. We're really talking about how a message looks as it is exchanged between endpoints. The name of a root node or how exactly the schema is structured doesn't directly relate to what the service is capable of doing, or even the method name for that matter. However, the forethought that goes into deciding on a more event-driven approach versus an RPC approach does impact how you build the service and infrastructure that uses the service message.

On building schemas in a distributed architecture, the tricky concept of **idempotence** must be addressed. Wikipedia defines **idempotence** as follows:

> *In computer science, the term idempotent is used to describe methods or subroutine calls that can safely be called multiple times, as invoking the procedure a single time or multiple times results in the system maintaining the same state.*

Source: http://en.wikipedia.org/wiki/Idempotence

Simply put, because it's never a good idea to rely on the infrastructure between distributed systems, the messages should ideally support repeated delivery without consequence. For instance, a typical request/response query (such as getting the address of a customer) is idempotent. It doesn't matter if I initiate this request fifteen times in a row; the state of the customer's address remains static (given that no external changes are made in between requests). However, if I execute a withdrawal command repeatedly, then I better expect my bank account to continually decrease.

So how do we account for this? The *Enterprise Integration Patterns* book from *Hohpe and Woolf* calls out two ways:

- Build de-duplication processes where duplicates are detected and ignored
- Define messages themselves to be idempotent

A non-idempotent RPC message may demand that my salary be increased by five thousand dollars. While I might appreciate that message accidentally traveling through our payroll system five or six times, my employer would not. An idempotent version of that message would instead declare what the current salary figure should be (such as fifty thousand dollars) so that the repeated transmission would result in the same value being present in the target system.

RPC and document-style services can be quite prone to this problem. What if you have repeated changes to an enrollment document published and the message bus processes them out of order so that the latest one is overwritten by the earlier one? You can try and exploit timestamps or sequence numbers and the like, but this remains a tricky issue.

One way to avoid this is to rely on event messages with required lookups by the subscriber. Deviating from our clinical trial scenario for a moment, let's consider the life cycle of employee changes in an HR system. A given employee record could get updated at a few distinct intervals in the day, and the opportunity exists for messages to slip out of sequence. However, if you have an event-style message that tells subscribers that the employee's data has changed (and nothing else), then the subscriber simply goes and pulls the latest employee profile from the source system themselves. It doesn't matter if I send that event message sixty times in a row; I'm not actually distributing any state data that is dependent on arrival order. The downside to this strategy is an increase in network traffic and an assurance that all subscribers can indeed access the source system.

While idempotence can't be built into every single integration scenario, it is a concept that should be considered carefully. However, if it can't be explicitly catered for, then due thought should be given to how your solution will handle the exceptional scenario in which a message might get duplicated several times, for whatever reason.

Canonical schemas

Once again, let's quote Wikipedia on **canonical models**:

> *Canonical Schema is a design pattern, applied within the service-orientation design paradigm, which aims to reduce the need for performing data model transformation when services exchange messages that reference the same data model.*

Source: http://en.wikipedia.org/wiki/Canonical_schema_pattern

Without designing a canonical intermediary data format, you can end up with a mess of point-to-point translations that leads to a brittle application:

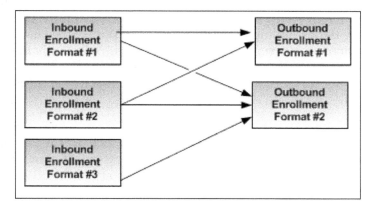

By injecting a common schema, you can reduce coupling between the source formats and destination formats. At any one point in time, a message only needs to be translated to or from the canonical format:

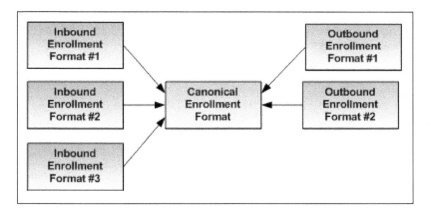

Where do we implement this in BizTalk solutions? One scenario in which canonical schemas can add a lot of value is while interacting with auto-generated schemas. The WCF LOB adapters available in BizTalk Server 2013 will automatically generate schemas that comply with the selected system interface. Naturally, these schemas exhibit extremely tight coupling to the destination platform. If we use these schemas in our orchestrations, or worse, in exposed services, we've instantly made either incremental or far-reaching change a more complicated endeavor. If we've exposed these schemas in our services, then we've also failed miserably at the SOA goal of abstraction.

Let's demonstrate an additional example. The LOB adapters expose **CRUD (create-read-update-delete)** types of operations on databases such as SQL Server. As we've discussed in the book so far, a service is a more business-oriented module that should extend higher than simply slapping a SOAP interface on low-level APIs. The **Enrollment** document-style schema I created earlier may actually be a canonical schema that sits in between a variety of input formats and destination systems. Let's say my database that stores enrollment information has the following structure:

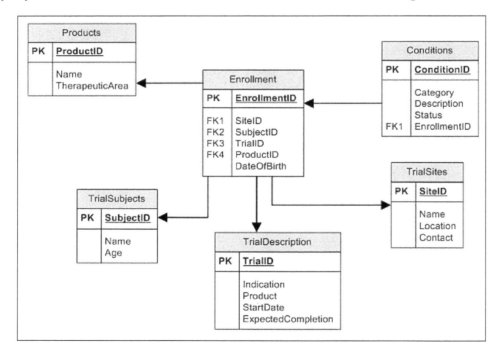

If I solicit schemas from the SQL Server WCF adapter for these tables, I'll end up with a series of message types. It would be a fairly poor decision to expose each schema as a distinct service operation. Instead, I have an intermediate enrollment schema that abstracts the more complex set of individual services needed to insert a new subject enrollment.

A well thought-out canonical schema typically doesn't simply have copies of the same nodes and structures from all the schemas that it relies on. While the canonical format clearly needs to capture the right data to serve its purpose, also consider how the logical composite entity should look and take a more business-centric view of the data. Specifically, remove redundant fields, reorganize elements into a natural hierarchy, reconsider data types, and evaluate occurrence and restriction boundaries.

Pitfall

Be careful about going overboard on canonical schemas and introducing accidental complexity. For messaging-only solutions, you may be fine with the schema formats demanded by the source and destination systems, depending on whether the solution must support multiple source/destination formats or not. When your scenario involves the injection of processing logic (for example, rules or orchestration), it definitely becomes more attractive to decouple components through the use of canonical schemas.

Another scenario is one in which BizTalk must receive messages from multiple parties that convey the same data, however, in different formats/standards. By using a canonical schema and transforming from all the various formats to your canonical format, you can streamline the internal processing (be this orchestration, BRE rules, or mapping to LOB formats) of these messages by applying it to your canonical format. Without a canonical schema, you would need to replicate your orchestrations, BRE rules, and maps to LOB schemas for each varying format.

Building and applying reusable schema components

Schemas in BizTalk Server 2013 can be built to support reusability in a variety of ways. Let's look at four of them:

1. If I want to put the content of one schema into the definition of another, I can either import or include it. When the target namespace between the schemas differs, the import option must be used. For example, let's say that we design a schema that represents a subject (or patient) that is planning to enroll in a drug trial:

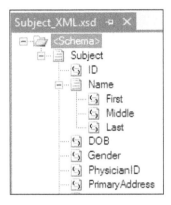

2. Next, we have a basic **Enrollment** schema that looks like this:

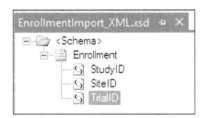

3. If we click on the uppermost node named **<Schema>** in the **Enrollment** schema, we get a set of global settings available in the Visual Studio **Properties** window. Select the ellipse next to the Imports property to launch the schema selection pane.

4. Clicking on the **Add** button will allow us to pick which schema in the project (or referenced projects) we wish to import.

5. After selecting the **Subject** schema, and before clicking on **OK** on the pop up, we can see the namespace prefix and action that we're about to perform:

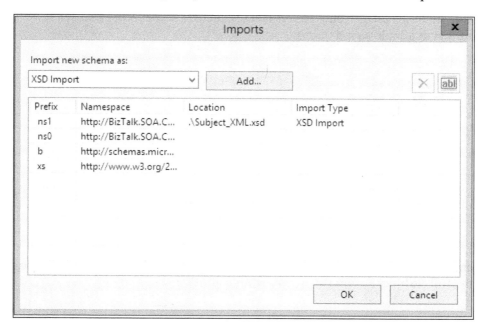

6. Once the import is complete, our schema tree view should look no different. However, if we glance at the XSD schema view pane, we can see a new `<xsd:import>` command injected at the top of the schema:

```xml
<?xml version="1.0" encoding="utf-16" ?>
<xs:schema xmlns="http://BizTalk.SOA.Chapter8/Import/Parent"
    xmlns:b="http://schemas.microsoft.com/BizTalk/2003"
    xmlns:ns0="http://BizTalk.SOA.Chapter8/Import"
    targetNamespace="http://BizTalk.SOA.Chapter8/Import/Parent"
    xmlns:xs="http://www.w3.org/2001/XMLSchema">
    <xs:import schemaLocation=".\subject_xml.xsd"
       namespace="http://BizTalk.SOA.Chapter8/Import" />
```

Exploiting the reusable imported schema

Let's create a new record in the **Enrollment** schema. The **Properties** window for that node includes an attribute called **Data Structure Type**. Note that we now have **ns1:Subject** available as a data type:

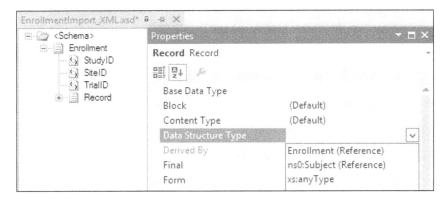

Choosing the **Subject** data type causes the previously created record to be replaced with the full **Subject** schema structure from our other schema:

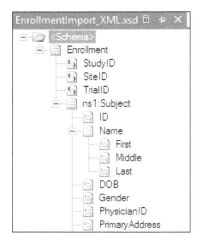

Note that changes made to the imported schema are automatically reflected in the importing schema.

If the schema you wish to reuse is in the same namespace as the importing schema, you have to perform a schema include. Including one schema in another is very similar to the import procedure. The only difference is that when you are choosing which schema to include on the XSD Import screen, you need to be ensure that you change the value in the drop-down list from the default value, XSD Import, to XSD Include. Visual Studio will ensure that you are not able to choose the XSD Import option if the schemas are in the same namespace. Likewise, it will not allow you to choose XSD Include if the schemas are in different namespaces:

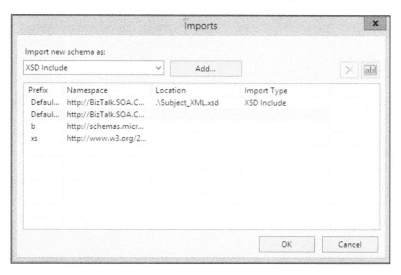

To illustrate the key difference between XSD Import and XSD Include, I updated the schemas so that the **Enrollment** and **Subject** schemas reside in the same namespace. The source of the **Enrollment** XSD file now includes an XML `<xsd:include>` statement pointing to the included schema. You will notice that the schema tree now has a ghosted Subject node at the top of it. We can now create a new record under the **Enrollment** node and point the **Data Structure Type** to **Subject**:

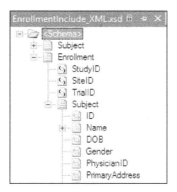

When you work with included schemas, you may experience some unexpected behavior generating XML instances for the schema. As the preceding schema stands, if I choose **Generate Instance**, the `Subject` node will be the one generated as the root node, not the expected `Enrollment` element. The way to get around this is to click on the uppermost **<Schema>** node, choose the **Root Reference** property, and explicitly define **Enrollment** as the root of the schema.

On the off chance that you wish to use another schema and make a variation to it, then this is where the redefine option comes in. In this scenario, you reference a schema (it must be in the same namespace) and you have the option of making modifications to it. You need to be cautious with redefinitions as you break your connection to the original schema.

The final type of schema reuse comes into play when designing global types that can be employed by other schemas. So far, we've seen the reuse of entire schemas, but what if we have a set of standard types that by themselves are not standalone messages but instead are snippets of data structures? For instance, let's take an address as an example. A typical address structure exists in all sorts of schema types and is probably duplicated over and over again. We could define a global address type and use that in all our relevant schemas.

Let's have a look at it:

1. First create a new schema and define a record that outlines the **Address** structure:

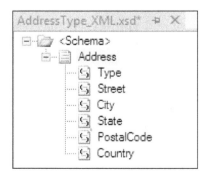

2. Next, click on the record name, select the **Data Structure Type** property, and manually type in a value such as `AddressType`. The Schema Editor now reflects the construction of a new global type:

```xml
<?xml version="1.0" encoding="utf-16" ?>
- <xs:schema xmlns="http://BizTalk.SOA.Chapter8/GlobalTypes"
    xmlns:b="http://schemas.microsoft.com/BizTalk/2003"
    targetNamespace="http://BizTalk.SOA.Chapter8/GlobalTypes"
    xmlns:xs="http://www.w3.org/2001/XMLSchema">
  - <xs:complexType name="AddressType">
    - <xs:sequence>
        <xs:element name="Type" type="xs:ID" />
        <xs:element name="Street" type="xs:string" />
        <xs:element name="City" type="xs:string" />
        <xs:element name="State" type="xs:string" />
        <xs:element name="PostalCode" type="xs:string" />
        <xs:element name="Country" type="xs:string" />
      </xs:sequence>
    </xs:complexType>
    <xs:element name="Address" type="AddressType" />
  </xs:schema>
```

3. The next thing to do is actually delete the **Address** node. This is because we don't actually need or want the element of the `AddressType` type in this schema. All we actually want is the type declaration, which survives after the record is deleted. Our schema now shows no nodes in the tree, but we can see within the XSD that a global type exists:

```
AddressType_XML.xsd

<Schema>

<?xml version="1.0" encoding="utf-16" ?>
- <xs:schema xmlns="http://BizTalk.SOA.Chapter8/GlobalTypes"
    xmlns:b="http://schemas.microsoft.com/BizTalk/2003"
    targetNamespace="http://BizTalk.SOA.Chapter8/GlobalTypes"
    xmlns:xs="http://www.w3.org/2001/XMLSchema">
  - <xs:complexType name="AddressType">
    - <xs:sequence>
        <xs:element name="Type" type="xs:ID" />
        <xs:element name="Street" type="xs:string" />
        <xs:element name="City" type="xs:string" />
        <xs:element name="State" type="xs:string" />
        <xs:element name="PostalCode" type="xs:string" />
        <xs:element name="Country" type="xs:string" />
      </xs:sequence>
    </xs:complexType>
  </xs:schema>
```

If we import this schema into our **Subject** schema (which we have to do in this case because they are in different namespaces) and create a new record called **Addresses**, we can now choose **AddressType** as the **Data Structure Type** for this record:

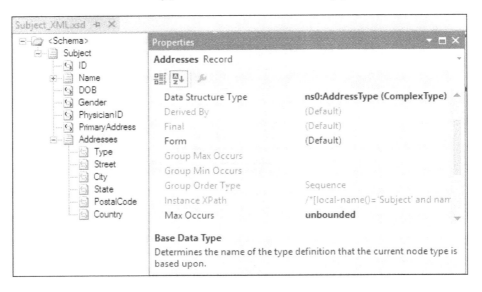

As you would hope, the relationship between **Subject** and **Address** is retained even when **Subject** is imported into the **Enrollment** schema. We've daisy chained three schemas in a very reusable way:

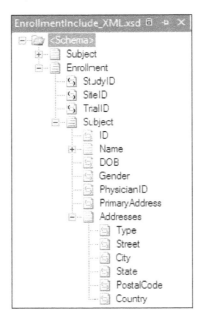

Finally, what's the impact of using imports/includes/redefines in your BizTalk-generated WCF endpoints? All three are supported by the **BizTalk WCF Service Publishing Wizard**. However, service consumers may experience issues when a schema possesses a redefine command, so use that with caution. Even with multiple nesting of included schemas, the WCF svcutil.exe command had no problem interpreting the contract. However, this is an area where interoperability can be a problem. As a best practice, try to limit excessive schema reuse if you cannot be sure of the types of clients consuming your service (this advice of course doesn't apply to canonical schemas).

There are many schools of thought as to how best reusable schemas should be defined. The primary differences are the types of elements/types that are considered global and the ones that remain local as well as whether namespaces need to be qualified or not. These variations have been well explored by Stephen Kaufman in his blog which also discusses the application of these patterns to BizTalk Server. This discussion is beyond the scope of this book; however, the blog series starting here is highly recommended reading: http://blogs.msdn.com/b/skaufman/archive/2005/04/21/410486.aspx.

Node data type conversion for service clients

You may have noticed that the Schema Editor provided by BizTalk Server 2013 delivers a comprehensive list of data types for schema nodes. In the following table, I call out a subset of the more common schema types, describe what they are, and mention what .NET type they convert to when consumed by the WCF svcutil.exe proxy generation tool:

BizTalk XSD type	Description	.NET type
anyURI	Can be any absolute or relative Uniform Resource Identifier reference	System.String
base64Binary	This holds Base64-encoded arbitrary binary data (for example, PDF and JPEG)	System.Byte[]
boolean	This supports the mathematical concept of binary value logic (0/1 or true/false)	System.Boolean
byte	This holds an 8-bit value	System.SByte
date	An object with year, month, and day properties	System.DateTime

BizTalk XSD type	Description	.NET type
dateTime	An object with year, month, day, hour, minute, second, and timezone properties	System. DateTime
decimal	This contains a subset of real numbers with support for a minimum of 18 decimal digits	System.Decimal
double	A double-precision, 64-bit floating point type	System.Double
float	A single-precision, 32-bit floating point type	System.Single
hexBinary	This represents arbitrary hex-encoded binary data	System.Byte[]
ID	Definition of document-global unique identifiers	System.String
IDREF	A reference to a unique identifier (ID)	System.String
IDREFS	A separated list of IDREF references	System.String
int	A 32-bit signed integer	System.Int32
long	A 64-bit signed integer	System.Int64
short	A set of 16-bit integers	System.Int16
string	A string of any set of allowable XML characters, including whitespace	System.String
Time	The instant of time recurring each day	System. DateTime

It's interesting to see how some types are handled in this table. Of course, these are conversion details for .NET only, and similar (but not necessarily the same) results can be expected for other platforms and languages. For maximum interoperability, stick with very common types, such as string and int. As you move into floating point numbers, consider using the decimal type instead of the float type so that you can get the maximum precision on your numbers and not fall prey to rounding errors.

One interesting data type to note, that I don't come across very often, is the ID/IDREF. ID/IDREF is a concept left over from DTD, where you can define relationships between XML nodes. The ID value acts as a primary key (and must be unique in the message), while the IDREF field points to the ID field.

In a schema, I have sections of dependent elements that are not structured in a way to enforce the relationship. For instance, recall that one version of my Enrollment schema has a repeating list of addresses in order to account for home, work, and alternate addresses. I may have a new element in this schema named **PrimaryAddress**, that references which of the included addresses we should treat as the default one. Using basic XML data types, there is no way to stipulate that the **PrimaryAddress** node can only contain a value that corresponds to the repeating list of addresses. However, if I update my schema to apply ID/IDREF data types to the corresponding address nodes and then validate the following XML snippet in the BizTalk Schema Editor, I get the exception `Reference to undeclared ID is 'Alternate'`:

```
<ns0:Subject xmlns:ns0="http://BizTalk.SOA.Chapter5/Import">
  <ID>ID_0</ID>
  <Name>
    <First>First_0</First>
    <Middle>Middle_0</Middle>
    <Last>Last_0</Last>
  </Name>
  <DOB>DOB_0</DOB>
  <Gender>Gender_0</Gender>
  <PhysicianID>PhysicianID_0</PhysicianID>
  <PrimaryAddress>Alternate</PrimaryAddress>
  <Addresses>
    <Type>Home</Type>
    <Street>Street_0</Street>
    <City>City_0</City>
    <State>State_0</State>
    <PostalCode>PostalCode_0</PostalCode>
    <Country>Country_0</Country>
  </Addresses>
  <Addresses>
    <Type>Work</Type>
    <Street>Street_0</Street>
    <City>City_0</City>
    <State>State_0</State>
    <PostalCode>PostalCode_0</PostalCode>
    <Country>Country_0</Country>
  </Addresses>
</ns0:Subject>
```

Hence, while it remains difficult to impossible to build strong relationship semantics into a schema, consider ID/IDREF if you need to enforce basic referential integrity in your service schema.

Node feature mapping for service clients

When you apply robust boundary and logic conditions to your service schema, it is critical to understand how those rules are translated from the WSDL to your client code.

Note that the **BizTalk WCF Service Publishing Wizard** is infinitely better than the classic **BizTalk Web Services Publishing Wizard** when it comes to respecting the initial schema. While the WCF wizard keeps all schema properties intact after metadata publication, the ASMX wizard removes occurrence limits, default values, and complex type groupings.

Element grouping

Let's first look at complex type grouping. When you erect a standard XSD schema, by default, the schema expects all the XML nodes to be in the sequential order set forth by the schema. However, you have options to be more flexible than that. The question, though, is how well do WCF clients support a schema structure possessing such flexibility? We can evaluate this by first setting up a Screen Result schema, which outlines the results of a physician screening of a drug trial subject. The original structure looks like this:

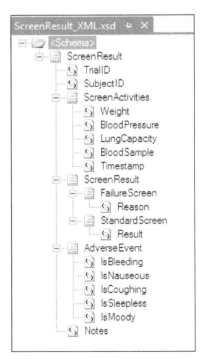

The **ScreenActivites** record contains elements explaining a sequence of steps that must be reported in a specific order. I can ensure that this is the case by clicking the **ScreenActivities** record, and setting the **Context Type** property equal to **Complex Content**:

1. As soon as that value is set, a **Sequence** group is added to the **ScreenActivites** node:

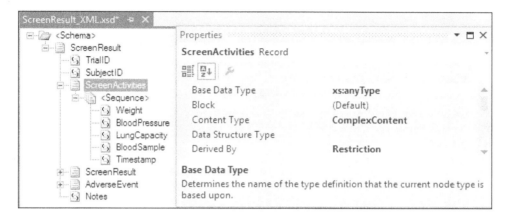

2. The second record of note, **ScreenResult**, will contain either a success or failure node based on the physician's evaluation of the screening visit. We want our schema to expect only one of these two possible values.

3. Once again, we can set the **Context Type** to **Complex Content** on this record. However, this time, after the **Sequence** group shows up, we should select it and flip the **Order Type** to **Choice**. This means that the schema expects one of the two records to be there:

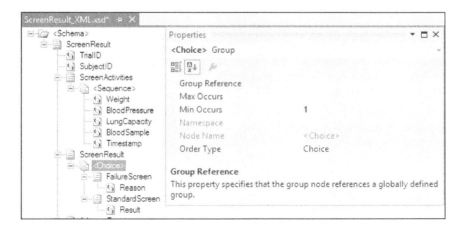

4. Finally, we have the **AdverseEvent** record, which holds a list of Boolean values about possible side effects we are keeping an eye out for. In this case, we can use an alternate way to dictate the record behavior.

5. After selecting the record and setting the **Group Order Type** to **All**, I've told the schema that all these nodes need to be here, but that they can exist in any order. One of the only real differences here is that there is no visual indication of the record's grouping behavior. I'll point out another difference in just a moment.

At this point, we want to expose this schema as a WCF service so that we can investigate how these grouping principles are (or aren't) applied in the WCF client that consumes it. I created a very simple, one-way WCF service (and metadata endpoint) using the **Expose schemas as web service** option in the BizTalk WCF Service Publishing Wizard. After starting the generated receive location (so that the service is enabled and browsable) I pointed my client application at the WSDL of the service.

Investigating the generated .NET types reveals something curious. The object representing the **ScreenActivities** node is defined like this:

```
public partial class ScreenResultScreenActivities {

        private string[] textField;

        /// <remarks/>
        [System.Xml.Serialization.XmlTextAttribute()]
        public string[] Text {
            get {
                return this.textField;
            }
        }
}
```

It does not contain all the sub types (**Weight, BloodPressure**, and so on) that were child nodes in the schema. This is because the **ScreenActivities** node had its **Sequence** characteristic set by changing its **Content Type** property. When we did this, the **Base Data Type** was automatically set to **xs:anyType**. Hence, the subsequent .NET class does not know about the actual contents of the **ScreenActivities** node. We can correct this by going back to our schema and removing **xs:anyType** as the **Base Data Type** and regenerating our WCF service endpoint:

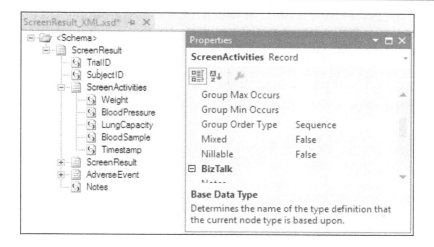

 When you set the complex type grouping behavior, just set the **Group Order Type** property instead of changing the **Content Type** property. This will prevent serialization problems down the line.

How does the generated .NET type class respect the schema grouping that we defined? You will notice in the following code snippet that, for the sequence node **ScreenActivities**, the corresponding class properties have order attributes in their serialization instruction:

```
[XmlElementAttribute(Form=XmlSchemaForm.Unqualified, Order=0)]
  public string Weight {
    get {
    return this.weightField;
  }
}
[XmlElementAttribute(Form=XmlSchemaForm.Unqualified, Order=1)]
  public string BloodPressure {
    get {
    return this.bloodPressureField;
  }
}
```

What about the **ScreenResult** element which has a choice grouping? In this case, the ScreenResult .NET object has an Item property that will hold either the FailureScreen or StandardScreen objects:

```
[XmlElementAttribute("FailureScreen", typeof(FailureScreen)]
[XmlElementAttribute("StandardScreen", typeof(StandardScreen)]
  public object Item {
    get {
    return this.itemField;
    }
    set {
       this.itemField = value;
  }
}
```

Finally, how is the concept of all XSD grouping handled by .NET client code? As you might expect, the code looks much like the sequence code, minus the mandatory node ordering attribute:

```
[XmlElementAttribute(Form= XmlSchemaForm.Unqualified)]
public bool IsBleeding {
  get {
        return this.isBleedingField;
      }
  set {
        this.isBleedingField = value;
      }
}


[XmlElementAttribute(Form= XmlSchemaForm.Unqualified)]
public bool IsNauseous {
  get {
        return this.isNauseousField;
      }
  set {
        this.isNauseousField = value;
      }
}
```

Overall then, XSD grouping clearly holds up pretty well when interpreted by WCF service clients.

Element properties

We now need to confirm how element properties are mapped from XSD definitions to .NET client code. Specifically, let's look at how occurrence limits nullability and default values are handled. I've gone ahead and modified our existing ScreenResult schema so that these new element properties are present. To do this, I made the following setting changes:

- The **ScreenActivities** node now has a minimum occurrence of 1 and a maximum occurrence of 5

- The **Timestamp** node, which is a **xsd:dateTime**, has its **Nillable** property set to **True**

- The **BloodSample** default amount is set to **Two Vials**

The resulting XSD looks like this:

```xml
- <xs:element minOccurs="1" maxOccurs="5" name="ScreenActivities">
  - <xs:complexType>
    - <xs:sequence>
        <xs:element name="Weight" type="xs:string" />
        <xs:element name="BloodPressure" type="xs:string" />
        <xs:element name="LungCapacity" type="xs:string" />
        <xs:element default="2 Vials" name="BloodSample" type="xs:string" />
        <xs:element name="Timestamp" nillable="true" type="xs:dateTime" />
    </xs:sequence>
  </xs:complexType>
</xs:element>
```

After rebuilding the WCF endpoint via the BizTalk WCF Service Publishing Wizard and then updating our client's service reference, we can see how these modified attributes are reflected. The **ScreenActivities** type does *not* capture the occurrence limits from the XSD but does show a default value for **BloodSample**, and a nullable type for the **Timestamp** property:

```csharp
public partial class ScreenResultScreenActivities {

        private string weightField;

        private string bloodPressureField;

        private string lungCapacityField;
```

```
private string bloodSampleField;

private System.Nullable<System.DateTime> timestampField;

public ScreenResultScreenActivities() {
    this.bloodSampleField = "2 Vials";
}
```

 Keep in mind that any well thought-out limits on XML node occurrences won't cascade down into the .NET clients that call your service.

Element restrictions

The last set of schema attributes to evaluate is restrictions placed on XML nodes. I've updated our existing **ScreenResult** schema by changing the following:

- The failure screen reason will only accept an enumeration
- The **Notes** field has a maximum field length of 150 characters
- A regular expression pattern has been added to the **SubjectID** field that looks for two letters and five numbers

All of these element restrictions are set by clicking on a schema node and changing the **Derived By** value to **Restriction**. This opens up an array of new attributes that can be applied to the selected node:

```
- <xs:element name="ScreenResult">
 - <xs:complexType>
  - <xs:sequence>
     <xs:element name="TrialID" type="xs:string" />
   - <xs:element name="SubjectID">
    - <xs:simpleType>
     - <xs:restriction base="xs:string">
         <xs:pattern value="[A-Z]{2}[0-9]{5}" />
       </xs:restriction>
      </xs:simpleType>
     </xs:element>
   + <xs:element minOccurs="1" maxOccurs="5" name="ScreenActivities">
   - <xs:element name="ScreenResult">
    - <xs:complexType>
     - <xs:choice minOccurs="1">
       - <xs:element name="FailureScreen">
        - <xs:complexType>
         - <xs:sequence>
           - <xs:element name="Reason">
            - <xs:simpleType>
             - <xs:restriction base="xs:string">
                 <xs:enumeration value="Adverse event detected" />
                 <xs:enumeration value="Incomplete data" />
                 <xs:enumeration value="Data not recorded properly" />
               </xs:restriction>
```

Once more, we can rebuild our BizTalk project, redeploy it, and rerun the **BizTalk WCF Service Publishing Wizard**. As we would hope, the enumeration that existed in the schema node is cleanly translated to a .NET enumeration type in the service client. However, neither the field length restriction nor the regular expression pattern flowed down to the generated .NET classes.

Also note that BizTalk Server appears to support all of the capabilities of the XSD standard, even if they aren't always exposed by the schema designer. An example of this is unique constraints (read more on this at `https://adventuresinsidethemessagebox.wordpress.com/2013/06/14/adding-a-unique-constraint-to-your-biztalk-schemas-to-prevent-duplicates`). You'll find that there is no way to enforce a unique constraint in your schema via the schema designer; however, if you edit the XSD file using a text editor, you can adjust the schema in any way that is supported by the XSD standard and BizTalk will respect that. As with field length and pattern restrictions, you'll find that unique constraints do not cascade into your .NET generated classes either. Therefore, you will need to ensure that you enforce schema validation on the server side as there will be no enforcement of constraints such as the unique constraint on the client side. Note that it's never a good idea to rely purely on client proxy code for validation.

So what can we glean from this investigation into node validation? While .NET translates an impressive amount of XSD validation logic into its service client objects, there are clearly gaps in the concepts that get mapped across. This means that you should be cautious about building too much data validation into your schemas if you expect your clients to adhere to it. Also, going overboard and meticulously configuring each schema node only makes later modification that much more difficult. For instance, setting default values and adding enumerations are great, but what happens when a default value changes or new enumeration choices are needed? It may be better to actually avoid these types of tempting restrictions in the spirit of abstraction and loosely coupling service expectations from client requirements. If you do need to rely on complex schema validation, then it might be a good idea to document your constraints in a data dictionary or a message implementation guide that can be shared with service consumers.

Exploiting generic schemas

While I've been preaching so far about all the benefits and capabilities of structured schemas, there are real cases where you need to be exceedingly flexible in the way you take data in. You may want to open up an inbound on-ramp that takes any sort of message in and let the message bus figure out how to type it and route it. Otherwise a particular message type may have a portion that expects variable content and you wish to accommodate any XML structure.

First, let's look at how to make a part of a specific schema expect generic content and see what the resulting WCF service endpoint would look like. We can add generic placeholders to an XML schema through the use of the XSD *any* node type. There are two key attributes of the any node which dictate how the XML parser treats the content embedded here. The **Namespace** property can contain any of these values:

Value	Description
##any	The default value; this means that the XML content can be part of any document namespace.
##targetNamespace	XML content must be associated with the target namespace of the document.
##local	Data not associated with any namespace is allowed.
##other	XML content associated with another namespace besides the target.
List of values	Data can be associated with any of the comma separated namespace values.

You have a variety of choices for how to qualify the XML content with a namespace. However, the second attribute of the any node is just as vital as the namespace instruction. The **Process Contents** property specifies how an XML parser should evaluate the XML content in the any node:

Value	Description
Strict	The default value, this means that the parser will look at the namespace of the XML content and must find a corresponding schema for validation.
Lax	The parser tries to find the schema and validate the XML content, but if it fails, it won't raise an exception.
Skip	The parser ignores the XML content and does not try to validate it.

So, if you have a namespace value of ##any and **Process Contents** is set to **Skip**, you can send along virtually any XML structure you'd like. Of course, you may still want to provide a bit of verification by limiting the allowable namespaces or still requiring the BizTalk parser to find a schema that matches the generic payload.

I went ahead and changed our **Enrollment** schema by adding a new **SiteSpecificData** record, which has an **Any** element underneath it. If my solution simply took this content and crammed it into a database field for archival purposes, I could be confidently lazy and accept any namespace and skip schema validation on that generic node:

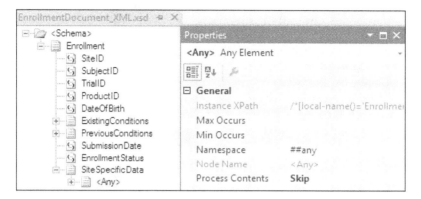

We can then publish this schema as a WCF endpoint and see how service consumers would interact with this open payload. The code in the auto-generated client object shows that the generic node expects nothing but an **XmlElement** object:

```
public partial class Enrollment{

        private string studyIDField;

        private string siteIDField;
        private string trialIDField;

        private Subject subjectField;

        private System.Xml.XmlElement siteSpecificDataField;
}
```

This is a fairly useful technique when you want to develop schemas that are expected to handle a variety of yet-unknown clients in the future.

The situation may also arise when you wish to make the entire payload of the service generic. That is, the service is capable of accepting any content, and the message bus is responsible for figuring out what to do with it. This is one situation where you cannot use the **Publish schemas as WCF service** option in the **BizTalk WCF Service Publishing Wizard**. You may recall my earlier statement that there is virtually no need to ever expose orchestration as services instead of exposing schemas. Well, here is that one fringe exception to that statement.

The **Publish schemas as WCF service** option of the **BizTalk WCF Service Publishing Wizard** always expects us to choose a schema from an existing assembly. We cannot choose simple types or generic types. Hence, we need to cheat and build a temporary orchestration that can force the wizard to build a service just how we want it. We start out by creating a new orchestration and adding a message of type **System.Xml.XmlDocument**. Next, we put a single **Receive** shape connected to a one-way logic receive port. The finished orchestration looks like this:

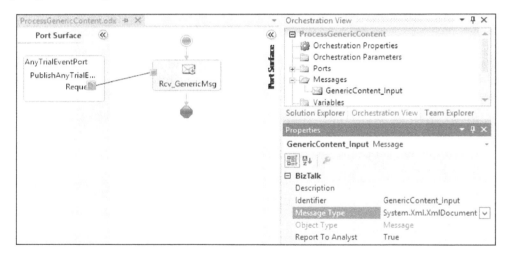

After deploying the updated solution, we should walk through the **BizTalk WCF Service Publishing Wizard** and choose to publish an orchestration port as a service:

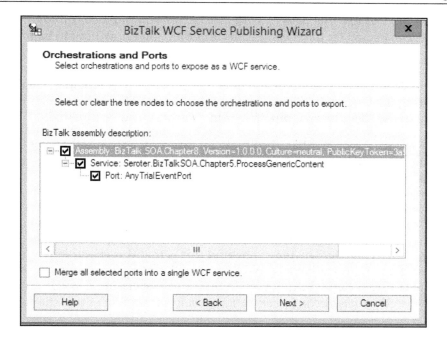

The WCF service reference in the client application defines a request message that accepts a generic object as its input:

```
public partial class PublishAnyTrialEventRequest {

    [MessageBodyMemberAttribute(Namespace="", Order=0)]
    public object part;

    public PublishAnyTrialEventRequest() {
    }

    public PublishAnyTrialEventRequest(object part) {
        this.part = part;
    }
}
```

Clearly you have to use this pattern with caution, as you must be confident that these messages are expected by the message bus and that you know how to handle each and every one that arrives. You must also consider validating incoming requests to ensure that clients aren't trying to inject messages into BizTalk that you would not expect them to. This can potentially be done by limiting what schemas are accepted by populating the Document Schemas property on the XML Disassembler pipeline component in the XMLReceive pipeline or in a custom receive pipeline.

Also, your service consumer has absolutely no direction as to the shape of the data that the service expects and must use some other means to inflate the request message. A message implementation guide would be almost necessary to satisfy such a scenario.

A final note is that you might find that the WSDL generated by BizTalk might not be as friendly and well-constructed as it would be if you published the WCF service based on schemas. The reason behind this is that this example was based on publishing an orchestration as a WCF Service. If you are implementing such a solution, do consider handcrafting your WSDL and associating it with your service as discussed in the *Constructing a contract-first endpoint* section of this chapter.

Service-oriented endpoint patterns

What can we do to make our endpoints as service-oriented as possible? We can retain our focus on reusability, abstraction, interoperability, and loose coupling in order to accomplish this. One way to do this is embrace data mapping and not be hamstrung by the idea that the bus should only accept a single canonical schema. If we don't force service callers to all implement a specific data format, we can instead grow our set of callers organically and bring on new clients with ease.

Building reusable receive ports

One key way to make our services as interoperable as possible is to offer a range of inbound transmission channels. While it would be ideal if all our service clients were running the latest versions of the .NET framework, in reality, we are frequently interacting with either dated or cross-platform service consumers. Also, while we may have all service consumers on the same platform, they may all define a particular data entity in slightly different ways. Let's look at how we'd accommodate each of these scenarios.

In this first scenario, consider an environment where our service callers each represent different vendors, and thus each have different service capabilities. One vendor has existing VPN access and is quite modern in their development framework and wants to use the TCP protocol. Another vendor is forced to go through a public Internet connection, and its service client only supports SOAP Basic Profile 1.1. As we've already discussed so far, neither of these considerations need to factor into the development of our BizTalk components. Let's assume we have a new schema that holds registration details for physicians wishing to administer a clinical trial for a new medicine. The corresponding orchestration takes in this physician registration message and processes it accordingly. Nothing in this orchestration has to influence which type of inbound receive channel we wish to use.

When this orchestration is deployed, we get to bond the logical receive port to the physical one. In this case, we have a single receive port but have the option of multiple receive locations. Each receive location corresponds to a different input mechanism, whether it be a classic FILE adapter or WCF channels such as HTTP or MSMQ. Given how easy it is to add new receiving endpoints, it is good form to offer multiple input channels that accommodate the widest range of consumers.

Now what if the physician registration message that my orchestration accepts was different than the format that each vendor had been transmitting for years prior? If I want the lowest service consumer impact, I'd want to let them send whatever format they use, and simply normalize it to the canonical format required by my orchestration. I have two real choices here:

- Create facade endpoints for each (new) service client so that each client has a strongly typed service to call. All of these facade endpoints can still be part of the same physical receive port, and maps are applied to get the data into a common format.

- Create a single, generic endpoint that onboards all registration messages and applies an assortment of maps to reshape the data into our common format.

Choosing the former option requires more maintenance for all parties, but follows better form. The latter option is quite flexible, but raises the risk of improperly formatted data reaching the bus.

So, when it comes to reusing receive ports, consider not only applying multiple receive locations but also adding multiple maps to accommodate a single receive location. A physical receive port offers a valuable level of abstraction to the message bus and any linked orchestrations so that we can control significant behavior at the outermost perimeter of the messaging infrastructure. We can use the same receive port over and over for a related process by simply standing up new input channels and applying new maps to the canonical format.

Constructing a contract-first endpoint

In *Chapter 3, Using WCE Services in BizTalk Server 2013*, we discussed the fact that BizTalk Server receive locations are inherently typeless; that is, they dictate no specific contract. While the BizTalk WCF Service Publishing Wizard does a fairly efficient job building metadata endpoints, there are simply cases where you want more control over the contract being exposed to service clients. Fortunately for us, the BizTalk WCF adapters do a nice job of allowing externally defined WSDL definitions to front the BizTalk endpoints.

In *Chapter 3, Using WCF Services in BizTalk Server 2013*, I alluded to the fact that you can technically host an HTTP-based WCF endpoint within the BizTalk in-process host; you don't have to use IIS. For the example we walk through here, I'll use that particular hosting pattern:

1. To legitimately do contract-first service development, you build a schema and WSDL file first and massage the resulting application to accommodate that contract definition. We can start out with a simple **SiteRegistration** schema, which provides all the details we need to associate a site with a particular clinical trial:

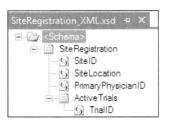

2. The next step is to create a basic WSDL, which uses this schema and defines the message exchange pattern and operations that our contract supports. My straightforward WSDL looks like this:

```
<?xml version="1.0" encoding="utf-8"?>
<wsdl:definitions name="HelloService"
  targetNamespace="http://BizTalk.SOA.Chapter8.ContractFirst"
 xmlns:wsdl="http://schemas.xmlsoap.org/wsdl/"
 xmlns:soap="http://schemas.xmlsoap.org/wsdl/soap/"
 xmlns:tns="http://BizTalk.SOA.Chapter8.ContractFirst"
 xmlns:xsd="http://www.w3.org/2001/XMLSchema">
 <!-- declare types-->
 <wsdl:types>
```

```
    <xsd:schema elementFormDefault="qualified" xmlns="http://
BizTalk.SOA.Chapter8.ContractFirst" targetNamespace="http://
BizTalk.SOA.Chapter8.ContractFirst">
    <xsd:element name="SiteRegistration">
      <xsd:complexType>
        <xsd:sequence>
          <xsd:element name="SiteID" type="xsd:string" />
          <xsd:element name="SiteLocation" type="xsd:string" />
          <xsd:element name="PrimaryPhysicianID" type="xsd:string"
/>
          <xsd:element name="ActiveTrials">
            <xsd:complexType>
              <xsd:sequence>
                <xsd:element minOccurs="0" maxOccurs="unbounded"
name="TrialID" type="xsd:string" />
              </xsd:sequence>
            </xsd:complexType>
          </xsd:element>
        </xsd:sequence>
      </xsd:complexType>
    </xsd:element>
  </xsd:schema>
  </wsdl:types>
<!-- declare messages-->
  <wsdl:message name="SiteRegistrationRequest">
    <wsdl:part name="part" element="tns:SiteRegistration" />
  </wsdl:message>
  <!-- decare port types-->
  <wsdl:portType name="CustomSiteRegistration_PortType">
    <wsdl:operation name="PublishSiteRegistration">
      <wsdl:input message="tns:SiteRegistrationRequest" />
    </wsdl:operation>
  </wsdl:portType>
  <!-- declare binding-->
  <wsdl:binding name="tns:CustomSiteRegistration_Binding" type="tn
s:CustomSiteRegistration_PortType">
    <soap:binding transport="http://schemas.xmlsoap.org/soap/
http"/>
    <wsdl:operation name="PublishSiteRegistration">
    <soap:operation soapAction="PublishSiteRegistration"
style="document"/>
      <wsdl:input>
```

```
          <soap:body use ="literal"/>
        </wsdl:input>
      </wsdl:operation>
    </wsdl:binding>
    <!-- declare service-->
    <wsdl:service name="CustomSiteRegistrationService">
      <wsdl:port binding="CustomSiteRegistration_Binding"
name="CustomSiteRegistration">
        <soap:address location="http://localhost:4044/
SiteRegistrationService"/>
      </wsdl:port>
    </wsdl:service>
  </wsdl:definitions>
```

While the BizTalk WCF Service Publishing Wizard produces a fairly clean WSDL file, we are clearly establishing more structural control by building these contracts by hand.

3. The next step is to switch to the **BizTalk Administration Console** and create a new one-way receive port/receive location combo. I've chosen the WCF-Custom adapter for the receive location, which means that the in-process, **BizTalkServerApplication** host is used:

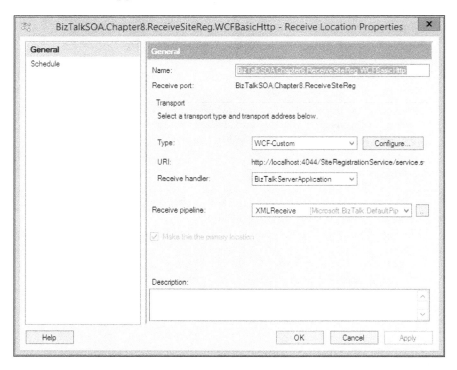

4. Now we need to configure this custom endpoint. Skip ahead to the Binding tab within the **WCF-Custom Transport Properties** window. I've decided that this custom WCF adapter will exploit the basicHTTP binding:

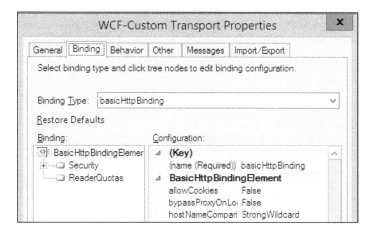

5. Now, we can switch back to the **General** tab and assign an HTTP address for this endpoint. I've chosen an arbitrary port number and URI (`http://localhost:4044/SiteRegistrationService/service.svc`) to represent this endpoint:

6. Finally, let's add a new behavior to this endpoint so that service clients can interrogate the WSDL. On the **Behavior** tab, we right-click the **Service Behavior** node and choose **Add Extension**. In the **Select Behavior Extension** window, we should choose the **serviceMetadata** entry. Then, we must be sure to flip the **serviceMetadata** property named **httpGetEnabled** to **True**. If you recall from our WCF discussion earlier, we use this behavior to explicitly turn metadata retrieval on and off:

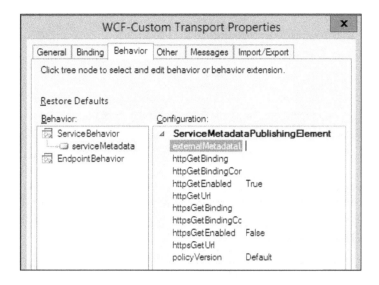

If we enable this receive location and browse to the chosen URL, we'll be presented with the standard WCF service description page.

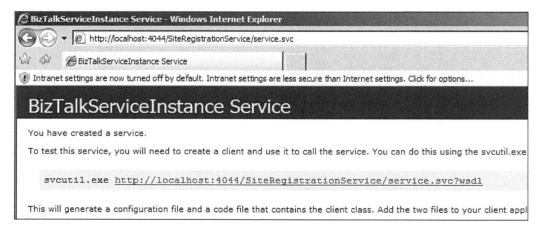

However, if we look at the available WSDL, we'll notice a generic BizTalkSubmit operation and no explicit schema. This makes sense because our receive location has absolutely no idea what type of data we plan on passing to it. Let's help it out, shall we? Go back to the receive location we created, open the adapter configuration window, switch to the **Behavior** tab and choose the **serviceMetadata** behavior listed there. This behavior has a property named **externalMetadataLocation** where we can specify which outside WSDL file should be a substitute for whatever the receive location would have generated on its own. I populated this property with the URL of my hand-built WSDL.

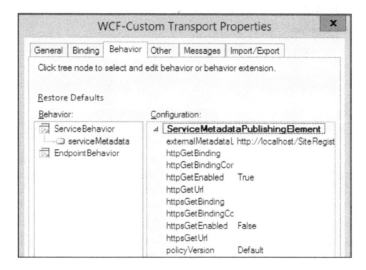

Pitfall

The WSDL file must be accessed through an HTTP or HTTPS channel by the adapter. If you try and point to a WSDL using a file system URI, the receive location will fail to start and throws an error. You can resolve this by placing the WSDL in an IIS web directory and referencing it there.

Another pitfall is that by using a handcrafted WSDL file, if you decide to make any binding changes on the receive location that you wish to be expressed in the WDSL you will have to update the WSDL file. This is in contrast to the auto-generated WSDLs which will always reflect the binding information of their associated receive locations. If you want more control over your auto generated WSDL, do consider making use of a WSDL Export Extension WCF behavior (see this article by Paolo Salvatori for more details: `http://blogs.msdn.com/b/paolos/archive/2009/05/22/how-to-throw-typed-fault-exceptions-from-orchestrations-published-as-wcf-services.aspx?PageIndex=2`).

Now if I browse this service again, I see that the custom WSDL file is served up instead of the auto-generated one:

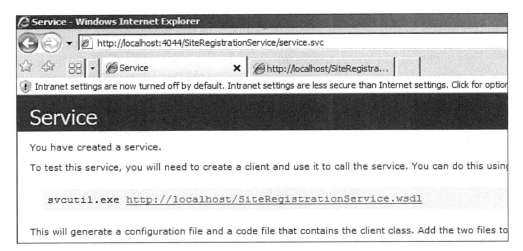

 Note that I could also use this pattern to accept generic content into my receive location and avoid the throwaway orchestration demonstrated in the previous section. Our custom-built WSDL could designate an arbitrary payload for our service operation.

This pattern demonstrates a clean way to attach type details to a WCF receive location in a very loosely coupled way. Note, however, that there is no practical reason to avoid hosting our services in IIS 8.0 and choosing the in-process hosting instead. The best part is that an endpoint hosted in IIS can still take advantage of the **externalMetadataLocation** property set in the corresponding receive location. Hence, this little trick isn't just for in-process hosting but, rather, is available to any WCF adapter in any hosting environment.

 Consider using the custom WCF adapters in all situations. In doing so, you get easy access to binding configurations and behaviors that are inaccessible from the transport-specific WCF adapters. Also, if you need to upgrade the capabilities of the port in the future, there is no need to create new ports and rebind existing processes.

Summary

Throughout this chapter, we looked at how to apply the basic SOA principles when designing our service schemas and inbound endpoint. Applying a level of forethought to our schema design prior to coding allows us to consider how our messaging solution should behave and how best to accommodate the current and future clients of our service.

In the next chapter, we will build upon these concepts and tackle the brave world of asynchronous messaging patterns.

9

Asynchronous Communication Patterns

The beauty of independence, departure, actions that rely on themselves.

– Walt Whitman

Arguably, the signature aspect of a service-oriented architecture based on messaging is the prevalence and embracing of the asynchronous message exchange pattern. In *Chapter 8, Schema and Endpoint Patterns*, we looked at how to construct practical schemas and design smart endpoints. Now we build upon those concepts and see how combining well-built messages and endpoints with an event-driven, asynchronous infrastructure can help us realize our aim of a loosely coupled architecture.

In this chapter, you will learn:

- The inherent value of asynchronous communication
- The patterns for implementing asynchronous processing in WCF solutions
- How to take advantage of asynchronous communication in BizTalk solutions
- Mechanisms for returning results from asynchronous operations
- The role of queue-based services

Why asynchronous communication matters

In earlier chapters, we discussed the benefits of chaining services together in an asynchronous fashion. I'm sure that for many developers, deciding upon asynchronous communication requires an enormous leap of faith. It feels much safer to simply make a linear series of synchronous calls where our client application only advances once we are assured that our message reached its destination. However, if you remain hesitant to about embracing asynchronous patterns, consider the wide range of benefits you will be missing out on. These benefits are as follows:

- **No client blocking**: By definition, a synchronous operation requires the caller to block and wait for the operation to return its expected response. The code can perform no other tasks. In an asynchronous model, the client engages in "fire-and-forget" behavior and relies on other mechanisms to determine any desired results from the service invocation.

- **Support for long-running processes**: This relates to the previous benefit, but it's worth flagging independently. When the client is freed from concerns of timeouts and blocking, they can safely trigger operations that take minutes or days to complete. A service invoked asynchronously can perform a variety of additional tasks when freed from the constraints of required responses.

- **Encourages event-driven, not procedural applications**: It's nearly impossible to build anything but linear applications when relying upon synchronous communication patterns. Call one service, wait for the result, and then call another. In an asynchronous world, both caller and services spawn events and rely less on strict procedural sequences, and instead, become more free-flowing in their processing.

- **Fewer operational dependencies**: This is a big one for me. If your solution utilizes a message bus, then applying asynchronous patterns means that you can engage in a very loosely-coupled relationship with the downstream recipients of your data. Experiencing a high burst of inbound data? No problem, as BizTalk Server will throw disproportionally more processing power at receiving messages than processing them. If no immediate response is expected, then BizTalk can gracefully scale down from a flood of requests. What if the downstream system is offline? Once again, this is of no real concern to the publisher because once they connect to the bus, they are no longer on the hook for handling infrastructure errors down the line.

Now, asynchronous programming isn't always easy, which is why it may not yet be part of your standard arsenal of patterns. Here are some challenges of asynchronous communication:

- **Building messages with required context**: When calling a series of synchronous operations on a stateful service, you have the luxury of the service retaining context of previous interactions. You can transmit small, discrete messages that only pertain to the current operation while knowing that the service can augment any gaps using knowledge retained from preceding calls. However, in a loosely-coupled, stateless, asynchronous environment, the messages need to encapsulate all the data needed by the service to handle independent service invocation.

- **Obtaining results to asynchronous calls**: Just because you execute a fire-and-forget function, it doesn't mean that you have no interest in the result of the service invocation. Even if the caller is able to obtain a result from the asynchronous service, they still need to determine the relevance of this message. What if the result came back after such a long period of time that a subsequent service call superseded it? Properly correlating relevant response events and data from the service back to the initiator can be a tricky concept fraught with opportunities to take a wrong turn.

- **Reliable delivery of data**: One of the most justified concerns regarding asynchronous programming is centered on reliability. When a developer calls a synchronous operation, they are able to proactively detect any infrastructure or service exceptions that may occur. The caller does not proceed until the service has completed its operation set. If you aspire to fully embrace asynchronous messaging patterns, then you will need to know that when you require reliability, it's there, and that any exceptions will be properly captured and handled by the service provider.

Throughout the remainder of this chapter, we will look at how to explicitly address these concerns and demonstrate ways to incorporate asynchronous patterns into your applications.

Using asynchronous services in WCF

WCF has support for both client-side and server-side asynchronous programming scenarios. By client-side programming, I mean that a service built with a request/response operation can appear asynchronous to the client. For example, let's look at a simple sequence diagram that shows what I mean:

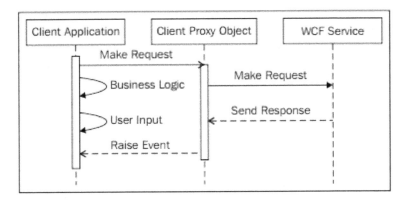

The WCF client proxy class is responsible for simulating the asynchronous communication, while the actual service still exposes only a synchronous operation. Let's look at an example of how we can physically create a client-side asynchronous experience in a WCF solution.

Creating the synchronous service

We start out by creating a new, empty Visual Studio 2012 solution. Then, we add a project of type WCF service library to the solution. This project type automatically adds an interface class, service class, and an application configuration file. I changed the interface class content so that it reflects the adverse event object that we will work with throughout this chapter. An adverse event is a patient experience with a drug that has caused them problems. My service interface (and corresponding data classes) now looks this:

```
[ServiceContract(Namespace="http://BizTalkSOA.Chapter9")]
public interface IAdverseEventSync
{
    [OperationContract]
    AdverseEventAction SubmitAdverseEvent(AdverseEvent NewAE);

}
```

```csharp
[DataContract(Namespace="http://BizTalkSOA.Chapter9")]
public class AdverseEvent
{
    [DataMember]
    public string Product { get; set; }
    [DataMember]
    public int PatientID { get; set; }
    [DataMember]
    public int PhysicianID { get; set; }
    [DataMember]
    public AECategoryType Category { get; set; }
    [DataMember]
    public DateTime DateStarted { get; set; }
    [DataMember]
    public ReportedByType ReportedBy { get; set; }
    [DataMember]
    public string Description { get; set; }
}

[DataContract(Namespace="http://BizTalkSOA.Chapter9")]
public class AdverseEventAction
{
    [DataMember]
    public string SubmissionID { get; set; }
    [DataMember]
    public string Product { get; set; }
    [DataMember]
    public int PatientID { get; set; }
    [DataMember]
    public bool doCeaseMedication { get; set; }
    [DataMember]
    public bool doReduceDosage { get; set; }
    [DataMember]
    public bool doAdmitHospital { get; set; }
    [DataMember]
    public bool doScheduleFollowup { get; set; }
    [DataMember]
    public string AdditionalNotes { get; set; }
}

[DataContract]
public enum AECategoryType
{
```

```
    [EnumMember]
    InjectionSoreness = 0,
    [EnumMember]
    Swelling = 1,
    [EnumMember]
    Headache = 2,
    [EnumMember]
    Bleeding = 3,
    [EnumMember]
    Sickness = 4,
    [EnumMember]
    Rash = 5,
    [EnumMember]
    Other = 6
}

[DataContract]
public enum ReportedByType
{
    [EnumMember]
    Patient = 0,
    [EnumMember]
    Physician = 1,
    [EnumMember]
    SalesRep = 2,
    [EnumMember]
    Other = 3
}
```

Note that we have a single, synchronous service operation defined. This operation accepts an adverse event and returns the resulting action that the submitter should take.

We now need an actual service implementation of this interface. In a separate class file, I have my very simple operation that looks like this:

```
public AdverseEventAction SubmitAdverseEvent(AdverseEvent NewAE)
{
  AdverseEventAction AEAction = new AdverseEventAction();
  AEAction.SubmissionID = Guid.NewGuid().ToString();
  AEAction.PatientID = NewAE.PatientID;
  AEAction.Product = NewAE.Product;
```

```
//initialize values
AEAction.doAdmitHospital = false;
AEAction.doCeaseMedication = false;
AEAction.doReduceDosage = false;
AEAction.doScheduleFollowup = false;
AEAction.AdditionalNotes = "";

TimeSpan aeDuration= DateTime.Now.Subtract(NewAE.DateStarted);

if (NewAE.Category == AECategoryType.InjectionSoreness &&
  aeDuration.Days > 3)
{
  AEAction.doReduceDosage = true;
}

return AEAction;
}
```

For this basic scenario, we will check whether someone is still experiencing soreness more than three days after a drug injection. Our next step is to actually host this WCF service, so that it is visible to the outside world. Up until now, we focused primarily on self-hosting, but I'm going to switch gears and take advantage of IIS 8.0 and **Windows Process Activation Services (WAS)** for hosting our WCF services.

Let's add a WCF Service Web Site project to our existing Visual Studio solution.

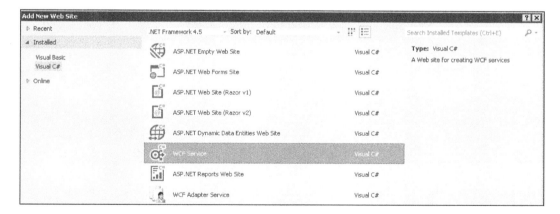

Once again, we are provided with some sample classes and implementation objects by this Visual Studio project type. We can freely delete the `Service1.cs` class files as we won't be putting actual service implementation logic into this host container. Next, we have to add a reference to our existing WCF service library project. After this, we change the directive at the top of the `Service.svc` file so that it points to the service type residing in our referenced library. This single line at the top should read as follows:

```
<%@ ServiceHost Language="C#" Debug="true"
  Service="BizTalkSOA.Chapter9.ServiceLibrary.
  AdverseEventSyncService" %>
```

Almost there. All that remains to do is use the WCF Service Configuration Editor under **Tools** to update the `web.config` file to accurately reflect our referenced service configuration. We only need to modify the service name and the endpoint contract.

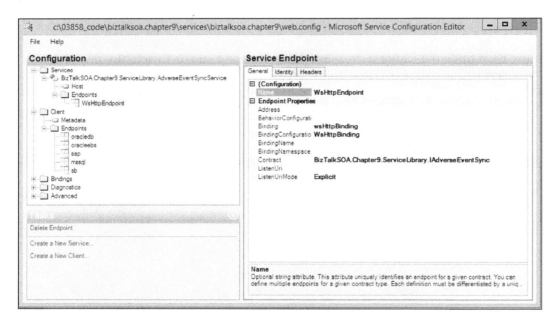

You may notice that we do not need to add either of the base address or service address in order for this service configuration to be complete. When a service is hosted within IIS 8.0, the base address is equal to the address of the `.svc` file.

We can confirm a successful configuration by opening IIS 8.0, locating our new service, and browsing the .svc file. You should see the standard WCF service introduction page.

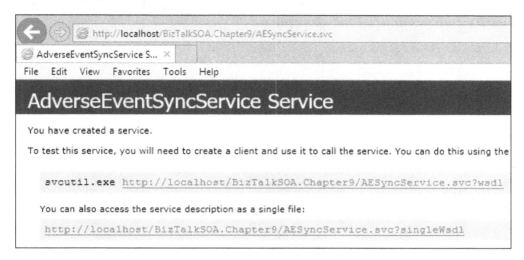

Building a client-side asynchronous experience

Now that our synchronous service is up and running, let's see how we can interact with it from the client perspective. Go ahead and add a new Console Application project to our existing Visual Studio solution. Right-click on the new project and choose to add a new Service Reference. After plugging in the URL of our IIS-hosted service, resist the temptation to immediately click on the **OK** button. Instead, let's visit the options we get after clicking the **Advanced** button.

Under the **Client** heading, notice a checkbox labeled **Allow generation of asynchronous operations**. Under this checkbox, you will find two radio options, one labeled **Generate task-based operations** and the other **Generate asynchronous operations**. To begin with, let's ensure that the checkbox is ticked, and let's select the **Generate asynchronous operations** option.

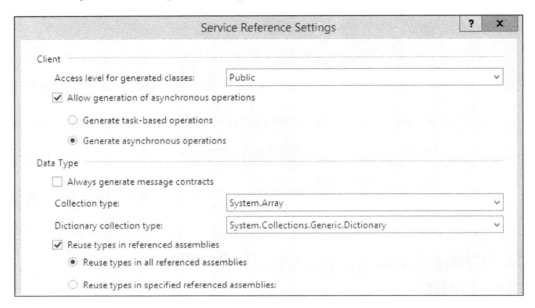

As a result of this wizard, we end up with a proxy class and application configuration files. Because I plan on using this same client application over and over again throughout this chapter, I've gone ahead and changed the **Name** attribute of the endpoint configuration in the application configuration file to something more descriptive such as AESyncEndpoint. Even though we checked the **Generate asynchronous operations** box earlier, absolutely nothing prevents us from calling this service in the traditional synchronous manner that it exposes. Such an example looks like this:

```
class Program
{
  static void Main(string[] args)
  {
      CallSyncServiceSync();

  }

  private static void CallSyncServiceSync()
    {
```

```
      Console.WriteLine("Calling sync service ...");
      AdverseEventSyncClient client =
        new AdverseEventSyncClient("AESyncEndpoint");
    try
      {
      AESyncServiceReference.AdverseEvent newAE =
        new AESyncServiceReference.AdverseEvent();

      newAE.PatientID = 100912;
      newAE.PhysicianID = 7543;
      newAE.Product = "Cerinob";
      newAE.ReportedBy =
        AESyncServiceReference.ReportedByType.Patient;
      newAE.Category = AESyncServiceReference.AECategoryType.
        InjectionSoreness;
      newAE.DateStarted = new DateTime(2008, 10, 29);

AESyncServiceReference.AdverseEventAction result =
  client.SubmitAdverseEvent(newAE);

Console.WriteLine("Service result returned ...");

Console.WriteLine("Should the patient reduce dosage? {0}",
  result.doReduceDosage.ToString());

client.Close();

Console.ReadLine();
      }
catch (System.ServiceModel.CommunicationException)
  { client.Abort(); }
  catch (System.TimeoutException) { client.Abort(); }
  catch (System.Exception) { client.Abort(); throw; }
}
```

As we discussed earlier, while there is no problem with this pattern per se, we limited the ability to do anything else until the emboldened statement returns a response. What if there is significant logic to determine the appropriate action for an adverse event? What if a nurse actually needs to review the event prior to disseminating a course of action?

There are a couple of ways to perform client-side asynchronous calls, but we'll start by detailing the legacy-style mechanism that was added back in .NET Framework 3.5. If we dig into the service reference's `Reference.cs` file, we will find a generated statement that reveals a new client-side event that was generated as a result of our choice to generate asynchronous operations when we first added the service reference.

```
public event System.EventHandler
  <SubmitAdverseEventCompletedEventArgs>
  SubmitAdverseEventCompleted;
```

Our client code can now register a handler for this event, and have it fire when the service response is eventually returned. The client no longer needs to wait until after executing the service request to continue processing other items. The client cod looks as follows:

```
class Program
{
  static void Main(string[] args)
  {
      //CallSyncServiceSync();
      CallSyncServiceAsync();
  }


  private static void CallSyncServiceAsync()
        {
  Console.WriteLine("Calling sync service (async) ...");
  AdverseEventSyncClient client = new AdverseEventSyncClient
    ("AESyncEndpoint");

    try
    {
      AESyncServiceReference.AdverseEvent newAE = new
        AESyncServiceReference.AdverseEvent();
      newAE.PatientID = 100912;
      newAE.PhysicianID = 7543;
      newAE.Product = "Cerinob";
```

```
    newAE.ReportedBy =
      AESyncServiceReference.ReportedByType.Patient;
    newAE.Category = AESyncServiceReference.AECategoryType.
      InjectionSoreness;
    newAE.DateStarted = new DateTime(2008, 10, 29);

    client.SubmitAdverseEventCompleted +=
      new EventHandler<SubmitAdverse
      EventCompletedEventArgs>
      (client_SubmitAdverseEventCompleted);

  client.SubmitAdverseEventAsync(newAE);

  client.Close();
  }
  catch (System.ServiceModel.CommunicationException)
    { client.Abort(); }
  catch (System.TimeoutException) { client.Abort(); }
  catch (System.Exception) { client.Abort(); throw; }

  for (int i = 0; i < 10; i++)
  {
  Console.WriteLine("Doing other important things ...");
  }
  Console.ReadLine();
}
static void client_SubmitAdverseEventCompleted
  (object sender, SubmitAdverseEventCompletedEventArgs e)
  {
    Console.WriteLine("Service result returned ...");

    Console.WriteLine("Should the patient reduce dosage? {0}",
      e.Result.doReduceDosage.ToString());

    Console.ReadLine();
  }
}
```

There are a number of interesting things to note here. Note that I registered a completed event handler, called the asynchronous version of the service operation, and closed my proxy class. Also note that the event handler has a strongly-typed argument that knows about the data members of my service result. This is the result of the client execution:

.NET Framework 4.5 greatly simplified the experience of creating asynchronous wrappers for WCF Services asynchronously through the introduction of the `async` and `await` keywords (note that these new functions are in no way relegated to WCF Service clients, and can be applied in any general .NET code). Through the usage of these keywords, you no longer need to worry about explicitly declaring events and event handlers; the resulting code looks a lot more like it would if you were writing regular synchronous code.

Taking advantage of this new functionality requires us to select the **Generate task-based operations** option in the service reference advanced menu when generating the service reference rather than the **Generate asynchronous operations** option that we chose previously. Note that you can't support the classic style of asynchronous programming as well as this new method at the same time. If you inspect the generated proxy code based on the service reference, you'll find that the `SubmitAdverseEventAsync` operation's signature is quite different, as shown here:

```
public System.Threading.Tasks.Task
    <BizTalkSOA.Chapter9.ServiceClient.
    AESyncTaskServiceReference.AdverseEventAction>
    SubmitAdverseEventAsync(BizTalkSOA.Chapter9.
    ServiceClient.AESyncTaskServiceReference.AdverseEvent NewAE) {
        return base.Channel.SubmitAdverseEventAsync(NewAE);
}
```

This method returns a `Task` object that wraps the response from the service operation rather than returning the response directly. Consuming the response is quite simple, as expressed here:

```
class Program
{
    static void Main(string[] args)
    {
        CallSyncServiceAsyncTask();

        for (int i = 0; i <= 10; i++)
        {
            Console.WriteLine
                ("Main thread counter - " + i.ToString());
                Thread.Sleep(1000);
        }

        Console.ReadLine();
    }

    private async static void CallSyncServiceAsyncTask()
    {
        Console.WriteLine("Calling sync service
            (async with Task) .");
        AESyncTaskServiceReference.AdverseEventSyncClient
            client = new AESyncTaskServiceReference.
            AdverseEventSyncClient();

        try
        {
            AESyncTaskServiceReference.
                AdverseEvent newAE = new
                AESyncTaskServiceReference.AdverseEvent();
            newAE.PatientID = 100912;
            newAE.PhysicianID = 7543;
            newAE.Product = "Cerinob";
            newAE.ReportedBy = AESyncTaskServiceReference.
                ReportedByType.Patient;
            newAE.Category = AESyncTaskServiceReference.
                AECategoryType.InjectionSoreness;
            newAE.DateStarted = new DateTime(2008, 10, 29);

            var result = await
                client.SubmitAdverseEventAsync(newAE);
```

```
            Console.WriteLine("Asynchronous (Task based)
              Service result returned ...");

            Console.WriteLine("Should the patient
              reduce dosage? {0}",
              result.doReduceDosage.ToString());
             client.Close();
        }
        catch (System.ServiceModel.CommunicationException)
          { client.Abort(); }
        catch (System.TimeoutException) { client.Abort(); }
        catch (System.Exception) { client.Abort(); throw; }
        }
    }
```

Note that in the preceding block of code, we have not had to engage in any tricky activities such as registering events and event handlers as we would have with more classic styles of asynchronous programming. As `CallSyncServiceAsyncTask` is marked as an asynchronous method (by virtue of the usage of the `await` keyword), the `Main` method will continue executing at the same time as the `CallSyncServiceAsyncTask` method executes, as demonstrated in the following screenshot:

```
 file:///c:/03858_code/BizTalkSOA.Chapter9/Projects/BizTalkSOA.Chapter9.Servic...
Calling sync service (async with Task) ...
Main thread counter - 0
Asynchronous (Task based) Service result returned ...
Should the patient reduce dosage? True
Main thread counter - 1
Main thread counter - 2
Main thread counter - 3
Main thread counter - 4
Main thread counter - 5
Main thread counter - 6
Main thread counter - 7
Main thread counter - 8
Main thread counter - 9
Main thread counter - 10
```

Be completely aware that these techniques only simulate asynchronous behavior on a natively synchronous service. You are still beholden to service timeouts and other characteristics of a typical synchronous execution.

Working with server-side asynchronous services

As I just mentioned, the previous technique is simply a way to call synchronous services in a non-blocking fashion. What if you want to design and expose a truly asynchronous service? This is quite an easy task in WCF. In our existing WCF service library project, I added a brand new class to hold the asynchronous service. This interface has the following definition:

```
[ServiceContract(Namespace = "http://BizTalkSOA.Chapter9")]
public interface IAdverseEventAsync
  {
      [OperationContract(IsOneWay=true)]
      void SubmitAdverseEvent(AdverseEvent NewAE);
  }
```

The IsOneWay attribute is the key to creating a truly asynchronous service.

 Having a service operation simply return void is not the same as making that operation asynchronous. While that may give the impression of exploiting a "fire-and-forget" pattern, in fact, the client executing the code is interacting with a request/response operation and, must still wait until the service completes before progressing further.

Next, we need a new service class that implements this interface. Once that is in place, we must revisit our WCF service host project and add a new .svc file whose directive points to our service class that we just created. All that's left is to update the web configuration file for the service host container by adding an entry for the new service.

This client application call is completely asynchronous. If I add a 30 second delay in the service implementation or throw an exception in the service code, the client will still move ahead immediately after the operation is invoked. However, the operation *does* wait until a successful connection to the server has been achieved and the appropriate HTTP 200 code is returned. Once the client is assured that service infrastructure is up and running, it will continue processing. Understand that this means that the caller has no real assurance that the operation has completed successfully; so this may not be appropriate for scenarios where critical data is passed or guarantees of once-only delivery are required.

Using asynchronous services in BizTalk with WCF

BizTalk Server natively promotes an asynchronous messaging pattern and readily embraces an event-driven architecture. What BizTalk adds to the standalone WCF patterns we've seen earlier is the injection of a message broker. This middle layer loosely couples the enterprise systems on both ends of the service call while enabling a new set of messaging capabilities not available in standard service implementations.

Consuming asynchronous services

Consuming asynchronous services from within BizTalk Server is an especially straightforward task. However, the huge caveat is that BizTalk Server 2013 cannot typically execute WCF services whose isOneWay flag is set to true. Wait, so doesn't that mean that BizTalk *does not* support asynchronous services? For me, it's a matter of perspective. BizTalk *can* still consume WCF services in an asynchronous manner from orchestration processes. Let's see how.

First, modify the existing IAdverseEventSync interface to include an operation that returns no data:

```
[OperationContract]
void UpdateAdverseEvent(AdverseEvent modifiedAE);
```

For my implementation of this service, I included a processing delay of 30 seconds, and wrote a message to the machine's Application Event Log afterwards. To ensure that our service host reflects this new operation, rebuild the service library and service host container projects.

Next, add a new BizTalk Server Project to the existing Visual Studio solution. Create a new schema that represents the canonical Adverse Event entity; mine looks like this:

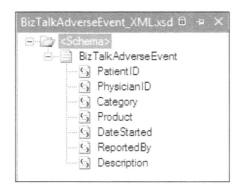

At this point, we need to reference the existing WCF service so that we can acquire the metadata necessary for BizTalk to consume it. Remember that we don't do **Add Service Reference** for BizTalk projects, but rather **Add Generated Items** and choose **Consume WCF Service**, as **Add Service Reference** will create a proxy class, whereas **Consume WCF Service** will generate the BizTalk artifacts.

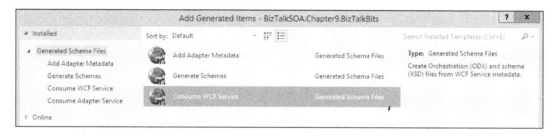

After plugging in the WCF service URL to the wizard, we end up with the schemas we are seeking. We will have to transform the Adverse Event data from the canonical format to the service-specific structure; so add a new BizTalk Map that performs this task.

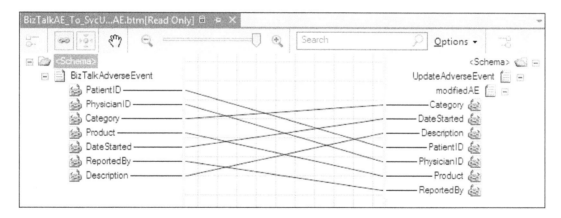

Finally, let's design an orchestration that takes in the canonical message, transforms it to the service format, calls the service, and writes a message to the machine's Application Event Log. The orchestration that I built is arranged like as follows:

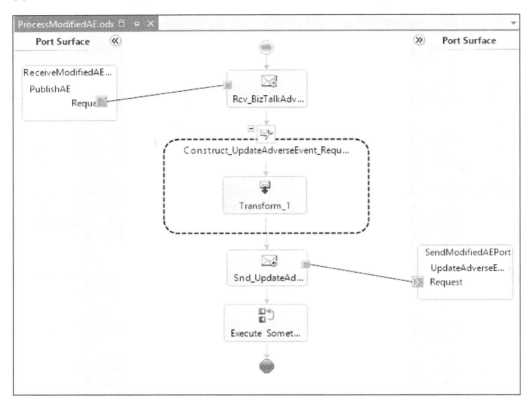

A key thing to note is that I created my own one-way orchestration send port because the orchestration port type autogenerated by the BizTalk WCF Service Consuming wizard is a two-way port that handles both the request message and empty response acknowledgement. In my case, I don't want to wait for the response and prefer to simply continue my workflow process. In essence, I am telling BizTalk Server to treat this service invocation asynchronously.

At this point, we can build and deploy the BizTalk project. In the BizTalk Administration Console, we create the receive port/location necessary to pick up the canonical schema format. As we decided to abandon the autogenerated type for our orchestration send port, the autogenerated bindings (which are also request/response) are equally unusable. So, we define a new static one-way send port that utilizes the WCF-WSHttp adapter. The values in this adapter configuration should match our service. This means that the address URI should match, the SOAP action should be properly set, and the security settings should be in sync with the service's expectations.

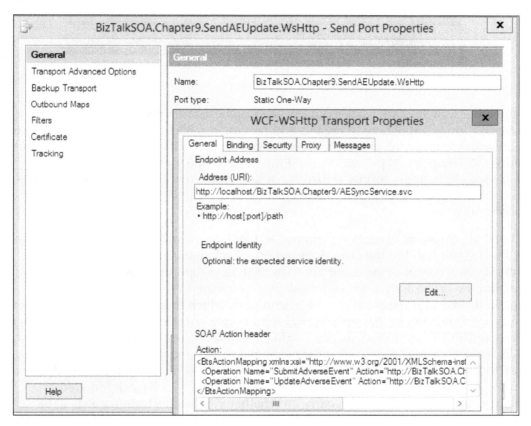

After binding the orchestration to the new ports and starting all relevant components, the solution can be tested. Remember that our synchronous service has a 30 second delay inside. So, if this orchestration behaves like a typical service client (that is, if it waits to proceed until the service completes), we should not expect to see the orchestration's final log message prior to the log message of the service. However, that's not what happens in the scenario that we just built. Testing what we built earlier, we can clearly see that the orchestration completes more than 30 seconds before the service finishes its processing.

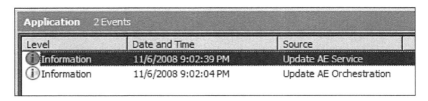

Remember how BizTalk works; our one-way orchestration port means that the orchestration is publishing to the bus and moving on. It's now up to the send port to successfully deliver the message. The send port still sees the service as synchronous and won't complete its processing (and thus deletes the message from the MessageBox) until the service returns its acknowledgement. The send port behaves in a "store and forward" fashion where the message is persisted until transmitted successfully.

What if we throw an exception from our service? By default, the send port message will be suspended, but the error does not flow back to the orchestration. The orchestration completes without knowing that an exception occurred. What if we *want* the orchestration to catch business exceptions? We could turn **Delivery Notification** on for the orchestration's send port, which means that the orchestration waits for confirmation that the physical send port successfully delivered its message. However, this doesn't work as you might expect, as the orchestration still progresses to its next step immediately after the message leaves the orchestration. The safest way for the orchestration to catch any service exception is to switch back to the request/response pattern and apply the **Scope** shapes, which catch targeted or general exceptions. So, do plan early on whether your orchestration needs to be aware of exceptions encountered while calling the service.

Exposing asynchronous services

Exposing BizTalk processes through asynchronous channels is also a clear-cut task. Once again, you cannot typically expose WCF services from BizTalk that have the `isOneWay` attribute set to `true`. There is no option in the BizTalk WCF Service Publishing Wizard to do so. However, because of the loosely-coupled nature of BizTalk's messaging engine, a straightforward void service behaves in a similar fashion to a true one-way service.

Let's start out with a very basic orchestration that takes in our canonical Adverse Event schema and then purposely causes an exception. In my case, I perform a "divide by zero" calculation. Note that one-way orchestration logical receive ports do not have the option to attach a Fault Message. On logical two-way ports, because we know the caller is expecting a response, we can define a specific fault message to return instead of the expected result data.

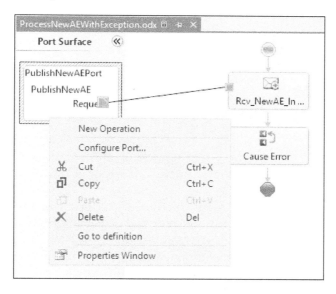

Once our BizTalk project is redeployed, we should walk through the BizTalk
WCF Service Publishing Wizard in order to produce a service on-ramp for this
orchestration. Construct a new service and endpoint for the WCF-WSHttp adapter
and manually assemble the service contract by choosing the **Publish schemas as
WCF service** option.

Now, this service is technically a request/response service. We can verify this by
looking at the resulting WSDL for the service and observing that our `PublishNewAE`
operation has both a request and response message. However, it is critical to
understand that as far as the service is concerned, its operation is completed when
the message reaches the `MessageBox`, not after (all) the subscribers are done with it.
Therefore, the service client only needs to wait until the message is published and is
not impacted by actions of downstream subscribers.

To prove this, all we have to do is call this service. Before we can do that, let's bind our orchestration to the receive port that was autogenerated by the BizTalk WCF Service Publishing Wizard. After starting the receive location and orchestration, we can reference this service from our client console application, which we built previously. Let's add a new Service Reference to the console application and point to the fresh WCF service we just built (if you so desire, nothing prevents you from choosing the advanced option of generating client-asynchronous proxy objects). We can call this service just like any other WCF service:

```
private static void CallBizTalkSyncService()
  {
    Console.WriteLine("Calling BizTalk sync service ...");
    AdverseEventServiceClient client =
      new AdverseEventServiceClient
    ("BizTalkAESyncEndpoint");

    try
    {
      BizTalkAdverseEvent newAE = new BizTalkAdverseEvent();
      newAE.PatientID = "100912";
      newAE.PhysicianID = "7543";
      newAE.Product = "Cerinob";
      newAE.ReportedBy = "Patient";
      newAE.Category = "Injection Soreness";
      newAE.DateStarted = new DateTime
        (2008, 10, 29).ToShortDateString();

      client.SubmitNewAdverseEvent(newAE);

      Console.WriteLine("Service result returned ...");

      client.Close();
      Console.ReadLine();
    }
    catch (System.ServiceModel.CommunicationException)
      { client.Abort(); }
    catch (System.TimeoutException) { client.Abort(); }
    catch (System.Exception) { client.Abort(); throw; }
  }
```

Sure enough, the service completes successfully, while the BizTalk Administration Console reveals a suspended orchestration resulting from the orchestration exception. So, if subscriber exceptions don't flow back to the client application, does it mean that nothing bubbles back to this WCF client as a result of an asynchronous service invocation? What you'll find is that any error encountered while physically publishing the message results in an exception flows back to the client. For instance, if the website hosting the service is unavailable, a receive location is offline, an exception is encountered in the receive pipeline or inbound map on the receive location, or no subscribers were found, then you will see that error in the client application. If a subscriber has any issue processing the message, then these errors stay local to the BizTalk Server.

So, while BizTalk does not expose truly asynchronous services, the fact that one-way service operations only extend to MessageBox publication means that, in essence, the messages are of a "fire-and-forget" fashion. How the messages are processed is not the concern of the publisher, and BizTalk shields the service caller from these details.

Getting results from asynchronous invocations

In many cases, the "fire-and-forget" nature of asynchronous communication may be applied only to prevent client blocking, not because there is no desire to find out the result of the service call. The options for retrieving service results depend heavily on the types of service clients and expected availability of both ends of the service transactions.

Ideally, you'd want your service client to be able to make outbound calls and also host inbound ones. This sort of solution where both the client and service can send messages to each other independently is called a duplex service. In this fashion, our client could makes an asynchronous call, and the service could delivers an out-of-band response event that the client would handle, accordingly. However, this approach is neither interoperable nor accommodating to clients and services that are online at different times.

A service designer who is most interested in supporting the widest range of consumers will offer both polling and service callback options. For the polling scenario, the service updates a repository that is agreed upon on completion, and it remains the client's responsibility to poll this repository to discover the service output. This repository can be a database, filesystem, queue, or even a URL in the case of the service building a "resource" as a completion output and the service client issuing RESTful calls for the said resource. Polling also works well in cases where we don't know whether both the service and client are online at the same time. By making use of an intermediary repository, the service can be unavailable, but its resulting output is residing in a location accessible by the client at any time.

The problem with polling is that it's both unpredictable and expensive. By unpredictable, I mean that the client cannot know whether the result will come back in one second, three seconds, or thirty seconds, and therefore must have an algorithm to poll at distinct times, and hope for the best. It's expensive because the client must inevitably waste processing cycles polling for something that may or may not return in a timely fashion. While not optimal for performance, this mechanism works well in cross-platform scenarios where providing generic access to shared repositories is straightforward.

Client callbacks are a solid choice when both the client and service are online simultaneously, and both ends of the service transaction use WCF as their service technology. WCF has hidden much of the complexity of this technique and exposed a powerful way to alert users to results of asynchronous processing.

Building WCF services that support client callbacks

WCF has rich support for client callbacks and efficiently handles service response events. What you need in order to support duplex patterns is a service contract that requires sessions, and one of the two available duplex bindings in WCF: NetTcpBinding and WSDualHttpBinding. Duplex bindings are designed for scenarios where you want to open a two-way communication between endpoints and potentially send numerous messages both ways. However, this technique also fits the bill if you simply want a single result returned from an asynchronous invocation. Let's take a look at how to set up this exchange pattern to accomplish the following scenario:

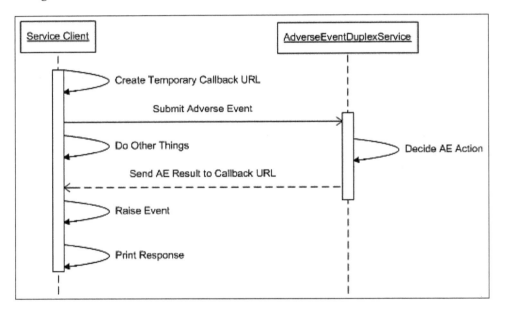

First of all, we need new service interfaces to accommodate our duplex scenario. Our first interface represents the service operation called by the client, and the second interface represents the client operation invoked by the service.

```
public interface IAdverseEventDuplex
{
    [OperationContract(IsOneWay = true)]
    void SubmitAdverseEvent(AdverseEvent NewAE);
}
public interface IAdverseEventDuplexCallback
{
```

```
    [OperationContract(IsOneWay=true)]
    void AEResult(AdverseEventAction aeAction);
}
```

Now that we have the interfaces, we need to decorate the primary service interface with the attributes necessary to support the WCF client callback capability. Specifically, we need to apply both a session requirement and callback contract to the service. The callback contract references an interface that must be implemented by the service client, as follows:

```
[ServiceContract(
  Namespace = "http://BizTalkSOA.Chapter9",
  SessionMode=SessionMode.Required,
  CallbackContract=typeof(IAdverseEventDuplexCallback))]
public interface IAdverseEventDuplex
{
  [OperationContract(IsOneWay = true)]
  void SubmitAdverseEvent(AdverseEvent NewAE);
}
```

Our subsequent service implements the IAdverseEventDuplex interface. Note that we extract the client's callback mechanism from the OperationContext object and then proceed to execute the client's AEResult function:

```
[ServiceBehavior(InstanceContextMode=
  InstanceContextMode.PerSession)]
public class AdverseEventDuplexService : IAdverseEventDuplex
{
  public void SubmitAdverseEvent(AdverseEvent NewAE)
  {
    System.Diagnostics.EventLog.WriteEntry
      ("Duplex Service", "New AE received");

    AdverseEventAction aeAction = new AdverseEventAction();
    aeAction.PatientID = NewAE.PatientID;
    aeAction.Product = NewAE.Product;
    aeAction.doAdmitHospital = true;
    //access callback object
    IAdverseEventDuplexCallback callback =
      OperationContext.Current.GetCallbackChannel
      <IAdverseEventDuplexCallback>();

    //sleep for two minutes
    Thread.Sleep(120000);

    callback.AEResult(aeAction);
  }
}
```

Now that we have a service implementation defined, we can add this to our existing WCF Service host container project. To do this, add a new .svc file and ensure that the service directive points to this new service class. Finally, we have to add a new service endpoint in the configuration file associated with this service. I used the WsDualHttpBinding so that we can see how to perform callbacks over the HTTP protocol. Our duplex service is now hosted by IIS 8.0 and available for browsing and execution.

On the client side, we need to create a class that implements the anticipated callback interface, and pass that class as context to the duplex service. First, we add a service reference to the duplex service hosted in IIS 8.0. Because this is a duplex service with a callback contract, the client proxy constructor now accepts an additional parameter:

```
public AdverseEventDuplexClient(
  InstanceContext callbackInstance, string
  endpointConfigurationName) :
base(callbackInstance, endpointConfigurationName) {}
```

Note that InstanceContext is now part of the constructor signature. This acts as the pointer that points back to the client object that will be executed when the callback occurs. In our client code, we need to first create a class that implements the callback interface we defined earlier.

```
class AECallbackHandler : IAdverseEventDuplexCallback
{
  public void AEResult(AdverseEventAction aeAction)
  {
    Console.WriteLine(
      "AE result for patient {0} says it is {1}
        that they should be admitted to a hospital",
      aeAction.PatientID,
      aeAction.doAdmitHospital.ToString());

    Console.ReadLine();
  }
}
```

At this point, we have all that we need to call our service and receive an asynchronous response. The code needed to execute our service operation looks like this:

```
private static void CallDuplexService()
  {
    Console.WriteLine("Calling duplex service ...");
```

```
//create instance context
InstanceContext context = new InstanceContext
    (new AECallbackHandler());
AdverseEventDuplexClient client =
    new AdverseEventDuplexClient(context, "AEDuplexEndpoint");
try
{
    AdverseEvent newAE = new AdverseEvent();

    newAE.PatientID = 100912;
    newAE.PhysicianID = 7543;
    newAE.Product = "Cerinob";
    newAE.ReportedBy = ReportedByType.Patient;
    newAE.Category = AECategoryType.InjectionSoreness;
    newAE.DateStarted = new DateTime(2008, 10, 29);

    client.SubmitAdverseEvent(newAE);

    Console.WriteLine("Doing other things ...");

    //Reader TODO; pick where to close this proxy AFTER callback
      is received
    //client.Close();

    Console.ReadLine();
}
catch (System.ServiceModel.CommunicationException)
    { client.Abort(); }
catch (System.TimeoutException) { client.Abort(); }
catch (System.Exception) { client.Abort(); throw; }
}
```

We created an `InstanceContext` object, which references our new `AECallbackHandler` class and passes that object into the proxy constructor. Once we execute our `SubmitAdverseEvent` operation (which if you recall has `isOneWay` set to `true`), we are free to do anything else we wish while waiting for the asynchronous response message.

What is happening behind the scenes? When using the `WsDualHttpBinding`, you actually end up with your service client briefly acting as a service host as well. That is, after you call the primary operation, a temporary endpoint is hosted by our client application. The HTTP address of this endpoint is passed along with the initial request so that the service knows where to send the response. We can demonstrate this technique in two ways. First, we can add an extended delay to our service implementation, which extends beyond the standard service timeout window. This proves that we are not making a pseudo-asynchronous call, which actually relies on a synchronous pattern. The second way to verify this concept is to turn on WCF diagnostics (applied by configuring the Diagnostics node of the client's configuration file via the WCF Service Configuration Editor) and watch the traffic that moves between the client and service. In fact, we can observe that our service request message has its temporary callback address stored in the `ReplyTo` node sent to the service.

Callbacks in WCF are a very powerful way to transmit data between clients and services in both directions.

BizTalk support for client callbacks

BizTalk has mixed support for WCF-based callbacks. On the receiving side, BizTalk does not have an explicit adapter for the `WsDualHttpBinding`, but does have "hidden" support for this WCF feature. When sending messages to services, BizTalk does not support duplex communication. However, there are mechanisms for mirroring this behavior as well.

First, let's look at the scenario where BizTalk is the service consumer. This is where BizTalk Server's capabilities shine and enable the most flexible and interoperable ways for services to send data back to calling clients. What are we really trying to accomplish? In essence, we want a service to tell the client that something happened well after the initial connection was concluded. In a straight WCF scenario, the core challenge is devising a way to transmit data in a non-client-blocking and WCF-compliant way. In the loosely-coupled, server-side BizTalk environment, we have two ways to retrieve data from services.

First off, BizTalk can call a service, get back a token, and then poll for changes stored within a repository, which is agreed upon. The token is needed so that we can poll for our unique result. Think of getting back a Federal Express tracking number when shipping a product and using that tracking number to poll their website for status updates. Within an orchestration, a loop can be set up to poll the repository (such as database, SOAP endpoint, RESTful HTTP resource) at an interval that is agreed upon, and only proceeds once the expected result is returned by the polling instance. This model is perfectly acceptable, but it does force the orchestration to wastefully poll when the repository has yet to be updated by the service.

The better way to receive callbacks into BizTalk is to rely on BizTalk adapters, which natively accept a "push" from the service. This can be a BizTalk WCF service endpoint, which is executed by the target service, or something more rudimentary such as BizTalk listening for a file or receiving an e-mail. In these cases, an orchestration is bound to this callback receive location and only proceeds once the data is absorbed by the BizTalk adapter. This provides BizTalk with a wide range of options to receive responses to asynchronous service invocation.

What about BizTalk Server 2013 acting as the service provider for others? In this case, we can also exploit all the native BizTalk adapters when sending callback information to client applications. For instance, a service client can instantiate a BizTalk orchestration and expect a response once the process is complete. Because the client does not know when BizTalk will finish the workflow, they want to exploit a transport mechanism that will reach them whether they are online or offline. In this case, the client puts an e-mail address in the request message header, and BizTalk utilizes dynamic send ports to send the expected e-mail acknowledgement once the long-running process is complete. You essentially have the entire BizTalk adapter stack at your disposal when choosing how to send notifications back to service clients.

How about actually using the WCF duplex bindings to receive messages into BizTalk and send a response later? On the surface, this doesn't seem particularly easy. There is no BizTalk adapter for the `WsDualHttpBinding`, and no way to define a callback contract in a receive location or orchestration. Nonetheless, it is indeed possible to apply the `WsDualHttpBinding` and get duplex behavior from BizTalk Server.

First of all, we need an orchestration that contains a request/response logical port. In my case, I designed an orchestration that takes in our adverse event message, waits for three minutes, and concludes by sending an acknowledgement message. Why the 3 minute wait? I want to ensure that we are not simply doing a synchronous behavior that looks asynchronous, so I'm using a time interval outside the boundaries of the standard service timeout.

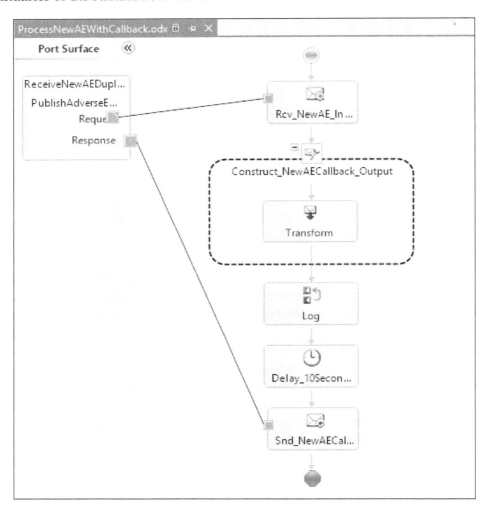

Once this orchestration is built and deployed, we next configure a physical request/ response receive port and location. The receive location should use the WCF-Custom adapter, which in turn applies the wsDualHttpBinding. By making use of this configuration, we are choosing to host our HTTP endpoint within the in-process BizTalk host service.

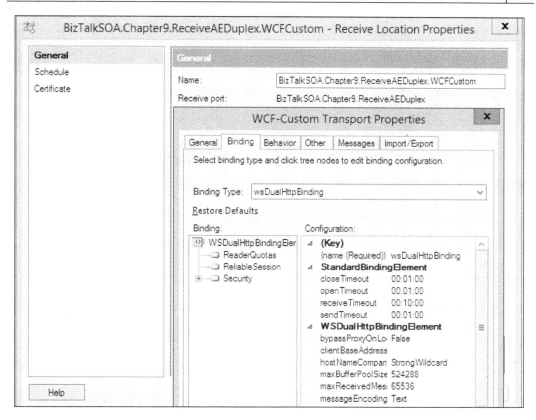

At this point, the BizTalk-based configuration is relatively complete. As I mentioned earlier, we don't have the ability to define the callback contract relationship within BizTalk. Also, the WSDL produced by the WCF-Custom receive location does not match the structure produced from a standard WCF service containing callback instructions. So what do we do? The easiest thing to do is define your own WCF contract that represents the BizTalk endpoint and messages.

First, we need data contract representations of the XSD messages circulating within BizTalk Server. Fortunately for us, WCF's svcutil.exe tool can take XSD schemas and generate corresponding WCF data contracts. For instance, the following command produces a class file corresponding to our adverse event schema:

```
svcutil BizTalkAdverseEvent_XML.xsd /dconly
```

Pitfall

The /dconly command in the svcutil.exe tool only works on schemas where the ElementFormDefault value is set to Qualified. Hence, this is yet another good reason to namespace qualify all of your BizTalk schemas.

Once we have class files for both our request and callback schemas, we next need the actual interface definition for the interaction. I defined one interface for the outbound request, and then a callback interface that handles the response from BizTalk.

```
[ServiceContract(
  Namespace= "http://BizTalkSOA.Chapter9.
    BizTalkBits.BizTalkAdverseEvent_XML",
  CallbackContract=typeof(IBizTalkAdverseEventDuplexCallback),
  SessionMode = SessionMode.Required)]
public interface IBizTalkAdverseEventDuplex
{
  [OperationContract(IsOneWay = true, Action =
    "PublishAdverseEvent")]
  void PublishAdverseEvent(BizTalkAdverseEvent
    BizTalkAdverseEvent);
}

public interface IBizTalkAdverseEventDuplexCallback
{
  [XmlSerializerFormat]
  [OperationContract(IsOneWay = true, Action =
    "PublishAdverseEventResponse")]
  void AEResult(BizTalkAdverseEventAction
    BizTalkAdverseEventAction);
}
```

What we have here is a typical service contract that supports callbacks. A few key items of note: first, the namespace applied to the service contract is the value used for the XML payload. Thus, I used the namespace value of the inbound schema. Secondly, the name of the parameter in the PublishAdverseEvent operation signature will be the name of the root node in the message. Hence, I chose to name the parameter after the data type to ensure a properly built schema. Thirdly, the callback operation requires the XmlSerializerFormat directive for its response from BizTalk. Without explicitly switching from the default DataContractSerializer, the callback parameter will not be properly interpreted. Finally, the SOAP action of the callback operation must be equal to the name of the initial operation with a Response suffix. So, which values in this contract do not matter to BizTalk? The interface names and operation names are completely irrelevant. Feel free to use values that best describe the interaction taking place.

Before we use this contract in our client code, we should set up the appropriate endpoint in the client application's configuration. In this case, our endpoint contract is the one constructed earlier, the binding is the `wsDualHttpBinding`, and the address should match the value specified by our in-process receive location.

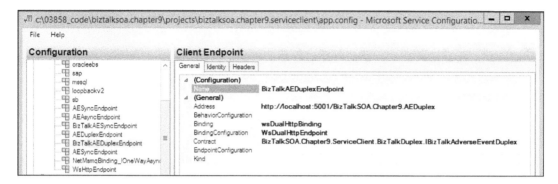

Now, we can dive into our client code. Because we don't have a proxy class available, we'll need to dive into the lower levels of WCF and interact directly with our channel. In this case, we capitalize on the `DuplexChannelFactory` object, which enables us to assign the instance context containing the callback object:

```
private static void BizTalkAEDuplexEndpoint()
{
    Console.WriteLine("Calling BizTalk duplex service ...");

    //create instance context
    InstanceContext context = new InstanceContext
      (new BizTalkAECallbackHandler());

    //need to use factory since don't have proxy available
    DuplexChannelFactory<IBizTalkAdverseEventDuplex> factory =
    new DuplexChannelFactory<IBizTalkAdverseEventDuplex>
    (context, "BizTalkAEDuplexEndpoint");
    IBizTalkAdverseEventDuplex channel =
      factory.CreateChannel();

    try
    {
      BizTalkAdverseEvent newAE =
      new BizTalkAdverseEvent();
      newAE.PatientID = "100912";
      newAE.PhysicianID = "7543";
      newAE.Product = "Cerinob";
```

```
newAE.ReportedBy = "Patient";
newAE.Category = "InjectionSoreness";
newAE.DateStarted = new DateTime
   (2008, 10, 29).ToShortDateString();
newAE.Description = "none";

channel.PublishAdverseEvent(newAE);

//Reader TODO; pick where to close this proxy
   AFTER callback is received
//((IClientChannel)channel).Close();
//factory.Close();

Console.WriteLine("Doing other things ...");
Console.ReadLine();
}
catch (System.ServiceModel.CommunicationException)
   { ((IClientChannel)channel).Abort(); }
catch (System.TimeoutException) {
   ((IClientChannel)channel).Abort(); }
catch (System.Exception) { ((IClientChannel)channel).
   Abort(); throw; }


}
```

Much like our earlier duplex example, we have a class
(BizTalkAECallbackHandler), which implements our callback contract and deals
with the operation invocation in the proper manner.

So is this it? Not quite. When we transmit a message from the client, our BizTalk
bus throws an exception. As we are not using WCF message contracts (which are
typically created by service references) but rather data contracts to make our request,
the payload is wrapped with the operation name (PublishAdverseEvent). The
problem is, BizTalk Server doesn't have any message type or subscriptions that
match the root value.

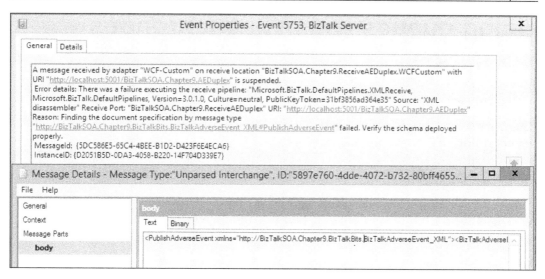

This is where a very handy WCF adapter capability comes to the rescue. If you can recall, the **Messages** tab of the adapter configuration enables us to specify where to find the body of the inbound message. Typically, we keep the default value of Body, which simply yanks out the structure contained in the SOAP message body element. For this situation, we need to dig a bit deeper and pull out the node beneath the SOAP body's root element. This is accomplished by setting the Path value, which in our case, looks like this:

```
/*[local-name()='PublishAdverseEvent']/*
   [local-name()='BizTalkAdverseEvent']
```

> Note that the parameter in this adapter is called Path and not XPath. This is on purpose. This XML search string only works in a forward fashion so the complete XPath universe is not available. That is, you cannot execute XPath commands that take a gander up and down the XML node tree.

With this change in place, we can now publish messages to BizTalk, and rely on the receive location to maintain the necessary duplex session while waiting for the orchestration to respond. While fairly hidden from public view, BizTalk does indeed support this interesting WCF binding and makes it possible to design rich callback scenarios between WCF service clients and BizTalk Server.

Using queues within asynchronous scenarios

Queue-based technology is an underrepresented but powerful way to exchange data and events between disconnected clients.

There are two technologies available within the Microsoft stack that provides an asynchronous message queuing mechanism: MSMQ and Azure Service Bus. MSMQ has been around since Windows NT4 and Windows 95 as a feature, while Azure Service Bus was released in 2012.

BizTalk Server supports both queuing mechanisms by providing dedicated adapters. MSMQ is supported using the WCF Adapter and using `netMsmqBindings`, while Azure Service Bus is supported by the new SB-Messaging adapter.

Why introduce yet another layer in your service communication? BizTalk has queuing logic, so what benefit do we get by having our service client send a message to an external queue that BizTalk acts upon?

First of all, you get delivery assurance in the case of the service being offline. As you are not travelling over an inherently unreliable transport such as HTTP, you can be confident that your message will arrive only once at its destination because of the intermediary queue. Also, a queue enables you to implement a level of soft throttling by allowing the queue to get pummeled by inbound requests but allows the service to process them at its leisure.

What we will demonstrate first is how to put MSMQ on both ends of a BizTalk solution. That is, the client application calls a BizTalk WCF endpoint that uses MSMQ as its transport, and when the processing is complete, BizTalk sends its concluding message to a service over an MSMQ channel.

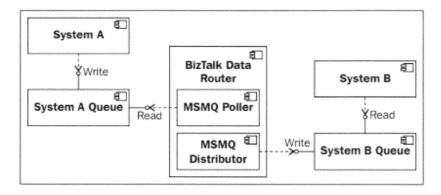

As with all other WCF bindings, the developer's interactions with MSMQ are fairly transparent and do not actively impact the client code. A developer does not need to understand any of the plumbing behind MSMQ and only needs to flip the appropriate binding switches to use the queuing transport.

Before building any BizTalk bits, how about we create the actual queues that our solution will use. To access the MSMQ panel in Windows Server 2012, we visit the **Computer Management**, expand the **Services and Applications** node, and highlight the `Messaging Queuing` node. Here, we can create two private transactional queues that will house our information while in transit between client and service.

Now we erect the terminating service, which publishes a final acknowledgement message to a dedicated queue. For our scenario, we have a customer satisfaction system that is interested in knowing when adverse events have been resolved. This system wants to send surveys to those who have interacted with our company and gauge their opinions of our efficiency. The first step to build our service is to build our interface contract. We will keep it fairly simple.

```
[ServiceContract(Namespace = "http://BizTalkSOA.Chapter9")]
public interface ISatisfactionSystem
{
    [OperationContract(IsOneWay = true)]
    void ProcessClosedAE(ClosedAE closedAE);
}


[DataContract(Namespace = "http://BizTalkSOA.Chapter9")]
public class ClosedAE
{
```

```
        [DataMember]
        public string AEID { get; set; }
        [DataMember]
        public string Product { get; set; }
        [DataMember]
        public string ResolutionDescription { get; set; }
        [DataMember]
        public DateTime CloseDate { get; set; }
}
```

I've highlighted the fact that service operations used on MSMQ service endpoints must be designated with a one-way messaging pattern. This is a rare example of endpoint selection playing a primary role in contract design.

 Earlier, I mentioned that BizTalk Server 2013 does not support truly asynchronous services that have their IsOneWay flag set to true. That's not entirely true. WCF service contracts associated with the MSMQ transport require that the IsOneWay flag is equal to true, and BizTalk readily supports this. Hence, unlike other WCF bindings, the MSMQ binding requires you to be aware of which transport you are planning to use when designing the contract.

Next, our contract needs to be implemented by an actual service. In this case, our service will simply write a notification in the machine's event log when a message has been received from the queue:

```
class SatisfactionSystemService : ISatisfactionSystem
{
    public void ProcessClosedAE(ClosedAE closedAE)
    {
        System.Diagnostics.EventLog.WriteEntry
          ("Satisfaction System Service",
          "Adverse Event Closed Event Received for case " +
          closedAE.AEID);
    }
}
```

Finally, we have to host our service. In this case, we can once again exploit our existing WCF Service project and add a new individual service (the .svc file) to it. After this is in place with the appropriate service directive, we simply need to append a new service endpoint in our configuration file.

The MSMQ service endpoint is configured using the `netMsmqBinding` with the path to the private queue as the service address. As we are hosting our service within IIS 8.0, we do not need a separate MEX endpoint for MSMQ, but rather, can simply apply a standard HTTP metadata behavior to our service.

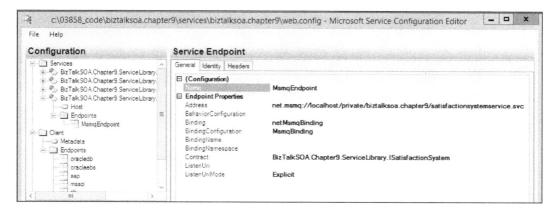

The final part of this service is the deployment. After building the service, we should confirm that the Net.Msmq Listener Adapter Windows service is running, as this is what WAS in IIS 8.0 uses to read from our queue.

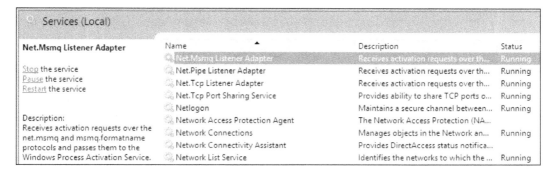

Lastly, we need to specifically enable the MSMQ protocol for our web application. This is accomplished by visiting the **Advanced Settings** of our application in IIS and ensuring that our Enabled Protocols contains both `http` and `net.msmq`. We can validate that our configuration is successful by visiting our service URL and seeing our service page displayed.

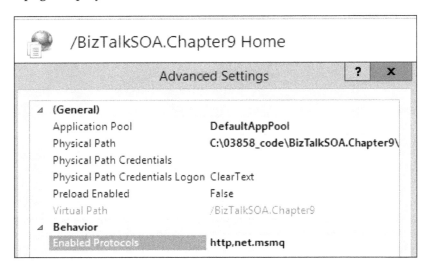

Let's get started with building the BizTalk pieces of our application. We start with a new event-style schema representing an adverse event that is considered "resolved" by the primary safety system. The schema contains a few key nodes, which explain the resolution information that the subscriber needs to update their system.

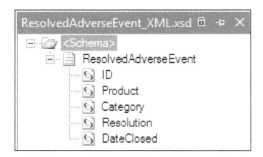

In order to get the artifacts necessary for BizTalk to consume this service, we should choose to **Add Generated Items** to our project, and then choose **Consume WCF Service**. Here, we point to the WSDL endpoint associated with our service and end up with the schemas and binding files we sought. We need to map our resolved adverse event from the format received by our service to the structure expected by our destination service.

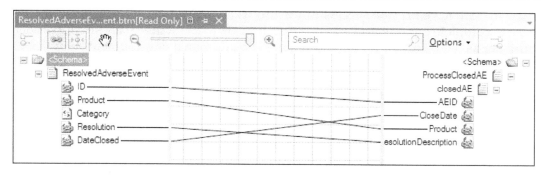

After building and deploying this sample, we need to assemble the necessary messaging ports from within the BizTalk Administration Console. First, import the binding generated by the BizTalk WCF Service Publishing Wizard to produce our concluding WCF-NetMsmq adapter send port. After adding both a "message-type"-based subscription and BizTalk map to the send port, we build a simple FILE receive location to test our destination service. To prove that BizTalk successfully publishes to the queue, we should turn off the IIS 8.0 application pool associated with our service so that the messages are not automatically extracted from the queue by the service. If everything is set up correctly, we should be able to pick up a message and see BizTalk drop it to the designated queue.

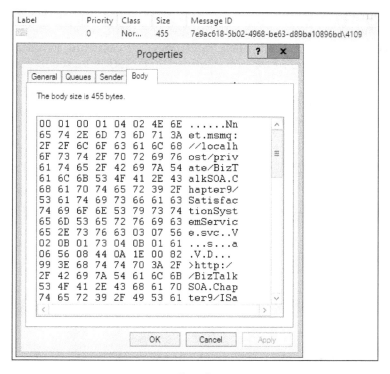

Now that we have BizTalk successfully acting as an MSMQ service consumer, it's time to complete our scenario and promote BizTalk to the status of an MSMQ service provider as well. Luckily for us, this requires no additional development activities. Instead, we can switch our inbound receive location from being FILE-based to WCF-NetMsmq-based. In this case, we configure the in-process adapter to point to the private queue created earlier in this section.

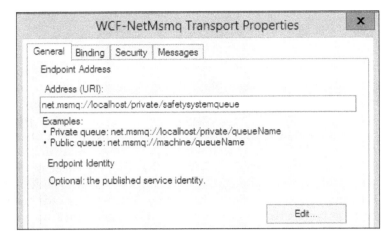

As we want our upstream service client to interrogate our BizTalk WCF endpoint for metadata, we should generate an IIS-hosted endpoint, which reveals our service contract. To do this, launch the BizTalk WCF Service Publishing Wizard and generate a metadata endpoint for our existing WCF-NetMsmq receive location:

Using the wizard, we want to expose a service with a one-way operation that will publish a message to the queue. If we are successful, a client application will be able to reference the MEX endpoint and import all the objects and configurations necessary to call the BizTalk hosted service. Remember that our MEX WSDL, while hosted as an HTTP endpoint, should show a service address that is MSMQ-based.

```
- <wsdl:service name="SatisfactionSystemService">
  - <wsdl:port name="MsmqEndpoint" binding="tns:MsmqEndpoint">
      <soap12:address location="net.msmq://localhost/private/satisfactionsystemqueue" />
    - <wsa10:EndpointReference>
        <wsa10:Address>net.msmq://localhost/private/satisfactionsystemqueue</wsa10:Address>
      </wsa10:EndpointReference>
  </wsdl:port>
</wsdl:service>
```

If you recall from earlier BizTalk + WCF discussions, we discovered that a BizTalk receive location needs to be in an **Enabled** status in order for the service to be online. Once again, MSMQ is an exception. As there is a layer between the client and BizTalk endpoint, our BizTalk receive location (or BizTalk itself!) can be offline, and the client application can still confidently distribute messages to the service. Once the BizTalk receive location returns to an active state, messages are read from the queue.

Now that we have successfully received and sent messages from MSMQ, we will now look at using Azure Service Bus queues. We will start by receiving messages from a queue and writing them to the filesystem using a BizTalk messaging only solution.

As the BizTalk SB-Message adapter requires ACS for authentication, we will need to create the namespace for the Azure Service Bus using a PowerShell script. This is because when creating the namespace using the Azure Portal, the only option available for authentication is SAS. To be able to create a namespace with ACS authentication enabled, we will need to resort to using the following PowerShell script for Azure:

```
New-AzureSBNamespace -Name <Your Namespace> -Location
  <Your Location> -CreateACSNamespace $true
  -NamespaceType Messaging
```

 The BizTalk SB-Messaging adapter does not support partitioned queues. When creating queues using the Quick Create option in the Azure Portal, partitioning is enabled by default. Instead, you must use Custom Create where you have the option to deselect partitioning.

Once the namespace has been created, we can now create two queues called `btsinbound` and `btsoutbound` using the Azure Portal, and select **Custom Create** to deselect the default **Enable Partitioning** setting.

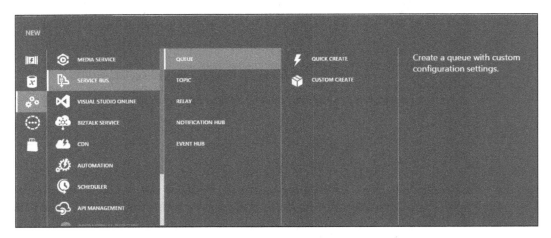

Once the queues have been created, we can now configure a BizTalk messaging only solution for receiving and sending messages to the Azure Service Bus Queues.

For the Receive Location, the URL is set to `sb://packtacs.servicebus.windows.net/btsoutbound`, and the send port destination URL is set to `sb://packtacs.servicebus.windows.net/btsinbound`.

Authentication for both receive and send adapters is set to the Azure Service Bus ACS credentials, as shown here:

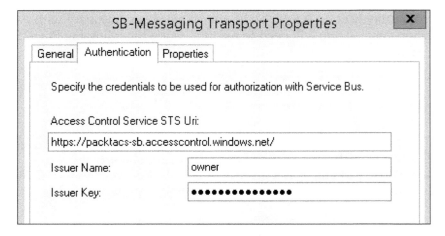

A simple console application is used to put messages onto the Azure Service Bus queue using the Azure Service Bus SDK:

```
private static void SendMsg()
    {
        Uri uri = ServiceBusEnvironment.CreateServiceUri
            ("sb", "packtacs", string.Empty);
        ServiceBusEnvironment.SystemConnectivity.Mode =
            ConnectivityMode.AutoDetect;
        TokenProvider tokenProvider =
            TokenProvider.CreateSharedAccessSignatureTokenProvider
            ("Writer", "3GZPtvOtFx1YgVjcMkkIqoshwvj28qVWmmAUXnMieg4=");

        MessagingFactory factory =
            MessagingFactory.Create(uri, tokenProvider);
        var customer = new CustomerEntity
        {
            Address1 = "Address line 1",
            Address2 = "Address line 2",
            CustomerNumber = 10034,
            FirstName = "Mahindra",
            LastName = "Morar"
        };

        //BrokeredMessage bm = new BrokeredMessage(customer);
        BrokeredMessage bm = new BrokeredMessage
            (customer, new DataContractSerializer
            (typeof(CustomerEntity)));

        MessageSender sender =
            factory.CreateMessageSender("btsoutbound");
        sender.Send(bm);
        factory.Close();
    }
```

When using the BrokeredMessage class to serialize a custom DataContract object, the default serialization encoding is binary. To serialize as XML, overload the constructor to use the DataContractSerializer, which will use text/xml serialization instead.

Running the console application will place a message in the btsoutbound queue. The BizTalk receive adapter will read the queue, and the send adapter subscribing to the receive port will write the message to a local folder.

Following is the serialized XML `CustomerEntity` received by the BizTalk SB-Messaging adapter:

```
<Customer xmlns="http://www.packt.com"
  xmlns:i="http://www.w3.org/2001/XMLSchema-
  instance"><Address1>Address line 1</Address1>
  <Address2>Address line 2</Address2>
  <CustomerNumber>10034</CustomerNumber>
  <FirstName>Mahindra</FirstName>
  <LastName>Morar</LastName>
</Customer>
```

This message is then copied to the file pickup folder of the receive adapter where a subscribing send port writes the message to an inbound Azure Service Bus queue. Another console application is used to read the messages sent to the inbound queue sent by BizTalk.

BizTalk has very strong support for MSMQ and Azure Service Bus. In scenarios with very disconnected clients possessing volatile uptime or specific throttling requirements, an intermediary queue offers a convenient way to reliably transfer data between systems.

Summary

Asynchronous patterns offer a valuable means for interacting with services. While synchronous services are very easy to use and excel at functions with immediate responses, these types of services also cause long-term scalability issues and require client blocking. Asynchronous services promote a more event-driven design, and the technological advances in callback mechanisms mean that we can embrace this pattern with confidence.

In this chapter, we saw how BizTalk Server 2013 exploits asynchronous messaging through its adapters and orchestration. Coming up next, we look at how to create rich, service-oriented orchestrations that can take advantage of the rich data flowing through the BizTalk bus.

10
Orchestration Patterns

No one can whistle a symphony. It takes a whole orchestra to play it.

– Halford E. Luccock

So far, we've looked at how to use BizTalk Server to design both, service endpoints and contracts, as well as exploit the powerful BizTalk messaging bus to support asynchronous messaging patterns. Now it's time to investigate how to incorporate service implementation patterns using BizTalk Server's orchestration engine. While an optional component of any BizTalk solution, orchestration enables a rich set of scenarios that messaging-only solutions are incapable of accommodating. As with the previous chapters in this book, this discussion will assume a base knowledge of BizTalk orchestration so that we can jump right into the implementation of occasionally complex concepts.

In this chapter, you will learn:

- Why orchestration matters
- What it means for an orchestration to utilize "MessageBox direct binding"
- How to build message-type-agnostic orchestrations
- How to take advantage of dynamic service ports
- The way to support multiple initiating message exchange patterns from within a single orchestration
- How to chain orchestrations together in a loosely coupled fashion
- The role of orchestration transactions in compensating service exceptions

Why orchestration?

At its core, orchestration is an executable business process that acts upon messages passing through the service bus. In the BizTalk world, orchestration has both a design-time and runtime aspect. At design time, a developer uses a predefined palette of activities, which are linked together to form a business process. The runtime orchestration engine is a server service that coordinates all aspects of orchestration execution, ranging from starting up and terminating orchestrations to load balancing and monitoring the orchestration processing health.

In many cases, a purely messaging-oriented solution is exactly what our situation calls for. However, we often need the flexibility to introduce a long-running, stateful interception of messages which may contain business logic, control flow, data processing, aggregation, exception handling, and transactions. This is the value of orchestration. What is the value of orchestration in a service-oriented architecture? Let's look at some of the key value-addition scenarios:

- **Service abstraction**: One of the greatest ways to exploit orchestration is to create new services by aggregating existing ones. Instead of requiring clients to call a chained series of system services in order to accomplish an overarching business task, we can create an orchestration that provides a single interface to the clients and orchestrates the set of system services itself. Even if there is only a single system service, we can use orchestration to provide a more abstract and generic interface that hides system-specific service details.

- **Orchestration as a service**: Business processes can be decomposed from large flows to more modular, reusable bits. Instead of creating a monolithic orchestration that rigidly enforces a complex business process, we can look for opportunities to break that process apart and, in essence, create new orchestration "services" that perform encapsulated, discrete tasks. These orchestrations can be reused by other processes or service interfaces, thus maximizing our investment in process modelling.

- **Orchestration containing process, not logic**: It may be tempting to enclose logical calculations alongside the process flow that makes up an orchestration. However, orchestration is not a replacement for writing services and components that perform business algorithms. We should treat orchestration as the coordinator of a process, not as the origin of all information needed by the process. This means that flow control calculations should be externalized in segmented locations such as the **Business Rules Engine** (**BRE**), external services, or custom-built components, whenever possible. An orchestration isn't yet another place to stash code but rather a mechanism for executing agile business processes. However, a case may arise where a bit of business logic is appropriate in an orchestration, so don't treat this pronouncement as a hard-and-fast rule but rather as a broad recommendation!

What is MessageBox direct binding?

The easiest way to link orchestration with messaging endpoints is to create logical ports in orchestrations and bind them to physical ports at runtime. A developer using this technique will know for sure that an orchestration will exchange messages with the appropriate ports. However, this mechanism of orchestration communication is more point-to-point oriented than event driven. What if relevant messages for an orchestration could arrive via multiple receive ports? Or how about trying to anticipate all the possible parties interested in a message that your orchestration is sending out?

The tight coupling produced by binding orchestration ports to physical ports is not the most service-oriented way to design orchestration communication. Instead, MessageBox direct binding is the cleanest way to sever the one-to-one relationship between the messaging and orchestration architectural layers. The way it works is that the "activating" receive shape that instantiates the orchestration maintains a subscription based on the message type in combination with any "filter" applied to the receive shape. Any message that hits the MessageBox and meets this subscription criterion will get delivered to this orchestration. For any "non-activating" receive shape (such as receive shapes present elsewhere in the orchestration), the subscription is based on the message type and a correlation set made up of additional subscription attributes.

The greatest benefit of this technique is that orchestrations can absorb messages that match specific data criteria instead of focusing on the data publisher. When we send messages on MessageBox direct bound ports, we get the benefit of broadcasting messages without identifying an individual target. As we'll see later in this chapter, there are cases where you want to use MessageBox direct binding but still need to target a specific consumer and this is entirely possible.

How do you apply `MessageBox` direct binding? While creating a new logical receive port in an orchestration, you get the option of choosing a target binding. In the book so far, we've typically used a **Specify later** binding, which allows us to hook up logical and physical ports at deployment time. However, note that we also have the option to choose **Direct** binding from this orchestration port creation wizard.

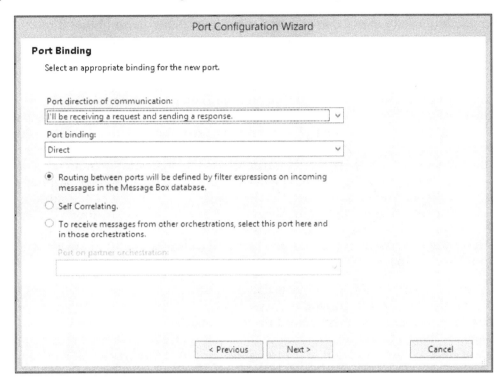

While creating a logical send port in an orchestration, the experience is similar to that while choosing direct binding. The difference here is that the filters will now need to be applied on the send ports that messages should be routed to.

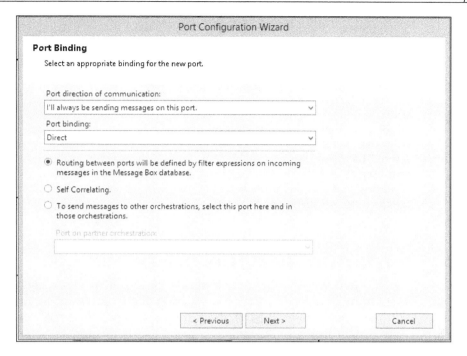

For orchestrations that use direct bound ports, you will see a much different "binding" view in the BizTalk Administration Console. Specifically, you'll notice that there are no ports to bind! The only activity required is the binding of the orchestration to a specific host.

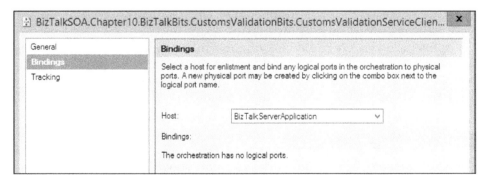

Throughout this chapter, we'll make heavy use of `MessageBox` direct bound ports in order to demonstrate this technique in a variety of scenarios.

Pitfall

What's the downside of `MessageBox` direct bound ports? For one, careless usage can lead to unanticipated messages reaching your orchestration, or worse, infinite loops. Consider an "activating" receive, which is direct bound solely on the message type (that is, no additional filter is applied). If you decide to send this same message out of your orchestration later on (via any type of port binding), you will unexpectedly find that this original orchestration starts up all over again! The proper application of direct binding requires forethought of subscription criteria and situational modelling of instantiation scenarios, and you will often need to provide much more specific filter criteria than just the message type.

Using dynamic service ports

In all the BizTalk solutions we've built so far in this book, the focus was on static ports with URIs set immediately after the code was deployed. However, there exist a number of legitimate cases where BizTalk does not know where to distribute a message until additional runtime-only context is provided. For example, when you configure a send port with an SMTP adapter in BizTalk Server, you are required to explicitly provide the recipient's email address. Any time this port is invoked, that particular email address is applied. But what if the corresponding message could be emailed to any of a number of addresses? You could choose to set up a series of static send ports and summon each one individually, based on decision logic from the orchestration. However, this is not a particularly flexible mechanism as it requires changes to the orchestration whenever an email target is added or removed. A better strategy is to apply dynamic ports and perform a runtime query of the endpoint address. We could look up the e-mail recipient (via Business Rules, custom component, message value) and set that value in a single spot within the orchestration. When changes to the recipient list are necessary, the only thing that must undergo a change is the user lookup mechanism and not the orchestration itself.

Defining the service

Let's demonstrate how this would work in a situation with services. As we saw in the previous chapter on asynchronous programming, a service client may invoke a service and expect a response well after the initial connection has been closed. To truly be loosely coupled and support multiple callers, our solution should not hard-code the return address of the service inside the invoked orchestration. Instead, to encourage reusability, this orchestration should extract a `reply to` value from the message itself and dynamically set the return destination that it will use.

For this scenario, BizTalk will accept data in, process it, and send a notification to an awaiting service when processing is complete. Our first step is to define these services that are anticipating a message from BizTalk. There is a simple contract, which expects a status update to be sent to the service endpoint.

```
[ServiceContract (Namespace="http://BizTalkSOA.Chapter10")]
public interface IAdverseEvent {
  [OperationContract]
  void UpdateAEStatus(AdverseEventStatus status);
}

[DataContract]
public class AdverseEventStatus {
  [DataMember]
  public string AE_ID { get; set; }
  [DataMember]
  public AEStatusCode StatusCode { get; set; }
  [DataMember]
  public string Comments { get; set; }
}

public enum AEStatusCode {
  Received,
  Pending,
  DataError,
  InReview,
  Resolved
}
```

I've gone ahead and created a pair of service classes that implement this interface and write differing messages to the machine's **Application Event Log**. Please note that the **Application Event Log** is only being used in this example for demonstration purposes and would not be the typical choice for such tracking; do consider CAT tracing or BAM tracking or an equivalent tracking solution for real life scenarios.

```
public class AdverseEventService : IAdverseEvent {
  public void UpdateAEStatus(AdverseEventStatus status) {
    EventLog.WriteEntry(
    "AE Client Application #1 (HTTP)",
    "Status for AE " + status.AE_ID + " is " +
    status.StatusCode.ToString());
  }
}
```

Next, we need to create a **WCF Service** website project in Visual Studio and define a pair of .svc files whose Service directive points to the service class(es) we just created. Our new service requires a valid application configuration, so I created service definitions that utilized an HTTP endpoint for one service and a **NetTcpBinding** endpoint for the other. We do not need to specify an address (or base address) for our services when they are hosted by IIS 7.0 or higher as these will be automatically resolved for us based on our website bindings. I also added a metadata behavior to both so that BizTalk can interrogate the service for its contract.

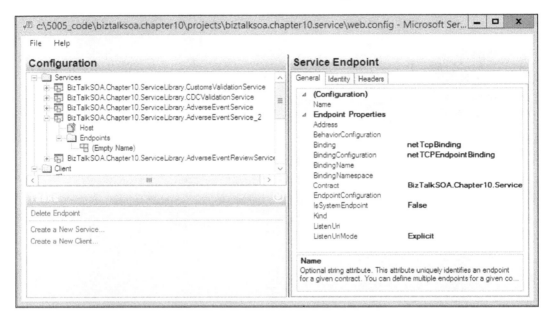

Configuring IIS/WAS to host the service

Once our service has been successfully built, we have to remember to add the **NetTcp** protocol to the IIS web directory. Remember that we do this by viewing the **Advanced Settings** of our virtual directory and setting **Enabled Protocols** to the desired values.

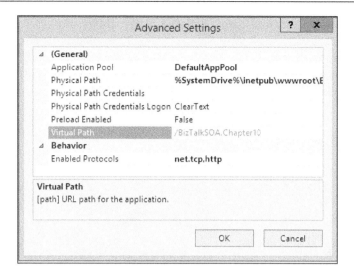

Building the BizTalk solution

Once these services are in place, we should next build the actual message that our BizTalk process will accept. Throughout this chapter, I will be using a modified version of the **Adverse Event** message we created in *Chapter 9, Asynchronous Communication Patterns*. This version of the message is structured as so:

For this scenario, I've designed a new schema (`BizTalkAdverseEventWithCallback`) that includes the `BizTalkAdverseEvent` schema. This schema is comprised of a `Header` and `Message` element. The `Header` is made up of values BizTalk requires to successfully execute a callback, while the `Message` record is made up of the included `BizTalkAdverseEvent` schema.

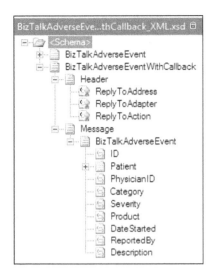

Note that I've distinguished the `Header` fields so that I can easily extract them from within my orchestration. Now we're ready to build an orchestration that takes in this message and sends a response to the service interface specified in the message header.

After accepting the initial `BizTalkAdverseEventWithCallback` message into the orchestration, we next set a series of orchestration variables equal to the callback attributes present in the inbound message.

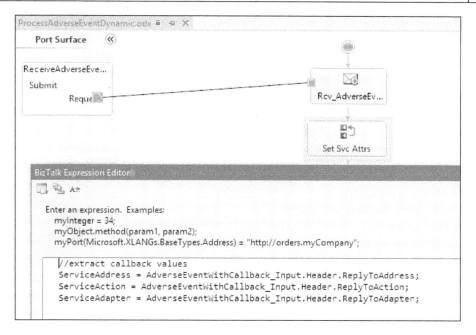

Before we can continue, we must auto-generate the items needed to call the service. Now, because every destination service will conform to the single WCF contract, we can point to either of the two services we built, get the service schema, and be confident that we can send this message to any possible endpoint that applies the same service contract. We utilize the **BizTalk WCF Service Consuming Wizard** to query our service and extract the necessary files. Once we have our schema generated, we should distinguish the StatusCode element so that we are able to set its value from within the orchestration itself.

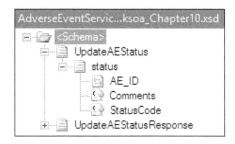

A BizTalk map is required in order to instantiate this service response message. In our case, we only need to map the ID of the adverse event from the source schema to the destination.

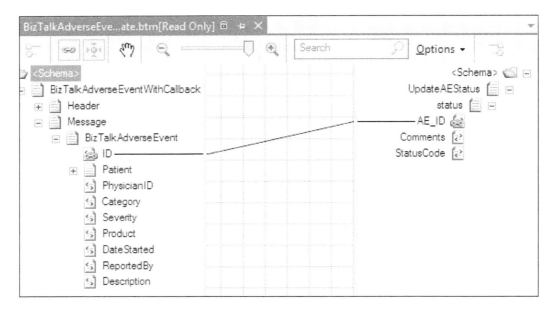

Back in our orchestration, we drop the **Construct, Transform**, and **Assignment** shapes onto the design surface. Directly below that trifecta, we should add a **Send** shape, which will be responsible for sending our service response message. Before configuring our message construction operations, we need to create the one-way dynamic port that the orchestration will use to transmit the final message. Add a new configured port to the orchestration and on the **Port Binding** tab of the wizard, our direction should be set to **I'll always be sending messages on this port** and the port binding set to **Dynamic**. When you have a dynamic port in an orchestration, you are expected to set the address of the endpoint before the port is executed.

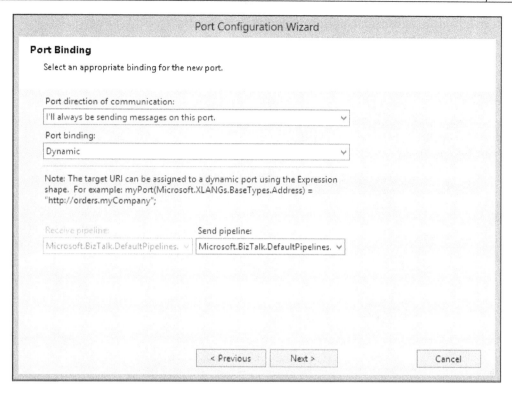

Returning to our **Construct** shape, we set the **Message Constructed** property of the **Construct** shape equal to a message of the type of the service response. Within the **Transform** shape, we pick the map we just created. The real fun begins in the **Assignment** shape, which is used to set the relevant transport details for the dynamic send port, which is directly below the **Transform** shape. Here I first set the StatusCode element of the outbound message and set four critical context attributes. First, we set WCF-specific attributes WCF.Action and WCF.SecurityMode to values that match the service endpoint. Next, we set transport-specific attributes, including the actual endpoint address and which adapter BizTalk should use.

```
AdverseEventStatus_Output.parameters.status.StatusCode =
  "Received";
//ServiceAction is the orchestration variable
AdverseEventStatus_Output(WCF.Action) = ServiceAction;
AdverseEventStatus_Output(WCF.SecurityMode) = "None";

//uses orchestration variables
SendDynamicAEStatusUpdatePort(Microsoft.XLANGs.BaseTypes.Address)
= ServiceAddress;
SendDynamicAEStatusUpdatePort(Microsoft.XLANGs.BaseTypes.Transport
Type) = ServiceAdapter;
```

You may not be as familiar with setting the `Microsoft.XLANGs.BaseTypes.TransportType` attribute as, typically, dynamic port adapters are determined based on the prefix contained in the endpoint URI. For instance, setting the `Microsoft.XLANGs.BaseTypes.Address` to `FILE://C:\temp` or `mailto:user@domain.com` enables BizTalk to automatically determine which adapter to use (in this example, FILE and SMTP). For HTTP-based endpoints, simply prefixing a URI with `http://localhost/MyService` does not specify which adapter (SOAP, HTTP, or WCF) should be applied. Hence, we explicitly added a directive to help BizTalk choose the proper endpoint adapter.

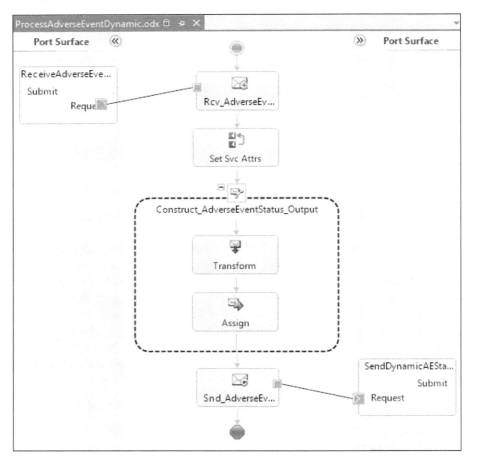

Configuring the BizTalk solution

Once our BizTalk project is completed (including the addition of an orchestration receive port to accept inbound messages), we deploy it. During the deployment process, a new, auto-generated dynamic send port is created. We should confirm this by visiting the **Send Ports** section of our application in the BizTalk Administration Console.

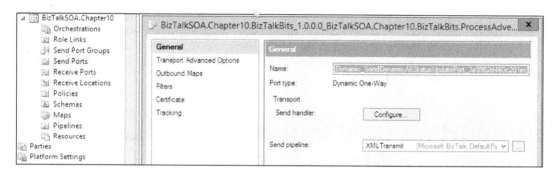

After creating a valid input receive location, we should send instance files into our orchestration and confirm that our two different service endpoints get called, depending on the header values of the input message. Sending in multiple instance files (two with HTTP callbacks and one with a TCP callback address) yields the following result in my Event Log:

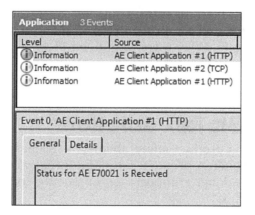

Dynamic ports are a great way to loosely couple the endpoints from your orchestration and rely on message-based context data (or external lookups) to determine the exact destination.

Pitfall

There is a performance-related behavior characteristic of dynamic send ports that you should be aware of before you choose to employ them for WCF services. When you use static WCF send ports, the channel stack gets cached by default and effectively gets reused when the adapter is called. With a dynamic send port, this is not the case; the channel stack is rebuilt each time the port is called. The result of this is that you might encounter a performance hit. An alternative solution that suggests using static WCF send ports while allowing for the URL to be dynamically overridden is explored in this blog post: `https://jamescorbould.wordpress.com/2014/06/17/using-a-static-send-port-like-a-dynamic-send-port/`.

Supporting dual initiating message exchange patterns

Back in *Chapter 7, Planning Service-oriented BizTalk Solutions*, we looked at **Message Exchange Patterns** (**MEP**) and evaluated differences between them. We concluded that asynchronous patterns can be more service-oriented and loosely coupled than synchronous patterns. However, there are cases where you want a single business process to accommodate invocation by either mechanism. In certain scenarios, the caller has no interest in the outcome, but in other situations, the caller requires resolution about the service outcome. You could choose to build two distinct processes that each support a distinct MEP, but this is fairly inefficient and challenging to maintain. What if we want to build a BizTalk orchestration with the least amount of effort required that can be invoked either synchronously or asynchronously?

Building the BizTalk solution

In keeping with our "drug product safety" theme, this scenario works with a "product complaint" schema. A product complaint is typically an issue that a customer has with the packaging, appearance, or reaction to the drug. The schema we are using looks like this:

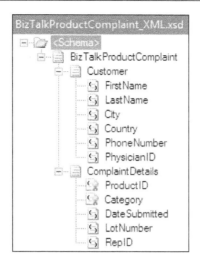

The follow-up message for a product complaint submission should contain a tracking number, assigned case agent identifier, and a status.

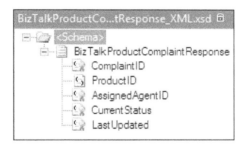

Now, let's build the orchestration. Because we are going to support both asynchronous (one-way) and synchronous (two-way) service clients, our orchestration needs to be even more loosely coupled from its endpoints than normal. That is, instead of binding to a specific receive port at runtime, we are going to use the MessageBox direct binding in order to abstract away the service endpoint as much as possible.

The orchestration begins by receiving a product complaint and executing a bit of pre-defined logic. In our amazingly simplistic case, our robust product complaint handling consists of a message being written to the Application Event Log. I can only assure you that actual biotechnology companies apply a bit more rigor to these types of input.

We must connect this **Receive** shape to an orchestration port whose **Port Binding** tab is set to **I'll always be receiving messages on this port** and whose port binding is **Direct** with **Routing between ports will be defined by filter expressions on incoming messages in the Message Box database**.

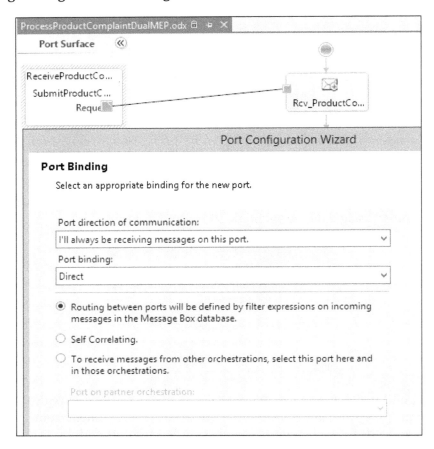

The question is, how do we know that this orchestration consumer is waiting for a response (synchronous) or not? Luckily for us, the BizTalk receive port stamps messages with a unique set of properties when those message participate in request-reply operations. At the end of our orchestration, we have a **Decision** shape, where we check to see if this orchestration was executed by a synchronous caller. The following conditional statement is the basis for the decision:

```
BTS.EpmRRCorrelationToken exists ProductComplaint_Input
```

The `EpmRRCorrelationToken` is what the `MessageBox` uses to associate a response message with the port instance waiting to send a result to a caller. I exploited the "exists" orchestration function, which returns a Boolean indicating whether the particular context property is present in the designated message.

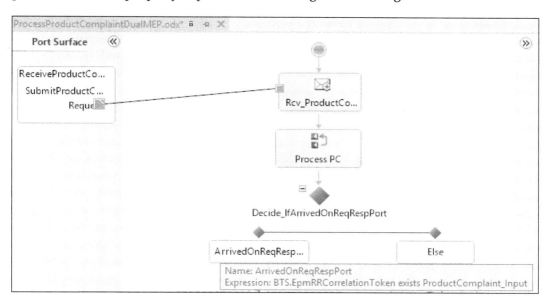

So, if the message did arrive via a request-reply messaging port, the left-hand side of the **Decision** shape gets executed. After transforming the `BizTalkProductComplaint` message into the corresponding `BizTalkProductComplaintResponse` message, we have a bit more manipulation of the message left to do. Specifically, we must copy all the context values from the source message to the destination (which copies the `EpmRRCorrelationToken` into the target message) and set the Boolean `BTS.RouteDirectToTP` to `true`. The `RouteDirectToTP` is used by the `MessageBox` to look for messages to route back to request-reply ports and the `EpmRRCorrelationToken` directs the `MessageBox` to WHICH port instance is waiting for a result.

```
ProductComplaint_Output(*) = ProductComplaint_Input(*);
ProductComplaint_Output(BTS.RouteDirectToTP) = true;
```

Finally, we send the response message out of the orchestration using a `MessageBox` direct bound port. We want to make sure that all the context properties necessary for request-reply routing are properly promoted in our outbound message. The only way to ensure this is to apply a "forced promotion" trick. That is, create a new correlation set that contains `BTS.CorrelationToken`, `BTS.EpmRRCorrelationToken`, `BTS.IsRequestResponse`, `BTS.ReqRespTransmitPipelineID`, and `BTS.RouteDirectToTP`. On the send port that distributes this outbound message to the `MessageBox`, set **Initializing Correlation Sets** to the set we just created. By doing this, we can be assured that these routing-critical values are visible to the BizTalk engine.

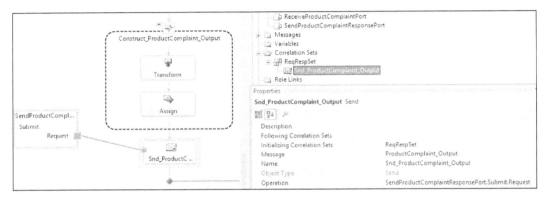

Our orchestration is now built to support dual invocation, but let's prove it. First, we need to generate two service endpoints via the **BizTalk WCF Service Publishing Wizard**. These services are built using the **Publish schemas as WCF service** option and are identical except for the fact that one service expects a response while the other does not.

Configuring the BizTalk solution

After deploying our BizTalk project (and binding the orchestration to the target host), we are able to test our orchestration. To do so, I've created a new Visual Studio Console Application that maintains service references to both the one-way and two-way BizTalk WCF service endpoints. When calling both services, we observe the following results:

```
file:///c:/03858_code/BizTalkSOA.Chapter10/Projects/BizTalk
Calling one-way service ...
Call complete ...

Calling two-way service ...
Call complete ... response status is Received
```

Sure enough, we've enabled our orchestration to support dual MEPs while not requiring us to butcher our business process or create redundant orchestrations. Note that we could also have decided to put an abstraction layer above our business process orchestration in the form of wrapper orchestrations, which each handle synchronous and asynchronous callers, respectively. This pattern would eliminate any hint of routing logic from the core orchestration but would also introduce additional layers to manage.

Chaining orchestrations using business rules

In *Chapter 7, Planning Service-oriented BizTalk Solutions*, we talked about how to chain orchestrations together. The simplest way to do so (from a developer's perspective) is to use the **Start Orchestration** or **Call Orchestration** shapes and explicitly invoke one orchestration from another. While this strategy is easy to develop and allows for transfer of more than just message data (such as variables and ports), it's also a very tightly coupled and inflexible way to connect stages of a business process if they are prone to change. If this is the case, you should pursue a route of `MessageBox` direct binding which enables fully encapsulated, reusable orchestrations that can be invoked by a wide number of clients (for example, services or other orchestrations).

What if your business process consists of a number of discrete steps that are subject to change over time? That is, let's assume a process by which an inbound "adverse event" must pass through a set of business logic and human review stages prior to commitment into the enterprise system. As I see it, you have three possible solutions to this situation:

- Put the entire process into a single orchestration. On the plus side, there is only one artifact to maintain, but on the downside, this process must maintain a rigid structure with no capacity to accommodate isolated change.

- Use the **Call Orchestration** or **Start Orchestration** shapes to link each separated stage of the process in a sequential manner. This is a better option because we have isolated each process into more management pieces, but we are still engaged in tight coupling with less optimal means for supporting a reordered or enhanced sequence of steps.

- Completely wall off each orchestration from the next and rely on `MessageBox` direct binding and a dynamic lookup to choose the next step of the process that should be invoked. Each orchestration acts as a distinct service with clear boundaries which awaits a chunky message consisting of the entire context needed to make a decision. This model also supports common "repair and resubmit" patterns where messages that fail at a discrete step can exit the process, undergo correction, and return to the flow.

Pitfall

Usage of the call orchestration shape results in the child orchestration being executed within the context of the parent orchestration. The start orchestration shape and direct `MessageBox` binding result in the message being sent to the `MessageBox` and instantiating a new orchestration instance. While the latter is not necessarily a bad thing, consideration should be given to the fact that extra latency will be introduced because of the extra `MessageBox` hop and more system resources will be required to manage the extra orchestration and routing of the message to it.

Building the BizTalk solution

Let's look at how to construct this optimal third option. Our adverse event process currently contains three steps:

1. Receive and log the inbound adverse event.

2. Apply a set of business rules to categorize the adverse event.

3. Evaluate the current work queue and assign the proper case agent to follow up on the adverse event.

As we analyze the business process further, we may find that additional steps are injected into this flow or the flow may become less sequential and have the option of taking a variety of twists and turns.

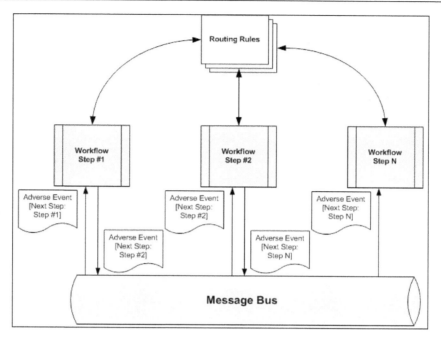

First, we need the schema that not only describes the adverse event but also contains the means for routing this adverse event from orchestration to orchestration. As with the earlier demonstration of dynamic ports, our message should be comprised of a header and a body. In this case, the header is actually the message bus routing instructions, and the body is the included (reused) adverse event schema.

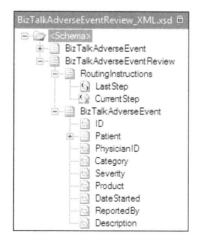

Now it would be foolish to expect our service client to know or care about the internal routing procedures of our BizTalk solution, so we don't want to reveal this particular (non-abstract) schema to the outside world. Instead, our process should accept the standard adverse event message, and a map responsible for instantiating our routing-friendly message should be applied at the receive port tier. This map sets the **CurrentStep** routing instruction to the first stage of adverse event processing (**Initial Receive**).

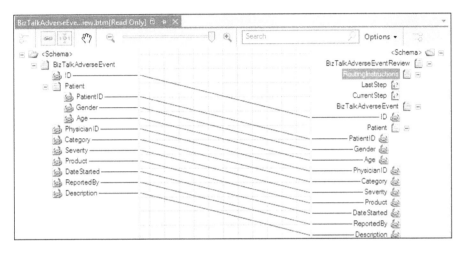

Because we are using `MessageBox` direct binding to control process flow, we will need to promote the routing instruction node expected by our orchestration filters.

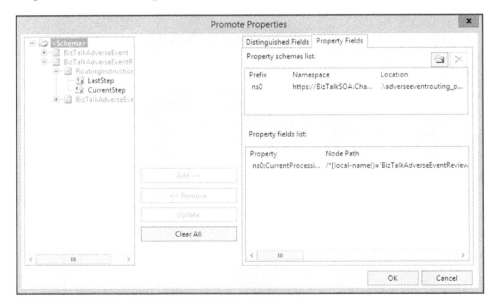

Before we start building our set of orchestrations, we need to devise a scheme for electing which step to execute after the current one. We want this information stored outside the orchestration(s) itself so that future changes to the flow do not require updates to existing components. This scenario cries out for the BizTalk Business Rules Engine. The BRE enables us to store logical conditions in a centrally managed and accessible storage medium that can be updated independently of components that rely on it.

Upon opening the **Microsoft Business Rules Composer** application, we choose which artifacts serve as the "facts" for our rule set. In this case, the BizTalkAdverseEventReview schema has all the information we need. I like using friendly references to my XML nodes instead of XPath statements, so I went ahead and created a BRE vocabulary that replaces XPath references with English language snippets.

Next, we must define the rules that BizTalk will apply when a particular stage of the broader workflow process is reached. In this simple case, I look at what the previous state was and set the next one. In a real-world example, you'd most likely apply a bit of additional logic to see which particular path you need to follow instead of blindly and sequentially moving from one stage to the next. From the following image, you can see that I have defined three rules that shuffle the adverse event between the available process steps.

The great thing about the BRE is that the individual rules that make up a rule set are completely hidden from the calling application. A consumer of rules may only invoke a policy and does not explicitly identify which rules in a policy to call. In this manner, it would be amazingly simple to reorder existing steps or add completely new ones while not requiring any changes to rule consumers.

Now that we have our data schema, a property schema and a set of routing rules, we are ready to build the orchestrations that make up our overarching business process. In the first orchestration, the topmost **Receive** shape should accept the `BizTalkAdverseEventReview` message type and have a filter that restricts the receipt to only messages set for an **Initial Receive** state. We immediately connect this shape to an orchestration receive port that is set to receive direct bound messages.

After walking through any logic specific to this processing step, we must next call our BRE policy in order to stamp this message with its updated routing instructions. While it is possible to call the BRE from code, it's much simpler to apply the **Call Rules** orchestration shape and choose the policy and corresponding input message.

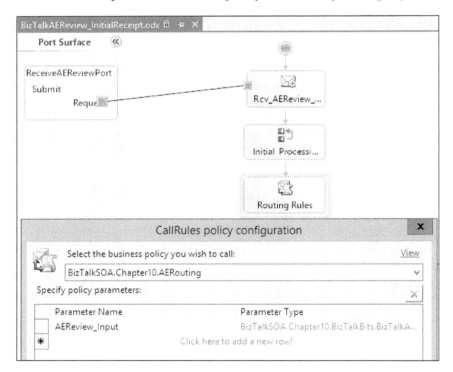

Pitfall

Be aware that, by passing a message through the BRE, the original message is actually copied and a "new" message is returned. This is important because all pre-existing context values are stripped from the messages departing the **Call Rules** shape. If you had a value in the message context that is required by downstream consumers, make sure to add those values back to the message before shipping it out of the orchestration.

Finally, we send the message back to the `MessageBox` via a direct bound send port. The additional two orchestrations all closely resemble this one, except for two key differences: each has a distinct `filter` on the activating receive shape, and each writes a different message to my **Application Event Log**. When we build and deploy this solution, we must still create an initial on-ramp receive location to accept messages into the bus and have to remember to apply our routing-friendly map to the appropriate receive port. When everything is in place, we send in an adverse event message and acknowledge the completeness by watching the Event Log results.

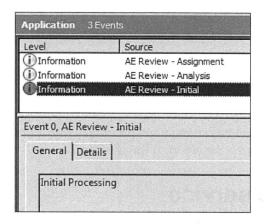

When you are looking to decompose workflow processes into more manageable sub-parts, consider the best possible options for the virtual recomposition that occurs at runtime. Designing this solution in a loosely coupled, rules-driven fashion will require additional forethought and planning, but in return you get a more future-oriented process that accommodates change.

The role of transactions in aggregated services

One of the principles of SOA that we discussed earlier in this book is the concept of abstraction. That is, shielding service clients from all sorts of implementation details with which they should not be concerned. One way to promote abstraction is through the use of aggregate services. Instead of having a service client call a series of required services that result in a new customer being added to a system, we should instead expose a single `CreateCustomer` operation that internally navigates the set of necessary system services. BizTalk orchestration is practically built for this situation. By injecting a stateful, cross-domain processing engine, our solution can coordinate a wide range of activities that our initiating service client never knows about.

However, one challenge with aggregating services in a single business process is figuring out how to effectively wrap these disconnected services into a single participating transaction. While BizTalk Server 2013 implements the idea of atomic transactions within orchestrations, this feature does not behave as you might suspect. In a truly atomic transaction, either all the enclosed operations are completed successfully or else none of them are. It is a means to prevent partial updates or anything that might leave the target system(s) in an inconsistent state. That said, a middleware solution can only provide a certain level of atomicity. In the case of an error within the orchestration's atomic transaction, changes to orchestration variables and messages are reversed, but the actual calls to adapter endpoints do not automatically get rolled back. Logistically, this makes sense. How do you reverse a message to the email adapter? How about calling a stateless web service? BizTalk Server integrates with a host of applications and protocols that don't share a common transaction scheme. This is where the concept of compensation arises. Within an orchestration **Scope** shape, we explicitly define a compensation action that should be executed in the case that this previously successful transaction needs to be rolled back. We can put any orchestration shape necessary into a compensation block if it helps us effectively reverse the effect of the transaction.

Defining the service

So, how do we correctly implement transactions in an aggregate service? What we want to do here is create a composite service that comprises three individual services. If any of these services fail, then any previously committed changes must be rolled back. In this case, I use the term *services* to represent a business service versus just being a WCF service. That is, the three services we want to aggregate are:

- Sending an email to the initiator of an adverse event indicating receipt of their message
- Inserting the adverse event into a tracking system
- Sending the adverse event to an investigator who reviews, categorizes, and validates the adverse event

All of these operations must succeed or else previously committed operations must be compensated. Both the second and third action have a WCF service component. We need a service operation that is able to insert into our destination system and a service that assigns the adverse event to an investigator. Our WCF service contract looks like this:

```
[ServiceContract(Namespace = "http://BizTalkSOA.Chapter10")]
public interface IAdverseEventReview {
  [OperationContract]
```

```
   string InsertNewAdverseEvent(AdverseEvent newAE);
   [OperationContract]
   void DeleteAdverseEvent(string aeID);
   [OperationContract]
   void PublishAEForInvestigation(AdverseEventCase newAECase);
}
[DataContract]
public class AdverseEvent {
   [DataMember]
   public string AE_ID { get; set; }
   [DataMember]
   public string ProductCode { get; set; }
   [DataMember]
   public string PatientId { get; set; }
   [DataMember]
   public string PatientGender { get; set; }
   [DataMember]
   public int PatientAge { get; set; }
   [DataMember]
   public string AECategory { get; set; }
   [DataMember]
   public string AESeverity { get; set; }
   [DataMember]
   public DateTime AE_Onset { get; set; }
   [DataMember]
   public string AdditionalNotes { get; set; }
}
  [DataContract]
public class AdverseEventCase {
   [DataMember]
   public string AE_ID { get; set; }
   [DataMember]
   public string CaseID { get; set; }
   [DataMember]
   public string Product { get; set; }
   [DataMember]
   public AEStatusCode Status { get; set; }
}
```

You will notice that I added a service operation that also deletes data from the adverse event system. I plan on executing this operation only in the case of compensating for a previously successful insertion. After all three of these service operations are implemented, we add them to the pre-existing WCF Service project and host the endpoints in IIS 8.0 as HTTP services.

Building the BizTalk solution

Back in our BizTalk project, we have to add a reference to this service in order to get access to the artifacts we need to successfully call each operation. Absent any worries about transactions, our straightforward aggregate orchestration should resemble the following figure:

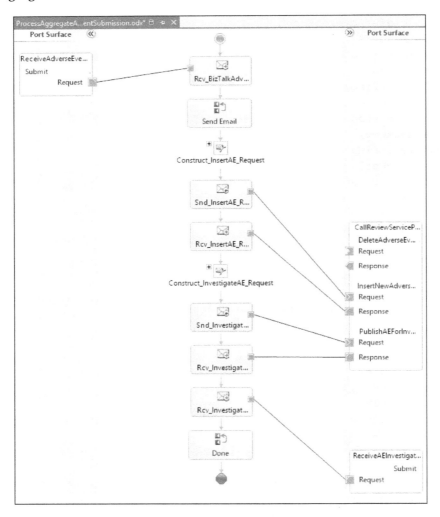

Note that our "investigator service" expects a response (outside the synchronous service call) that describes the final assessment of the investigator. This is done by initializing a correlation set (on the adverse event ID property) when the investigator service is called and following that correlation set when the subsequent out-of-band response is returned.

Now let's add some transactions. In order for an orchestration to contain transactions, the orchestration itself must be marked as transactional. This is done by clicking on any whitespace in the orchestration designer, finding the **Transaction Type** property, and setting it to a value such as **Long Running**. Wrap the **Send Email** Expression shape in an atomic transaction (using a **Scope** shape) and add a compensation section by right-clicking the scope and choosing **New Compensation Block**. For this example, I put an additional **Expression** shape in the compensation block to write a message to my Event Log.

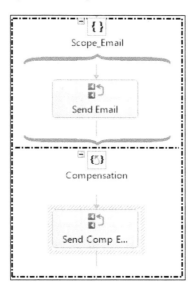

Next, we wrap the `InsertNewAdverseEvent` WCF service operation into a long-running transaction. After the service call is completed, we should set the ID of the adverse event to a member variable for later access. For this section's compensating action, we take the saved adverse event ID and pass that into the `DeleteAdverseEvent` WCF service operation.

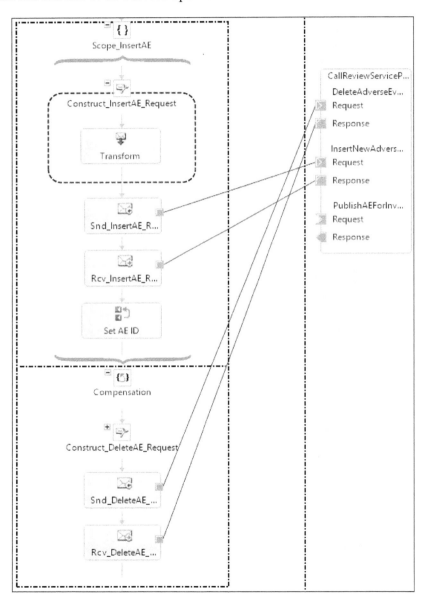

Because the investigator review is the last step of the process, there is no compensating action for the long-running transaction enclosing this operation. However, we do want to look at the result of the investigator review; if they find this adverse event to be illegitimate, then we should throw an exception because this service operation has, in essence, failed.

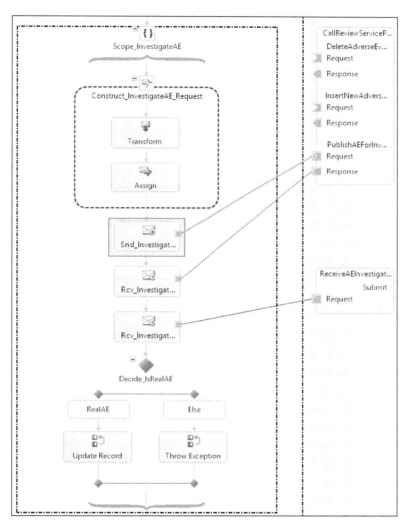

We want all three of these actions to behave as one, so we will next wrap all three transactions into one large, long-running transaction. Add a single **Catch Exception** block to the outermost transaction. This will catch any exceptions thrown by the contained transactions. Now, we could choose to put two **Compensate** shapes in this exception block in order to explicitly execute the compensation block of the first two transactions. However, this strategy is hard to maintain when there are many nested transactions. Instead, put a single **Compensation** shape in the exception block and choose the transaction of the outermost scope to compensate. What we are saying by doing this is that all the transactions contained within the outermost transaction should have their compensation logic fired in reverse execution order. This is much simpler than calling out each individual compensation block.

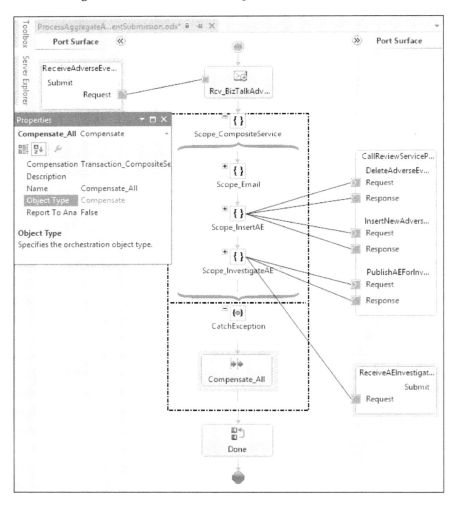

After we build, deploy, and bind this orchestration, we send in an initial request and watch our scenario play out. If we send an investigator response indicating a false adverse event, we are able to observe each compensation block being called in the reverse order of execution.

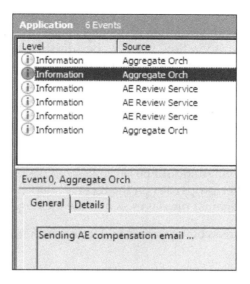

 Be especially careful in long-running transaction scenarios when you choose to reverse a service operation that you called previously. Changes made to a given system may spawn an entire set of processes (such as new records resulting in workflows being initiated) that might not get notified of a later change to the source record. Evaluate these scenarios prior to blindly deleting a record that you created at an earlier part of a transaction.

BizTalk Server 2013 provides solid support for modeling cross-domain transactions, but the usage of such transactions requires a fair amount of upfront design and consideration. However, to truly architect composite services, transactions need to become a familiar part of your orchestration arsenal.

Building message-type agnostic orchestrations

From time to time, you might find that you are building very similar orchestrations to process different types of messages. This goes against every basic tenet of development in that it doesn't promote reuse and causes maintenance nightmares. Imagine that your orchestration flow needs to be adjusted and you have to apply the change to each orchestration with the similar flow.

Luckily, orchestration messages do not have to be typed to a specific schema. When we discussed `MessageBox` direct binding, we mentioned that an orchestration's subscription, when direct binding is employed, consists of the message type of the activating message in combination with filter properties applied against the activating receive shape. To build a truly type-agnostic orchestration, the message type of the activating message should be set to `System.Xml.XmlDocument`. The result of this is that only the filter properties on the receive shape will be assessed during subscription evaluation against messages, while the message type is ignored.

There are some restrictions when it comes to dealing with untyped messages in orchestrations as follows:

- Maps can't be executed against untyped messages inside an orchestration
- Distinguished properties can't be inspected or set against untyped messages
- Only context properties that derive from the `MessageContextPropertyBase` base class can be inspected or set against untyped messages
- Untyped messages can't be asserted as typed XML-based facts to the BRE using the **Call Rules** shape

 We have already mentioned the danger of using `MessageBox` direct bound ports earlier in this chapter and have preached that proper thought needs to be put in place to ensure scenarios such as endless loops or missed subscriptions do not occur. The risk of these problems can be even more pronounced when the message type is taken out of the subscription evaluation equation. Do plan ahead to ensure that your untyped messaging subscriptions evaluate as desired.

Armed with an understanding of the restrictions that constrain us, we can leverage untyped messages to build loosely coupled and reusable orchestrations. To demonstrate the usage of message-type-agnostic orchestrations, we are going to design a solution that performs validation for different pharmaceutical patent-related events, these validations being in the form of web services hosted outside of BizTalk, and then returning the validation result back to the client. The solution needs to be flexible enough such that new events as well as new validation services can be catered for in the future without changes to the orchestration. A breakdown of the message flow in the solution is as follows:

- Event messages regarding pharmaceutical patents are received via two WCF receive locations contained within separate receive ports. The WCF services each expose one strongly typed operation allowing for the submission of a specific event type.

- The receive pipeline promotes the message type to the BTS.MessageType context property and some promoted properties from within the message to the message context including the product name to the ProductName context property and the country the event was registered in to the RegisteredCountry context property. The BRE Pipeline Framework component from **CodePlex** (https://brepipelineframework.codeplex.com/) is also used to set the ProcessStage context property on the incoming messages to ValidateEvent based on the BTS.MessageType context property of the incoming message.

- The message gets routed to a message-type agnostic orchestration that subscribes to messages with a ProcessStage context property value of ValidateEvent on which the BTS.MessageType, ProductName, and RegisteredCountry context properties exist, regardless of the value.

- The orchestration will use the BRE to decide what WCF services to call upon to validate the message based on the relevant context properties. It will then loop through each of the WCF services that is relevant for that given message, using direct binding to communicate with the send ports corresponding to the validation services.

- If validation in all the resolved WCF services passes, the orchestration will return a successful response to client. If any of the services fail, the orchestration will respond with the first failure message.

- If a successful message was returned to the client, the original untyped message will also be sent to the BizTalk MessageBox, with direct binding, to be directed for further processing. Before sending out the message, the ProcessStage context property will be set to ProcessMessage.

Defining the validation services

For the purpose of this example, we will create two validation services, one provided by the CDC and one provided by Customs. To make the example somewhat simpler, both services will implement similar interfaces; however, this constraint is in no way enforced on you if you decide to take this example further. The interfaces and corresponding data contracts will look like this:

```
[ServiceContract (Namespace="http://BizTalkSOA.Chapter10")]
public interface ICDCValidation {
  [OperationContract]
  ValidationResponse ValidateWithCDC(CDCValidationRequest
  request);
}
[ServiceContract(Namespace = "http://BizTalkSOA.Chapter10")]
public interface ICustomsValidation {
  [OperationContract]
  ValidationResponse ValidateWithCustoms(CustomsValidationRequest
  request);
}
[DataContract]
public class CDCValidationRequest {
  [DataMember]
  public string ProductName { get; set; }
  [DataMember]
  public string ProductClass { get; set; }
  [DataMember]
  public string RegistrationCountry { get; set; }
  [DataMember]
  public string PatentNumber { get; set; }
}
[DataContract]
public class CustomsValidationRequest {
  [DataMember]
  public string ProductClass { get; set; }
  [DataMember]
  public string RegistrationCountry { get; set; }
}
[DataContract]
public class ValidationResponse {
  [DataMember]
  public ValidationStatus ValidationStatus { get; set; }
  [DataMember(IsRequired=false, EmitDefaultValue=false)]
  public string ErrorMessage { get; set; }
}
```

```
public enum ValidationStatus {
  Success,
  Failure
}
```

The services are defined as follows:

```
public class CDCValidationService : ICDCValidation {
  public ValidationResponse ValidateWithCDC(CDCValidationRequest
  request) {
    ValidationResponse response = new ValidationResponse();
    if (request.PatentNumber.StartsWith("DG")) {
      response.ValidationStatus = ValidationStatus.Failure;
      response.ErrorMessage = "CDC rejects patent based events
      when their corresponding patent numbers start with DG";
    }
    else {
      response.ValidationStatus = ValidationStatus.Success;
      response.ErrorMessage = null;
    }
    return response;
  }
}
public class CustomsValidationService : ICustomsValidation {
  public ValidationResponse
  ValidateWithCustoms(CustomsValidationRequest request) {
    ValidationResponse response = new ValidationResponse();
    if (request.RegistrationCountry == "Antartica" &&
    request.ProductClass == "UnstableChemicals") {
      response.ValidationStatus = ValidationStatus.Failure;
      response.ErrorMessage = "Customs has enforced an embargo on
      unstable chemicals from Antartica";
    }
    else {
      response.ValidationStatus = ValidationStatus.Success;
      response.ErrorMessage = null;
    }
    return response;
  }
}
```

The service implementations are such that the CDC service will reject events if they contain a `PatentNumber` starting with DG, while the customs service will reject events if the `RegistrationCountry` is Antarctica and the `ProductClass` is UnstableChemicals.

The services are exposed via two separate endpoints, one with `basicHttpBinding` and one with `wsHttpBinding`, and hosted in IIS under the "Default Web Site" website. Theoretically, these services could be based on any synchronous binding such as `netTcpBinding`, or they could even be written in non .NET languages. If you want to use an asynchronous service with a callback, then the orchestration would need to be extended further; however, this is beyond the scope of this example. Authentication is also disabled to keep this example simpler.

```xml
<bindings>
  <basicHttpBinding>
    <binding name="BasicHttpEndpointBinding">
      <security mode="None" />
    </binding>
  </basicHttpBinding>
  <wsHttpBinding>
    <binding name="WsHttpEndpointBinding">
      <security mode="None" />
    </binding>
  </wsHttpBinding>
</bindings>
<services>
  <service name="BizTalkSOA.Chapter10.ServiceLibrary.
  CustomsValidationService">
    <endpoint binding="basicHttpBinding"
    bindingConfiguration="BasicHttpEndpointBinding"
    contract="BizTalkSOA.Chapter10.ServiceLibrary.
    ICustomsValidation"/>
  </service>
  <service name="BizTalkSOA.Chapter10.ServiceLibrary.
  CDCValidationService">
    <endpoint binding="wsHttpBinding"
    bindingConfiguration="WsHttpEndpointBinding"
    contract="BizTalkSOA.Chapter10.ServiceLibrary.
    ICDCValidation"/>
  </service>
</services>
```

Building the BizTalk solution

The logical place to start building this solution is the property schema, seeing as routing is going to be heavily based on context properties. We'll define the property schema with the following string properties, and in each case, we'll set the context properties to have a Property Schema Base property of `MessageContextPropertyBase` (this is achieved by clicking on each element and setting the property in the properties pane in Visual Studio), as this means we'll still be able to assess and set these context properties in orchestrations against untyped messages.

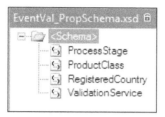

Next up, let's define two XML schemas corresponding to two different patent-related events. All elements are defined as strings and are mandatory. The `ProductClass` elements in both schemas are promoted to the `ProductClass` context property in the aforementioned property schema, and the `RegistrationCountry` and `NewRegistrationCountry` elements in the two schemas are promoted to the `RegisteredCountry` context property.

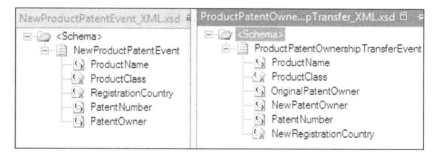

We'll also define a `ValidationResponse` XML schema, which will be returned to the service client and indicates whether all resolved validation services succeeded or not, with an optional error message. All elements are set to be distinguished so that they can be inspected in orchestrations without running XPath queries against the message.

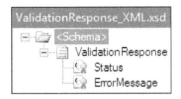

Next, we'll run the WCF Service Publishing wizard once for each of the two services we are going to create with the following configuration settings. In both cases, we'll choose the WS-Http binding to enable a metadata endpoint and to automatically create a receive location in the `BizTalkSOA.Chapter10 BizTalk` application. In both cases, we'll expose a single request-response operation, with the two event schemas as the request messages, and the `ValidationRespose` schema as the response schema in both cases. We'll choose to allow anonymous access to the service in both cases. Once the wizard has completed, we'll configure both receive locations to disable security in order to simplify the example.

We now want to create the receive pipeline that will promote the relevant context properties on the event message and set the `ProcessStage` context property to `ValidateEvent`, which will direct it to our untyped orchestration. In order to do this, we must first download the BRE Pipeline Framework from CodePlex (`http://brepipelineframework.codeplex.com`). We'll want to import the `BREPipelineFramework.AllVocabs.xml` export file from the `Vocabularies` subfolder in the `Program Files` folder (the default location is `C:\\Program Files (x86)\BRE Pipeline Framework\Vocabularies`) using the Business Rules Engine Deployment wizard. Once this is done, we can create our receive pipeline with the XML Disassembler pipeline component in the disassemble stage and the `BREPipelineFrameworkComponent` pipeline component in the validate stage. We'll want to set the `ApplicationContext` property to `Rcv_EventsToValidate` and the `ExecutionPolicy` property to `BizTalkSOA.Chapter10.UntypedMessaging`. We'll choose to use this receive pipeline on both of our WCF receive locations corresponding to the event registration services.

Now let's create the BRE policy that we'll actually use to set the `ProcessStage` context property to `ValidateEvent`. We'll open the Business Rules Composer application and create a new policy called `BizTalkSOA.Chapter10.UntypedMessaging` (which is the `ExecutionPolicy` property value we chose in the `BREPipelineFrameworkComponent` pipeline component). We'll add a new rule called `Set ProcessStage to ValidateEvent` to the policy and define the rule as in the following screenshot. The first predicate uses the `ApplicationContext` vocabulary definition from the `BREPipelineFramework` vocabulary (note that the value `Rcv_EventsToValidate` is what we set for the `ApplicationContext` property in the `BREPipelineFramework` pipeline component, which is part of the reason this rule will fire). The next two predicates are based on the `GetBTSContextProperty` vocabulary definition in the `BREPipelineFramework.SampleInstructions.ContextInstructions` vocabulary. The action is based on the `SetCustomContextProperty` vocabulary definition, which is also in the `BREPipelineFramework.SampleInstructions.ContextInstructions` vocabulary.

This rule will only fire if the `ApplicationContext` passed into the BRE is set to `Rcv_EventsToValidate` and only if the `BTS.MessageType` context property matches one of our two event schemas. The result of this rule is that the `ProcessStage` context property will be promoted with a value of `ValidateEvent`. At this stage, let's save the policy but not publish it as we will come back to it and add more rules later.

We'll now create a .NET class in a helper project that contains a private list called `validationServices`, has a public method to add strings to the list if they aren't already contained in the list, a public method to get a count of items in the list, a public method to extract a value at a specific index in the list, and contains public properties called `EventType`, `ProductClass`, and `RegistrationCountry`. The class is marked as Serializable to ensure that it can be used in orchestration variables outside of atomic scopes.

The purpose of this class is to behave as a fact which will be asserted to the BRE. Our orchestration will instantiate an instance of this class; set the `EventType`, `ProductClass`, and `RegisteredCountry` properties on it; and pass it into the BRE. The BRE will assess these values and choose which validation services will be executed by adding a value to the `validationServices` list.

```
[Serializable]
public class EventValidator {
  private List<string> validationServices = new List<string>();
  public string EventType { get; set; }
  public string ProductClass { get; set; }
  public string RegisteredCountry { get; set; }
  public void AddValidationService(string validationService) {
    if (!validationServices.Contains(validationService)) {
      validationServices.Add(validationService);
    }
  }
  public int GetCountValidationServices() {
    return validationServices.Count;
  }
  public string GetValidationServiceAtIndex(int index) {
    return validationServices[index];
  }
}
```

We'll need to build the helper project and add it to the GAC using the Gacutil tool to ensure that contained methods are available to the Business Rules Composer tool. We'll now open **Business Rules Composer** (if it was already open, close it and reopen it so that it refreshes its assembly cache from the GAC). Create a friendly BRE vocabulary called `BizTalkSOA.Chapter10` with .NET-based definitions corresponding to the Get property accessors for the `EventType`, `ProductClass`, and `RegisteredCountry` properties as well as for the `AddValidationService` method. We'll use the following names and display names for the vocabulary definitions corresponding to the mentioned class member.

Member	Name	Display name
get_EventType	GetEventType	The event type of the event being evaluated
get_ProductClass	GetProductClass	The product class of the event being evaluated
get_RegisteredCountry	GetRegisteredCountry	The registered country of the event being evaluated
AddValidationService	AddValidationService	Validate the event by executing the validation service {0}

Now that we've created our vocabulary definitions, we can add some more rules (as per the following screenshots) to the `BizTalkSOA.Chapter10.UntypedMessaging` policy in Business Rules Composer, and we can choose to publish and deploy it.

The following rule is used to add the `ValidateWithCustoms` validation instruction to the list of validations to execute if the registered country for the event in question is the USA.

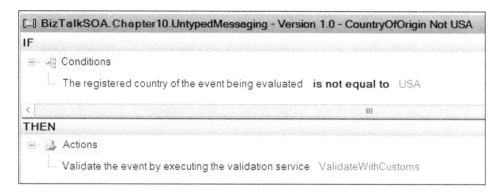

The next rule is used to add both the `ValidateWithCDC` and `ValidateWithCustoms` validation instructions to the collection if the type of event being evaluated is `ProductPatentOwnershipTransferEvent`.

And finally, the following rule is used to add the `ValidateWithCDC` validation instruction to the collection if the product class of the event being evaluated is Biohazard.

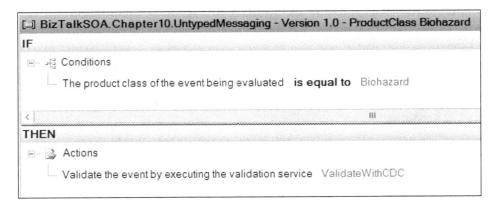

The result of these rules is that if the registered country is not USA, then regardless of the event type, the event will be validated with customs. If the event type is not `ProductPatentOwnershipTransferEvent`, then the event will be validated with the CDC and with customs. If the product class is Biohazard, then the event will be validated with the CDC. If multiple rules get fired that result in the same validation service being executed, they will not get duplicated since we built a duplicate detection check into the `AddValidationService` method in our helper class. Of note is that this BRE Policy does not actually perform the CDC and customs validation; all it does is resolve who needs to perform validations by adding a value to a list.

Now to bring this together we will start building our untyped orchestration. We'll start by creating the orchestration and defining two multi-part message types in the **Orchestration View** window, one corresponding to an untyped message for which we will set the type to the .NET class `System.Xml.XmlDocument` and the second for the validation response which we will set to the `ValidationResponse` schema.

Next up, we'll create two port types. One will be a request-response port type taking in the untyped multi-part message for the request and the validation response multi-part message for the response. The other will be a one-way port type taking in the untyped multi-part message for the request. We'll now create a receive port based on the request-response port type and two send ports based on each of the port types. All the ports will be configured to use direct `MessageBox` binding.

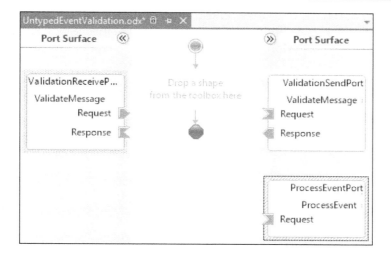

Now let's define some orchestration messages and variables as follows:

- **Messages**:
  - ○ untypedMessage: Based on the untyped multi-part message, this event message will trigger the orchestration.
  - ○ untypedMessageToProcess: Based on the untyped multi-part message, this copy of the original event message will be sent out of the orchestration for further processing if all the resolved validation services succeed.
  - ○ validationResponse: Based on the validation response multi-part message, this is used to hold the validation status of each of the validation services called on and will also be used to return the validation status to the WCF service client.

- **Variables**:
  - ○ counter: An integer with an initial value of 1, which is used to iterate through the resolved validations.
  - ○ eventValidator: This is based on the custom .NET resolver class we created earlier. A reference will need to be added to the helper assembly in order to use this class for our variable.
  - ○ placeHolderResponse: Based on System.Xml.XmlDocument, this variable will be used to create a successful validationResponse message, which will be used in the case that no validation services are resolved.

Let's drag a receive shape onto the orchestration designer and set it to be an activating receive shape, receiving the `untypedMessage` message. Click on the ellipsis in the **Filter Expression** property in the properties window and set up the filters as shown in the following screenshot. This results in the orchestration having an activation subscription based on messages with a `ProcessStage` context property value of `ValidateEvent` and having any values in the `ProductClass`, `RegisteredCountry`, and `BTS.MessageType` context properties.

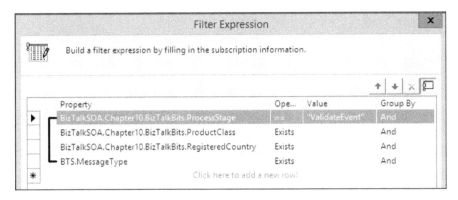

Next, we are going to use a BizTalk expression shape to set up the resolver object as in the following code. Doing this copies the `ProductClass`, `RegisteredCountry`, and `BTS.MessageType` context properties from the untyped message into the object.

```
eventValidator.EventType = untypedMessage(BTS.MessageType);
eventValidator.RegisteredCountry =
  untypedMessage(BizTalkSOA.Chapter10.BizTalkBits.
  RegisteredCountry);
eventValidator.ProductClass = untypedMessage(BizTalkSOA.Chapter10.
  BizTalkBits.ProductClass);
```

We are then going to drag a Call Rules shape into the orchestration design surface, configuring it to call the `BizTalkSOA.Chapter10.UntypedMessaging` BRE Policy, and passing in the resolver class as a fact. The result of this is that the BRE Policy will assess properties on the resolver object and add validation services to call to the contained list.

Before we get to the point of actually calling on validation services, we need to cater for a scenario whereby no validation services have been resolved. If validation services have been resolved, we will call on them sequentially until all of them succeed or one of them fails. If one of them fails, we'll send back the failure response message, and if all of them succeed, we'll send back the last response message. In case no validation services are resolved, we'll need to send back a pre-prepared validation response. We'll do this by dragging a Construct shape to the orchestration design surface, configured to construct the `validationResponse` message, with a contained **Message Assignment** shape with the following expression:

```
validationResponse.Body = new System.Xml.XmlDocument();
placeHolderResponse.LoadXml(@"<ns0:ValidationResponse
  xmlns:ns0=""http://BizTalkSOA.Chapter10.BizTalkBits.
  ValidationResponse""><Status>Success</Status>
  </ns0:ValidationResponse>");
validationResponse.Body = placeHolderResponse;
```

Now, to call the validation services, we are going to use a loop shape which is set to continue looping while the counter variable is less than or equal to the count of validation services in the `eventValidator` resolver variable and while the status on the most recent validation response message is `Success`. The loop expression will be as follows.

```
counter <= eventValidator.GetCountValidationServices() &&
  validationResponse.Body.Status == "Success"
```

When we send out the validation message to be routed to the relevant send port, we will need to promote the name of the validation service to the `ValidationService` context property for routing purposes. In order to do so, we will need to reuse the correlation set trick mentioned earlier in the chapter, whereby a correlation set can be used to force property promotion on a message sent out of an orchestration. However, BizTalk orchestrations have a constraint that a correlation set can only be initialized once. Thus, this wouldn't work without our loop without a further trick. In order to ensure that the correlation set only gets initialized a single time, we need to create a scope within our loop and declare the correlation set there. We'll also declare a message called `validationMessage` based on the untyped multi-part message in this scope.

Now that we've set up the scope, we will use a **Construct / Message Assignment** shape to set up the `validationMessage` message by making a copy of the original `untypedMessage` and then setting the `ValidationService` context property to the validation service value contained within the `eventValidator` object (based on the current iteration of the loop). We can achieve this via the following expression:

```
//Message Assignment
validationMessage.Body = untypedMessage.Body;
validationMessage(*) = untypedMessage(*);
validationMessage(BizTalkSOA.Chapter10.BizTalkBits.
ValidationService) = eventValidator.GetValidationServiceAtIndex(count
er - 1);
//Tracing
Microsoft.BizTalk.CAT.BestPractices.Framework.Instrumentation.
TraceManager.WorkflowComponent.TraceInfo("{0} - Currently on loop
{1}", callToken.ToString(), counter);
Microsoft.BizTalk.CAT.BestPractices.Framework.Instrumentation.
TraceManager.WorkflowComponent.TraceInfo("{0} - Calling validation
service {1}", callToken.ToString(),
eventValidator.GetValidationServiceAtIndex(counter - 1));
```

Of special note in the preceding code is the trace statements based on the CAT Instrumentation Framework. No good SOA or integration solution would be complete without a level of instrumentation that makes troubleshooting the application easier. The beauty of this instrumentation framework is that it is based on **Event Tracing for Windows (ETW)**, which is a highly efficient alternative to common logging frameworks and is quite safe to use in production builds rather than just in debug build profiles. In the case of the above you would see the counter value as well as the validation service at the index of the counter in the trace logs.

Next up, we'll send out the `validationMessage` to our request-response send port while initializing a correlation set that will promote our `ValidationService` context property. After that, we'll use a receive shape to receive a `validationResponse` message. The key here is that, on the send ports that correspond to the validation services that this orchestration calls, we will need to employ outbound maps that transform each of the relevant events to the data contract of the given service operation, and we will also need to employ an inbound map that transforms the response message from the service operation to the internal `ValidationResponse` format that the orchestration expects.

Finally, we'll increment the counter variable so that the loop can progress appropriately.

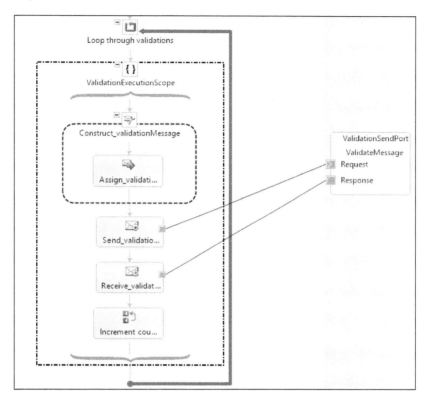

The final part of the orchestration is to return the response back to the client and to send the message on for further processing. Because we have to send out two messages, we shall use an atomic scope to ensure that there is only one persistence point back to the BizTalk `MessageBox` database rather than two, which will deliver better performance. Marking this scope as atomic requires us to revise the transaction type of the orchestration itself to be long running, since an orchestration with the default transaction type of none can't contain nested transactions. In this scope, we will need to construct and send out the `untypedMessageToProcess` message if all the validation services returned successfully. The **Message Assignment** shape should contain the following expression:

```
untypedMessageToProcess.Body = untypedMessage.Body;
untypedMessageToProcess(*) = untypedMessage(*);
untypedMessageToProcess(BizTalkSOA.Chapter10.BizTalkBits.
   ProcessStage) = "ProcessMessage";
```

The scope and contained shapes would look like the following screenshot:

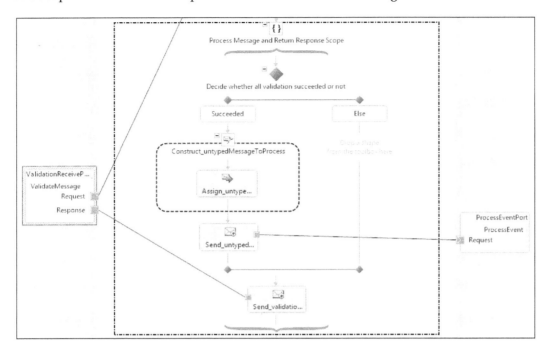

Bringing it all together

In order to finally stitch this solution together, we will now need to right click on our BizTalk project and choose the **Add Generated Items** option, then select the **Consume WCF Service** option for each of the validation services, pointing the wizard at the WSDL corresponding to each service. This will generate the schemas and binding files corresponding to the given service. With the generated schemas, you can then create maps between the event schemas and the validation service request data contracts as well as between the validation service response data contracts and the internal ValidationResponse schema.

Next up, import the generated binding files into the BizTalk application via the BizTalk Administration Console, thus generating send ports related to the services. You would need to add a filter to the send ports based on the ValidationService context property having a value specific to the validation service operation in question and you'll need to apply the relevant inbound and outbound maps. Finally, you will need to edit the **SOAP Action Header** section of the WCF send ports such that rather than containing BTSActionMappings, they just contain the SOAP action for the service operation that the send port corresponds to.

We can now use SOAPUI to call the event registration services, and based on the values chosen in the request, we will either get a success or failure response.

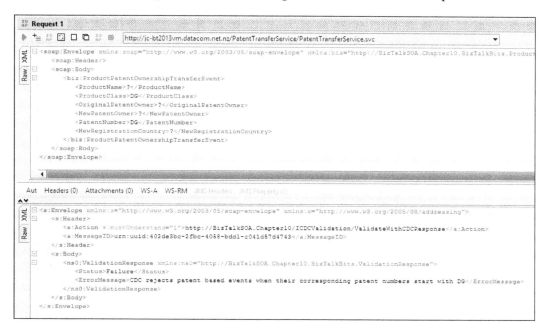

The CAT Instrumentation Trace logs provide valuable information as shown next. Note the GUID value 33fac74b-0c84-4fa1-bed5-5fe80953f8aa, which is based on our callToken orchestration variable that can be used to correlate the trace statements for a single instance of our untyped orchestration.

```
EventTrace
[2]2104.2B60::03/04/2015-22:11:46.954 [Event]:TRACEIN:
    BizTalkSOA.Chapter10.BizTalkBits.UntypedEventValidation.
    segment2() => [33fac74b-0c84-4fa1-bed5-5fe80953f8aa]
[2]2104.2B60::03/04/2015-22:11:46.955 [Event]:
    33fac74b-0c84-4fa1-bed5-5fe80953f8aa - Currently on loop 1
[2]2104.2B60::03/04/2015-22:11:46.955 [Event]:
    33fac74b-0c84-4fa1-bed5-5fe80953f8aa -
    Calling validation service ValidateWithCustoms
[1]2104.1F9C::03/04/2015-22:11:48.260 [Event]:
    33fac74b-0c84-4fa1-bed5-5fe80953f8aa -
    Currently on loop 2
[1]2104.1F9C::03/04/2015-22:11:48.260 [Event]:
    33fac74b-0c84-4fa1-bed5-5fe80953f8aa -
    Calling validation service ValidateWithCDC
```

```
[1]2104.2A68::03/04/2015-22:11:48.968 [Event]:
    TRACEOUT: BizTalkSOA.Chapter10.BizTalkBits.
    UntypedEventValidation.segment6
    (...) = <void> <= [33fac74b-0c84-4fa1-bed5-5fe80953f8aa]
```

Reflecting on the implemented solution

Here are some of the important points to be aware of regarding the solution we have implemented:

- As new events are implemented, there is no need to make any change to our orchestration. The new requirements would be limited to the creation of the new event schemas, new WCF services to be published, for the new receive location to stamp a `ProcessStage` context property to `ValidateEvent` (potentially with the existing pipeline if it is suitable), business rules to be adjusted if required, and new maps to the relevant validation service operations.

- As new validation services are implemented, there is no need to change the orchestration at all. The new requirements would be limited to creating new send ports corresponding to the validation service operations, new maps from the relevant event messages to the validation service request data contract, a new map from the validation service response data contract to the internal `ValidationResponse` message, and new business rules that specify the scenarios in which the new validation service operation should be called upon.

- In this example, we created two validation services with one operation each. Thus, we have two send ports. If one of the validation services contained two operations, we would actually need one send port for each of the operations. The reason for this is that we need to be able to choose which outbound maps are executed and what SOAP Action to attach to the WCF request message. If the number of send ports were to become a concern, then the concern could be addressed by dynamically choosing which map to execute and what SOAP action to apply; however, this discussion is beyond the scope of this chapter.

- For the sake of brevity, there is no exception handling implemented in this orchestration. For a production-ready orchestration, it is recommended that SOAP faults conforming to both SOAP version 1.1 and 1.2 are catered for and that routing failures, timeouts, and delivery notification failure exceptions are all catered for when calling the validation services.

- In rare circumstances, the HTTP session made by the client might get torn down before BizTalk is able to deliver the response message back to the client. While this will result in a failure on the receive location, it won't stop the orchestration from sending the message on for further processing. To prevent problems, the processing orchestrations would either need to implement a level of idempotence (such that if the WCF client submits the same message again it will result in the same outcome) or the untyped orchestration will need to ensure that the response message was successfully returned to the client before it delivers the event message for further processing. Another option might be to consider making the event registration services into one-way services, with the validation results being sent back to the client asynchronously.

- By using friendly display names in our BRE vocabulary definitions, we've ensured that our BRE Policies are easy to understand. The benefits are even more realized if you use a tool such as BizTalk Documenter (https://biztalk2013documenter.codeplex.com/), which will document your BRE Policies for you.

- Through the usage of the validation resolver class that was instantiated and set in the orchestration and then passed to the BRE for resolution, we demonstrated how business logic should be separated out of orchestrations and placed in .NET assemblies instead. Orchestrations should primarily be used to orchestrate workflows rather than contain business logic.

- In a real life scenario, you might want to consider employing authentication, authorization, and XML validation on your WCF receive locations to ensure that you block garbage data from entering into your solution, which could possibly result in cryptic errors.

- In our AdverseEventReview example, we kept the routing instructions (LastStep and CurrentStep) within our message bodies and promoted these elements to ensure we could route based on them. In this example, we do not tamper with the message bodies at all and use only the context for routing. When you build your solution, do consider which approach would be the best fit for you.

- We briefly demonstrated the use of the CAT Instrumentation Framework for tracing purposes. In a fully implemented solution, the usage of the framework would most likely be extended to trace the entrance and exit of an orchestration, potentially to capture the timings of each scope in the orchestration and perhaps the entire orchestration itself, possibly some details about the untyped request message such as the `ProductClass`, `RegisteredCountry`, and `BTS.MessageType` context properties, and perhaps the status returned by each validation service. The framework can be downloaded from `http://btscatifcontroller.codeplex.com/releases/view/138246`. The CAT Instrumentation Framework Controller, which allows you to enable and disable tracing based on severity as well as by type (orchestration, WCF Service, Business rules, and so on), can be downloaded from `https://btscatifcontroller.codeplex.com/`.

Summary

In this chapter, we looked at a variety of orchestration usage scenarios that exploit BizTalk in a service-oriented fashion. Through the use of dynamic ports and direct binding, we can create very loosely coupled processes that are capable of reuse. By not directly connecting a batch of related orchestrations but rather relying on external routing rules, we make our orchestration act like encapsulated services whose execution sequence can be determined on the fly. And lastly, by leveraging untyped messages in orchestrations, we explored how to create reusable and flexible orchestrations that do not require changes to be made as more message types are implemented and need to be handled by said orchestrations.

In the next chapter, we'll look at how to take these service-oriented BizTalk artifacts and effectively version them so that new capabilities can be supported while causing minimal impact to existing clients.

11
Versioning Patterns

To improve is to change; to be perfect is to change often.

– Winston Churchill

Until this point, we looked at how to design and build many of the core components of a service-oriented architecture using BizTalk Server 2013. One of the most prominent aspects of SOA is the capacity to support change. This chapter focuses on how to change service components while introducing the least amount of impact to existing clients.

In this chapter, you will learn the following topics:

- The importance of versioning your SOA solution
- The types of components of an SOA that may undergo versioning
- Strategies for versioning schemas
- How to version endpoints
- How to version long-running orchestrations
- Ways to lengthen the life of production services and delay the need to explicitly introduce changes

Why versioning?

When I talk about versioning I don't mean simply updating code and pushing an updated set of libraries to target locations. A traditional, monolithic application is typically updated by rebuilding the entire solution and deploying the complete package to desktops or servers. This makes deployments fairly burdensome, but on the plus side, the developers are confident that the changes being made only affect entities within the discrete application boundaries.

A solution based on a SOA pattern is much easier to deploy because functional modules may stand alone if principles of encapsulation and loose coupling are correctly applied. Changes made to a single service shouldn't necessarily impact every component of the application and force a massive redeployment of the entire system. However, this flexibility comes at a cost. Unlike classic applications with discrete boundaries, SOA applications have components with a potentially disparate set of clients outside of the initially deployed application boundary. A service developer cannot know for sure who the clients for a given service are and therefore must treat future modifications differently than developers working in monolithic applications. Specifically, service developers need to apply changes through distinct new versions while keeping existing versions in a frozen state.

So true versioning means that multiple distinct versions are accessible simultaneously instead of simply overwriting the existing code base. This is important because those who rely on a particular service built and tested their applications around a specific behavior and SLA present at a specific point in time. This is even more important with the growing trend of public APIs, which are widely accessed and depended on. We must be careful to not impact these existing clients in way that fundamentally changes their contract with our service. Here lies the challenge; we need to provide a level of continuity to the existing clients while at the same time providing new or modified capabilities to clients that need them.

Note that a design pattern that lends itself well to an easy versioning of services is to exposed services with a message contract based on key/value pairs. Adding or removing elements that are supported by the service will typically not require any change to the service contract, taking away a lot of the frequently encountered pains associated with versioning. It should be noted that this doesn't lend itself well to the SOA principle of having well-defined contracts, so do choose carefully when you apply this concept. You can read more about mapping schemas based on key/value pairs to hierarchical schemas at https://code. msdn.microsoft.com/windowsdesktop/BizTalk-Mapper-Patterns-dd10187b.

A **version** of a component is typically comprised of both a major and minor version indicator. As a rule of thumb, the minor version is incremented for backwards-compatible changes while the major version is reserved for breaking changes. What is a backwards-compatible change as it relates to services? Backwards-compatible changes are the ones that produce no ill-effect or altered behavior for the existing clients. For example, switching a message parameter from being required to optional does not require service clients to alter any portion of their application. There may be functional implications that clients have to address in future releases of their own application, but a change of this type doesn't fundamentally alter the service contract. In another case, adding new service operations to an existing contract is considered a backwards-compatible change. Clients who use the existing contract are not impacted by the addition of new operations to the contract.

Major version updates are applied for breaking changes. For instance, if the service has a new mandatory parameter added to an existing service operation, then the client's contract is broken and their application will probably raise an exception. Similarly, adding non-optional elements to the schema of the response message being transmitted by the service will typically result in a breaking change. That is, if I add a new required field to a schema, clients built against the original contract will obviously not be able to satisfy this new requirement without rebuilding their application.

Pitfall

Even though the addition of new optional elements is typically considered a non-breaking change, some clients may still fail to adjust to this change if they use an aggressive XML/XPath strategy for reading response messages and rely on nodes being present at a specific position in the tree. If the client expects the Name node to be the fourth node from the root and the response message contains new (optional) nodes preceding the Name node, the client will encounter an error. This risk highlights the need for using a strong unit testing tool such as BizUnit so that you can automate the testing of positive and negative cases.

You should also take into account who the target audience of these services are and weigh up interoperability risks. If the target audience is fully composed of .NET applications, then it is safe to say that testing for breaking changes from .NET clients only will be sufficient. However, if you have a mixture of different types of clients, or you want to ensure that you have room for interoperability in the future, then you must consider whether your changes are breaking from a wider perspective.

In an architecture where reusable services are the goal, a pattern of versioning instead of *rebuild + redeploy* is the key to long-term success.

What service aspects may undergo changes?

In an SOA solution, there are four key areas that are subject to change: contract, address, binding, and implementation.

Let's take a look at the contract. As we discussed in *Chapter 7, Planning Service-oriented BizTalk Solutions*, contracts explain which operations the service exposes and the types of messages and exchange patterns supported by this service. So, as you can imagine, there are cases when all of those items are subject to change. A widely-used service, which provides an abstraction of business functionality is likely to be extended with new operations and capabilities. For example, when first created, a service may have operations for publishing both new and changed invoices. Sometime later, the service adds the capability to query and return existing invoices. Users may then request the capability to only return the status of a given invoice. Over time, our service has additional operations added while keeping the existing operations in place.

Similarly, a contract may adopt new versions of messages or entire new messages altogether. Inevitably, data schemas will undergo some changes as new fields are required or tighter restrictions are added to existing fields. When those modifications are made, our service contract must reflect the reality of the new message types that future operations can exploit. If you're willing to make a breaking change, then these updated messages can be applied to existing operations. However, breaking changes can be difficult to detect, so this reiterates the need for unit testing of all aspects of the service-oriented solution.

If a service needs to undergo significant changes, one of the best items to version is the address itself. This way, the client using an original version of the service has no opportunity to accidently collide with new or changed features and messages. By putting service changes at an entirely new URI, you are creating the ultimate "opt-in" scenario for clients.

As a WCF service matures, it's realistic that the binding will require changes. It's possible to introduce either breaking changes or backwards-compatible changes to a service binding depending on what is modified. Adding behaviors pertaining to data processing within the WCF server stack versus the transmission of data over the wire can often be backwards-compatible. For instance, we can add custom behaviors that perform message instrumentation, exception handling, or output caching without directly affecting service consumers. However, changing binding attributes or behaviors impacting security schemes, service timeout, or encoding strategy will result in a breaking change for the client application.

Finally, we can clearly expect the actual implementation logic of the service to mature over time. These can be incremental, backwards-compatible changes that address bugs, extend exception handling routines, or introduce processing efficiencies through caching. While many of these types of changes would not require service clients to be notified, it is critical to evaluate any change made to service implementation to determine whether or not it changes the behavior of the service in any way. Just because the interface doesn't change, it doesn't mean that the service hasn't undergone a functional modification that will cause the service to execute its logic in a way the client does not expect.

In order to maintain the confidence of service clients, we need to have a well-defined versioning and unit testing strategy that evaluates changes made to contracts, endpoints, bindings, and implementations and clearly articulates how to introduce such changes to your service layer.

How to version schemas?

Schemas define the messages that travel between our service endpoints and represent a core aspect of the service contract. As the need arises to reshape our schema to fit changing business needs, it's critical to understand the impact our choices have and strategies for minimizing impact on existing consumers.

What if we have an existing BizTalk schema exposed via a WCF service to client applications and decide to reorganize the underlying node structure of the schema? Alternately, what if we chose to remove existing schema elements and add new required ones? From our earlier discussion, this would seem to be a blatant breaking change. However, if you perform a vanilla exposure of a BizTalk schema as a service, these types of schema changes do *not* cause an immediate runtime exception in the client application, which is bound to earlier service versions.

At the beginning of this book, we talked about the fact that BizTalk receive locations are inherently "type-less". That is, they aren't explicitly tied to a specific schema format. Similarly, the BizTalk WCF service endpoints are not strongly typed to a particular message. This differs from the classic SOAP adapter service endpoints, where the designated schema was converted to a serializable .NET type and tightly bound to the service interface. If we updated a BizTalk-generated ASP.NET service with a new schema, then any legacy callers would receive errors about the now invalid data being sent over the wire. For the BizTalk WCF services, you can technically publish any object to a given endpoint, assuming you have not specified document schemas in your receive pipeline. The metadata associated with a WCF endpoint is purely reference data and not a binding part of the service interface. Let's prove that this is the case.

I've created a **Product** schema that we'll use throughout this chapter. Each product, or drug in our case, has attributes such as what it is used for, how often it should be taken, which countries have approved its use, and any critical safety issues to be aware of.

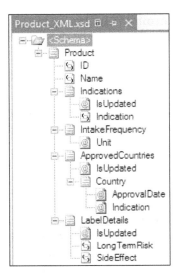

We then create a WCF service by exposing this schema as part of an asynchronous service contract, as shown in the following screenshot:

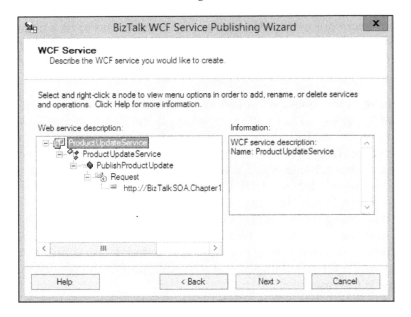

After starting up the corresponding receive location (and creating an associated send port, which spits our message to the filesystem), our client application is able to reference this service endpoint and interrogate its current metadata. Based on the types generated, our client builds up the product object and calls this service with the following code:

```
private static void CallProductUpdateV1()
{
Console.WriteLine("calling V1 service");

ProdUpdateSvc.ProductUpdateServiceClient client =
  new ProdUpdateSvc.ProductUpdateServiceClient
  ("ProdUpdateService");

  try
  {
    ProdUpdateSvc.Product prodInput =
      new ProdUpdateSvc.Product();
    prodInput.ID = "1234";
    prodInput.Name = "Watsonastic";

    ProdUpdateSvc.ProductIndications prodIndications =
      new ProdUpdateSvc.ProductIndications();
    prodIndications.IsUpdated = true;
    prodIndications.Indication =
      new string[] { "Oncology", "Immunology" };
    ProdUpdateSvc.ProductIntakeFrequency intakeFrequency =
      new ProdUpdateSvc.ProductIntakeFrequency();
    intakeFrequency.Value = "60";
    intakeFrequency.Unit = "Days";

    ProdUpdateSvc.ProductApprovedCountries approvedCountries =
      new ProdUpdateSvc.ProductApprovedCountries();
    approvedCountries.IsUpdated = true;
    ProdUpdateSvc.ProductApprovedCountriesCountry[]
      approvedCountry =       new ProdUpdateSvc.
      ProductApprovedCountriesCountry[2];
    approvedCountry[0] =
      new ProdUpdateSvc.ProductApprovedCountriesCountry();
    approvedCountry[0].ApprovalDate =
      DateTime.Parse("12/22/2001");
    approvedCountry[0].Indication = "Oncology";
    approvedCountry[0].Value = "USA";
    approvedCountry[1] =
      new ProdUpdateSvc.ProductApprovedCountriesCountry();
```

```
    approvedCountry[1].ApprovalDate =
      DateTime.Parse("08/10/2004");
    approvedCountry[1].Indication = "Immunology";
    approvedCountry[1].Value = "Germany";
    approvedCountries.Country = approvedCountry;

    ProdUpdateSvc.ProductLabelDetails labelDetails =
      new ProdUpdateSvc.ProductLabelDetails();
    labelDetails.IsUpdated = true;
    labelDetails.LongTermRisk = new string[]
      { "heart disease" };
    labelDetails.SideEffect = new string[]
      { "headache", "exhaustion" };

    prodInput.Indications = prodIndications;
    prodInput.IntakeFrequency = intakeFrequency;
    prodInput.ApprovedCountries = approvedCountries;
    prodInput.LabelDetails = labelDetails;

    client.PublishProductUpdate(prodInput);

    Console.WriteLine("V1 service completed");

    client.Close();
    Console.ReadLine();
  }
  catch (System.ServiceModel.CommunicationException)
    { client.Abort(); }
  catch (System.TimeoutException) { client.Abort(); }
  catch (System.Exception) { client.Abort(); throw; }
}
```

After confirming that our service works as expected, we can go ahead and change our existing **Product** schema. I switched the Indication field to the ID data type and made the Indication property of the Country node an IDREF data type. This forces a tighter restriction that says that only those indications for which this product is approved for can be associated with a given country's usage. I continued changing the schema by adding a new required element (Competitors) and renaming an existing element (Name to ProductName), as shown in the following screenshot:

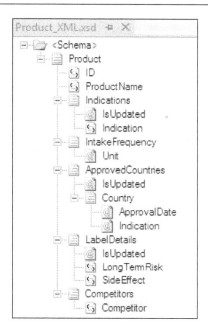

So in theory, these are all breaking changes. I've added restrictions to existing elements, added required elements, and changed the name of an existing element. After deploying the changes to BizTalk Server (and not updating our service contract) and calling our original service again, we see that everything behaves exactly as it did before. If we walk through BizTalk WCF Service Publishing Wizard again and overwrite our previous service with a new one (and make no changes to our client), we can still call our service with no errors. If we choose to update our service reference in the client application, then we are forced to address the contract changes represented in the generated .NET client types.

What does all this mean? Unless you apply data verification of some sort to a WCF behavior or to the receive pipeline, there is nothing preventing clients from publishing out-of-date, malformed, or in fact totally incorrect messages to the Bus. More importantly, from a client perspective, they will not get the same service behavior that they are used to getting. In my opinion, this is an essential reason to have a well-articulated (and practiced!) schema versioning strategy to ensure data mismatches are prevented. If it is your policy to never deploy breaking changes to a schema without explicitly versioning the schema (and service), you'll be in a good position to establish a consistent experience for service consumers.

So, how do you exactly version a schema? Your first thought may be to set the **Document Version** attribute that is part of the root schema node in the BizTalk Editor. However, this attribute is only an informational schema annotation and has no discernable impact on the processing of messages themselves by the parser. Similarly, the XSD standard itself defines a `Version` attribute on the root `<schema>` element, but again there is no semantic meaning attached to this value, and it is not supported in the BizTalk Editor environment.

The next choice is to explicitly add a `Version` attribute or element to your schema structure. While this method allows us to make MessageBox routing decisions based on the message version (assuming that you promote the node), it is still a content parameter and thus subject to client entry error and does not convey the true impact of changing a schema.

Versioning a schema through the namespace is the preferred mechanism. If you recall, the unique identifier for any message in BizTalk is typically the schema namespace plus the root node name. No two schemas should have the same combination of values, or else you run the risk of parser confusion within BizTalk Server. Because of the overall scope of the namespace, it is a prime candidate to communicate the version of a given schema. There are two choices I'd recommend when inserting version information into a namespace:

- **Numerical values**: It is perfectly acceptable to represent the schema version using the traditional numerical attributes such as:

  `http://BizTalkSOA.Chapter11/v1.1`

- **Date driven approach**: Instead of applying numerical values that denote no enterprise context, you can also use a date as the namespace version indicator:

  `http://BizTalkSOA.Chapter11/20081212`

  For many organizations, these dates would provide context to schema readers and associate the schema with major software milestones within the company.

There is no right or wrong choice between these two options. The numerical values provide greater granularity to designate major and minor changes, while the date-driven approach works well for enterprise services that are aligned with software platforms and organizational milestones. My only advice here is to pick a namespace versioning mechanism and apply it consistently across all schemas.

I'd be remiss if I didn't raise a warning about the impact of changing namespaces. If you are a seasoned BizTalk developer, you know that it's a real pain in the neck to accommodate namespace changes. Why? The schema namespace seeps into a myriad of locations within a BizTalk project:

- Schemas and imported/included references
- Maps and any custom XSLT within the map
- Pipelines and pipeline components
- Generated service metadata
- Business rules
- Orchestrations that contain custom XPath statements
- Helper components that execute against orchestration messages as XML documents

Changing namespaces should not be a task undertaken lightly. To that point, I'd recommend only changing namespaces (and thus versioning) for major versions. Minor versions that are assured to be backwards compatible do not need to have their schemas explicitly versioned.

 Where possible, try and eliminate the namespace portion of any XPath query you have to execute within maps, pipelines, orchestrations, or unit tests. If you simply use the `local-name()` function in your queries, then a namespace change will not break your existing XPath queries (assuming the queried node still exists following the schema update).

Schemas are arguably the most critical part of any BizTalk solution, and correctly applying versioning patterns to these schemas will enable your services to maintain their contractual agreements in a predictable way.

How to version endpoints?

The service endpoint is the gateway to the service. Clients who design, develop, and test against services on that endpoint expect consistent behavior. While there are non-breaking changes that we can introduce to our BizTalk WCF endpoints (for example, instrumentation or even internal mapping changes), we want to follow good practices when preparing to introduce new or modified capabilities to our service endpoints.

Let's look at an example here. Assume that we have a business process applied to the **Product** schema through the use of BizTalk orchestration. Our orchestration takes apart each section of the product and inserts or updates the relevant data into downstream systems:

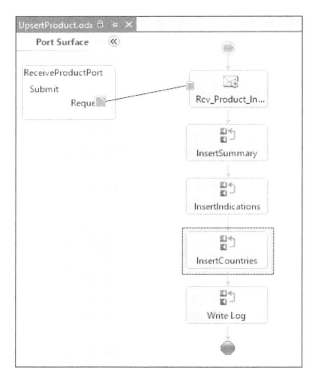

After deploying this orchestration, we bind its logical receive port to the WCF service receive port that we've created earlier in this chapter. When the business units come calling for **Manufacturing Locations** to be added to the product schema, we can apply namespace versioning and create a new orchestration that works with the updated schema type:

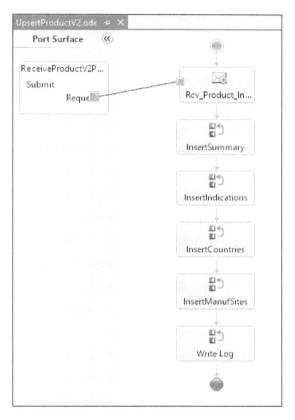

We need an additional endpoint to accommodate this new *schema + orchestration* combination. While we can attempt to reuse the existing endpoint or worse, overwrite it, we would rather leave our existing static endpoint and create a new distinct URI for service consumers. When we walk through **BizTalk WCF Service Publishing Wizard** this time, we should choose to *not* create a receive location for the service:

Once the service is created by the wizard, we should go to our existing receive port (that accepts the original product schema) and add a new receive location. This new receive location points to the latest service endpoint associated with the modified product schema:

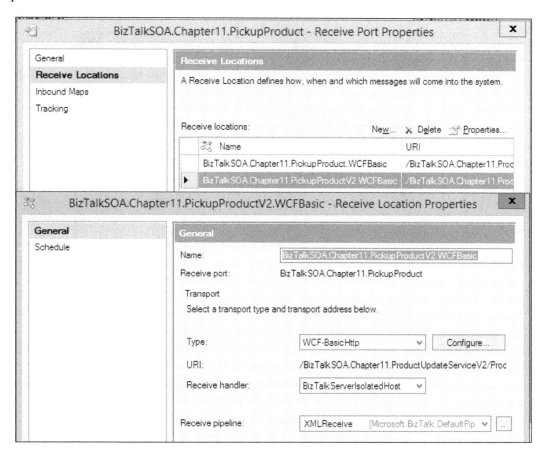

The new orchestration can now bind its logical receive port to this physical one. However, won't the orchestrations get confused? Now, I've bound two orchestrations to the same receive port, which in turn accepts two different types of messages. If we look at the subscriptions maintained by our orchestrations, we see that each one, while bound to the same receive port, is seeking a different message type:

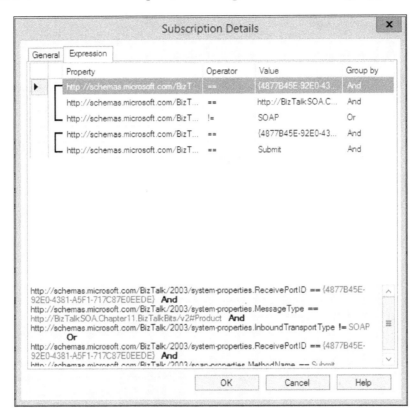

Instead of using BizTalk WCF Service Publishing Wizard to create a mirror image of the original WCF service, which only differs by URI, also consider versioning the service itself by altering the namespace of the service. This way, you can establish a distinct service definition that can be managed as a separate asset than the previous service version:

You may have looked at the last example and wondered "why create a whole new orchestration instead of trying to reuse and modify the old one?" In that example, the new orchestration does not introduce breaking changes to original clients but simply takes new data (if available) and adds to a system. So, it is indeed a candidate for reuse. However, how do we insulate our original service clients who are not ready (or willing) to upgrade their service contract to take advantage of the new schema? One word: maps.

BizTalk maps offer a powerful way to satisfy existing contracts while not sacrificing progress necessitated by business demand. For the preceding solution, we still need the two receive locations so that we host two distinct service URIs. However, we want to only maintain a single orchestration. To accomplish this, let's create a new map that takes the first version of the product schema and maps it to the second version:

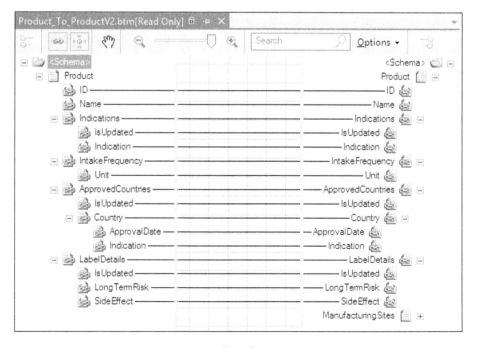

After deploying the updated assembly, we now apply this to the single receive port, which holds both receive locations. Remember that maps are applied based on message type, so this map will only be applied to the messages arriving via the original receive location:

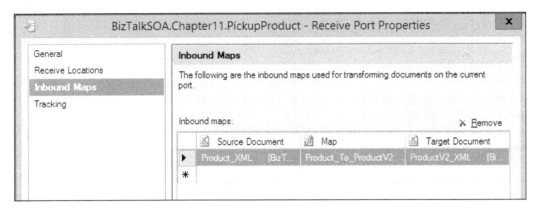

Now, when we call either of the service endpoints, we see that only the latest orchestration gets executed. Using this strategy, we can provide full continuity to legacy clients.

This principle also applies when talking about distributing messages to target systems through BizTalk send ports. In some cases, you will have an update to a canonical schema (and possibly the orchestration that operates on it) but certain downstream systems are not yet ready to consume the new standard entity. Once again, BizTalk maps to the rescue. We can apply maps to our send ports so that we gracefully downcast our new internal entities to the classic format expected by clients who are slow to change.

Creating endpoints for custom WSDLs

If we wish to use custom WSDL files instead of allowing BizTalk to define the metadata description, there are two ways to create endpoints that accommodate this. As we have seen in *Chapter 8, Schema and Endpoint Patterns*, you can define a WSDL document and associate it with a particular WCF receive location through the **externalMetadataLocation** setting of the **Metadata** behavior. However, how do we create the actual endpoints that use this WSDL?

The first choice is to exploit the **WCF-Custom** adapter and select an HTTP-based binding, which in effect enables BizTalk to act as an HTTP service host. There is no need to walk through wizards or create IIS services while still getting the advantages of the HTTP binding. Do note that you might experience differences in behavior between an in-process WCF endpoint and an IIS hosted endpoint in regard to queuing and other behaviors, and you will miss out on other capabilities of IIS, so don't make this decision lightly.

If you still wish to have a service hosted in IIS, you can do one of the two things. First, you can copy an existing BizTalk-generated service and rename the service file (`.svc`) and web application/directory. There is risk in getting this wrong, so you have the second option of creating a brand new endpoint. Since we don't want our service to produce any autogenerated description, we want to walk through **BizTalk WCF Service Publishing Wizard**, select the **WCF-CustomIsolated** adapter, and deselect the **Enable Metadata endpoint** option.

While we should choose to create a service from schemas, what we do on the following wizard pane is virtually irrelevant. The only thing that matters here is the message exchange pattern, which influences the type (one-way or request-response) of receive location generated for this endpoint. Why does the rest (service name, operation name, and message type) not matter? Remember that services generated by BizTalk for the WCF adapter have no contract logic embedded in the service itself. All we want is a physical endpoint that we can connect our custom WSDL to. Once the wizard completes, we can go into the generated project and remove the App_ Data folder, which contains the bits used for metadata generation. Finally, we can go into the receive location produced by the wizard and add a **Metadata** behavior with the **externalMetadataLocation** option pointing to our externally managed WSDL.

Using external WSDLs as a service's metadata source is a clean way to make backwards-compatible changes to services without going through the error-prone steps involved in overwriting a service via BizTalk WCF Service Publishing Wizard.

Having said that, BizTalk WCF Service Publishing Wizard is quite capable of regenerating existing services, allowing for tweaks and modifications, with minimal data entry. You can read more about this at the following link: `https://adventuresinsidethemessagebox.wordpress.com/2012/10/17/biztalk-wcf-service-titbits-organizing-your-biztalk-wcf-services-in-your-visual-studio-solution-regenerating-wcf-services-adding-wcf-services-as-a-resource-in-your-biztalk-application/`.

Let's say that we want to expose a service interface based on our **Product** schema and host that service using in-process HTTP via the WCF-Custom adapter. When creating the WSDL, we can make the (poor) choice of copying the XSD content of that schema directly, or we can reference the existing schema file. I created a WSDL file, which along with a copy of the **Product** schema, is hosted in IIS 8.0:

```
<?xml version="1.0" encoding="utf-8"?>
<wsdl:definitions name="ProductService"
    targetNamespace="http://BizTalkSOA.Chapter11"
    xmlns:wsdl=http://schemas.xmlsoap.org/wsdl/
    xmlns:soap="http://schemas.xmlsoap.org/wsdl/soap/"
    xmlns:tns="http://BizTalkSOA.Chapter11"
xmlns:bizsoa="http://BizTalkSOA.Chapter11.BizTalkBits/v1"
    xmlns:xsd="http://www.w3.org/2001/XMLSchema">

  <!-- declare types-->
  <wsdl:types>
    <xsd:schema targetNamespace="http://BizTalkSOA.Chapter11.
BizTalkBits/v1/Imports">
      <xsd:import schemaLocation=
        "http://chapter11:80/Product_XML.xsd" namespace=
        "http://BizTalkSOA.Chapter11.BizTalkBits/v1" />
    </xsd:schema>
  </wsdl:types>

  <!-- declare messages-->
  <wsdl:message name="PublishProductRequest">
    <wsdl:part name="part" element="bizsoa:Product" />
  </wsdl:message>
  <wsdl:message name="EmptyResponse" />

  <!-- declare port types-->
  <wsdl:portType name="PublishProduct_PortType">
    <wsdl:operation name="PublishNewProduct">
      <wsdl:input message="tns:PublishProductRequest" />
      <wsdl:output message="tns:EmptyResponse" />
    </wsdl:operation>
    <wsdl:operation name="PublishUpdatedProduct">
      <wsdl:input message="tns:PublishProductRequest" />
      <wsdl:output message="tns:EmptyResponse" />
    </wsdl:operation>
  </wsdl:portType>
```

```
<!-- declare binding-->
<wsdl:binding name="PublishProduct_Binding"
  type="tns:PublishProduct_PortType">
  <soap:binding transport=
    "http://schemas.xmlsoap.org/soap/http"/>
  <wsdl:operation name="PublishNewProduct">
    <soap:operation soapAction=
      "PublishNewProduct" style="document"/>
    <wsdl:input>
      <soap:body use ="literal"/>
    </wsdl:input>
  </wsdl:operation>
  <wsdl:operation name="PublishUpdatedProduct">
    <soap:operation soapAction=
      "PublishUpdatedProduct" style="document"/>
    <wsdl:input>
      <soap:body use ="literal"/>
    </wsdl:input>
    <wsdl:output>
      <soap:body use ="literal"/>
    </wsdl:output>
  </wsdl:operation>
 </wsdl:binding>

<!-- declare service-->
<wsdl:service name="PublishProductService">
  <wsdl:port binding="PublishProduct_Binding"
    name="PublishProductPort">
    <soap:address location=
      "http://localhost:8087/BizTalkSOA.Chapter11.
      ProductServiceCustom"/>
  </wsdl:port>
</wsdl:service>
</wsdl:definitions>
```

If I need to make a small, backward-compatible change to the schema associated with this service, the only thing I need to do is copy the `Product_XML.xsd` file to the web directory housing the WSDL file.

The other useful aspect of a hand-built WSDL is that we can add new operations to our service with little effort. If we use the same messages available in the WSDL (or even want to add references to new types), all we need to do is add a new operation to our `PortType` and `Binding` nodes in the WSDL.

Pitfall

Back in WSDL 1.1, we were able to do overloading of service operations. That is, we could have multiple operations named **PublishProduct** and have each one define a different parameter. This is great to name an operation name and provide newer messages in each copy. However, this capability was removed from the WSDL 2.0 specification. While WCF currently supports the WSDL 1.1 standard, the SOAP Basic Profile 1.1 additionally disallows operations with the same name existing within the same port definition. Regardless, overloading should be avoided in service-oriented design as we want our contract to have clear usage scenarios and limit the confusion for consumers.

Versioning long-running orchestrations

Orchestrations can be built to operate in a stateful, long-running fashion. This introduces a host of powerful service aggregation and coordination capabilities. However, it would appear to be quite difficult to ever find the right time to introduce a new version of such an orchestration. If we always have orchestrations dehydrated and waiting for messages, how can we ever hope to bring a new version online without being forced to tear down existing instances of the orchestration?

In this scenario, we want to initiate a manual review of any product label changes that have been introduced by the upstream systems. We need a new schema representing a product label review:

Next, we need a property schema that holds a pointer to the unique review
ChangeID review that this review schema retains during long-running processes:

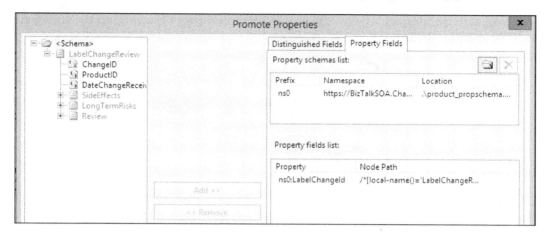

In order to inflate this review message, we need a map that takes the data from our
Product schema and maps it to the review schema:

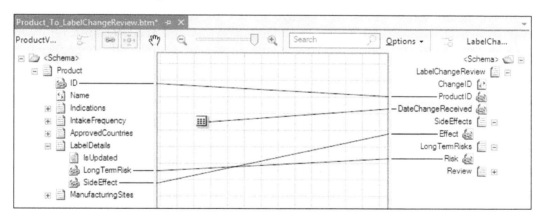

Because we'll be explicitly versioning our BizTalk assembly, I want to separate our new orchestrations from the various messages it uses by placing the orchestrations in a different assembly than the schemas and maps. Our workflow, not the underlying schemas, will undergo changes. After a new BizTalk project is added to the solution and the existing BizTalk project is referenced, we create a new orchestration that has messages defined for the **Product** message that starts the orchestration, and the review messages that are transmitted in and out of the orchestration:

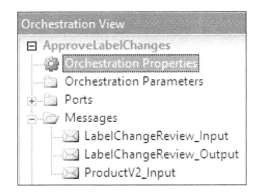

In this orchestration, the **Product** message arrives, the review message is constructed and review ID assigned, the review message is sent out, and at a later time, returned back to the waiting orchestration. The response message is then evaluated to see if the reviewer approved or denied the label change.

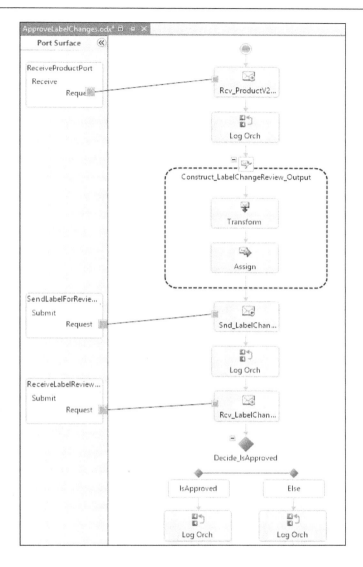

I've defined an orchestration variable that holds the version of this orchestration. Each **Expression** shape uses this variable when printing its status to the machine's Application Event Log. After creating the appropriate correlation type and set, and setting the necessary initializing and following attributes of the orchestration send and receive shapes, we can deploy this orchestration.

When we run this orchestration, we can see all of the version 1.0 designations. Before versioning our orchestration, let's initiate one more instance but leave it in a dehydrated state while it waits for the label review message to come back into BizTalk:

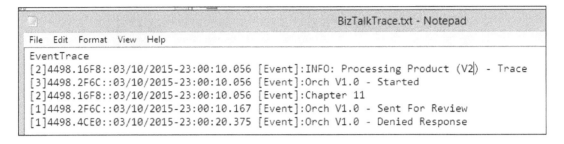

Back in Visual Studio.NET, we will change the actual assembly version of this project. To do this, we visit the project properties and look at the **Application** tab for the **Assembly Information** button. Clicking on this button reveals a set of assembly parameters, including the version. I changed my **Assembly Version** value to 2.0.0.0:

Next, I changed my internal orchestration variable so that we know that the version 2.0 orchestration is being executed when messages are written to the Event Log.

> If I were extremely clever, instead of manually setting the value of my version orchestration variable, I'd use an **Expression** shape at the top of my orchestration and set that variable's value to the following:
>
> ```
> System.Reflection.Assembly.GetCallingAssembly().
>     GetName().Version.ToString(4)
> ```
>
> This technique uses reflection to determine the version of the active assembly and will leave us with one less manual task when building a new version of an orchestration.

After deploying this project, we can see its distinct version designation by looking at the **Resources** section of this application in the BizTalk Administration Console:

Looking in the **Orchestrations** section of this application in the BizTalk Administration Console, we see our currently running orchestration and our new unbound, unenlisted one:

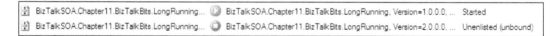

We want to bind this new orchestration to the same ports used by the original orchestration and then unenlist the original and enlist the new one.

> We do this so that any new messages arriving to BizTalk Server will only start with the new version of this orchestration and do not accidently run the out-of-date process. If we aren't careful about this, then we might end up having instances of both the old and the new versions of the orchestration spinning up when a new message that matches the relevant subscription is received.

If we send a new message in, we see the version 2.0 notifications in the Event Log:

```
                                        BizTalkTrace.txt - Notepad
File  Edit  Format  View  Help
EventTrace
[0]4498.3A14::03/10/2015-23:14:42.945 [Event]:Orch V1.0 - Started
[3]4498.3274::03/10/2015-23:14:42.945 [Event]:INFO: Processing Product (V2) - Trace
[3]4498.3274::03/10/2015-23:14:42.945 [Event]:Chapter 11
[0]4498.3A14::03/10/2015-23:14:43.029 [Event]:Orch V1.0 - Sent For Review
[2]4498.57FC::03/10/2015-23:15:01.318 [Event]:INFO: Processing Product (V2) - Trace
[2]4498.57FC::03/10/2015-23:15:01.318 [Event]:Chapter 11
[1]4498.A738::03/10/2015-23:15:01.318 [Event]:Orch V2.0 - Started
[1]4498.A738::03/10/2015-23:15:01.385 [Event]:Orch V2.0 - Sent For Review
```

As a best practice, we really should unenlist an old orchestration version and enlist a new orchestration programmatically within a single transaction. This helps minimize the window when no orchestration subscriptions exist. Refer to the BizTalk Help documentation topic entitled *Deploying and Starting a New Version of an Orchestration Programmatically* (http://msdn.microsoft.com/en-us/library/aa562027.aspx) for more details. In an ideal case, you should stop the inbound receive location to be 100 percent sure that no messages will come in during the orchestration switch-over.

An alternative strategy is to set a context property in your receive pipeline that denotes the receiving orchestration's version number, and you can have your orchestration's subscription based on this context property. Assuming that you have the means to update the version number that the pipeline component sets to the context at runtime (by reading the version number value from an SSO configuration store, using BRE Pipeline Framework or exposing the version number as a property of your custom pipeline component), you will be able to seamlessly direct messages from your old orchestration version to the new one without having to worry about timing issues.

Now what happens to our dehydrated orchestration associated with the version 1.0.0.0 assembly? If you recall, we unenlisted this orchestration, thus taking it out of regular usage by BizTalk. If we conclude this orchestration by sending back our associated product label review, which orchestration will it complete with? As you would hope, the original orchestration is still used when the product label review message returns to BizTalk.

```
                                              BizTalkTrace.txt - Notepad
File   Edit   Format   View   Help
EventTrace
[2]4498.0C30::03/10/2015-23:16:47.396 [Event]:Orch V2.0 - Denied Response
[1]4498.5C14::03/10/2015-23:16:47.397 [Event]:Orch V1.0 - Denied Response
```

> It is important to note that even though the orchestration is unenlisted and virtually invisible to BizTalk now, we get continuity so that the process that was agreed upon when this message was first received is the same process that brings resolution to the message. How is this possible? The unenlistment of our old orchestration removes any activation subscriptions (which prevents new instances of the old orchestration from starting up), but retains any existing subscriptions for active instances such as those anticipating a correlated response. Therefore, messages arriving into BizTalk will be accurately routed to the correct version of the running orchestration instances. If the new orchestration version is picked up where the old one left off, we'd inevitably run into both business and technical issues.

Once all the instances of your old orchestration version have completed and you are sure that you no longer need this version deployed, feel free to remove the orchestration assembly from the BizTalk Administration Console altogether. Keeping the number of deployed versions to a minimum helps keep confusion for support teams at bay, and reduces the risk that components that shouldn't be in a started state aren't started accidentally.

As you can see, BizTalk Server has fairly clean support for versioning even the longest running orchestrations. Note, however, that if your orchestration is not long running and you are able to negotiate periods of planned downtime during your deployments then the aforementioned process could possibly be considered overkill for your requirements and you might be better off adopting a file versioning strategy (which will be discussed shortly), and to perform your deployments with controlled shutdowns.

Versioning other BizTalk components

You may also want to consider how you should approach versioning other types of BizTalk components such as orchestrations that aren't long running, maps, pipelines, .NET helpers, WCF behaviors, or even pipeline components and mapping functoids. When it boils down to it, these are really just .NET assemblies and thus can be approached with a similar versioning strategy you'd follow for regular .NET assemblies with a few extra considerations.

The two paths you would typically take would be to increment the .NET assembly version and deploy the updated assembly alongside the existing assembly as detailed when discussing versioning long-running orchestration, or to overwrite the existing assembly while incrementing the file version, which will be discussed shortly.

One of the most important points you need to consider when deciding how to version these components is whether the change you're making is targeted at all the components that reference the updated assembly, a subset of these components, or new components only. When evaluating this, you of course need to assess whether you are introducing breaking changes to the changed components or not. If you're targeting all existing components then chances are you want to adopt a file versioning strategy. Otherwise, you will most likely need to adopt a .NET assembly versioning strategy with a side-by-side deployment to ensure that existing components continue to target the unchanged assembly, while new or updated components can target the updated assembly.

A further consideration is the type of assembly you're updating. Updating a BizTalk assembly that contains orchestrations, maps, or pipelines has far reaching consequences in contrast to updating a .NET assembly that contains a pipeline component, a mapping functoid, a helper class, or even a WCF behavior for that matter. The reason for this is that redeploying an existing assembly that contains BizTalk components often mandates that you shut the application down prior to the deployment. This usually isn't a problem if your BizTalk assembly only contains pipelines, but is almost always a problem if your BizTalk assembly contains orchestrations or maps, which are used within orchestrations or receive and send ports.

With orchestrations, you don't really have much of an option but to either negotiate downtime or do a side-by-side deployment; however, you do have more options with maps.

When your map is directly associated with an orchestration, receive port, or send port, then you'll find that you have no choice but to follow the same guidelines as you would to deploy a BizTalk orchestration. One way to get around this is to make use of dynamic transformation instead; in which case, no direct association or reference is made to the map.

You could always create your own dynamic transformation implementation by following guidelines such as those described in the article at `http://www.codeproject.com/Articles/13517/ Using-Dynamic-Maps-in-BizTalk`. An alternative, however, would be to leverage the in-built dynamic transformation capabilities of the ESB Toolkit or the BRE Pipeline Framework. Both of these frameworks support hot deployments for maps and are discussed further in *Chapter 12, Frameworks and Tools*, of this book.

Following on from this, another important point you need to consider is whether you will be allowed a period of downtime when deploying the new version of your component. Being allowed a period of downtime allows you to consider overwriting assemblies while adopting a file versioning strategy rather than forcing you down the path of deploying them side by side with a .NET assembly versioning strategy. If your changes are to a BizTalk assembly and that assembly is referenced by multiple BizTalk applications, then you would need to seek downtime for each of those applications if you weren't planning to perform a side-by-side deployment.

Lastly, you need to consider whether your component will support side-by-side versioning or not, as this might enforce extra constraints on you. By default, all .NET assemblies that are classified as containing BizTalk components must be signed with a strong named key and installed into the **Global Assembly Cache** (**GAC**) and thus support side-by-side versioning. This is also true for helper classes that you might want to reference from your BizTalk orchestrations or maps.

However, this isn't necessarily the case with BizTalk pipeline components, which you can opt not to sign. If this is the case, then there are a few extra considerations. If you want to overwrite an unsigned pipeline component, then you have to ensure that the updated DLL gets copied into the `Pipeline Components` subfolder of the BizTalk Server program files folder. You'll also find that if any host instances or IIS application pools have loaded the existing pipeline component into memory, then you will have no choice but to stop the said host instance or application pool in order to copy the updated assembly into the aforementioned folder. An alternative is to update the assembly name (possibly adding a version number as a suffix) when updating the assembly, but note that in this case, the new assembly will not target any existing pipelines that reference the pipeline component. These points should give you the hint that it is usually desirable to sign your pipeline component assemblies with a strong named key and install them in the GAC unless you have a very good reason not to do so.

File versions

When discussing how to version long running orchestrations or other BizTalk/.NET assemblies, we mentioned that you can version the .NET assembly version to load the old and new assemblies side by side. However, we also need a means of tracking version changes when making tweaks to existing components, whose assemblies we want to overwrite rather than deploy side by side with a new .NET assembly version. This is especially important when you have a BizTalk application deployed to an environment, have made changes to the source code in Visual Studio, but aren't sure whether your changes have been deployed to the environment or not.

If the .NET assembly version isn't being incremented, then the next best means of versioning your assemblies is through the use of the **File version** field:

If you deploy an assembly for which you've incremented the file version number, you will not notice any difference in the BizTalk Administration Console, Also, if you use the GACUTIL tool with the –l (list) switch, you'll see that the version number listed here is unchanged. The version numbers reflected in the BizTalk Administration Console as well as in the GAC are both the .NET assembly versions.

Where you will see the incremented version number is if you right-click on the assembly file in the file explorer, choose properties, and view the details tab. You'll notice that the incremented file version number is reflected in the **File version** and **Product version** records:

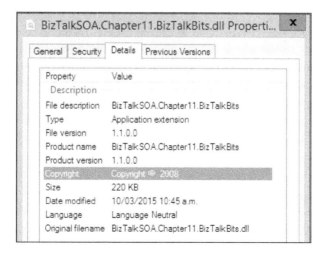

The most reliable place to check the file versions on your assemblies is in the GAC itself, since that is the single source of truth that BizTalk will use when loading assemblies. Assemblies compiled in .NET 4.0+ will be found in the `C:\Windows\Microsoft.NET\assembly\GAC_MSIL` folder by default; however, note that within this folder, you will see a subfolder per assembly name and a further subfolder per .NET assembly version/PublicKeyToken combination.

As a rule, you should always increment the file version on assemblies, which you change if the assembly has already been deployed to a nondevelopment environment. By doing this, you can always inspect the file version number of the deployed assembly rather than having to rely on jackhammering or reflection tools to try to figure out whether a change has been deployed or not.

 Even better, if you use an automated build server, get your automated build process to automatically increment the file version number for you in order to ensure that developers don't forget this step.

Versioning BRE components

Versioning BRE vocabularies and policies is very straightforward. In fact, the Business Rules Composer IDE doesn't actually give you the option to bypass the recommended versioning procedure for BRE artifacts. Once you have chosen to publish a BRE vocabulary or policy, it is not possible to unpublish it from the composer; you are forced to make a new version of the said vocabulary or policy if you want to make any changes.

Making a new version of a BRE artifact is easy. You can right-click on the top level of the vocabulary or policy and choose **Add New Version** to create a new version from scratch. Alternatively, you can choose to copy an existing version of the vocabulary or policy, right-click on the top level of the vocabulary or policy and choose **Paste Vocabulary Version** or **Paste Policy Version**. This allows you to use the copied version of the component as a starting point for the new version of the component.

While it is not possible to unpublish a published BRE vocabulary or policy, it is possible to copy an existing version, undeploy it if it is in a deployed state to set it back to a published state, delete it, paste the copied version, and then edit it.

Alternatively, you can even set the status of a published vocabulary or a published or deployed policy back to unpublished by updating relevant tables in the `BizTalkRuleEngineDb` database. This process is described at the following link:

`http://www.codit.eu/blog/2010/03/01/avoid-republishing-your-vocabularies-and-policies-with-the-business-rules-engine/`

Neither of these methods are recommended for BRE vocabularies or policies on environments except for development environments, or on versions of vocabularies or policies that have already been deployed to UAT or Production environments. If you do choose to follow one of these methods, then ensure that you have committed exported XML definitions for the existing version of the BRE components to a source control repository to ensure that you don't lose your current state.

Techniques for delaying change

Throughout this chapter (and hopefully the entire book!), we've been looking at building loosely-coupled services that accommodate flexibility and change. This includes direct bound ports that loosely coupled the messaging and orchestration layers, transforming messages at the edges to enable internal progression of components, applying explicit versioning attributes to schemas, and much more. Here, I'd like to investigate two ways to build solutions for volatile situations where change is constant and adaptability is vital.

Flexible fields

First, let's talk about situations where we want to future-proof parts of our schema that seem to be likely candidates for extension. In essence, we want to create a sort of flex field that enables us to stash additional information into the message even though there aren't explicit schema fields to hold that information. This is done through the use of the `xsd:any` element type. One example of using this is on an `Address` node where we want to allow parts of the organization to place country-specific or custom addressing attributes into the message without requiring us to create named elements just for them.

How about we build an actual example of this concept? I've created a new version of my `Product` schema (and changed the namespace to reflect this fact) and added a `DescriptionDetails` node. Here, I have a named element for the actual `Description` text, but have decided to also add a generic placeholder for details about this product that may only be relevant for a short time or for a specific audience. The `any` node allows any namespace and skips any attempt to match the contents to a particular schema:

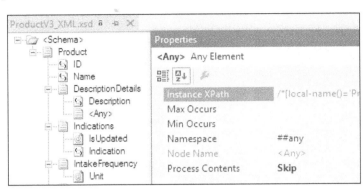

A bit earlier in this chapter, we handcrafted a WSDL file that we applied to an in-process HTTP receive location. Let's go ahead and extend that WSDL now in order to accommodate our new message type and operation and bypass **BizTalk WCF Service Publishing Wizard**. Our WSDL requires multiple small changes, which are as follows:

- A new namespace reference on the root node:

  ```
  <wsdl:definitions name="ProductService"
  ...
  xmlns:bizsoa3="http://BizTalkSOA.Chapter11.BizTalkBits/v3">
  ```

- A new type that references our (copied) schema that now resides on the web server:

  ```
  <wsdl:types>
  ...
      <xsd:schema targetNamespace=
        "http://BizTalkSOA.Chapter11.BizTalkBits/v3/Imports">
        <xsd:import schemaLocation=
          "http://chapter11:80/ProductV3_XML.
          xsd" namespace=
          "http://BizTalkSOA.Chapter11.BizTalkBits/v3" />
      </xsd:schema>
  </wsdl:types>
  ```

- A new message that points to the schema type needed:

```
<wsdl:message name="PublishProductV3Request">
    <wsdl:part name="part" element="bizsoa3:Product" />
</wsdl:message>
Addition of operation to the WSDL port type definition.
<wsdl:portType name="PublishProduct_PortType">
    ...
    <wsdl:operation name="PublishProductV3">
      <wsdl:input message="tns:PublishProductV3Request" />
      <wsdl:output message="tns:EmptyResponse" />
    </wsdl:operation>
</wsdl:portType>
```

- A new operation in the WSDL binding:

```
<wsdl:binding name="PublishProduct_Binding" type="tns:
  PublishProduct_PortType">
    ...
    <wsdl:operation name="PublishProductV3">
      <soap:operation soapAction="PublishProductV3"
        style="document"/>
      <wsdl:input>
        <soap:body use ="literal"/>
      </wsdl:input>
      <wsdl:output>
        <soap:body use ="literal"/>
      </wsdl:output>
    </wsdl:operation>
</wsdl:binding>
```

Once our WSDL is up to date, our service client can add/update its service reference to the WSDL. When we attempt to inflate the `Product` object in our client code, we can see that the `DescriptionDetails` member has a string-based attribute for the `Description` and an `XmlElement` attribute to hold the generic content.

In the code, I've built up this block of XML, which we will add to the `Product` object. It represents data about an advertising campaign for the product that will only be included in messages for a 45-day period. Instead of forcing the schema to be versioned over and over again to accommodate temporary data needs, we can place this data into our generic placeholder:

```
StringBuilder adBuilder = new StringBuilder();
    adBuilder.Append("<MediaBuy>");
    adBuilder.Append("<Agency>Demattia Partners</Agency>");
    adBuilder.Append("<StartDate>01/22/2009</StartDate>");
```

```
    adBuilder.Append("</MediaBuy>");

XmlDocument adDoc = new XmlDocument();
    adDoc.InnerXml = adBuilder.ToString();

    product.DescriptionDetails.Any = adDoc.DocumentElement;
```

When this client calls the service, we can see that BizTalk receives the message, and our temporary block of XML is nestled into the rest of the structure in a valid way:

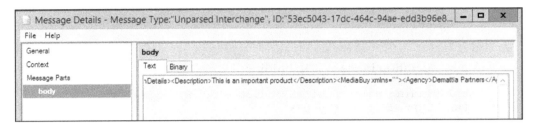

 This technique should not be a substitute for proper versioning of schemas. That is, you shouldn't place an xsd:any node at the end of every schema just so that you can avoid making changes in the future. A strongly-typed schema is a valuable commodity in the enterprise and the flexibility offered by the xsd:any node is no replacement for thoughtful design and diligent versioning.

Generic on-ramps

The previous technique demonstrated how to embed flexible elements into a strongly-typed interface. However, what are the options if you want a generic endpoint that can accept any number of different messages? In this scenario, we'll build an on-ramp to BizTalk Server that accepts any message the user provides. However, I'll show how we can encourage the developer to utilize a set of predefined message types when calling this loosely-typed service.

First, we need to build the generic endpoint. There are two options available. First, we can walk through **BizTalk WCF Service Publishing Wizard** and produce an endpoint. What data type would we use to generate a loosely-typed service? When using the classic SOAP adapter, we can create an orchestration that accepts a message of type `System.Xml.XmlDocument`, and then expose that orchestration as a service. However, this mechanism does not work the same when applying the WCF adapters. So, we should instead create a wrapper schema whose root node has a single child of the type `any` element. However, instead of walking through the wizard to produce such an endpoint, our second choice is to manually update an external WSDL with this wrapper schema and corresponding operation. Let's look at this second option in practice.

In the `wsdl:types` portion of my existing custom WSDL file, we need to add a new schema definition:

```
<wsdl:types>
  ...
  <xsd:schema xmlns="http://BizTalkSOA.Chapter11"
    elementFormDefault="qualified"
    targetNamespace="http://BizTalkSOA.Chapter11">
  <xsd:element name="ProductWrapper">
    <xsd:complexType>
      <xsd:sequence>
        <xsd:any namespace="##any" processContents="skip" />
      </xsd:sequence>
    </xsd:complexType>
  </xsd:element>
  </xsd:schema>
</wsdl:types>
```

As you can see, I have a `ProductWrapper` root node and allow any possible XML structure underneath it. Next, we need to add the appropriate message declaration to our WSDL:

```
<wsdl:message name="ProductData">
        <wsdl:part name="part" element="tns:ProductWrapper" />
</wsdl:message>
```

Now, we need to add our operation to the existing port type section and then update our WSDL binding:

```
<wsdl:portType name="PublishProduct_PortType">
  . . .
 <wsdl:operation name="PublishProductData">
  <wsdl:input message="tns:ProductData" />
  <wsdl:output message="tns:EmptyResponse" />
 </wsdl:operation>
</wsdl:portType>

<wsdl:binding name="PublishProduct_Binding"
  type="tns:PublishProduct_PortType">
 <soap:binding transport="http://schemas.xmlsoap.org/soap/http"/>
  <wsdl:operation name="PublishProductData">
    <soap:operation soapAction="PublishProductData"
      style="document"/>
    <wsdl:input>
      <soap:body use ="literal"/>
    </wsdl:input>
    <wsdl:output>
      <soap:body use ="literal"/>
    </wsdl:output>
  </wsdl:operation>
</wsdl:binding>
```

At this point, we are able to reference our WSDL from a client application, and we can then publish messages to the endpoint. However, we'd like to encourage developers to use a known set of types so that the message bus doesn't encounter a mess of unknown entities. What we can do is create the schemas that the bus should expect, create .NET objects out of those schemas, package the objects into a standalone assembly, and constantly provide fresh versions of these approved data types to our clients:

1. We start with a pair of schemas as per the following screenshot that describe the types of messages we expect our generic port to receive:

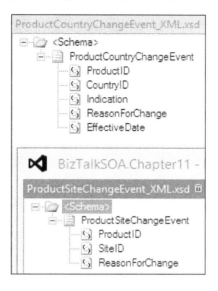

2. Next, we run the `xsd.exe` tool to build XML serializable objects for each schema. The command is as follows:

```
xsd /c /n:"BizTalkSOA.Chapter11.GeneratedTypes"
   "C:\BizTalk\Projects\BizTalkSOA.Chapter11\
   BizTalkSOA.Chapter11.BizTalkBits\
   ProductSiteChangeEvent_XML.xsd"
```

3. The resulting two C# class files should then be loaded into their own .NET assembly that can be shared with service clients. The generic service endpoint accepts an `XmlElement` object meaning that our typed classes need to be converted to XML for submission to the service. I wrote a helper function that I included in the assembly that holds the generated types. That helper function looks like this:

```
public static XmlElement ConvertObjectToXml
   (object inputObject)
  {
     XmlDocument tempXml = new XmlDocument();
     XmlSerializer serializer =
       new  XmlSerializer(inputObject.GetType());

     using (MemoryStream memStream = new MemoryStream())
     {
```

```
          serializer.Serialize(memStream, inputObject);
          memStream.Seek(0, SeekOrigin.Begin);

          tempXml.Load(memStream);
     }

        return tempXml.DocumentElement;
   }
```

4. In our service client, we first add a reference to our generic service endpoint. This gives us a service operation, which accepts `XmlElement`:

```
client.PublishProductData(|
void PublishProduct_PortTypeClient.PublishProductData (XmlElement ProductWrapper)
```

5. Next, we add a reference to our assembly containing the .NET types generated from the XSD schemas. Our client code inflates one of our strongly-typed objects and applies our helper function in order to cleanly send XML content to our service endpoint:

```
private static void CallGeneric()
   {
   Console.WriteLine("calling generic service first");

   ProdSvcGeneric.PublishProduct_PortTypeClient client =
      new ProdSvcGeneric.PublishProduct_PortTypeClient
      ("ProdServiceGeneric");

   try
   {
   ProductCountryChangeEvent countryChange =
      new ProductCountryChangeEvent();
   countryChange.CountryID = "90032";
   countryChange.ProductID = "322";
   countryChange.Indication = "Oncology";
```

```
countryChange.EffectiveDate =
  DateTime.Parse("12/29/2008");
countryChange.ReasonForChange =
  ProductCountryChangeEventReasonForChange.Approved;

client.PublishProductData
  (ConversionHelper.ConvertObjectToXml
  (countryChange));

Console.WriteLine("generic service completed");

client.Close();
Console.ReadLine();
}
catch (System.ServiceModel.CommunicationException)
  { client.Abort(); }
catch (System.TimeoutException) { client.Abort(); }
catch (System.Exception) { client.Abort(); throw; }
}
```

6. Now, we can create send ports in BizTalk Server, which subscribe to the message types sent via the generic endpoint. These send ports have subscriptions based on the BTS.MessageType so that we can clearly see that messages arriving via the generic port are treated the same as those coming in via strongly-typed WSDLs.

We're all done, right? Not yet. If you recall, we wrapped our generic payload in a ProductWrapper element. If we call our service as is, we get a suspended message in BizTalk saying that we have no subscriptions matching the inbound message (or an error saying message type not found if the ProductWrapper element isn't a BizTalk schema):

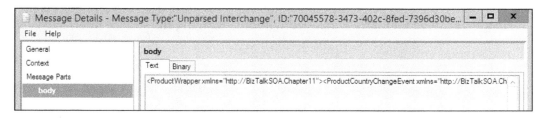

We need to rip off this header element and leave just the meaty center. This is where the new WCF adapters provide an easy solution. The **Messages** tab of the BizTalk receive location configuration allows us to specify the actual body of the inbound message:

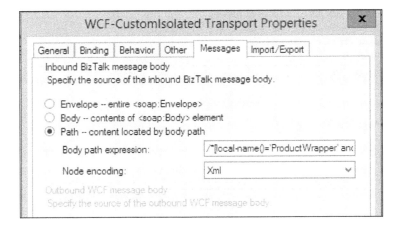

Instead of taking the entire SOAP body node, we can instead use a custom path to grab whatever is below the root node:

```
/*[local-name()='ProductWrapper' and
   namespace-uri()='http://BizTalkSOA.Chapter11']/*
```

Once this setting is applied, messages arriving to this receive location are appropriately parsed and our target payload is published to the MessageBox.

While a well-defined interface is an important part of a successful, reusable service-oriented architecture, there are cases where volatile business requirements will force a more creative approach to accommodate such cases. What we've seen is that you can create untyped endpoints while still providing a set of valid objects in a format that can be regularly versioned without changing the service interface itself.

Summary

It can be easy to fall into the lazy trap of simply taking an existing solution, making the changes to the necessary components, and overwriting those changes on the production servers. This chapter introduced you to strategies to version service artifacts and establish creative ways to build our services to accommodate changes. These strategies can be used in combination with the RESTful API versioning strategies discussed in *Chapter 4, REST and JSON Support in BizTalk Server 2013*, to ensure a high level of confidence that you know which components are deployed to which environment, and to ensure that you do not break existing interface versions that service consumers depend on.

In the next chapter, we start looking at tools and frameworks that you can leverage to build integration applications that closely follow SOA principles with ease.

12
Frameworks and Tools

A bad workman always blames his tools.

– Unknown

The old adage about a bad workman always blaming his tools couldn't be truer with technology, and this is especially true with the Microsoft integration stack. Armed with an understanding of the foundations of the .NET framework and tenets of integration, it is hard to find major functional gaps in mature integration technologies such as BizTalk Server, WCF, ASP.NET Web API, and Service Bus.

That said, having the right tooling can make the difference between a functioning and a finely tuned and orchestrated environment. There is much value to be added in areas such as service virtualization, additional decoupling, monitoring, and automated documentation.

In this chapter, you will be given an introduction to the following tools and frameworks and made aware of how leveraging them can help you build an effective SOA:

- ESB Toolkit
- BizUnit 4.0
- BizTalk 360
- AIMS for BizTalk
- BRE Pipeline Framework
- BizTalk Documenter
- Sentinet

This chapter only seeks to provide an introduction to the chosen tools and will not delve too deeply into their usage. Rather, it will aim to help you understand what you would use these tools for. Lots of further source material is available on the Internet, and we shall try to point you to some of the most reliable sources, or in other forms of publication to help you learn how to use these tools.

ESB Toolkit

The ESB Toolkit is an extension to BizTalk that aims to provide the means to implement **Enterprise Service Bus** (**ESB**) style patterns. You can read more about ESB patterns at http://en.wikipedia.org/wiki/Enterprise_service_bus. This is largely achieved via the introduction of new types of components called itineraries, resolvers, and adapter providers that mandate developers to implement a routing slip pattern. The routing slip pattern entails routing information or a routing slip being affixed to a message's context upon its receipt, with updates being made to the slip to track its progress as it reaches each additional stage of the route.

An itinerary is effectively the routing slip that gets affixed to the message. Microsoft has provided an extension to Visual Studio that lets you create these itineraries via a GUI-based editor. Once the itinerary has been developed and the developer has chosen to deploy it, Visual Studio will generate an XML representation of the itinerary, which will be deployed to the ESBItineraryDb database. Itineraries can be versioned as well, and multiple versions of an itinerary can be deployed at the same time.

When a message is received on an ESB toolkit-enabled receive location, the ESB Itinerary Selector pipeline component is used to resolve which itinerary should be affixed to the received message. This resolution can be done in a static fashion, where the itinerary name is hardcoded into the pipeline component. It can also be looked up based on a **Business Rules Engine** (**BRE**) policy taking the received message type and body into consideration. One can also choose to explicitly select a specific version of an itinerary or to leave the version unspecified, in which case the latest deployed version of the itinerary will be used. Keep in mind, however, that itineraries are cached by BizTalk host instances, and thus if you deploy a new itinerary version or choose to overwrite an itinerary version, it might not be read into the cache until the next refresh interval or host instance restart.

An itinerary is made up of on-ramps, off-ramps, and itinerary services. On-ramps and off-ramps represent BizTalk receive and send ports. Itinerary services are made up of messaging extenders, orchestration extenders, and off-ramp extenders. Messaging extenders are units of execution within receive or send pipelines of an on-ramp or an off-ramp, and thus, each messaging extender is contained within an on-ramp or off-ramp.

When you drag a messaging extender onto the itinerary design surface, you will be asked to choose a service name. This service name effectively defines what the unit of execution within the extender will be. Out of the box, Microsoft has provided a routing service and a transformation service for messaging extenders which cater for dynamic endpoint resolution and dynamic transformation, respectively. These itinerary services are extensible, however, and it is possible to create and register your own custom services, which can be leveraged in your itineraries. As previously mentioned, a messaging extender is contained within an on-ramp or an off-ramp and will be executed by the ESB Dispatcher pipeline component within receive and send pipelines.

Orchestration extenders are used to route messages to ESB Toolkit-aware orchestrations as part of the routing slip. These orchestrations will need to be designed with some specific considerations around activation filters and contained resolvers in order to be valid. They will also need to be registered in the ESB toolkit configuration files in order to appear in the itinerary design surface.

Finally, off-ramp extenders effectively let you route messages to your off-ramp.

Messaging and orchestration extenders allow you to nest resolvers within. These resolvers can be used to look up instructions for the containing messaging extenders. For example, the BRE resolver can be used to dynamically choose the transformation to execute against a message while the **Universal Description, Discovery, and Integration (UDDI)** resolver could be used to resolve transport details for a dynamic send port.

Both messaging extenders and resolvers are extensible, so it is possible to create your own implementations and register them for usage within itineraries. Some third-party products such as Sentinet provide custom resolvers, and additional custom messaging extenders and resolvers can be found in open source extensions of the ESB toolkit on CodePlex. Like orchestration extenders, these custom messaging extenders and resolvers must be registered in the ESB toolkit configuration file.

An additional important pipeline component that helps stitch an itinerary together is the **ESB Itinerary Cache** pipeline component, which is used in the send pipeline on a solicit-response send port as well as the receive pipeline on the same send port. The purpose of this pipeline component is to cache the itinerary on the message that is to be sent by the send port within the send pipeline and to then reapply the cached itinerary to the response message in the receive pipeline. This ensures that the itinerary flows through to the response message as the message context would otherwise be lost and the routing slip would not progress.

Bringing all these concepts together, the following itinerary is used to route messages to a solicit-response dynamic send port, performing messaging transformation and transport resolution based on BRE resolvers within the context of the receive pipeline on the receive location. Once the message has been sent to the target, the response message will be transformed within the receive pipeline on the send port with the transformation details looked up based on a BRE resolver before the message is routed back to the original receive location.

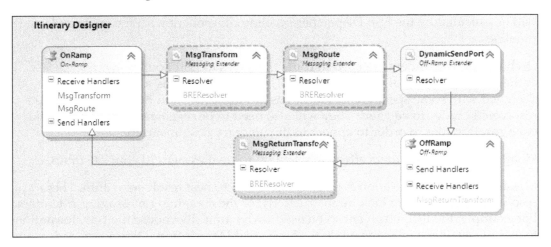

Beyond itineraries, there is additional value provided by the ESB Toolkit in the form of exception management and various other web services, such as transformation services and operations services, which allow you to request the status of a given BizTalk application.

Exception Management is delivered through the creation of the `ESBExceptionDb` database upon installation of the ESB Toolkit, which is used to capture details of exceptions encountered within BizTalk applications. The `Microsoft.Practices.ESB` BizTalk application, which can be imported into the BizTalk Administration Console upon installation of the ESB Toolkit, contains a send port called `ALL.Exceptions` that, by default, subscribes to all fault messages generated by BizTalk ports with routing for failed messages enabled. This can also be extended to cater for ports without this feature, based on subscriptions to **negative acknowledgement (NACK)** messages as detailed in this blog post: `https://adventuresinsidethemessagebox.wordpress.com/2012/12/19/routing-exceptions-on-send-ports-to-the-esb-exception-management-portal-without-turning-on-routing-for-failed-messages-part-2/`. By virtue of these subscriptions, the send port will log the exception details on the subscribed fault message to the `ESBExceptionDb` database.

Also contained within the ESB Toolkit is a sample Exception Management Portal, which can be used to visualize exception statistics and to display exception details contained within the `ESBExceptionDb` database. Do keep in mind however, that this is a sample portal, and you will need to ensure that you are confident in deploying and maintaining it and that you might meet some challenges while carrying out upgrades to your BizTalk environment.

While the ESB Toolkit isn't required to implement an ESB pattern or to build a SOA architecture in your BizTalk Server environment, the itinerary design pattern does encourage developers down these paths. The ESB Toolkit can be used to provide for the loose coupling required in a SOA environment and should definitely be considered. For more information about the ESB Toolkit, you can pick up the book *Microsoft BizTalk ESB Toolkit 2.1* by *Packt Publishing*.

BizUnit 4.0

BizUnit 4.0 is a declarative and extensible testing framework that can be used to create robust automated tests for integration solutions. It too is a community-driven open source project that can be found on **CodePlex** (`https://bizunit.codeplex.com/`).

Before delving into its capabilities, let's delve into two misconceptions regarding this framework that derive from its name. BizUnit is in no way relegated to BizTalk (even though it is commonly used to test BizTalk projects) beyond the fact that many BizTalk-specific test steps are catered for out of the box. BizUnit can be used to test pretty much any integration solution, and where the framework doesn't contain a test step that caters for your requirements, a custom test step can easily be written. The second misconception is that BizUnit is not relegated solely to unit testing. Arguably, BizUnit is at its best when used for integration testing since it shines when multiple steps are being stitched together. This doesn't mean that you can't unit test using BizUnit, which is still very much possible; just don't assume that this is solely a unit testing framework.

Now that we have that out of the way, let's dive into what makes this framework a great complement to integration solutions. The first standout point is the number of available test steps. Out of the box, you will find test steps that cater for file writing and reading, SQL database query execution, HTTP posting, SOAP, XML validation, host instance restarts, receive location / send port / orchestration disabling and enabling, and pipeline execution, to name just a few. This large list of test steps is further complemented by the multitude of community test step contributions, such as WCF, Oracle, AS2, and so on. Writing test steps couldn't be easier in BizUnit 4.0, and it is very feasible for you to build up a collection of test steps that cater for scenarios that might be specific to the way you do things within a project you're working on or within your organization.

The top level of a BizUnit test is a test case. A test case is made up of multiple stages: setup, execution, and cleanup. Each of these stages can contain zero to many test steps, as required. These test steps are the actual units of execution required to carry out the test. A test case can be built using code or in XAML. It is also possible to first write a test case in code and to have the XAML automatically constructed based on the code. Here is an example of a test helper method that is used to test the BRE Pipeline Framework to execute a pipeline passing in an input message and context file and to validate the output context based on a collection of XPath queries:

```
public static void BREPipelineFrameworkSendPipelineBaseTest
  (string InputFileName, string InstanceConfigFilePath,
  XPathCollection _XPathCollection, TestContext
  testContextInstance) {
    var _BREPipelineFrameworkTest = new b.Xaml.TestCase();
    var pipelineTestStep = new
      b.TestSteps.BizTalk.Pipeline.ExecuteSendPipelineStep {
        PipelineAssemblyPath = testContextInstance.TestDir +
          @"\..\..\BREPipelineFramework.TestProject\bin\debug\
          BREPipelineFramework.TestProject.dll",
        PipelineTypeName = "BREPipelineFramework.TestProject.
          Snd_BREPipelineFramework",
        SourceDir = testContextInstance.TestDir +
          @"\..\..\BREPipelineFramework.UnitTests\
          Sample Files\Input Files",
        SearchPattern = InputFileName,
        Destination = testContextInstance.TestDir +
          @"\..\..\BREPipelineFramework.UnitTests\
          Sample Files\Output Files\Output.txt",
        OutputContextFile = testContextInstance.TestDir +
          @"\..\..\BREPipelineFramework.UnitTests\
          Sample Files\Output Files\Context.xml",
        InstanceConfigFile = InstanceConfigFilePath,
    };
    _BREPipelineFrameworkTest.ExecutionSteps.
      Add(pipelineTestStep);
    var fileReadMultipleStepContext = new
      b.TestSteps.File.FileReadMultipleStep {
        ExpectedNumberOfFiles = 1,
        DeleteFiles = false,
        DirectoryPath = testContextInstance.TestDir +
          @"\..\..\BREPipelineFramework.UnitTests\
          Sample Files\Output Files",
        SearchPattern = "Context.xml",
        Timeout = 3000
    };
```

```
        var xmlValidateContextStep = new
          BREPipelineFramework.CustomBizUnitTestSteps
          .XmlValidationStep();
        foreach (KeyValuePair<string, string> pair in
          _XPathCollection.XPathQueryList) {
            var xPathDefinitionPropertyValue = new
              BREPipelineFramework.CustomBizUnitTestSteps.
              XPathDefinition {
                Description = "Property Value Test",
                XPath = pair.Key,
                Value = pair.Value
            };
            xmlValidateContextStep.XPathValidations.Add
              (xPathDefinitionPropertyValue);
        }
        fileReadMultipleStepContext.SubSteps.
          Add(xmlValidateContextStep);
        _BREPipelineFrameworkTest.ExecutionSteps.
          Add(fileReadMultipleStepContext);
        var bizUnit = new b.BizUnit(_BREPipelineFrameworkTest);
        bizUnit.RunTest();
    }
```

BizUnit provides a base class called `TestStepBase`, from which your test steps must derive. You are able to add whatever properties, constructors, and helper methods that help you achieve your goals to the said class. However, the real logic will live in the `Execute` and the `Validate` methods, which you will need to override from the base class. The `Execute` method will carry out the logic required by the test step, while the `Validate` method will be used to ensure that the instance of the class has been correctly populated with all the required properties. The following snippet is the source code for the out of the box `DelayStep` which is used to introduce a delay between test steps in your test case. This should help demonstrate the simplicity of creating a test step:

```
namespace BizUnit.TestSteps.Time {
  public class DelayStep : TestStepBase {
    private int _timeOut;
    public int DelayMilliSeconds {
      set { _timeOut = value; }
      get { return _timeOut; }
    }
    public override void Execute(Context context) {
      context.LogInfo("About to wait for {0} milli seconds...",
        _timeOut.ToString());
      Thread.Sleep(_timeOut);
```

```
        context.LogInfo("A delay of {0} milli second has
          successfully completed.", _timeOut.ToString());
      }
      public override void Validate(Context context) {
        // _timeOut - no validation required
      }
    }
  }
}
```

Beyond the TestStepBase base class, BizUnit also offers two other base classes that
can be used to great effect, SubStepBase and DataLoaderBase. Classes that derive
from SubStepBase can be used to nest substeps within a TestStep. An example use
case for this class is to validate a message, potentially based on XML validation or
binary comparison with an expected output file.

The DataLoaderBase class is used to load data into a test step. A typical use case
for the DataLoaderBase class would be in a test step that sends a request to a target
system, such as a WCF service. Classes derived from DataLoaderBase could even
be taken a step further to manipulate a message before it is read in to the test step,
allowing you to minimize the number of input files that need to be saved in your
test project.

Both of these base classes allow for a test step author to create his class with a level
of agnosticism with regards to how a source file will be provided to his test step, or
how validation will be performed. While writing the test step, the author need not be
concerned about how the data will be fetched nor how validation will be performed,
which opens the door to the test step being used in all kinds of creative ways. Here is
a snippet of the community-provided WCFRequestResponseTestStep that is used to
call a WCF Service, with a request loaded in via a data loader, which then validates
the response based on a collection of substeps:

```
public class WcfRequestResponseTestStep : TestStepBase {
  private Stream _request;
  private DataLoaderBase dataLoader;
  public DataLoaderBase DataLoader {
    get { return dataLoader; }
    set { dataLoader = value; }
  }
  public WcfRequestResponseTestStep() {
    SubSteps = new Collection<SubStepBase>();
  }
```

```
public override void Execute(Context context) {
  _request = dataLoader.Load(context);
  //Do stuff to call the WCF service based on the request and
  populate the response stream
  foreach (var subStep in SubSteps) {
    try {
      // Try the validation and catch the exception
      response = subStep.Execute(response, context);
    }
    catch (Exception ex) {
      context.LogException(ex);
      throw;
    }
  }
}
```

So why would you want to use BizUnit rather than just create a Visual Studio unit test method? The primary reason is that, with BizUnit, rather than concentrate on building all the plumbing required to implement your test scenario in your test method, you can leverage the existing test steps that are provided out of the box in the BizUnit framework. Where a test step doesn't already exist, you are able to write your own custom test steps, and if you design these well, they can be reused in future projects. A developer who is familiar with BizUnit is empowered to implement complicated test scenarios with relative ease and can take advantage of the framework's extensibility points to implement whatever custom validation he wants to. All of this could potentially be achieved using Visual Studio unit tests, and in fact, you could even build up your own library of helper classes to achieve the same outcome. However, the fact that BizUnit provides a substantial variety of test steps out of the box should, at the very least, prompt you to consider using the framework.

In closing, SOA environments are ever-changing beasts that require the constant extension of an existing code base. Frameworks like BizUnit provide a lot of value by enabling developers to create predictable tests that can be run when changes are made to a solution to ensure that existing functionality has not been broken as well as to test that new functionality fulfills the given requirements.

Monitoring tools

Monitoring integration platforms can be a large challenge given their black box like nature. As a result, BizTalk support teams typically need to be composed of specialists, as a deep understanding of the product is required to be able to troubleshoot problems. A large degree of trust also needs to be provided to support teams due to the lack of granular access rights while accessing the BizTalk Administration Console.

While these problems can be circumvented in relatively smaller organizations by having one or two dedicated BizTalk support specialists on board, such a solution doesn't scale well for a large SOA. This would typically require a larger team to deal with the increased surface area of the BizTalk environment and a high level of proactive support to ensure the health of the environment.

A wide array of tools, such as the BizTalk Health Monitor, the ESB Exception Management Portal, BAM, Message Box Viewer, BizTalk Terminator, Performance Monitor, and the Windows Event Log, would need to be accessed on a semi-regular basis to perform support functions. The knowledge required to use these various tools raises the barrier to entry for support personnel who want to focus on BizTalk support.

Enterprise monitoring tools, such as **Systems Centre Operation Manager (SCOM)** or HP OpenView, can be used to provide a consolidated view of the health of the infrastructure used to host BizTalk Server as a well as a view of the health of BizTalk application components through the use of BizTalk-specific plugins. These platforms, being focused on much more than just BizTalk Server, require a level of specialization. The costs might also be prohibitive for small- to medium-sized organizations.

As a result of the difficulties involved in BizTalk operations monitoring, multiple third-party monitoring solutions have sprung up that focus on BizTalk Server alone, using their targeted focus to solve common problems that are experienced by BizTalk support teams. Two of the most standout products are introduced next, both of them focusing solely on BizTalk Server and thus having the luxury of providing targeted solutions to make the lives of BizTalk support personnel easier and consolidate the number of tools that support personnel need to use on a daily basis.

BizTalk 360

BizTalk 360 is a monitoring tool that was designed and developed based on the experiences of BizTalk specialists who encountered many of the gaps in the BizTalk Server platform we discussed and decided to address them.

BizTalk 360's features are based on four core pillars, and some of the primary features based on each of these pillars are listed here:

- **Operations and administration**:
  - ○ BizTalk 360 provides a single portal from which all BizTalk configuration, management, monitoring, and reporting can be carried out.
  - ○ This portal contains many productivity tools that provide functionality such as the ability to search for components, providing a consolidated event viewer tool that aggregates events from across the multiple servers in a BizTalk group, the ability to run and schedule Message Box Viewer reports, and an integrated knowledge base.

- ° The portal provides a graphical message flow visualizer that displays the route that messages have taken through BizTalk. This is especially useful in loosely coupled applications where it isn't always immediately obvious to support teams where a message originated from or is destined to be delivered to.

- ° The portal contains views that help you to diagnose whether and why your BizTalk environment is undergoing throttling.

- ° The portal provides a consolidated view of the health of backup/DR SQL Agent jobs.

- ° The portal also provides tools, such as an advanced event viewer, custom SQL queries, and so on, that will reduce the need for people to have direct access into BizTalk servers and SQL databases.

- **Security and audit**:

  - ° Unlike the BizTalk Administration Console and other out of the box tools, granular user access rights can be configured to allow specific users to only have access to a nominated set of features or components to manage within the BizTalk 360 portal.

  - ° BizTalk 360 audits all changes and management activities that are carried out via the management portal, including activities such as finding out who disabled a receive location. One would typically have no visibility of such activities using the BizTalk Administration Console.

  - ° As all support activities are catered for using a web portal, no RDP access is required to the servers, except perhaps for infrastructure-level support.

- **All your data in one place**:

  - ° The BizTalk 360 portal provides views of components that would otherwise require access to an array of MMCs and IDEs (for example, BAM portal, ESB portal, Business Rules Composer, Event Viewers, Message Box Viewer, and so on). In some cases, these views are read only, while in others, they provide equivalent functionality compared to the primary store for the given component.

- **Monitoring**:
  - ○ BizTalk components such as receive locations, orchestrations, and send ports can be monitored with automatic alerting in case they enter an undesired state.
  - ○ BizTalk 360's data monitoring capability allows users to set up monitoring for various data points available in BizTalk server, such as message box, tracking, EDI, ESB, and BAM data. For example, users can watch out for suspended instance counts for a specific application with a specific error code, and if the count reaches certain thresholds, a notification can be generated and sent. Some actions, such as terminating the instances, can also be automated.
  - ○ Alerting can be based on thresholds whereby alerts won't be sent out until a certain number of errors have been encountered and duplicate errors can be suppressed.
  - ○ The desired states of monitored components can be explicitly set so that, in cases where you expect a send port to be stopped, BizTalk 360 won't generate alerts.
  - ○ Monitoring is also extended to the OS/infrastructure layer with alerting based on CPU/memory usage, the status of Windows services, disk space, and event logs on the BizTalk Server as well as the underlying SQL server(s) for the BizTalk group.
  - ○ Monitoring can generate heartbeats to SOAP/RESTful endpoints to ensure the correct HTTP status code is returned by the endpoint.
  - ○ Monitoring can generate messaging threshold-based alerts similar to BAM alerts to notify support teams when abnormal levels of activity are encountered.

 You can read more about BizTalk 360 on the official website at http://www.biztalk360.com/.

AIMS for BizTalk

AIMS for BizTalk is a monitoring solution differentiated with a focus of proactive self-learning and intelligent alerting with reports providing additional technical and business-oriented insight about BizTalk. AIMS was created to simplify and automate the complex task of integration monitoring by a team with a strong belief that traditional monitoring where users need to select parameters and thresholds fail. In addition, it provides proactivity to prevent really costly downtime and processing issues and also caters for process insights.

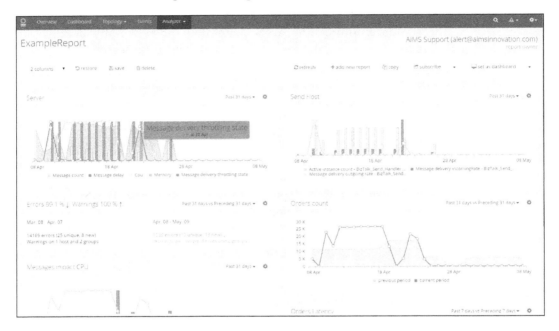

AIMS' feature set centers around monitoring and business insight. A subset of the key features provided by AIMS for BizTalk are as follows:

- Proactive monitoring based on self-learning of normally observed behavior patterns with dynamic thresholds. This allows AIMS to easily detect any anomalies and their impacts on the BizTalk environment and then send out a proactive warning pinpointing the situation and possible impacts.

- Reactive monitoring, which provides alerts on errors occurring on your BizTalk environments. This feature also provides notifications about components stopping or getting started.

- Custom monitoring, which allows you to apply an additional set of monitoring rules on any port or orchestration. You can select between message count, message delay, and message volume in any time range and will receive an alert if deviations are detected.

- AIMS will audit changes to your BizTalk environment. AIMS detects any un-deploys/redeploys, component status changes, and changes in messaging patterns. These changes are logged and presented by AIMS either as a dashboard component or within an e-mail report.

- AIMS provides an automated, real-time topological map of your BizTalk environment, from a high-level server view down to observed messaging patterns, highlighting dependencies between ports and orchestrations.

- A daily **Application Performance Index (APDEX)** score, which provides a very quick view into the performance of your BizTalk environment on the current day.

- Visualization of statistics for the current period in comparison to previous periods for the purpose of trend analysis.

- Displays correlation of different statistics such as CPU versus message counts that can help during root cause analyses.

- Allows for comments to be added to specific events, providing further instruction for specific support personnel to undertake or to mark an event as ignored.

- Provides the ability to build customized reports based on out-of-the-box building blocks.

 You can read more about AIMS for BizTalk on their website at `http://www.aimsinnovation.com/`.

The BRE Pipeline Framework

The BRE Pipeline Framework is an open source project located on CodePlex (`https://brepipelineframework.codeplex.com/`) that allows for the execution of BRE policies in BizTalk pipelines. The primary goal of the framework is to encourage developers to build loosely coupled solutions that do not rely on orchestrations where they are not warranted. This is achieved by providing utility functionality and extensibility such that custom utility can also be implemented. This utility can all be called upon in a conditional fashion, using the BRE as a container for the conditions and actions, from within a pipeline via the provided pipeline component. Some of the out-of-the-box features of the framework are as follows:

- Getting and setting context properties—in the case of out-of-the-box context properties, enumerations are provided for property names and namespaces to reduce chances of errors and promote awareness of the various properties

- Read configuration from SSO configuration stores or from **Trading Partner Management (TPM)** party configuration

- Execute queries based on regular expressions, XPath, or string searches in message bodies

- Get and set message part properties

- Cache and reapply context properties to a message

- Execute maps conditionally, potentially stringing multiple maps together within a single pipeline

- Updates to message bodies in a streaming fashion, including updating element names, namespaces, and values

- Custom ETW trace statements that will be executed from within BRE policies based on the CAT Instrumentation Framework

- Providing debug traces of condition evaluation and rules firing to help troubleshoot issues

- Providing friendly vocabularies for all of the out-of-the-box utility, which is very automatic documentation generation friendly

This utility is all delivered in the form of vocabularies based on .NET facts. The framework also allows for the more traditional XML based facts, which allow you to run XPath queries to assess and manipulate message body values. Lastly, the framework also caters for SQL-based facts that allow you to query and update data in SQL databases.

The BRE Pipeline Framework addresses one of the primary difficulties associated with the BRE. In order to make use of a vocabulary definition, an instance of a corresponding fact must be passed into the policy during execution, and this applies regardless of the fact type. This challenge is circumvented by providing the ability to easily instantiate various types of facts. This is done by allowing for two BRE policies to be run within the pipeline, one called an **Instruction Loader Policy** (which is optional), which resolves the facts that are required and instantiates them, and a secondary policy called the **Execution Policy**, which allows for the instantiated facts to be assessed and manipulated appropriately. The instruction loader policy caters for the various types of facts in the following manners:

- In the case of .NET facts, the fully qualified class name and assembly name are specified in the Instruction Loader Policy, which results in an object instance of that class being asserted as a fact to the Execution Policy.

- In the case of XML facts, the XML document type must be specified in the Instruction Loader Policy so the Execution Policy knows which vocabulary definitions are valid against the message body. The message type context property can be inspected in the Instruction Loader Policy so that you can dynamically choose what the XML document type is.

- In the case of a SQL fact, a connection string to the database instance must be specified in the Instruction Loader Policy, along with the name of the database and the name of the table. Utility is provided to read in the connection string from an SSO configuration store application so that sensitive credentials don't need to be contained in BRE policies if integrated security is not an option.

If the only utility required is that catered for by the framework out of the box, an Instruction Loader Policy is not required at all. On the flip side, if you want to inject your own utility classes into your Execution Policy, you just need to ensure that your utility classes derive from the base classes provided for by the framework and you can use an Instruction Loader Policy to instantiate an instance of your class and assert it into your Execution Policy.

One additional feature of note is that the BRE Pipeline Framework pipeline component allows the developer to set a property called `ApplicationContext`. This property is used to pass some additional context into the BRE Policies that are called about the calling pipeline. The property would typically be set to the pipeline name, or if the pipeline component was used multiple times within the pipeline (for example once prior to disassembly and once post disassembly), then it would be set to the pipeline name plus the pipeline stage. This `ApplicationContext` can be evaluated in conditions within the called BRE Policies, thus allowing for certain rules to only fire when nominated pipelines call the policy. This allows for a single policy to contain rules for an entire application, with the `ApplicationContext` being used to quickly filter which rules get fired for which pipeline, potentially in combination with more conditions if more dynamism is required.

An Execution Policy consists of rules that assess message content and context, resulting in actions being fired for rules on which all conditions evaluate to `True`. Actions can be used to update the message content and context. An example of a rule within an Execution Policy is shown here. In this case, if the application context passed in as a property value from the pipeline component is `Test_ReplaceDocumentNamespaceAndPrefix`, the framework will replace the target namespace of the root node of the message body with `http://brepipelineframework` and replace the namespace prefix with `bre`.

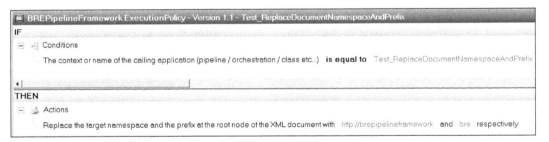

There is some overlap between the BRE Pipeline Framework and the ESB Toolkit in that both of them can be driven based on the BRE for resolution purposes, and for the most part, logic is executed within the context of a BizTalk pipeline. Where they differ is that the ESB Toolkit introduces a completely new development paradigm in the way of itineraries that implement the routing slip pattern and is largely focused on dynamic endpoint resolution. BRE is only one of the choices for resolution in the ESB toolkit, with other resolution mediums catered for as well. In contrast, the BRE Pipeline Framework is closer to vanilla BizTalk development in that it doesn't introduce any new types of development artifacts, and its primary focus is utility rather than endpoint resolution. There is no reason the two frameworks should not be used to complement each other within the same solution.

The BRE Pipeline Framework fits in nicely in a SOA environment because it promotes loose coupling through the ease of assessing and manipulating message context for routing purposes. Being based on the rules engine that is packaged with BizTalk Server, rules can be updated at runtime with minimum downtime experienced by service consumers. Another strong point is that it promotes reusability since utility is provided as self-contained units rather than in the form of monolithic components and thus can be reused across services. Finally, pipelines by their very nature lend themselves very well to unit testing, thus ensuring the testability and reliability of your environment, including the detection of breaking changes to routing rules.

BizTalk Documenter

The BizTalk Documenter is a community-driven, open source project located on CodePlex (`https://biztalk2013documenter.codeplex.com/`) that caters for the automated generation of documentation for your BizTalk environments. The project is active and has seen multiple releases in the last few years, which include new features and support for both BizTalk Server 2013 and 2013 R2. Some of the key features of the BizTalk Documenter are as follows:

- Documentation of BizTalk receive and send ports, including adapter configuration, tracking settings, pipelines, maps, and adapter handlers
- Documentation of core BizTalk artifacts, including schemas, maps, pipelines, orchestration, BRE vocabularies and policies, and party configuration
- In depth documentation of orchestrations, including contained orchestrations
- Selectivity in the form of being able to filter by application, orchestrations, and BRE vocabularies and policies
- Ability to generate snapshot images of entire orchestrations
- Ability to output to `.chm` help files or word documents

One of the keys to a successful SOA, or any integration environment in general, is having an understanding of how the implemented solutions fit together to ensure that changes can be planned such that they introduce the least amount of disruption possible. Having good documentation also ensures that getting developers who aren't familiar with the environment up to speed can be without hassle. The BizTalk Documenter is a quick and easy way to inventory your existing environments, and it should be used regularly to capture the state of your environments.

Sentinet

Sentinet is a product created by **Nevatech** (http://www.nevatech.com) that provides a service repository and caters for service virtualization. Comparisons could be drawn between some of the contained service repository features and Microsoft's own UDDI services; however, the Sentinet product goes well beyond this in scope.

Sentinet's repository feature provides a centralized store from which one can discover information about all registered services within an organization. Populating the registry is a simple task when dealing with SOAP services as Sentinet will allow you to load the service's metadata into its database by pointing to the service's WSDL. Once a service's metadata has been consumed, the WSDL will be accessible from a Sentinet-provided URL, removing the need for you to directly expose WSDLs from individual target services.

Once the service has been registered it can then be managed further. New versions of the service can be added, the state of a service can be graduated from draft to active through to retired, and additional endpoints can be added to the service. Creating a new version of the service can be done by loading the new version's WSDL file, or potentially, by cloning the existing version and making changes manually, or finally, by going a contract first route and manually constructing the service based on XSD schemas that can be uploaded to Sentinet. You are even able to define header and fault contracts while creating a new service version. Once your changes have been committed, you'll be able to access the WSDL for your new service version, even if you haven't actually gone to the effort to implement the service yet.

Sentinet also allows for RESTful services to be registered in the repository. At this stage, the process to register such a service is more manual than for SOAP; however, the benefits are much the same.

Another benefit of adding services to the repository is that Sentinet provides a BizTalk ESB Toolkit resolver that allows you to fetch configuration details for a given endpoint at runtime to be used by dynamic send ports. Changes can now be made to the service's configuration, and as long as these changes are registered in Sentinet, no updates will be required within your BizTalk itinerary to connect to the service.

The next reason to register services in Sentinet is that doing so makes them candidates for Service Virtualization.

Service Virtualization is defined by Wikipedia as a method to emulate the behavior of specific components in heterogeneous, component-based applications such as API-driven applications, cloud-based applications, and service-oriented architectures. It goes on to suggest that the primary goal of Service Virtualization is to remove dependencies in agile teams by being able to provide virtual services or service stubs, to ensure that teams that depend on them are not blocked from progressing with their own tasks. The Sentinet product takes this concept further by delivering real value add that can be leveraged in production scenarios.

In order to virtualize a service, one must first create Sentinet nodes. These are effectively IIS virtual applications that will be used to host Sentinet virtualized endpoints. Once this has been done, one can choose to virtualize any registered services, effectively exposing contained operations via a new facade endpoint contained within the Sentinet node virtual application. By virtualizing a service, one can choose to expose said service with different authentication means, completely different transports, and even different protocols by exposing SOAP operations in a RESTful manner.

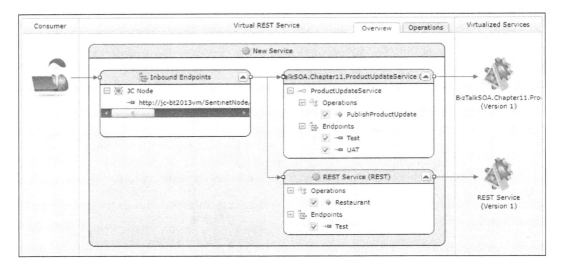

One can even choose to create composite virtual services, picking and choosing operations to expose from various services. As previously mentioned, SOAP operations can be exposed via RESTful virtual services as well. Sentinet provides the tools to map URL parameters to an inbound SOAP message body via configuration, largely trivializing such a task. Sentinet also provides inbound and outbound pipelines, during which you can also run XSLT transformations against request and/or response messages if required.

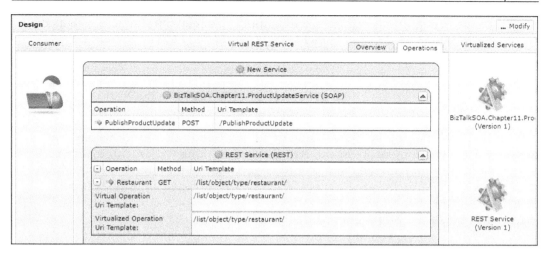

This is just scratching the surface of functionality contained within Sentinet.
Additional features that make the product worth considering are:

- Monitoring of virtualized services, including success/failure counts,
  durations, message sizes, and even message payloads.

- Advanced security methods, such as STS, based on Azure ACS or ADFS
  and SAML tokens in a totally configuration-driven fashion and the ability
  to easily lock down services based these means as well as more traditional
  means, such as on nominated Windows users/groups. This would normally
  be quite difficult to implement in BizTalk, typically requiring development of
  a custom WCF behavior.

- Creation of mock virtualized services, which return a preset response. This
  is especially useful for testing purposes prior to implementation of the target
  services.

- Exposing services via Sentinet nodes allows you to avoid exposing BizTalk
  servers externally via reverse proxies or similar means and, instead, allows
  you to only expose the Sentinet nodes, lowering the surface area of exposed
  services.

- The ability to transform XML messages into JSON and vice versa in
  inbound/outbound pipelines.

- Azure integration readiness, with support for relay bindings as well as the `netMessagingBinding`, which allows for messages to be consumed from Service Bus queues or topics.

- Extensibility, in that Sentinet provides .NET interfaces that allow you to build your own custom pipelines, behaviors, and access control rules that can be used across your virtualized services.

All up, Sentinet is a product that should definitely be considered for usage in a serious SOA environment. The benefits would scale along with the number of services that are implemented and would largely reduce the strain of governing a complex SOA. More information about the synergies between BizTalk Server and Sentinet can be found in a blog series at `http://soa-thoughts.blogspot.co.nz/2013/12/sentinet-service-virtualization-part-1.html`.

Further reading

Some additional noteworthy tools that you would be wise not to ignore are listed here, and you can find an even larger list on the TechNet wiki (`http://social.technet.microsoft.com/wiki/contents/articles/5208.biztalk-server-2010-tools.aspx`):

- **The ContextAccessor functoid** (`http://contextaccessor.codeplex.com/`): This project contains a custom pipeline component and mapping functoid that allows you to access a message's context properties within maps executed within a receive pipeline or an orchestration.

- **Loopback Adapter** (`http://www.twoconnect.com/loopback-biztalk-adapter-free-download/`): This is an adapter that allows you to loop back a message via a BizTalk send port, enabling some interesting patterns based on loose coupling.

- **BizTalk Deployment Framework** (`https://biztalkdeployment.codeplex.com/`): This framework enables the automated build of near one-click installers for BizTalk solutions. It is especially powerful when combined with a build server.

- **BizTalk Server Functoids Project Wizard** (`https://sandroaspbiztalkblog.wordpress.com/2012/08/06/biztalk-mapperextensions-functoid-wizard/`): This project provides a wizard that will build the skeleton Visual Studio project and contained class required to build a custom mapping functoid.

- **BizTalk Server Pipeline Component Wizard** (`https://btsplcw.codeplex.com/`): This project provides a wizard that will build the skeleton Visual Studio project and contained class required to build a custom pipeline component.

- **CAT Instrumentation Framework and Controller** (`https://btscatifcontroller.codeplex.com/`): This project provides a UI that allows you to enable and disable traces based on the **Event Tracing for Windows (ETW)** based CAT Instrumentation Framework. It enables you to choose what type of components trace statements should be captured for and allows you to filter based on severity level. You can choose whether to capture traces synchronously to DebugView or asynchronously to a text file.

- **BizTalk NoS Ultimate** (`http://www.biztalk360.com/nos/`): This is a paid Visual Studio add-in that aims to improve developer productivity. Some of the more compelling features are a simplified exploration of dependencies between BizTalk components, comparing source code to deployed assemblies (also known as jackhammering), and pipeline / pipeline component testing.

- **BizTalk Mapper Extensions UtilityPack** (`https://btsmapextutilitypack.codeplex.com/`): This project contains a diverse collection of custom mapping functoids that add a lot of utility to your BizTalk solutions without the need for custom coding.

- **BizTalk Map Test Framework** (`https://mtf.codeplex.com/`): This framework enables developers to build robust unit tests for BizTalk maps, well beyond the capabilities of the out-of-the-box map testing classes.

- **DanSharp XmlViewer** (`https://dansharpxmlviewer.codeplex.com/`): This project provides a UI that allows you to test out XPath queries against a given XML message or to click on a node within a message to get the corresponding XPath query for that node.

Summary

There is no shortage of tooling available to complement your SOA aspirations, and this chapter will have given you an insight into some of the options available to you. This is merely a short list, and each tool mentioned will have alternatives available. There are entire genres of tooling that haven't even been touched upon in this chapter.

The best thing that you can do is prioritize areas in which tooling could help you reach the next level of maturity by filling a gap and choose the tool that best fits your need.

In the next chapter, we will look at new ways to connect on-premise and cloud-based applications/services using Azure.

13

New SOA Capabilities in BizTalk Server 2013 – Azure Hybrid Patterns

Once you have eliminated the impossible, whatever remains, however improbable, must be the truth.

– Spock, Star Trek

With the advent of cloud computing, there is now more demand for bridging on-premises applications to cloud-hosted applications and services.

A hybrid cloud solution is when applications or services are spread across two or more private, public, or community clouds.

A private cloud is an infrastructure dedicated to a single organization. There are two variations on this, on-premises private cloud and an externally hosted private cloud. An on-premises private cloud is hosted within an organization's own data center, while an externally hosted private cloud is located in a public data center with resources dedicated solely to your organization.

A public cloud belongs to a service provider who hosts the infrastructure and is generally available to the public. Customers who use this, typically share the same infrastructure resources with other customers with limited configuration and security options.

A community cloud is shared infrastructure between several organizations that is governed and managed by all participants.

With hybrid solutions, there are many obstacles to overcome, such as limited bandwidth, secure channels, and data solvency, to name a few.

In this chapter we will discuss the following:

- Advantages of hybrid solutions
- What SOA patterns hybrid solutions tend to use
- Special security considerations
- Monitoring assets on the ground and on the cloud

Advantages of a hybrid solution

Creating a hybrid solution provides many advantages compared to a totally on-premises application or service. Some of the key benefits of shifting to a hybrid solution are as follows:

Reduced operating costs

By paying only for what you actually use, you can reduce the operating costs involved. Extra resources may be purchased at any time and then relinquished once peak loads have subsided.

For this to work effectively, you would host resource-intensive processing in the cloud, which can be scaled when required and back down again after the results of the processing are returned to the on-premises application.

Freeing up on-premises infrastructure resources

On-premises infrastructure resources can be made redundant or freed up by moving systems into the cloud, thus reducing licensing costs.

Allowing burst capacity

Most cloud infrastructures provide the capability to dynamically scale resources up horizontally and vertically as demand increases or down as demand tapers off. This offers a big advantage when dealing with burst type loads.

Improved service levels

Hybrid solutions provide better availability service levels, as the cloud components can easily be scaled up as demand increases. Also, cloud infrastructure tends to be more resilient to failure.

On the other hand, cloud-based integration services lack inbuilt persistence points and retry logic. When you design an integration solution for the cloud, you should provide persistence points within a process flow and retry logic for connections to on-premises resources. This will deliver a more resilient solution.

Reduced capital expenditures

This is one of the biggest advantages of cloud computing: moving from a capital expenditure model (**CAPEX**) to an operational expense model (**OPEX**).

Testing and trialing innovative ideas can easily be accomplished without having to outlay any infrastructure requirements. Normally, you just purchase extra cloud resources when required and have them up and running within minutes.

Improved system availability and disaster recovery

Cloud infrastructure is built on a robust architecture, providing resiliency and redundancy.

Most cloud resources are normally duplicated to other resource groups in a totally separate rack. Geo-replication is also provided as an option for total disaster recovery.

Wider audience reach

By hosting some of the components of a system on the cloud, it allows a wider reach of consumers as these services are not obscured by corporate firewalls.

In these scenarios, components that handle sensitive information normally reside on-premises and public-facing APIs are hosted in the cloud, where a secure channel connects the distributed components.

Disadvantages of a hybrid solution

Implementing a hybrid solution does have some disadvantages, namely:

- **Security**: The hybrid solution is solely reliant on the provider to provide best practices in protecting your data from unauthorized access.

- **Provider dependency**: Normally called **vendor lock-in**. This is when it becomes difficult to move your resources from one vendor to another. An example that could make it difficult would be the amount of data to transfer to another vendor.

- **Technical issues**: Diagnosing and fault finding system errors that have components distributed across several networks.

SOA patterns used in hybrid solutions

A typical hybrid solution will have resources distributed between cloud infrastructure and on-premises resources behind a corporate firewall.

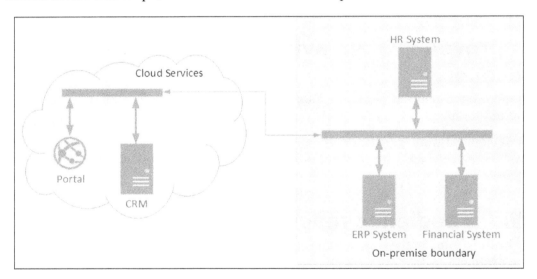

Before deciding on a hybrid solution, there are several key considerations that must be taken into account. Cloud integration solutions should provide the following benefits:

- **Scalability**: Allows the system to accommodate more demand by adding more resources horizontally or vertically. Horizontal scaling (or scaling out) lets you adjust the number of instances while vertical scaling (or scaling up) allows you to change the size of the instance.

- **Elasticity**: The ability to dynamically grow and shrink resources, depending on the demand.

- **Security**: Managing access to resources in a secure manner.

- **Robustness**: Handling failures, network interruptions, and so on in a graceful manner.

- **Flexibility**: To vertically or horizontally scale the resources.

- **Configurability**: Providing tools or APIs to configure the environment.

There are two types of cloud integration patterns:

- **Cloud-to-cloud**: Commonly referred to as SaaS integration. This is where applications and services connect to each other via the cloud.

- **Cloud-to-enterprise**: Also commonly known as hybrid integration. This is where there is a secure connection between cloud-based and on-premises services/applications.

On-premise applications tend to have low network latency and very seldom encounter network connectivity issues; cloud services, on the other hand, tend to have higher network latency and network transients. Without the proper business logic in place to handle connectivity issues, there is a risk of losing information.

There are many scenarios where data cannot be moved into the cloud and must be accessible by applications that are hosted externally. The most common way of connectivity was via a secure connection through a firewall and NATs.

Now there are other alternatives using BizTalk Services, as described in the following sections.

BizTalk Services Hybrid Connection

BizTalk Services Hybrid Connections provides a convenient way to connect Azure Websites and Azure Mobile Services to on-premises resources behind your firewall. It is one of the fastest ways to build hybrid applications as it does not require a VPN gateway or firewall changes to allow inbound traffic. It works by installing a connection agent service onto an on-premises server that connects to the local resource. The connection agent then listens for any connections from the Hybrid Connection in Azure.

The most obvious scenario where you would use a Hybrid Connection is when a resource is not designed as a Microsoft WCF service, in which case you might want to employ Service Bus Relays instead. External devices simply access the on-premises resources in the same manner as if they are connecting to a local resource.

A good example for using a Hybrid Connection is if you wish to connect directly to an enterprise (on-premises) database, as shown in the following diagram:

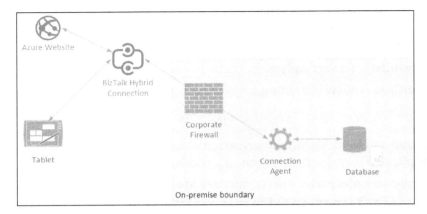

Azure Relay Services

Azure Relay Service is very similar to Hybrid Connections. However, the main difference is Relay Services only supports WCF applications that use the WCF Relay bindings.

As described in *Chapter 6, Azure Service Bus*, Relay Service is another option for providing connectivity for hybrid solutions, by delegating listening for incoming requests to the cloud-hosted Service Bus.

In the following diagram, we see a typical scenario where an on-premises WCF service needs to be exposed externally. By using an Azure Service Bus Relay, the external consumers connect to the endpoint hosted on the cloud, which relays the requests to the on-premises service:

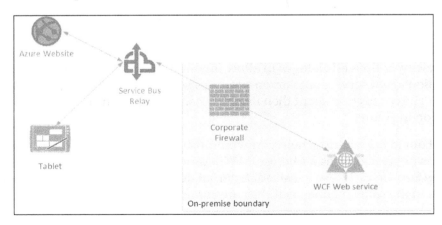

BizTalk Adapter Service

This adapter enables your cloud application to communicate with on-premises LOB systems.

The following LOB systems are currently supported:

- Microsoft SQL Server
- Oracle Database
- Oracle E-Business Suite
- SAP
- Siebel eBusiness Applications

The Adapter Service consists of a WCF LOB target adapter that is installed on an IIS server, located on-premises. One end of this adapter connects directly to your resource, and the other end connects to an Azure Service Bus, using your service namespace.

When a message arrives at your BizTalk Service in Azure, it is placed on Service Bus and is monitored by the on-premises LOB adapter. The adapter then executes the CRUD operation and returns the response via the Service Bus.

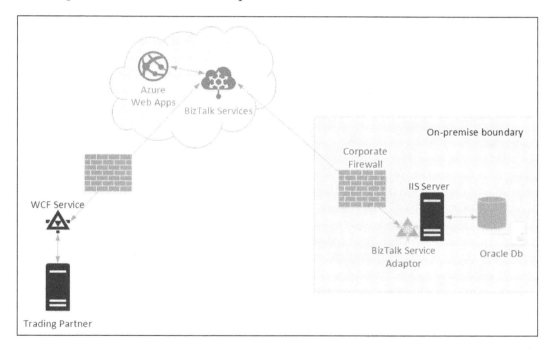

BizTalk Server Adapters

BizTalk 2013 now includes new adapters that allow on-premises services and applications to extend to the cloud.

These new adapters have been mentioned in the previous chapters, but I will list them here again as these adapters may typically be used for hybrid solutions also. Remember that these adapters are available for both BizTalk receive locations and send ports.

The WCF-BasicHttpRelay and NetTcpRelay adapters

The WCF-BasicHttpRelay and NetTcpRelay adapters allow sending and receiving messages through the Azure Relay Service using BizTalk as the service broker between an on-premises application and a cloud-based application.

In the following diagram, the enterprise applications expose their APIs using one of BizTalk's WCF Relay adapters. The WCF Relay adapter makes an initial outbound connection to the Service Bus Relay, which establishes the connection to the cloud. Whenever the tablet device requires resources from the applications residing on-premises, it sends a request to the Service Bus Relay, which forwards the message to BizTalk's WCF Relay adapter:

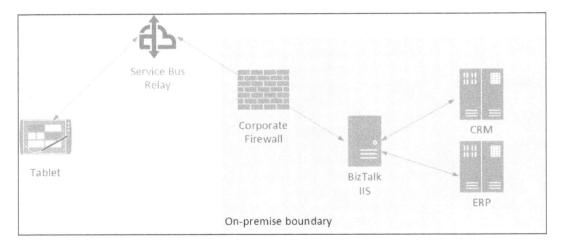

This scenario is a typical hybrid pattern to employ when you need to expose on-premises resources as WCF services, using BizTalk as a service broker.

The SB-Messaging adapter

This adapter provides first-class integration with Azure Service Bus Queues and Topics. Using this type of connectivity allows many cloud-based integration patterns to be utilized (publish/subscribe, disconnected clients, load management, and so on).

In the following solution, the SB-Messaging adapter monitors the specified Azure Service Bus Topic for any new messages by polling the endpoint. When a new message arrives on the Queue from the tablet device or any other client application, BizTalk will read it off the queue for processing:

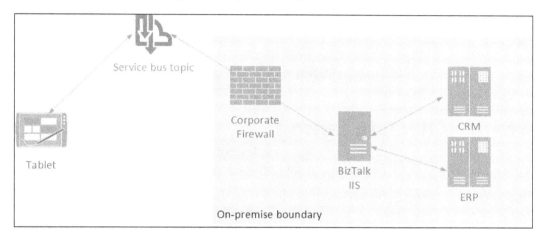

The BizTalk WCF-WebHttp adapter

The BizTalk WCF-WebHttp adapter allows developers to support RESTful API type calls that are lightweight. Many SaaS providers are adopting REST as the default protocol to use in order to consume their services.

The WCF-WebHttp adapter offers the option to expose your on-premises applications as RESTful services by using BizTalk and IIS to host the services. This is an especially useful capability to expose RESTful APIs for enterprise applications that do not provide any web service capability.

Using the WCF-WebHttp adapter in a practical example was discussed in *Chapter 4, REST and JSON Support in BizTalk Server 2013.*

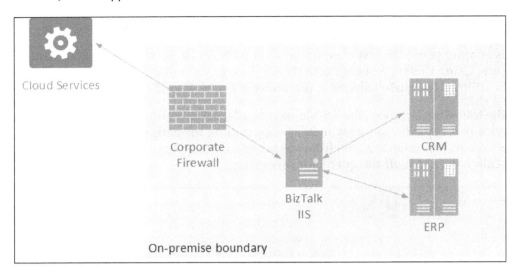

Azure SQL Data Sync

In some scenarios, it is beneficial to store a subset of data on the cloud in order to reduce network latency between a cloud application and on-premises databases.

This, however, brings forth another problem with data synchronization between on-premises and cloud-hosted databases. By using the SQL Azure Data Sync service, which is built upon the Microsoft Sync Framework, the databases can be scheduled to synchronize at intervals of between 5 minutes to a month without writing any code.

Synchronization may be set up in a singular or bi-directional manner between any combination of cloud and enterprise databases. You also have the option to synchronize down to tables and columns within a database.

 If you require near real-time data synchronization, you may want to consider AlwaysOn availability groups instead.

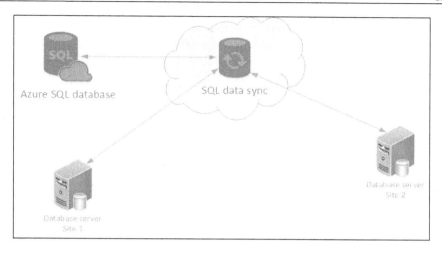

Microsoft Azure Caching

Although this section is not part of integrating applications, it is still worth a mention as Azure Caching plays an important role in hybrid solutions to provide scalability.

Microsoft Azure Caching provides a robust caching mechanism in scenarios where networking connectivity is limited in bandwidth or is subjected to networking transients between cloud and on-premises applications.

However, to use this feature, your application would be required to make use of caching in the data access layers unless caching was already implemented from the initial design.

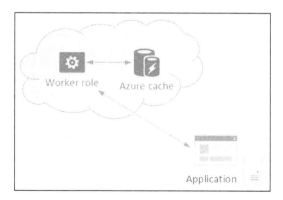

 Azure Caching is intended for code execution on the cloud and in the same data center.

Database sharding

This is another pattern worth discussing when developing hybrid solutions. Database sharding is horizontally partitioning data in a table. It improves scalability with storing and accessing vast amounts of data.

In a hybrid solution, the on-premises table schemas would be replicated in a cloud hosted database. Data intended for cloud resources would then be stored on the cloud partition.

Special security considerations

Security concerns are one of the primary hindrances to large-scale adoption of cloud computing today. When you move applications to the cloud, you cannot rely on traditional security measures as you are no longer in control. You tend to gain a sense of security because the networking and infrastructure hardware is managed by world-class security practices.

As with all applications, the greater the surface area that is exposed, the greater the chances of exposing a security vulnerability. Most cloud technologies and services are exposed as endpoints rather than in-memory communication pathways. This increases the surface area that may potentially be exploited.

With hybrid data storage, it is normally good practice to only place less critical data on the cloud and leave all sensitive data on-premises, where you have total control over access.

 If storing sensitive data on the cloud, you should consider some form of encryption mechanism.

Providing a first-class authentication and authorization mechanism is the first line of defense for your services. This should be based on industry-proven standards, such as two-factor authentication or token based security, where authentication is managed by another identity management service.

Auditing all service calls and authentication requests is another form of defense against attacks. In some cases, it is possible to be alerted when malformed requests are actively being sent.

Monitoring assets on the ground and on the cloud

As with any service or application, monitoring should be one of the top priorities in the overall solution design. It is important to monitor how well the overall system is functioning and how quickly issues are resolved when they arise. Without proper monitoring and alerting in place, there is no means to check the health of a system and to manage any **service level agreements** (**SLA**) that are in place.

Monitoring hybrid solutions is not an easy task as components of the system are now distributed across different locations and connected by networks that may vary in bandwidth and reliability. You also have fewer configuration options for cloud-hosted components and are reliant on the data center to provide their own monitoring tools.

With Microsoft Azure, you can use Azure Diagnostics to gather performance and diagnostic information about your components running on each infrastructure node. Azure Diagnostics has been specifically designed for cloud applications to minimize the impact on performance when collecting diagnostic data.

It is highly configurable by specifying what information to collect, whether it be data from performance counters, event logs, IIS logs, or crash dumps.

More information about collecting data using Azure Diagnostics can be found at `https://msdn.microsoft.com/en-us/library/gg433048.aspx`.

Another recently released monitoring service from the Microsoft Azure team is called **Application Insights**. It works by installing an SDK package into your application to send telemetry data to the Azure Portal. The SDK is available to support multiple platforms and development languages. These applications or services do not need to be deployed onto the Azure platform.

> More information about this service can be found here at `http://azure.microsoft.com/en-us/services/application-insights/`.

There are also many other third-party products available for monitoring private, public, and hybrid clouds.

To provide a centralized view of the captured diagnostic data from your hybrid solution, there are a few options, as described next.

If your organization is currently using System Center Operation Manager on-premises, there is a System Monitoring Pack available for Azure applications. The default configuration monitors the state of the hosted service and roles, ASP.NET performance counters, memory utilization, and processor performance.

With System Center Operations Manager, you can configure alerts to be raised when various counters have exceeded the specified thresholds and automate tasks to be executed. For example, the ability to spin up additional web instances if the web response times are becoming too long.

Another option is to configure Azure Diagnostics to persist the captured data to blob storage, as shown in the following diagram. Then, at regular intervals, copy the data stored in blob storage to a centralized database situated on-premises. Applications running on-premises would also write diagnostic information to this same database. A reporting tool, such as Microsoft Reporting Services, would then be used to send alerts and reports on the captured data:

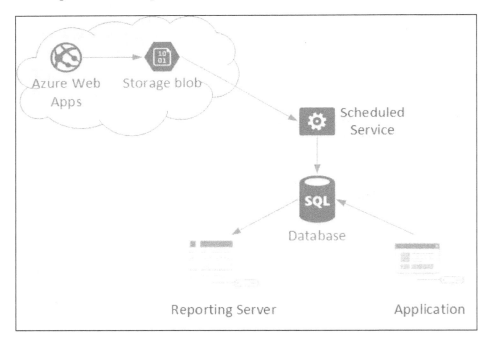

> Ensure that the diagnostic information repository is secure, as it may yield security information and information about the internal structure of your system. All communication between the Azure storage and the on-premises applications should be over a secured channel, such as HTTPS.

Handling scalability, availability, and performance

Organizations tend to move applications to the cloud because of cost savings and the scalability factor. In doing so, an additional level of management complexity is added due to resources being shared by other tenants who may introduce risk by affecting your applications. Some of this risk may be mitigated by providing multiple instances of the application or by opting for premium tier offerings, which provide dedicated resources rather than shared resources.

For a mission-critical application to handle high demands, these factors must be considered carefully during design and must be developed from the beginning, instead of being added to the solution afterwards.

Components of a solution that are quite chatty should be kept in close proximity to each other and not distributed across networks.

Scalability

Using cache in solutions is one of the most significant options you can use to enhance the scalability of an application. Typically, cache should be used when frequently querying static data from persistent storage, such as databases and blob storage. However, you must consider the amount of required cache memory and the expiration policy. For a hybrid solution, you can use Azure cache to minimize traffic between cloud and on-premises resources for slow-changing data, instead of querying the on-premises resource for every request.

Using multiple Azure Worker roles is another option to use when processing asynchronous tasks. More roles may be bought online to handle the extra demand. In a hybrid scenario, messages would be sent to an Azure Service Bus Queue from on-premises applications and then picked up by several Azure Worker roles to process the data asynchronously.

Availability

To ensure high availability, a cloud provider may use a combination of load balancing, partitioning, and resource management.

Most cloud providers offer redundancy by creating three copies of storage resources on different rack systems in the same data center. This ensures high availability of data if a hardware device fails. When this does occur, the Fabric Controller will transparently switch to another copy of the storage resource.

Geo-replication is also available on some cloud providers where, data in a primary location is asynchronously replicated to a secondary location. There is no dependency between these locations other than the transferring of data.

Microsoft recommends having a minimum of two compute instances to ensure high availability of services. This is because the virtual machine that hosts the compute instance may be rebooted by the Fabric Controller after a planned maintenance event. The Fabric Controller will never place two compute instances on the same virtual machine. This is to ensure both instances never get rebooted at the same time.

Performance

One of the major hurdles with hybrid solutions is network performance between the cloud and on-premises network infrastructures. Applications and services migrated to the cloud may need to be optimized for cloud architecture. This may include a significant redesign of the solution.

Placement of the data is very important with hybrid solutions. Tightly coupled data may not allow the application to perform well if it needs to be distributed across domains.

Most cloud providers offer effective management tools that allow performance monitoring of applications. Using these tools offers the ability to adjust the resources dynamically.

Summary

In this chapter, we've discussed hybrid solutions and architectures. We have learned the benefits of moving to a hybrid solution and also discussed some of the issues that are inherently associated with cloud infrastructures.

We looked at different options to connect on-premises and cloud-hosted resources using BizTalk Server and other Azure products.

We also discussed how to design scalable cloud applications using caching and multiple compute instances. Another important point that we touched upon was how to monitor hybrid solutions using System Center Operations Manager and how to leverage Azure Diagnostics and Application Insights.

In the next chapter, we shall take a look at some of the new features in BizTalk Server 2013 R2, Azure and beyond.

14
What's New and What's Next?

The Times They Are A-Changin'.

– Bob Dylan

The world of the Microsoft integration specialist is currently in flux. The last decade and a half has been spent building robust frameworks and mature practices to deliver comprehensive integration solutions on-premises, with a large focus on understanding and implementing SOA applications. However, the last few years has seen a monumental shift in focus from the traditional way of doing things in the integration space towards rapid time to market, reduced capital expenditure, and the proliferation of lightweight solutions. This creates new demands of integration specialists as well as untold opportunities.

There are many factors that have resulted in these changes. Some of them are listed as follows:

- The rise of smartphones, tablet devices and mobile **apps** demanding levels of scalability well beyond what was previously thought possible

- The creation of the **API economy** which has seen a rising preference for RESTful APIs

- Increased enterprise adoption of the public cloud for **Infrastructure as a Service (IaaS)**, **Platform as a Service (PaaS)**, and **Software as a Service (SaaS)** solutions.

Microsoft has recognized that their product line needed to be adjusted to account for these industry trends and this has resulted in many updated and new product offerings. The last few years have seen the introduction of the **Microsoft Azure Public Cloud** and **Azure Pack, BizTalk Server 2013 R2, Service Bus** (in Azure and on-premises), **MABS (Microsoft Azure BizTalk Services), ASP.NET Web API, Windows Server AppFabric, Azure API Management**, and very recently the new **Azure App Services** platform.

In this chapter you will be introduced to the following technologies which should get you started on a further journey to enrich your knowledge of the modern day Microsoft integration landscape:

- BizTalk Server 2013 R2
- Azure App Services
- Azure API Management

BizTalk Server 2013 R2

BizTalk Server 2013 R2 was released in late 2014 and is an incremental update to BizTalk Server 2013. There are a few key improvements and features that were delivered in this version of the platform (a subset of which will be discussed further), and it also provides platform alignment with the newest versions of SQL Server (SQL Server 2014) and Windows Server (Windows Server 2012 R2).

JSON support

One of the key improvements in BizTalk Server 2013 R2 is that Microsoft now provides out of the box support for JSON messages, making the consumption and exposure of RESTful APIs that much easier with BizTalk Server 2013 R2. This could all be achieved in BizTalk Server 2013 as well with the use of custom components however the design time experience has now been streamlined and JSON messaging is now supported by Microsoft. JSON support is provided through the following components:

- JSON Schema Wizard
- JSON Decoder Pipeline Component

JSON encoder pipeline component

The JSON Schema Wizard allows you to generate XSD schemas for XML structures corresponding to JSON message formats. The experience of using this Wizard is somewhat akin to that of using the Flat File Schema Wizard in that the Wizard intelligently builds the XSD schema for you based on an instance of a JSON message.

The difference between the flat file schema wizard and the JSON schema wizard is that the generated schema is not based on any schema extensions; it is just a vanilla XSD schema that is representative of the JSON message. It is altogether possible for you to create an XSD schema representing a JSON message by hand if you are keen to do so, as it is possible for you to extend a JSON schema that is generated by the JSON schema wizard.

The generated schema will contain a root node name and namespace as specified in the wizard, with the contents of this node being representative of the JSON message. Thus the root node can be viewed as a wrapper for the JSON contents.

When a JSON message is received on a BizTalk receive pipeline, it can be processed by the JSON Decoder pipeline component in any pipeline stage (ideally in the decode stage, but you are not constrained in your selection), which will convert the message from JSON into XML. The generated XML will then be wrapped in a root node name and namespace as specified in the parameters of the JSON decoder pipeline component. Converting the JSON message to XML allows you to take advantage of the BizTalk features that you would already be used to such as mapping, promoting and distinguishing properties, running XPATH queries against the message, and executing business rules against the message. If these features aren't important to you and you just want to deliver the message in its original JSON format, you can always make use of a pass through pipeline which will also reduce the amount of time taken to process the message.

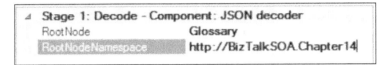

Likewise on the outbound front, you can make use of the JSON Encoder pipeline component in any stage of a send pipeline (again chances are that you will want to use this in the encode stage unless you have an explicit need to use it in another stage). This pipeline component will convert any XML messages (note that they don't have to be based on schemas that were generated with the JSON schema wizard) into their corresponding JSON formats. Once again if the message that is being processed by the send pipeline is already in a JSON format then there is no need to use the JSON decoder pipeline component, and a pass through pipeline can be employed thus reducing the amount of time required to process the message.

Service bus adapter improvements

BizTalk Server 2013 provided the Service Bus Adapter that was used to connect to Azure Service Bus queues and topics. Since then Microsoft made the strategic decision to discourage the usage of **Access Control Service** (**ACS**) for Service Bus and move towards the simpler **Shared Access Signature** (**SAS**) authentication mechanism. ACS is still supported by Service Bus, however it can only be implemented for Service Bus using PowerShell rather than through the Azure Portal.

SAS is based on a signature that is provided in the HTTP Authorization header of a message. The signature is calculated based on a SAS Key Name (much like a token), and a SAS Key (much like a token secret), with the Key Name being provided within the Authorization header for identification purposes while the Key is only used to hash the signature. The URL of the Service Bus resource as well as an expiry time which is included in the header are also used during the hashing of the signature. Service Bus is aware of which Key is associated with which Key Name and is thus able to decrypt the signature to verify its authenticity. Specific permissions such as send, receive, and manage can also be assigned to a SAS key thus allowing for different levels of privilege being assigned to consumers.

Following is a sample SAS Authorization HTTP header for illustration purposes:

```
Authorization: SharedAccessSignature
sr=https%3a%2f%2fpacktservicebusqueue.servicebus.windows.net%2fTes
tQueue&sig=F7ST4ys2OWaS1A03lhS4kYusIAp7shk9xls4evTw0dg%3d&skn=Pack
t&se=1432980105
```

Creating a SAS Authorization header is not difficult at all. Following is a code snippet which will allow you to generate the header contents:

```
public static string GetSASToken(string resourceUri, string
keyName, string key)
  var expiry = GetExpiry();
  string stringToSign = HttpUtility.UrlEncode(resourceUri) + "\n"
  + expiry;
  HMACSHA256 hmac = new HMACSHA256(Encoding.UTF8.GetBytes(key));
  var signature =
  Convert.ToBase64String(hmac.ComputeHash(Encoding.UTF8.GetBytes
  (stringToSign)));
  var sasToken = String.Format(CultureInfo.InvariantCulture,
  "SharedAccessSignature sr={0}&sig={1}&se={2}&skn={3}",
  HttpUtility.UrlEncode(resourceUri),
  HttpUtility.UrlEncode(signature), expiry, keyName);
  return sasToken;
}
```

Leveraging SAS in BizTalk Server 2013 required the usage of the WCF-Custom adapter with the netMessagingBinding binding in combination with the `transportClientEndpointBehavior` WCF endpoint behavior, both of which are contained within the `Microsoft.ServiceBus` assembly (this assembly can be obtained via NuGet). This assembly has seen many updates, including ones with breaking changes (the `transportClientEndpointBehavior` behavior's parameters were totally overhauled in one of the updates), which has made the upgrade path for the assembly somewhat trickier. The reason the WCF-Custom adapter needs to be used on BizTalk Server 2013 is because the SB-Messaging adapter only supports ACS.

Furthermore, the on-premise version of Service Bus, labeled **Service Bus for Windows Server (SBWS)** does not support ACS, and only supports SAS or Windows Authentication, thus the aforementioned methods were absolutely necessary to integrate SBSW with BizTalk Server 2013 since ACS was not an option.

BizTalk Server 2013 R2 now provides support for SAS authentication for Service Bus Queues and Topics. SBSW is now also supported on the SB-Messaging adapter in BizTalk Server 2013 R2.

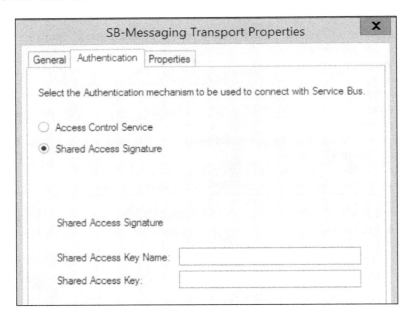

Note however that the relay binding adapters such as the WCF-BasicHttpRelay adapter still only support ACS, and if you want to use SAS you will have to use the relevant relay binding on a WCF-Custom adapter in tandem with the `transportClientEndpointBehavior` endpoint behavior.

In order to make the `transportClientEndpointBehavior` endpoint behavior available, you will need to download and install version 2.1 or above of the `Microsoft.ServiceBus` assembly which is available on NuGet. This assembly needs to be installed into the GAC and the following entry would need to be made in your `machine.config` files (note that there are alternatives to editing `machine.config` files to register WCF extensions, such as adding the extensions to your `web.config` or BizTalk `config` files, or registering the extensions on your WCF Adapter Handler):

```
<add name="transportClientEndpointBehavior"
type="Microsoft.ServiceBus.Configuration.
TransportClientEndpointBehaviorElement, Microsoft.ServiceBus,
Version=2.1.0.0, Culture=neutral,
PublicKeyToken=31bf3856ad364e35"/>
```

The above entry is based on version 2.1.0.0 of the `Microsoft.ServiceBus` assembly, and will need to be adjusted based on the version of the assembly you install in the GAC. You could now create a receive location based on the WCF-Custom adapter that uses one of the relay bindings (these too are contained within the `Microsoft.ServiceBus` assembly and might need to be registered in your `machine.config` or alternative configuration file), and then configure the `transportClientEndpointBehavior` endpoint behavior on the receive location to enable SAS. Note that this trick will work on any version of BizTalk Server above 2010.

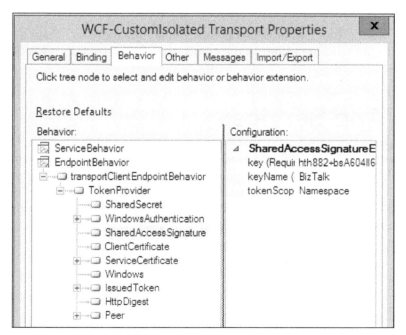

The WCF Service Publishing Wizard also doesn't include any options to create Service Bus Relays based on SAS, with ACS being the only option, but you can always update the generated web.config file of your service in order to swap ACS out with SAS. In order to do so you must perform the aforementioned steps to register the `transportClientEndpointBehavior` endpoint behavior, and then edit the section in the auto-generated `web.config` file for your BizTalk WCF Service relating to the `transportClientEndpointBehavior` behavior such that it is configured to use SAS instead of ACS, as follows:

```
<endpointBehaviors>
  <behavior name="sharedSecretClientCredentials">
    <transportClientEndpointBehavior>
      <tokenProvider type="SharedAccessSignature">
        <sharedSecret issuerName="" issuerSecret="" />
        <sharedAccessSignature keyName="BizTalk" key=
        "hth882+bsA604Il67rYIVawr6wOTlWQroDrZo62ecEs=" />
      </tokenProvider>
    </transportClientEndpointBehavior>
  </behavior>
</endpointBehaviors>
```

This trick will also work on any version of BizTalk Server above 2010, though since the WCF Service Publishing Wizard does not support Service Bus Relays on BizTalk 2010 you would need to add the relay endpoint to your `web.config` manually.

The Service Bus adapter can now be taken seriously for more use cases against queues and topics running either in the cloud or on-premise with BizTalk Server 2013 R2.

Azure App Services

Microsoft Azure BizTalk Services (MABS) was Microsoft's first attempt at providing an integration PaaS in Azure. While the platform was somewhat limited in functionality, it did help to illustrate the promise of implementing integration solutions in the cloud, even when some of the targets were on-premise. This was made possible through hybrid connections which requires an agent service to run on-premise that aids with inbound connectivity from Azure, much like a Service Bus Relay, and of course through having BizTalk Server on-premise to provide further connectivity with on-premise components.

Rather than build upon MABS, which was a platform that was very isolated from the other Azure PaaS offerings, Microsoft has taken the best of what MABS had to offer and built a brand new platform called Azure App Services. Azure App Services stitches together what used to be Azure Websites, Mobile Services, and MABS into a single integrated offering with great potential for synergies. This new platform now consists of Web Apps, Mobile Apps, API Apps, and Logic Apps.

All four types of Apps share a common backbone, in which HTTP/REST are first class and scalability is king. The primary differences between Web Apps, Mobile Apps, and API Apps is that each of these is optimized for certain use cases, while Logic Apps are more specialized but is also built from the same cloth. Web Apps are targeted at your more traditional web site or web service use cases while mobile apps are targeted at building mobile applications, with all the associated goodness such as single sign-on, push notifications, and offline syncing. It is important for integration developers to be aware of these platforms, given that it is likely that we will be providing integration for applications based on Web Apps and Mobile Apps a whole lot more in the future.

API Apps and Logic Apps will be of tantamount interest to integration developers but are in preview mode at the time this chapter was written so we shall give you an overview of them rather than get into too much detail, as changes are sure to come in the near future.

API Apps are primarily targeted towards building RESTful APIs with enterprise grade security, easy consumption based on Swagger based metadata, and tight integration with hybrid connections to enable connectivity to on-premise components. While the promise is that you can on board APIs to the platform even if they were developed in Java, PHP, node.js or Python, chances are that you will be interested in the .NET implementation.

Microsoft has built the .NET implementation of API Apps upon the ASP.NET Web API platform with some extensions to support Swagger for documentation purposes, as well as a new Visual Studio publish profile.

Following are examples of WebAPI model and controller classes which are used to expose a RESTful API with a GET operation to retrieve a contact from a static list based on a provided identifier (with a 404 exception being thrown if the ID is not found) as well as a POST operation to add a contact to the list.

```
public class Contact : IComparable
  public string Id { get; set; }
```

```
        public string Name { get; set; }
        public string EmailAddress { get; set; }
        public int CompareTo(object obj)
          if (obj == null) return 1;
          Contact otherContact = obj as Contact;
          if (otherContact != null)
            return this.Id.CompareTo(otherContact.Id);
          else
            throw new ArgumentException("Object is not a Contact");
        }
      }

    public class ContactsController : ApiController
      static List<Contact> contacts = new List<Contact>();
      [HttpGet]
      public Contact GetById(int id)
        foreach (var item in contacts)
          if (item.Id == id)
            return item;
          }
        }
        var resp = new HttpResponseMessage(HttpStatusCode.NotFound)

          Content = new StringContent(string.Format("No contact with
          ID = {0}", id)),
          ReasonPhrase = "Contact ID Not Found"
        };
        throw new HttpResponseException(resp);
      }
      [HttpPost]
      public void Post(Contact contact)
        contacts.Add(contact);
      }
    }
```

Publishing the API App is as simple a process as right clicking on your Visual Studio project, choosing publish, providing your Azure subscription credentials, and filling in the following wizard screen:

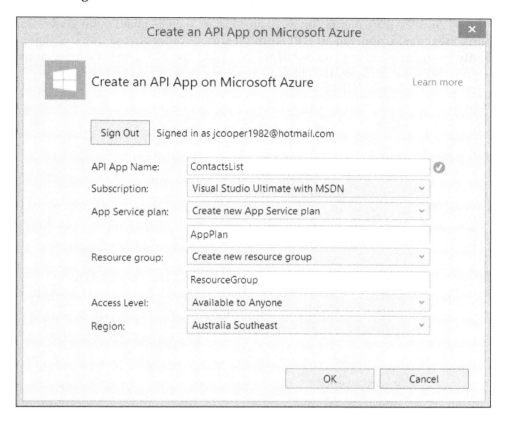

Once your App has been published, if you browse to the API's URL appended with /swagger you can view the Swagger UI which is reminiscent of the help page that used to be generated for ASMX web services. You can even submit requests to your API operations from the Swagger page and view the response. Similar to WSDL, Swagger allows for documentation of your APIs, as well as client code generation. Enabling Swagger support in an API App is a simple process, and .NET will generate a friendly Swagger page for you out of the box. You can also use SDK extensions to add comments for each operation to your Swagger page if you so please.

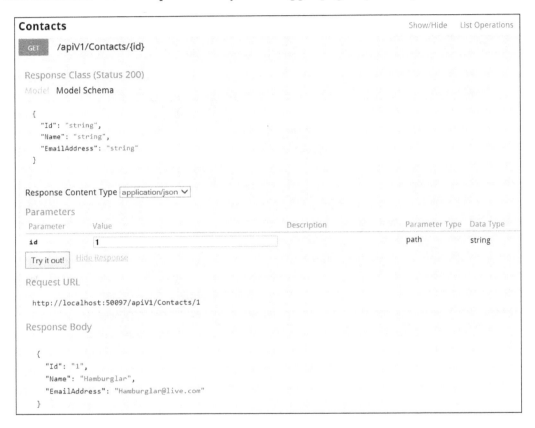

To further sweeten the deal, adding an authentication provider to your API such as Azure Active Directory, Facebook, Google, or Twitter can all be done through configuration rather than code, greatly simplifying the development experience.

It's fairly clear that API Apps provide a fantastic way to expose RESTful APIs. Logic Apps cater for the next level of integration capability by providing more connectors (similar to BizTalk adapters) and an orchestration layer. Even at this early stage the list of available connectors is pretty thorough. A small sample of available connectors are listed as follows by classification:

- Traditional connectors such as POP3, SMTP, FTP, SFTP, File, and HTTP

- Data connectors such as Azure Blob Storage, DB2 database, SQL database, Oracle database, and Informix database connectors

- Integration focused connectors such as AS2, EDIFACT, Business Rules, XSLT Transformation, XPath Extractor, and XML Validator

- Social connectors such as Twitter, Facebook, Yammer, and Twilio

- Enterprise connectors such as DropBox, SAP, Salesforce, Office365, and SharePoint

A subset of these are shown in the following image:

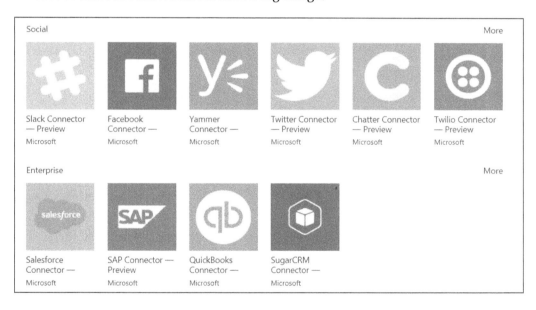

The list of connectors is ever growing, and the real kicker about these connectors is that under the hood they are all just API Apps. Thus when you deploy your own API Apps to Azure App Services you can utilize them within a Logic App just like any other connector. Swagger metadata is used for each operation within an API App to expose the relevant parameters and return types in a strongly typed fashion to the Logic App design surface so that the connectors can be displayed in a friendly fashion.

During the current stage of the Logic App preview custom API Apps can't be shared across subscriptions, but Microsoft has conveyed their eventual goal of creating an API marketplace where each API owner will have the opportunity to share or even monetize their APIs.

In the following screenshot you can see how the Swagger generated for the POST method on the `ContactController` WebAPI controller class (which was discussed previously in the API App example) has been used to list the parameters for the contactslist connector within the UI. Also of note is that the input values for these parameters are based on outputs from the preceding POP3 connector, with the outputs being strongly typed based on the **Get Email** operation of the POP3 connector. Clicking on the ellipses alongside the input parameters on the contactslist controller would provide a list of all the available parameters based on the preceding connectors. You can even use functions such as concatenate to manipulate the outputs from connectors, or apply conditional and looping logic:

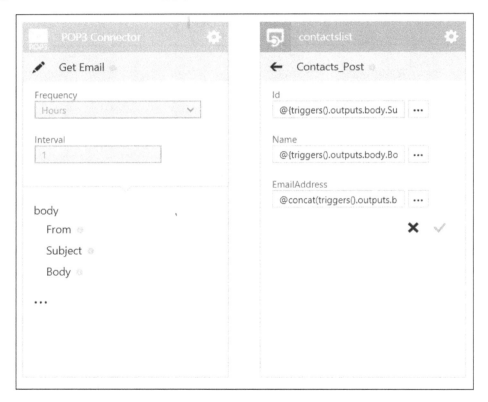

Operations on connectors can be classified as either triggers or actions. Trigger operations can be used to start up an instance of a Logic App while action based operations are used in connectors that follow the trigger. It is possible to manually trigger a Logic App via the Azure Portal, but note that this will result in the trigger connector being skipped so might result in undesired behavior. In the case of custom API Apps you will need to decorate trigger methods appropriately otherwise they will be treated as actions. Some creative trigger operations are based on notifications rather than polling, such as the Twitter connector which has a trigger operation based on Twitter's notification API thus is near real time.

Another very impressive point is that a lot of the out of the box connectors wrap all the OAUTH implementations of their targets in a very friendly manner, typically requiring the user associated with the target to log in to the target application and authorize the Logic App to act on their behalf at design time. This would be quite a difficult feat to achieve in BizTalk Server so it is good to see an immediate differentiating factor between the two platforms.

Under the hood, Logic Apps are stored as JSON, which can be edited manually by clicking on the "Code View" button in the Logic App designer. Inspecting the JSON can help give you a finer appreciation for how the connectors hang together. From the ALM perspective, Microsoft's current implementation during the preview period is to allow you to store the JSON corresponding to a Logic App within Visual Studio and to deploy the Logic App from there as well. Note however that there is currently no UI to design a logic App in Visual Studio.

Azure App Services as a platform also offers much in the way of scalability options. Similar to Azure Virtual Machines you choose from a Basic, Standard, or Premium tier, each with different base capabilities, and then choose the scale of the individual VM. With the Standard and higher tiers you can also take advantage of auto scaling to cater for peaks and troughs in demand.

S1 Standard ★	S2 Standard	S3 Standard
1 Core	2 Core	4 Core
1.75 GB RAM	3.5 GB RAM	7 GB RAM
50 GB Storage	50 GB Storage	50 GB Storage
5 SNI, 1 IP Custom domains / SSL	5 SNI, 1 IP Custom domains / SSL	5 SNI, 1 IP Custom domains / SSL
Up to 10 instances Auto scale	Up to 10 instances Auto scale	Up to 10 instances Auto scale
Daily Backup	Daily Backup	Daily Backup
5 slots Web app staging	5 slots Web app staging	5 slots Web app staging
Traffic Manager Geo availability	Traffic Manager Geo availability	Traffic Manager Geo availability
54.63 NZD/MONTH (ESTIMATED)	109.26 NZD/MONTH (ESTIMATED)	218.52 NZD/MONTH (ESTIMATED)

While these are still early days for Logic Apps, Microsoft has made it clear that this platform is not intended only for one-way or request-response type patterns only, but that it can also support more complex patterns such as scatter/gather and publish/subscribe content based routing. To lower the barrier to entry for Logic Apps, Microsoft has also created templates based on common integration patterns which will allow you to quickly spin up a new logic app based on a pre-existing template. A subset of the available templates is depicted as shown:

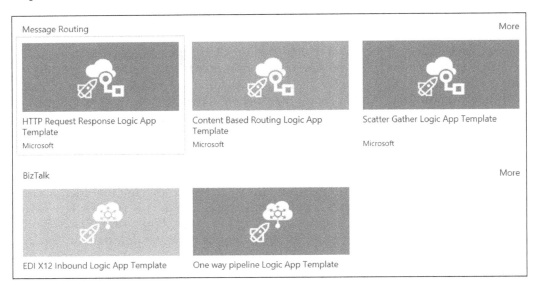

There is of course a lot more to Azure App Services, enough to fill a whole other book, but the above should give you a taste of what the platform has to offer and get you excited about its capabilities. There is no doubt that we will see a lot of evolution in this platform so don't be surprised if the features in the final product or in further releases far surpass what has been discussed here.

Azure API Management

Azure API Management is an Azure PaaS offering that provides a powerful governance layer for RESTful services. It provides many of the most common features of mature RESTful services and encapsulates them such that developers don't have to worry about explicitly building them into their backend services. Some of the key features of Azure API Management are listed as follows:

- Service virtualization
- Service throttling / rate limiting
- Scalability
- Importing and exporting API metadata via Swagger/WADL
- VPN connectivity to your back end services where they aren't exposed over the internet
- Security via OAUTH 2.0 based authentication and IP filtering
- Request validation
- Caching
- Transformation (message bodies and headers)
- Access Control (including a developer portal)
- Monitoring

That's an intimidatingly large list of features so let's discuss where the value add is. Modern frameworks for building RESTful frameworks such as .NET Web API make implementation of bare bones APIs easy, and allow you to concentrate on your business requirements rather than getting too caught up in the plumbing of the service.

However building a robust public API require a whole lot more thought regarding many of the aforementioned bullet points, and ignoring these raises the risk of embarrassing failures, both in terms of functionality and usability. This is not to say that these features can't be built or tacked on using readily available frameworks, but in the age of PaaS the incentive to implement custom plumbing features is much lessened.

Where Azure API management comes in is that it allows you to treat these features as after thoughts. Worried about your service failing when there are too many concurrent requests being made? If you're using Azure API management then you don't need to worry about it while you've implementing the backend service, and can instead delay this implementation till later when you are ready to apply governance policies around the service via Azure API management. This is of course only one example of where Azure API Management adds value.

Rather than walk through each of the aforementioned features (which don't comprise the full list of functionality anyways), let's walk through an example of how Azure API Management can be used to add value to your service. As a very first step you should log in to the Azure Management Portal and create a new API Management instance. You'll be asked to select a base URL which will be appended with `.azure-api.net`. Note that all your virtualized services will use this URL as a base address, so choose carefully. You can also choose to use your own custom domain name at a later stage if you want. You'll also be asked to select a subscription, a region, your organization's name and administrator's e-mail address before Azure will be ready to provision your instance.

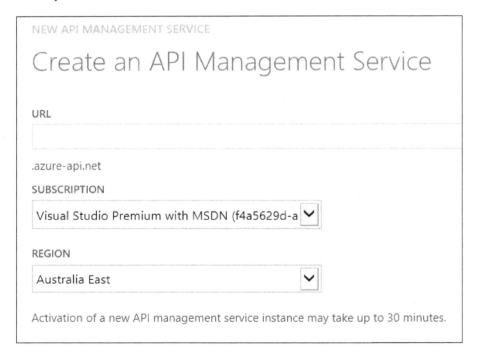

Once your instance has been created, if you browse to it in the Azure Portal you'll notice there are a few tabs of interest. The first one is called Scale which gives you a host of scalability options. The default tier of scale is developer which equates to a single API Management compute unit. The standard tier allows you to scale up to a maximum of four compute units, granting you more scalability. Finally the premium tier allows you to assign multiple regions, each with a maximum of ten compute units. You can even bypass the ten compute unit restriction, though in order to do so you will need to contact Microsoft as the feature is not enabled by default.

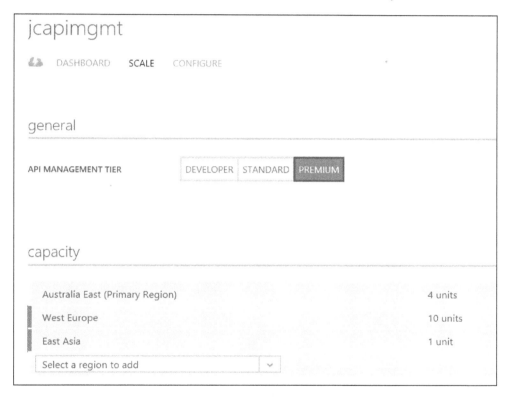

The Configure tab gives you a few additional options, namely the ability to configure custom domain names, both for your API endpoints as well as for the developer portal, as well as the ability to establish a VPN connection to your premises. The latter feature is especially handy if your backend services aren't currently exposed externally, though note that this feature is only available for the premium tier of API Management.

If you browse back to the Dashboard tab, you'll notice that there is a button at the bottom of the screen called Manage. Clicking this will take you to the API Management Administrator Portal where you can manage your backend APIs.

I've chosen to use the MashApe **Yoda Speak** API as my backend API which I will use throughout the remainder of this demonstration. The API has a single operation which converts an input sentence to one that Yoda from Star Wars would say (an API of the utmost use for all enterprises). To follow along with this example you will need to browse to `https://www.mashape.com/ismaelc/yoda-speak` and either sign in to MashApe or create a login. Once you've done so if you click on the Applications button and choose the relevant application (unless you created one manually it will be called Default Application) and then click the **Get the keys** button you will be presented with an API Key that you can use when calling on the API.

In order to call on the API operation you will need to perform an HTTP GET request to the `https://yoda.p.mashape.com/yoda?sentence={0}` URL where `{0}` is the URL encoded sentence that you want to convert. You will also need to supply your API key in the X-Mashape-Key header otherwise you will be met with a **401** unauthorized exception. Calling on the API operation results in the Yoda speak version of your input sentence being returned in the response body.

Back to the API Management Portal, let's now add an API called Yoda. You'll be asked to provide a URL suffix which will be added on to the base URL for your API management instance, the base URL for the backend API, a description, and you'll have to choose whether your API will support HTTP, HTTPS, or both. Fill in this screen as follows to proceed with the example.

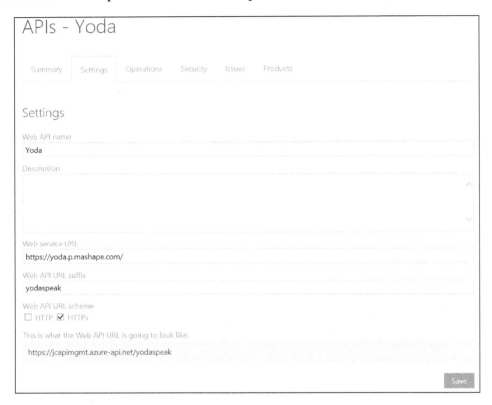

Once that's done, let's browse to the operations tab and click add operation. Here we have to specify the HTTP verb that we are going to associate with this operation, the URL template for the backend operation, an optional URL rewrite template in case you want to format your operation differently from the backend service, and a display name which will be the name of the operation on your virtualized API.

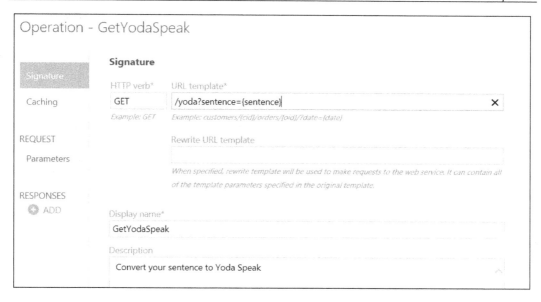

In order to actually publish our API to external developers, or to test it using the Developer Portal we need to add it to a product. A product is simply a collection of APIs to which developers can subscribe to. You can configure a product such that subscriptions must be approved by the administrator (which is handy if you're seeking to monetize your API), or you can make it completely open so that no approval is necessary. When you create an Azure API Management instance, two products called Starter and Unlimited will be automatically created, though you can remove these if you like, and you can also create your own ones. For now we will add our API to the Starter product from the Products tab under our API.

We're now ready to attempt to call our API. You could call the API using any common HTTP tools such as Fiddler, but in this case let's actually use the test tool that is provided in the API Management Developer Portal. To access the Developer Portal go back to the Dashboard tab for your API Management instance in the Azure Management Portal and click the Browse button. This will now take you to the Developer Portal, though you will be logged in as the administrator of the API Management instance rather than as a developer, thus will be able to see all APIs, even if they aren't associated with a product.

In the Developer Portal you will now need to browse to the APIS tab, choose the Yoda API, highlight the **GetYodaSpeak** operation and click on the **Try It** button. In order to call the API you will need to enter a value into the sentence parameter, and you'll need to add your X-Mashape-Key value that is associated with your MashApe application.

You'll notice that the Ocp-Apim-Subscription-Key request header has been automatically populated with a masked value. This header is mandatory on all requests made to APIs exposed by Azure API Management, and each developer who signs up to use your API will have their own unique value for this key per product subscription they make. This key can be viewed or regenerated from the developers profile page in the developer portal.

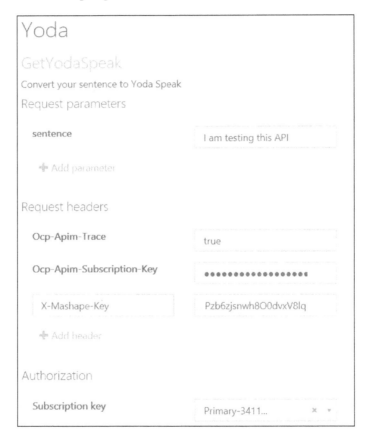

After submitting your request, you'll see the response HTTP code, latency, response headers, and response body, and you can see that our input sentence has now been converted into Yoda speak as expected.

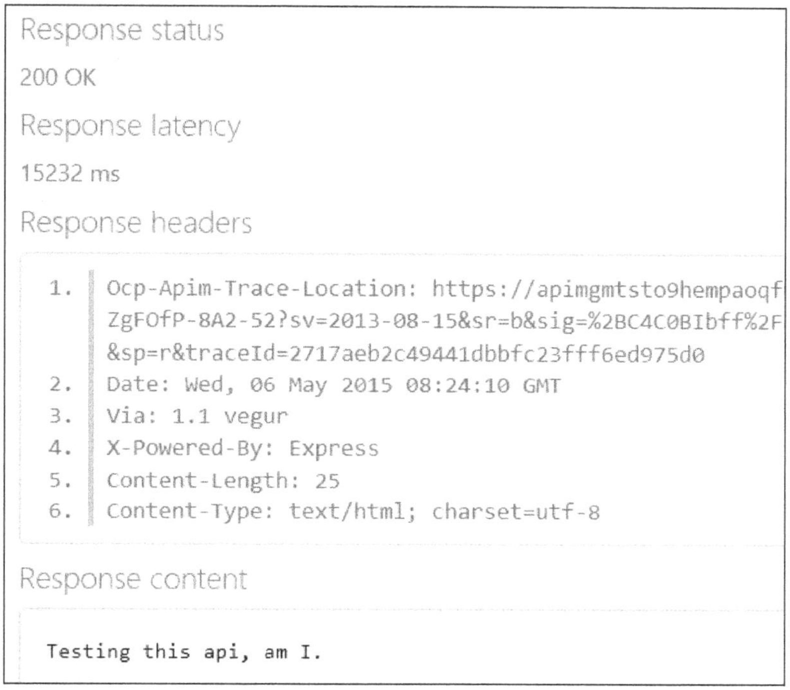

```
Response status

200 OK

Response latency

15232 ms

Response headers

  1.  Ocp-Apim-Trace-Location: https://apimgmtsto9hempaoqf
      ZgFOfP-8A2-52?sv=2013-08-15&sr=b&sig=%2BC4C0BIbff%2F
      &sp=r&traceId=2717aeb2c49441dbbfc23fff6ed975d0
  2.  Date: Wed, 06 May 2015 08:24:10 GMT
  3.  Via: 1.1 vegur
  4.  X-Powered-By: Express
  5.  Content-Length: 25
  6.  Content-Type: text/html; charset=utf-8

Response content

  Testing this api, am I.
```

So far all we have done is wrap the target API and haven't really added much value yet. You'll notice that the response latency in the above screenshot was quite high, possibly due to an unoptimized backend API. It would be ideal if we could cache the result based on the input sentence in order to reduce the load on the back end service and reduce the response latency. And what if we want to automatically submit the MashApe API key so that the developers using our managed API don't have to worry about authorization against the backend API. Lastly, what if we want to throttle our service such that it can't be called more than five times per minute per developer. All these features can be tacked on to your back end service with little effort using Azure API Management.

Back to the Developer Portal, let's start by browsing to the **GetYodaSpeak** operation defined in the Yoda API and open the caching tab. Here we can tick the Enable check box and type in sentence under query string parameters as well as select a caching duration. If you save this and attempt to call the API operation again you'll notice that subsequent calls with the same sentence parameter value are much faster to respond, in the double digit milliseconds even! Do keep in mind that there are limitations on how large your cached items can be (at the time of writing the limit is 2MB).

In order to automatically apply the relevant MashApe authorization header to the request, we will need to browse to the Policies tab in the Administrator Portal. Here you'll be presented with three list boxes, one to select a product, one to select an API, and one to select an API operation. For now let's select the Yoda API and the **GetYodaSpeak** operation and leave the Product blank.

What you'll immediately notice is that the caching details we entered for the **GetYodaSpeak** operation have actually been inserted into a policy. In fact, we could have set up the caching from the policy tab exclusively rather than from within the API operation definition.

You'll also notice that the policy is divided into an inbound and outbound section and that there are a whole lot of different policy statements that you can use within your policy on the right hand side of the screen. To BizTalk developers policies and policy statements should immediately draw parallels to pipelines and pipeline components. At this stage it isn't possible to create your own custom policy statements, but this is somewhat counteracted through the ability to augment policies through the use of **Policy Expressions**. Policy Expressions effectively provide you a subset of .NET classes that you can leverage within your policies through the use of C# like syntax. You can read more about Policy Expressions here—`https://azure.microsoft.com/blog/2015/04/27/policy-expressions-in-azure-api-management/`. The list of out of the box policy statements is quite thorough, and Microsoft keeps adding more useful policy statement with each update.

In order to set the MashApe API key on messages before they get sent to the backend API, we would need to use the Set HTTP Header policy statement in our inbound policy, and you'll notice that we'll be provided with options on what to do in case the header already exists on the message when it is being processed by the policy. Below is a policy statement snippet that will insert the MashApe key into the relevant header, overriding the header if it already exists on the inbound message.

```
<set-header name="X-Mashape-Key" exists-action="override">
  <value>API key value goes here </value>
</set-header>
```

Before we get into throttling, I will draw your attention back to the three list boxes at the top of the policy screen again. These list boxes are used to select the scope at which the policy you've configured will be applied. In our previous example we applied the policy to the Yoda API on the GetYodaSpeak operation irrespective of the product (note that an API can be added to as many products as you want). You could also choose to apply a policy at the API scope, in which case it will be applied to all operations on the API, or on a combination of product and API in which case the policy will only apply to APIs which are subscribed to based on a given product. The final policy that will be applied when an API operation is called upon will be an amalgamation of all the policies that would apply to the called operation across the various scopes.

Let's set the APIs and Operations list boxes back to their default values, and select the **Starter** product in the **Product** list box (you'll recall that we associated the Yoda API with this product). You'll notice in this case that there is already an existing policy with a limited call rate and a set usage quota policy statement set to the inbound policy. This is because the default Starter product comes pre-configured with rate limiting policies, so you don't actually need to do any further work to apply rate limitations on the Yoda API as long as it is being subscribed to by interested developers based on the **Starter** product. If you associate the Yoda API with further products then you'll need to consider whether any throttling is required on those products and then apply it on those products as well, or you could always choose to apply your throttling at a lower level.

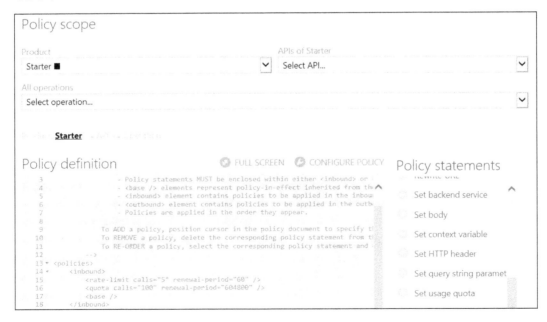

One final item of interest that I'll point out to you is that Azure API Management provides administrators with the ability to retrieve rich tracing information for their API operations. In order to do this the Administrator must call on the relevant API operation with the Ocp-Apim-Trace header set to a value of true (note that only administrators of APIs are able to make use of this header). Doing so will result in a trace log being generated in JSON format, with the URL to retrieve the log being included in the Ocp-Apim-Trace-Location header in the response message. This trace file gives you a good idea of the policies have been applied and at what point any failures might be encountered. This makes troubleshooting your APIs a whole lot easier.

API Management also provides you with rich monitoring of your APIs, giving you an idea of the number of requests that were made against the service, the bandwidth used, and even the number of errors encountered. This information can be viewed on the summary tab of your API in the Administrator Portal.

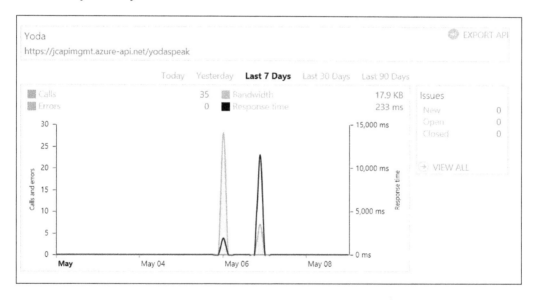

One final note is that you can easily generate Swagger for your virtualized service by clicking on the Export API button in the summary tab of your API in the Administrator Portal. The Swagger generated for the demonstrated API would look like the following, and as you can see it documents the usage of the API with a good level of detail.

```
{
  "swagger": "2.0",
  "info": {
    "title": "Yoda",
    "description": "",
    "version": "1.0"
  },
  "host": "jcapimgmt.azure-api.net",
  "basePath": "/yodaspeak",
  "schemes": [
    "https"
  ],
  "paths": {
    "/yoda?sentence={sentence}": {
      "get": {
        "description": "Convert your sentence to Yoda Speak",
        "operationId": "GetYodaSpeak",
        "parameters": [
          {
            "name": "sentence",
            "in": "query",
            "description": "The sentence to convert",
            "required": true,
            "type": "string"
          }
        ],
        "responses": {}
      }
    }
  }
}
```

This only scratches the surface of what is possible using Azure API Management. It is definitely a tool that all Microsoft Integration developers should at the very least have a play with, if not get intensely familiar with. The potential to leverage API Management, to add robustness and developer friendliness into your backend services is huge, and means you don't have to invest a huge effort in building all the goodness provided by the platform into your backend services themselves. And of course don't ignore the potential of combining Azure API Management with Azure App Services, Service Bus (keeping in mind that Service Bus entities can be interacted with via a RESTful API) queues, topics, or relays, BizTalk Server, and ASP. Net Web API or WCF-WebHttp services to deliver even more API goodness.

Summary

SOA is all about architecture, not products. The point of this book was to demonstrate real, concrete examples of the principles and patterns of SOA through the use of BizTalk Server 2013 and Microsoft Azure. Using these technologies doesn't automatically make you service oriented, and using legacy technologies doesn't mean you are not service oriented. Even your choice of transport and protocols isn't enough to qualify you as being service oriented or not. What does qualify a solution as being service oriented is an effort to internalize the core concepts of loose coupling, abstraction, encapsulation, interoperability, and reuse and aggressively apply them wherever they makes sense. Products like BizTalk Server, Azure App Services, Service Bus, ASP.NET Web API, WCF and protocols or architectures such as SOAP/REST are simply tools that allow you to apply your service-oriented principles in a software solution.

We hope that this book triggered new ideas in your mind and offered you innovative ways to tackle the problems that you currently face and will face in the future. There is a large amount of tooling available to fulfill the promises of SOA, and never have we been more enabled to fulfill these promises than now. The momentum in the IT industry shows every sign of increasing at an exponential rate, and there is no question that the principles of SOA will serve you well if you know how to utilize them, and in this we wish you good fortunes.

Index

X

Thank you for buying
SOA Patterns with BizTalk Server 2013 and Microsoft Azure
Second Edition

About Packt Publishing

Packt, pronounced 'packed', published its first book, *Mastering phpMyAdmin for Effective MySQL Management*, in April 2004, and subsequently continued to specialize in publishing highly focused books on specific technologies and solutions.

Our books and publications share the experiences of your fellow IT professionals in adapting and customizing today's systems, applications, and frameworks. Our solution-based books give you the knowledge and power to customize the software and technologies you're using to get the job done. Packt books are more specific and less general than the IT books you have seen in the past. Our unique business model allows us to bring you more focused information, giving you more of what you need to know, and less of what you don't.

Packt is a modern yet unique publishing company that focuses on producing quality, cutting-edge books for communities of developers, administrators, and newbies alike. For more information, please visit our website at www.packtpub.com.

About Packt Enterprise

In 2010, Packt launched two new brands, Packt Enterprise and Packt Open Source, in order to continue its focus on specialization. This book is part of the Packt Enterprise brand, home to books published on enterprise software – software created by major vendors, including (but not limited to) IBM, Microsoft, and Oracle, often for use in other corporations. Its titles will offer information relevant to a range of users of this software, including administrators, developers, architects, and end users.

Writing for Packt

We welcome all inquiries from people who are interested in authoring. Book proposals should be sent to author@packtpub.com. If your book idea is still at an early stage and you would like to discuss it first before writing a formal book proposal, then please contact us; one of our commissioning editors will get in touch with you.

We're not just looking for published authors; if you have strong technical skills but no writing experience, our experienced editors can help you develop a writing career, or simply get some additional reward for your expertise.

SOA Patterns with BizTalk Server 2009

ISBN: 978-1-84719-500-5   Paperback: 400 pages

Implement SOA strategies for Microsoft BizTalk Server solutions

1. Discusses core principles of SOA and shows them applied to BizTalk solutions.

2. The most thorough examination of BizTalk and WCF integration in any available book.

3. Leading insight into the new WCF SQL Server Adapter, UDDI Services version 3, and ESB Guidance 2.0.

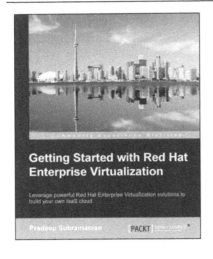

Getting Started with BizTalk Services

ISBN: 978-1-78217-740-1   Paperback: 180 pages

Leverage powerful Red Hat Enterprise Virtualization solutions to build your own IaaS cloud

1. Create integration solutions on the cloud with Windows Azure BizTalk Services.

2. Understand the different capabilities of BizTalk Services and how to use them effectively.

3. Connect enterprises together in scalable and flexible ways that go beyond what traditional on-premises integration products (such as BizTalk Server) can manage.

Please check **www.PacktPub.com** for information on our titles

Microsoft BizTalk ESB
Toolkit 2.1

Discover innovative ways to solve your mission-critical integration problems with the ESB Toolkit

Andrés Del Río Benito   Howard S. Edidin   [PACKT] enterprise

Microsoft BizTalk ESB Toolkit 2.1

ISBN: 978-1-84968-864-2   Paperback: 130 pages

Discover innovative ways to solve your mission-critical integration problems with the ESB Toolkit

1. A comprehensive guide to implementing quality integration solutions.

2. Instructs you about the best practices for the ESB and also advises you on what not to do with this tool.

3. A sneak view of what's new in the ESB Toolkit 2.2.

WCF Multi-layer Services
Development with Entity Framework
Fourth Edition

Create and deploy complete solutions with WCF and Entity Framework

Mike Liu   [PACKT] enterprise

WCF Multi-layer Services Development with Entity Framework
Fourth Edition

ISBN: 978-1-78439-104-1   Paperback: 378 pages

Create and deploy complete solutions with WCF and Entity Framework

1. Build SOA applications on Microsoft platforms.

2. Apply best practices to your WCF services and utilize Entity Framework to access underlying data storage.

3. A step-by-step, practical guide with nifty screenshots to create six WCF and Entity Framework solutions from scratch.

Please check **www.PacktPub.com** for information on our titles

www.ingramcontent.com/pod-product-compliance
Lightning Source LLC
Chambersburg PA
CBHW081453050326
40690CB00015B/2787